D0502408

The Founders at Home

Also by Myron Magnet

The Dream and the Nightmare:
The Sixties' Legacy to the Underclass

Dickens and the Social Order

Edited by Myron Magnet

The Immigration Solution: A Better Plan Than Today's

Modern Sex: Liberation and Its Discontents

What Makes Charity Work?:
A Century of Public and Private Philanthropy

The Millennial City: A New Urban Paradigm
for 21st-Century America

The Founders at Home

The Building of America,
1735–1817

MYRON MAGNET

W. W. NORTON & COMPANY
New York London

Printed in the United States of America
First Edition

For information about special discounts for bulk purchases, please contact
W. W. Norton Special Sales at specialsales@wwnorton.com or 800-233-4830

Manufacturing by Courier Westford
Book design by Helene Berinsky
Production manager: Devon Zahn

Library of Congress Cataloging-in-Publication Data

Magnet, Myron.
The founders at home : the building of America, 1735–1817 /
Myron Magnet. — First Edition.
p. cm.
Includes bibliographical references and index.
ISBN 978-0-393-24021-4 (hardcover)
1. Founding Fathers of the United States—Biography. 2. Statesmen—United States—
Biography. 3. United States—Politics and government—Philosophy. I. Title.
E302.5.M19 2014
973.2—dc23
2013020095

W. W. Norton & Company, Inc.
500 Fifth Avenue, New York, N.Y. 10110
www.wwnorton.com

W. W. Norton & Company Ltd.
Castle House, 75/76 Wells Street, London W1T 3QT

1 2 3 4 5 6 7 8 9 0

For Barbara, Julia, Alec, and Trevor

CONTENTS

PART THREE
The Republicans

The Founders at Home

INTRODUCTION

The Americanness of the American Revolution

THE *FOUNDERS AT HOME* recounts the American Founding from 1735 to 1817 in a series of biographies that together help explain why the American Revolution, of all great revolutions, was the only successful one, resulting in two centuries and more of unexampled freedom and prosperity. By contrast, the French Revolution, illuminated by America's example and Enlightenment thought, began in blissful optimism but collapsed into a blood-soaked tyranny much worse than the monarchy it deposed. It spawned a military dictatorship that roiled Europe and half the globe for over a decade with wars of grandiose imperial aggression that slew at least three million. And the result of twenty-five years of turmoil? The Bourbon monarchy, minus the Enlightenment of its earlier incarnation, settled plumply back on its throne.

The Russian Revolution switched one despotism for another; and a century later, after the millions of deaths from its purges, slave camps, and purposely inflicted famines, Russia remains a despotism, without rights or justice. We all get only one life: imagine someone born under the billowing flags of the new Soviet Union in 1917 who had to live that whole single life without the freedom so much as to speak the truth of the squalid, oppressive reality he saw in front of his own eyes.

One single life—and what you can make of the one you have depends so much on what others have done to mold the time and place in which you live.

The Founders knew that truth so well that they announced their nationhood by significantly changing John Locke's catalog of natural rights. The shift began in the Virginia Declaration of Rights, in which George Mason emended Locke's right to "Lives, Liberties and Estates" to "Life and Liberty, with the Means of acquiring and possessing Property, and pursueing and obtaining Happiness and Safety."[1] Two months later, Thomas Jefferson penned the final pithy formulation of "Life, Liberty and the pursuit of Happiness" in the Declaration of Independence. The pursuit of happiness! Who but the Americans made a revolution to vindicate the paramount right of each individual to try to make the most of his life by his own effort as he sees fit?

A key reason the Revolution succeeded was its strictly limited scope. The Founders sought only liberty, not equality or fraternity. They aimed to make a political revolution, not a social or economic one, and they didn't seethe with an Old-World intensity of social rancor or class rage.[2] Their Lockean social-contract political philosophy taught them that the preservation of individual liberty was the goal of politics. Its basis was the surrender of a portion of man's original, natural freedom to a government that would protect the large remainder of it better than any individual could do on his own—the freedom to make your own fate, think your own thoughts, and own your own property without fear of bodily harm, unjust imprisonment, or robbery. The Founders' study of history taught them that the British constitution under which they had lived—"originally and essentially free," as Boston preacher Jonathan Mayhew described it—was the ideal embodiment of such a contract.[3] It was "the most perfect combination of human powers in society," John Adams wrote in 1766, "for the preservation of liberty and the production of happiness"—until George III began to violate it.[4] So Americans didn't take up arms to create a new world order according to some abstract theory. They sought only to restore the political liberty they had actually experienced for 150 years, and they constructed their new government to preserve it.

Because democratic self-government requires a special kind of culture—one that fosters self-reliant selves—the Protestantism of the Founding Fathers also helped the Revolution succeed. Their Protestant worldview placed an intense value on the individual—his conscience, the state of his soul, his understanding of Scripture, his personal relation to God, his salvation. It was an easy step for them to assume that, as each man was endowed by his Creator with an immortal soul immediately related to God, so he was similarly endowed with rights that are "not the Donation of Law," as Constitution signer William Livingston put it, but "prior to all political Institution" and "resulting from the Nature of Man."[5] It was easy for them to assume, therefore, that the individual, not the state, took center stage in the human drama. They saw the state as merely instrumental to the fate of the individual.

But their Protestantism also gave them a history that helps explain why the colonists didn't need or want a social revolution. The many non-Anglican Dissenters among them had already had such a revolution: they had had to uproot themselves from their relatives and friends, from "the fair cities, villages, and delightful fields of Britain," fleeing religious persecution into "the arms of savages and barbarians" in pursuit of liberty of conscience, as Mayhew put it in 1763.[6] The Plymouth Pilgrims, who wrote a literal social compact in the middle of the Atlantic Ocean, were only the first wave of a tide of such immigrants fleeing persecution: English and Scottish Presbyterians, Baptists, and Quakers; German pietists; French Huguenots; and others followed. In the eighteenth century, their offspring—John Jay, for example, descended from New York's huge contingent of Huguenot refugees from Catholic oppression, or Livingston, whose Presbyterian great-grandfather fled Scotland for Holland after the Stuart restoration—had as lively a sense of lucky escape from the Old Country's murderous religious tyranny as had American Jews whose forebears had escaped Russian pogroms and the Nazi Holocaust in the twentieth century. They had as acute a sense of having had to start their lives over again in a land that afforded them almost providential religious and political freedom, safety, and opportunity. They cherished liberty with the clarity and concreteness that only the experience of oppression confers.

It was that historical understanding that made Founders like Livingston or James Madison begin their journey to revolution with an assertion of freedom of conscience, which led to freedom to examine and judge for yourself, to think your own thoughts and speak and write them—and all the rest, since they knew that liberty is seamless. An "equal TOLERATION of Conscience," Livingston wrote, "is justly deem'd the Basis of public Liberty in this Country."[7] To Madison, for whom America "offer[ed] an Asylum to the persecuted and oppressed of every Nation and Religion," an established, official, obligatory religion, with dogmas you must profess, though it is seemingly "distant from the Inquisition, . . . differs from it only in degree. The one is the first step, the other the last in the career of intolerance."[8] Even George Washington, who never knew that his great-great-grandfather, an Anglican cleric, suffered religious persecution at the hands of Cromwell's Puritans, often liked to speak of America, with an endearing mix of Old and New Testament echoes, as "a Land of promise, with milk & honey," which offered a refuge to "the poor, the needy & the oppressed of the Earth; and anyone therefore who is heavy laden."[9] He wasn't alone among the colonists in thinking of the settlement of America in terms of the Israelites' providential deliverance from Egyptian tyranny to the Promised Land.[10]

Others had made their own personal social and economic revolution by uprooting themselves from home and coming to America for economic opportunity. From laborers signing on as indentured servants, up to younger sons of gentlefolk with no inheritance in prospect, immigrants came to make their own fortunes as best they could. If they believed their rights came from nature, not from government, they believed the same thing of their property, as people had believed from biblical and classical times and as Locke had reemphasized in the modern era. In explaining the origin of property rights, Locke had remarked of the State of Nature that "in the beginning all the World was *America*," where people create property by working "the wild Common of Nature." Their labor made the land and its produce their own, since "*labour makes the far greatest part of the value* of things, we enjoy in this World"—in fact, he calculated, "of the *Products* of the Earth, useful to the Life of Man 9/10 are the *effects of labour*."[11] Human effort, in other words—guided by human intelligence and imagination, the greatest of all natural resources—transforms the raw material of nature into something of use: we don't eat grain but bread, for example, which we then take to market over roads we have built to exchange for other products of human industry.

The colonists, because they and their ancestors had created wealth out of a wilderness, took for granted, with Locke, their right to their own property. And though they believed in the inborn equality of natural rights, they assumed, with Madison, that in a society where every man has the right to pursue his happiness and forge his fate, the unequal distribution of talents will naturally and unobjectionably produce inequality of wealth.[12] So economic equality—as opposed to an equality of rights and equality under the law—was no part of their revolutionary goal. Quite the reverse: "an equal division of property," Madison pronounced in *Federalist* 10, would be an "improper" and "wicked project."[13]

Colonists without personal experience of Old World oppression, or oft-heard family memories of it, knew from history and Scripture—from tales of Pharaoh and Herod, of Caesar, Nero, and Caligula, of Bloody Mary and the Stuarts—that even though government exists to preserve liberty, it too often has been freedom's destroyer. Even more vividly, they knew from the presence of slavery in their own midst just what monstrosities of organized cruelty and licensed oppression men are capable of inflicting on one another, given the power to do so; and, with tragic irony, the knowledge of their homegrown injustice made them all the more determined never to submit to the Crown's efforts "to make us as tame, & abject Slaves, as the Blacks we Rule over with such arbitrary Sway," as Washington vowed in 1774—a vow whose full import he grasped only late in life.[14] From *Magna Carta* and from the Glorious Revolution of 1688 the colonists knew that Englishmen had had to resist tyranny at swordpoint and reassert the strict limits that the social contract had placed on royal power. They knew what it had cost to assure, as Prime Minister William Pitt the Elder put it, that "The poorest man may in his cottage bid defiance to all the forces of the Crown. It may be frail, its roof may shake; the wind may blow through it; the storm may enter, the rain may enter—but the King of England cannot enter; all his force dares not cross the threshold of the ruined tenement." Or as the Jacobean chief justice Sir Edward Coke (pronounced cook), whose *Institutes of the Laws of England* every colonial lawyer had read, phrased it more succinctly 150 years earlier, "A man's house is his castle."

So when, after 150 years of letting Americans run their own affairs, the British government began to meddle malignly with their liberty once twenty-two-year-old George III became king in 1760, following the death of his grandfather, George II, the colonists unsurprisingly responded with outrage. After decreeing new colonial customs duties and stricter enforcement in 1764, London imposed its first direct levy on the colonies in 1765 in the Stamp Act, taxing every colonial newspaper, journal, legal document, almanac, playing card, and other paper product, in flagrant contravention of the "standing Maxim of English Liberty," as Livingston had quoted it more than a decade earlier, " 'that no Man shall be taxed, but with his own Consent.' "[15] As George Washington wrote to a friend, "I think the Parliament of Great Britain hath no more Right to put their hands into my Pocket, without my consent, than I have to put my hands into your's, for money."[16] Property doesn't belong to the government, and the social contract gives government no right to tell you what to do with your own.

The American Revolution, then, was doubly limited in its aims: limited to making only a political change without altering social or economic arrangements, and determined to set strict limits to its new government, fearful that any governmental power beyond the barest minimum necessary to protect liberty too easily could become a threat to liberty itself. So apprehensive were the Founders on this score that the governmental structure they erected after the Declaration of Independence proved too weak to perform its essential function of protecting their lives, liberties, and properties adequately, prolonging the Revolutionary War and increasing the hardships of the men who fought it. With great misgivings, the Founders had to create a new Constitution to give government the necessary powers, but their most urgent concern was to make those powers limited and enumerated, hedged round with every check and balance they could think of to prevent tyrannical abuse.

With similar prudence and modesty, when they wrote the new Constitution the Founders nursed no grandiose illusions that they were going to change human nature by altering the structure of government. Except for Thomas Jefferson, they didn't believe in human perfectibility, as did some of the French *philosophes* whose worldview Jefferson had absorbed from his years in Paris as well as from his voluminous reading. The Founders certainly didn't aspire to create something like the New Soviet Man. They had a very clear-eyed assessment of human nature. After all, their social-contract theory rested on a psychology that acknowledged what Patrick Henry called, conventionally enough, "the depravity of human nature," with its lusts, aggression, and greed no less inborn than its rights.[17] They tried to create a republic that would flourish with human nature as it is, with all its cross-grained passions and interests. They never forgot, as Alexander Hamilton cautioned, "that men are ambitious, vindictive, and rapacious."[18]

Still, they weren't cynics. Despite human nature's failings, they believed men capable of virtue, as history, literature, observation, and introspection taught them. Not all men, and not all the time; but if "there is not sufficient virtue among men for self-government," Madison observed in *Federalist* 55, then only "the chains of despotism can restrain them from destroying and devouring each other."[19] The question that vexed many throughout the Founding was what conditions virtue needed to thrive. What kind of culture and education would nourish it? Could it survive in a large republic? Would commerce and investment stifle it, especially since they breed luxury, which "the Voice of History" teaches, wrote Livingston, is "a Kind of political Cancer, which corrodes and demolishes the best regulated Constitution"?[20] Just look at "*Rome*; e'er-while the Nurse of Heroes, and the Terror of the World; but now the obscene Haunt of sequestered Bigots, and effeminate Slaves," he wrote in 1753; and for the next three decades Americans worried that liberty couldn't survive a culture of riches, with its "musicians, pimps, panders, and catamites," as one signer of the Declaration of Independence fretted.[21] In such a money-corrupted culture, some Founders worried, legislators and offices would be for sale.

The best answer to that fear was the example of the Founders themselves—men of luminous public spirit, who had no hesitation in "appealing to the Supreme Judge of the world for the rectitude of our intentions" in the Declaration of Independence. And that is the last, and largest, reason why the American Revolution succeeded where others failed. Its leaders were men of extraordinary character, intelligence, wisdom, and, in the case of Washington, the Founding's presiding genius, of heroic private virtue too. They had the unshakeable courage to "pledge to each other our Lives, our Fortunes and our sacred Honor" to assure the Revolution's success. Already social leaders, professional successes, or both, they had no psychological need to exalt themselves, and certainly not by abasing or terrorizing others, like such revolutionary sociopaths as Robespierre or Lenin. They never dreamed of placing themselves above the laws that they had made as the people's representatives, and they wholeheartedly agreed with Madison that if the "spirit that nourishes freedom" should "ever be so far debased as to tolerate a law not obligatory on the legislature as well as on the people, the people will be prepared to tolerate any thing but liberty."[22] And when they had played their parts and done their duty, they were content, indeed eager, to go home.

That so many great men came together at that time and place to do such great deeds is one of history's most profound miracles. That's why I thought it instructive to tell the story of the Founding through a series of biographies: to show not just what the Founders did but to dramatize who they were, what made and drove them, what they said in their own words about the meaning and rationale of their enterprise. Men, not abstract forces, made the Revolution, framed the American government, and set it in motion. They had ideals and purposes that they articulated with vigorous eloquence and successfully embodied in historical reality with steadfast dedication. The "who" and "why" of the Founding is as important as the "what," especially if we want to use the past to understand and judge the present, and shape the future.

Chapter One introduces New Jersey governor William Livingston, a passionately intellectual signer of the Constitution, who in the hugely influential magazine he edited and wrote in the early 1750s laid out the Lockean and constitutional rationale that the colonists wielded two decades later to justify their revolt to themselves and to the world. Chapter Two presents two of the Lee brothers who grew up in princely Stratford Hall, Virginia, and played central Revolutionary War roles—one as a Continental Congressman and signer of the Declaration of Independence, the other as a key wartime diplomat and propagandist for the American cause—along with their cousin, a dashing, though tragic, Revolutionary War commander, who also lived in Stratford. The saga of these fourth-generation Americans, who worked as a team for the cause of independence, dramatizes why people whose ancestors had built the country out of wilderness by their own efforts and at their own expense were not likely to take orders from London about how to run it over a century later.

The commanding figure of Part Two of the book, "The Federalists," is George Washington, unquestionably the Founding's key figure, who won the war, presided over the legendarily amicable and successful Constitutional Convention, and invented the office of president of the United States, setting the country on what, based on a lifetime of profound reflection and an unusual wealth of experience, he believed its course should be. The Founding's visionary in chief, he had a genius for recognizing and managing gifted people and motivating them to use all their considerable ingenuity to fill out the details of his idea. Part Two also paints a portrait of the underappreciated John Jay, the first chief justice of the United States. He was in fact the early republic's most canny diplomat, who with classic American initiative took the bit between his teeth to win a much more advantageous treaty ending the Revolution than anyone imagined possible (especially America's French allies), and whose later Jay Treaty gave the new nation the long interval of peace that Washington believed it needed to grow and prosper.

Completing Part Two is a portrait of the childless Washington's brilliant young protégé, the fatherless Alexander Hamilton, whose economic system brought into being the opportunity society that Washington wanted. To Treasury secretary Hamilton, who came to America a penniless immigrant, economics was soulcraft: only political liberty and a diversified economy, with a multitude of career possibilities, could allow individuals to develop all the talents that were within them: talents that would otherwise molder away in disappointment and frustration—and that, developed, would increase the prosperity of all. It's telling that in founding the mint, Hamilton made sure to provide coins of very small denominations, so that the humblest of Americans could participate in his opportunity economy, pursue their happiness, and rise as high as their abilities would permit.

Part Three, "The Republicans," depicts the third and fourth presidents, Thomas Jefferson and James Madison, such close friends and allies that Madison served not just as Jefferson's secretary of state but in effect as his prime minister or even co-president. "When Madison was asked his opinion by a common friend, he *very often* replied by putting the question, 'What says Mr. Jefferson?'" a contemporary recounts of the Jefferson administration. "Ask Jefferson for information, and he would not infrequently answer, 'Go to Mr. Madison—that was his measure—he knows a good deal more about it than I do.'

On being told this, Madison would smilingly say, 'It was *his measure, not mine*. I only *helped* to carry it into execution.'"[23] Chapter Eight tries above all to portray Jefferson's extraordinary, original, Enlightenment mind—not without its conflicts, though. Chapter Nine, an account of Madison as the Father of the Constitution, examines America's extraordinary Founding document both in theory and in practice. And Chapter Ten, on Madison's presidency, shows how so profound a theorist proved a surprisingly weak and irresolute chief executive, the legacy, perhaps, of standing so long first in Washington's and then in Jefferson's shadow.

The Founders at Home had its origin in a relatively recent visit to Monticello, which, though a lifelong architecture buff, I had never seen before. I was electrified—not just by the brilliance of its design, but because the house struck me as a vivid embodiment of Jefferson's soul, speaking in the most direct and personal way of his ideals and worldview. On the same Virginia trip, I saw, also for the first time, Mount Vernon, the work of art through which Washington, like Jefferson a gentleman-architect, expressed his deepest longings and most cherished values as he enlarged and improved the house, and sculpted and perfected the landscape, for over forty years, until the very last day of his life. I visited Montpelier, then in the midst of an extraordinarily ambitious project to restore it to the house that Madison had built but that a twentieth-century enlargement had swallowed up. The experience was like being at the excavation of Pompeii, breathlessly watching a long-lost past come back to light.

So I was hooked. As I thought of retelling the story of the Founding through biographies, so as to convey the immediacy and concreteness of the experience of the men who created it, it occurred to me that not only the words the Founders wrote but also the houses they built would bring their living reality home all the more vividly. Because they were trying to create a new nation where Americans would be truly at home, the houses they themselves inhabited (and in most cases designed and built) offer a vivid glimpse, in the most up close and personal way, into the ideal of life they imagined for themselves and for their countrymen. So each biography includes a description of the subject's house—all of them open to the public and richly worth visiting. It's an overstatement to say that they are haunted by the spirits of the great men who conceived and lived in them; but when you visit, you will know that you are in their presence.

PART I

The Firebrands

I

Conceived in Liberty: William Livingston and the Case for Revolution

When did the American Revolution begin? John Adams thought it started long before the shots rang out at Lexington and Concord in April 1775—even before Bostonians stained their harbor dark with tea in December 1773 or British redcoats shot down Americans in cold blood in the Boston Massacre of March 1770.

"But what do we mean by the American Revolution?" Adams asked in a revisionist 1818 essay. "Do we mean the American War? The Revolution was effected before the War commenced. The Revolution was in the minds and hearts of the people; a change in their religious sentiments, of their duties and obligations. . . . *This radical change in the principles, opinions, sentiments, and affections of the people was the real American Revolution.*" Anyone who wants to trace that cultural revolution and understand how it fused the American colonists into an independent nation, Adams advised, need only read the pamphlets, newspapers, and even handbills that flooded America between 1760 and 1775.[1] However spectacular, the war, Adams wrote Jefferson in 1815, "was only an effect and consequence" of that revolutionized worldview.[2]

In fact, though, the cultural transformation Adams described had started even earlier than the 1755 Harvard graduate remembered. It began in New York, with a shy but intellectually fiery lawyer named William Livingston, the editor and chief writer of a pathbreaking weekly magazine that from November 1752 to November 1753 disseminated throughout the colonies the world-shaking Lockean ideas of government by consent and the right of the people to depose a tyrannical king. Livingston's pugnacious *Independent Reflector* won fervent subscribers not only in New York but also in Philadelphia, Boston, and beyond, and colonial newspapers reprinted the magazine's essays for years afterward. Benjamin Franklin was an enthusiastic reader, and James Madison recalled that his fellow Princeton students read the *Reflector*'s essays avidly two decades later and strove to emulate what he called their "energy and eloquence" in their public-speaking assignments.[3] Livingston thundered out impassioned polemics for the next quarter century; but although he also served in the Continental Congress and the Constitutional Convention, and as New Jersey's governor for fourteen years, no mark he made on the fate of the continent proved as fateful as the one he imprinted on the American mind in those twelve pivotal months in the mid-eighteenth century.

SHY THOUGH HE WAS, Livingston was to the manor born—to Livingston Manor, a 160,000-acre principality his grandfather Robert had wrested from the Hudson Valley forest in the late seventeenth century. Robert's clergyman-father had fled Scotland for Holland with his family when his Presbyterian scruples barred him from swearing allegiance to Charles II after the Restoration, so Robert had grown up fluent in Dutch as well as English, a skill that greased his way to riches when he reached the New World in 1673. A Boston fur merchant hired the nineteen-year-old newcomer as his agent in Dutch-speaking Albany, gateway to the lush, beaver-thronged woodlands of the New York colony that England had seized from Holland only nine years earlier. The enterprising youth won the Albany fur traders' confidence and soon set up in the lucrative trade for himself. Mastering the Iroquois language, he became secretary of the Board of Indian Commissioners, with privileged access to the pelt supply. As another step in his single-minded self-advancement, in 1679 he married Alida Schuyler Van Rensselaer, widow of the recently deceased head of the vast Van Rensselaer patroonship surrounding Albany, and entered "ye Ranke of honest men," as one merchant put it, in welcoming Robert into the Dutch establishment and the Dutch Reformed Church.[4]

Only so honest, however. Though not himself a pirate, Robert did later act as lead financier of his friend Captain William Kidd's fabled 1696–99 piratical rampage, and many thought his own business methods verged on piracy, starting with his acquisition of Livingston Manor.[5] In 1684, he got a royal patent confirming his title to 2,000 virgin acres on the Hudson River's east bank below Albany, which he had bought from the Mohicans for 300 guilders' worth of cloth, guns, and kettles. The next year he bought 300 more acres 20-odd miles to the east. But in 1686, he somehow finagled a patent of ownership declaring the two widely separated parcels to be "adjacent," thereby giving him title to the land in between and magically transmuting 2,300 acres into 250 square miles, while also making him lord of the manor (a term of ownership, not a title of nobility). A new royal patent in 1715 gave the manor a seat in the colonial Assembly, cloaking generations of Livingstons with the political might of their own pocket borough.[6]

In 1691, New York's royal governor appointed Robert victualer to the Albany and New York City garrisons, to feed the soldiers at a set fee, regardless of the real cost of the provisions. The soldiers fared so ill that the next governor complained that Robert "has made a considerable fortune by his employments in the Government, never disbursing six pence but with the expectation of twelve pence[;] his beginning being a little Book keeper, he has screwed himself into one of the most considerable estates in the province. . . . [H]e had rather be called knave Livingston than poor Livingston."[7] In 1710, a new governor settled some of the 3,000 Palatine German refugees from war and famine, who had come to America under Queen Anne's protection, on Livingston Manor to produce tar for the Royal Navy, while Robert was to provision them. A winter of spoiled meat and not much of it sparked armed revolt, which redcoats quashed. Most of the Germans fled to more hospitable spots, and the disgusted governor branded Robert "ye most selfish man alive."[8]

When Robert died, rich and powerful, in 1728, his shrewd son, Philip, added thousands more acres to the Livingston domain and supplemented its industrial-scale saw-mill with New York's first iron-works in 1741. By 1765, it smelted ore from Livingston land into 1,500 tons of America's best iron each year. The manor produced beef, flour, hides, dried peas, and timber, too, shipped down the Hudson in Livingston vessels, along with the bales of furs for costly hats, to New York, the West Indies, and Europe.[9]

William Livingston, the youngest of the six sons (and three daughters) of Philip and his wife, Catherine Van Brugh, came into the world on November 30, 1723, in the family home in Albany. With the step-gabled ends of its houses facing the street, Dutch style, and their stoops scrubbed clean daily, the little frontier town looked like a stage set of Vermeer's Holland improbably dropped down into the north woods. Its thrifty, burgherly manners echoed Dutch culture, too, and William probably went to school at the Dutch church where he'd been baptized—though, as the son of a rich merchant and a relative of all the colony's patroon grandees, he later spoke nostalgically of "the ease and affluence in which we were bred."[10] Each summer, the Indians came to Albany to sell their furs, and a camp of wigwams sprouted around the town. Livingston got to know them and their language well when his new tutor, a Yale-trained minister, went to serve as a missionary to the Mohawks and took his eleven-year-old pupil to live with them in the woods for all of 1735—good fur-business training, Livingston's father thought.[11] That year, a world away in London, Alexander Pope published his *Epistle to Arbuthnot*, and Handel's *Ariodante* premiered at Covent Garden.

At thirteen, rather than the more usual seventeen, Livingston went to Yale, and he emerged after graduation in 1741 transformed, not by the Presbyterian orthodoxy of the college's teaching but by the riches of its library, which electrified him. Above all, he devoured Locke, especially the *Letter on Toleration*, whose urbanely reasonable case for freedom of thought and religion—with its mild observation that you'd no sooner swallow a monarch's prescription for your bodily than for your spiritual health, neither of which concerns the state—resonated with Livingston's deepest intuitions. Given Yale's reputation in those early days for fierce republicanism, the budding intellectual probably studied Locke's *Two Treatises of Government*, along with the other classics of seventeenth-century English republicanism that he later cherished in his own large library—James Harrington's *Oceana*, for instance, which like Locke's *Second Treatise* argued for a government based on consent, protecting the natural rights of life, liberty, and religious freedom through a system of checks and balances; or Algernon Sidney's *Discourses*, which maintained that men have "the liberty of setting up such governments as best please themselves"; that they have not just the right but indeed the duty to rebel against, and even kill, tyrants who threaten their liberties; and that justified rebellion only makes a nation stronger.[12]

From Sidney, Livingston also learned the importance of a culture of virtue: "Liberty," Sidney had written, "cannot be preserved if the Manners of the People are corrupted"—"manners" meaning in that age a combination of customs and values.[13] Like Livingston, many of the Founding generation avidly read these republican writers, and many joined him in poring over Joseph Addison's *Cato*, a now stilted-seeming 1712 verse drama about a heroic champion of Roman republicanism against Julius Caesar's military dictatorship, who served the colonists as a model of all that they meant by republican virtue. At Yale, Livingston also read the wildly popular magazines that Addison wrote with Sir Richard Steele—the *Tatler* and the *Spectator*—which in their breezy, conversational way sought to cultivate in their readers the skeptical good sense and educated taste that, almost by reflex, judge everything freely, politics included. He also read (and later imitated) the era's greatest writer, Alexander Pope, whose poetic satires proved the power of public ridicule to curb abuses.

The skeptical rationalism Livingston learned from these English writers only strengthened when the evangelical revival movement known as the Great Awakening convulsed Yale in his last years there and swept his fellow students, most of them studying for the Presbyterian ministry, into its enthusiasm, which many found an emotional liberation from the sifting of theological minutiae key to Yale's teaching. Keenly curious, Livingston went to hear the Awakening's celebrity preachers, George Whitefield and Gilbert Tennent, in 1740, but he remained unawakened, choosing to steer with cool Enlightenment reason between the dogmatism of his teachers and the hysteria of his fellow students. "I can never persuade myself," he told a classmate, "that such Convulsions, . . . trances, groanings, . . . Shakings, . . . Ecstasies . . . are any Sign that Christianity prevails amongst a people."[14]

LIVINGSTON'S FATHER planned to split the chores of his empire among his six sons, sending several as merchants to New York City and the West Indies, and anointing William the family lawyer. That William had a talent for drawing and wanted to study painting was of no interest to his ruthlessly determined father, who apprenticed him in 1742 to New York City's leading attorney, James Alexander, a rich, intelligent Scottish immigrant with no flair for teaching. The young clerk began copying wills, deeds, and so on, in that pre-photocopier, pre-computer age, and reading, often from dawn until midnight, the then-standard text, Volume One of Sir Edward Coke's *Institutes*, a property-law treatise that seemed to get longer the more he read, he lamented, "so that 'twas impossible to attain the conclusion thro' all the ages of Eternity."[15] In 1745 the frustrated clerk complained in a pseudonymous newspaper column that "To make a young Fellow trifle away the Bloom of his Age, when his Invention is Readiest, his Imagination Warmest, and all his Faculties in their full Vigour and Maturity" was "Drudgery . . . fit only for a Slave."[16]

His next pseudonymous article, a year later, unluckily failed to conceal his identity, and it got him instantly fired, for it lampooned his boss's wife. When Mrs. Alexander, an heiress at the top of New York's pecking order, wouldn't let her daughter accept a valentine from

Trinity Church's young organist as beneath her status, Livingston—who hated pretension as only someone born to rank and wealth but not to social ease and charm can—exploded with contempt in a piece in the *New-York Weekly Post-Boy* entitled *Of Pride, arising from Riches and Prosperity.* Asserting what would become an insistent American sense that "Real Dignity and Worth are personal and intrinsic" rather than external qualities (as he later wrote in the *Reflector*), Livingston rebuked his boss's wife, not by name but recognizable as New York's "haughtiest and most insolent Woman," for forcing her daughter to a crude breach of good breeding, properly understood. After all, he said, with more radical egalitarianism than he perhaps intended, God himself "makes no Difference between the Monarch and the Beggar; but considers the universal Race of Men as his Children and Family." When Livingston couldn't deny Alexander's outraged accusation that he was the author, the ex-clerk found himself back in Albany four months before his four-year apprenticeship would have ended.[17]

His father got him a clerkship with New York City's other top lawyer, William Smith, Sr., and made him take it. In July 1746, with a sinking heart, the twenty-two-year-old returned to the grindstone and found . . . he liked it. The English-born, Yale-educated, broadly cultivated Smith proved an amiable teacher, who believed that wide general reading was key to making a good lawyer, a precept his bookish clerk embraced.[18]

Livingston was not just absorbing the law in Alexander's and Smith's offices but also marinating in a journalistic and political tradition that within a few years he would carry on. Alexander had been the editor and main writer of America's first opposition newspaper, the *New-York Weekly Journal*, which he founded in 1733 and modeled on an English magazine of the 1720s, *Cato's Letters*, by radical Whigs John Trenchard and Thomas Gordon, later also Livingston's model for the *Independent Reflector.* Alexander, who sometimes simply reprinted Trenchard and Gordon's essays, wholeheartedly endorsed their theory of limited monarchy, in which the laws, backed by a free press, protect everyone's basic rights against invasion by all state authorities, from the king on down—including especially, when Alexander and Smith wrote, New York's royal governor, William Cosby.[19]

Sparking the first constitutional crisis in British America—and the most celebrated trial of the pre-revolutionary era—Cosby had set out to sue one of his councilors in a dispute over the spoils of office. Fearing that no jury would support his dubious claim, however, he asked the Supreme Court to sit as a nonjury Exchequer Court, an exotic ploy that outraged New Yorkers, who thought that trials without juries violated the rights of free-born British subjects. When Chief Justice Lewis Morris, owner of the sprawling Morrisania manor in Westchester, forbade the maneuver as illegal, Cosby fired him and elevated loyal supporter James De Lancey, thirty, to the chief justiceship instead. "THE PEOPLE of this city," Alexander thundered in his January 1734 issue, "think, as matters now stand, that their LIBERTIES and PROPERTIES are precarious, and that SLAVERY is like to be entailed on them and their posterity, if some past things be not amended."[20]

Alexander published his articles anonymously; the only name on the *Weekly Journal*'s masthead was its printer's, John Peter Zenger, one of the 3,000 Palatine German refugees who had reached America in 1710, the biggest German immigration of colonial times. When Zenger also printed two broadside ballads deriding the authorities for starting to "chop and change" the colony's judges, Cosby had him arrested in November 1734 for seditious libel in the ballads and in the newspaper, setting impossible bail of ten times his net worth. Two grand juries agreed that the ballads were libelous but professed bewilderment as to who might have written or published them, and so refused to indict. Cosby, exasperated, ordered his attorney general to bring charges on a so-called "information," a device that, while arguably legal, was as arbitrary and irregular as an Exchequer Court.[21]

Alexander and Smith volunteered as Zenger's lawyers, and their opening statement highlighted the trial's threat to British constitutional rights. They began by challenging the legitimacy of the commissions of two of the three presiding judges, including newly minted

Chief Justice De Lancey, who served "during pleasure" of the governor rather than "during good behavior" (for life, that is), as was customary in England. As any reader of *Cato's Letters* would know, officials who serve at pleasure can easily decline into henchmen of the executive officer who can fire them. De Lancey met the challenge by disbarring the two lawyers for their impudence—though even he couldn't sit still for the prosecutor's shameless jury-rigging that put Cosby's baker, shoemaker, and tailor in the jury pool. For this part of the trial, at least, he required fair play.[22]

THE DISBARRED Alexander and Smith (both reinstated in 1737) enlisted as their replacement America's most famous lawyer, Benjamin Franklin's older friend Andrew Hamilton of Philadelphia, who, according to historian of New York William Smith, Jr. (once Livingston's fellow clerk), "had art, eloquence, vivacity, and humor, was ambitious of fame, negligent of nothing to ensure success, and possessed a confidence which no terrors could awe."[23] Hamilton purposely turned the case into an epochal constitutional showdown, beginning with his opening statement on August 4, 1735, when he materialized in the courtroom as a complete surprise to the judges and prosecution, and announced himself as Zenger's lawyer. "I'll save Mr. Attorney the trouble of examining his witnesses," Hamilton said, and "confess that [Zenger] both printed and published the two newspapers" for which he's being prosecuted. The real question was whether they were true or false.[24]

Hold on, Chief Justice De Lancey interrupted—correctly objecting that the law of that era said that a libel is no less libelous for being true. After all, as the prosecutor had noted, government, which protects our lives, religion, and property, is too essential to allow people to weaken or subvert it by publishing scandal, whether true or false, about the officials who administer it. The jury's duty is only to decide if Zenger published the papers, and it must then leave it to the Court to decide if they are libelous.[25]

Not necessarily, Hamilton countered. The jury's duty includes considering whether the law at issue invades the basic rights of Englishmen, and if so, jurors should ignore it as illegitimate. "This of leaving it to the judgment of the Court *whether the words are libelous or not* in effect renders juries useless," Hamilton observed.[26]

Why didn't the chief justice, who'd had no qualms about disbarring Alexander and Smith for similar effrontery, stop Hamilton in his tracks? Because, beyond his eminence and courtroom charisma, no trivial matters—along with his good sense not to attack the judges personally—Hamilton had also sounded one of the deepest chords of British jurisprudence, and even the arrogant young De Lancey didn't dare cut him off. "The people of England," the defense attorney argued, striking the keynote of Sir Edward Coke's teachings, have rights that "nature and the laws of our country have given us" since time immemorial. Chief among these, Hamilton said, paraphrasing the key thirty-ninth chapter of *Magna Carta*, are that "their liberties and properties" cannot be taken away "without the judgment of a jury of their equals," and no one can stop them from "exposing and opposing arbitrary power . . . by speaking and writing truth."[27]

All the precedents the prosecution cites for criminalizing truthful speech as libel, Hamilton noted, are cases from the Star Chamber, the arbitrary court of royal officials that Charles I, in particular, wielded as an infamous weapon of tyranny before the Long Parliament abolished it in 1641. They come from "the reign of an arbitrary prince," in which "judges, who held their places at pleasure" (like De Lancey) presided over juryless proceedings, brought by informations rather than indictments, trampling the "ancient and sacred right of trials by grand and petit juries" that normally protect the liberties of Englishmen—and that the Glorious Revolution thankfully reasserted in 1688, Hamilton reminded his hearers.[28]

Zenger, though shamefully charged by a Star Chamber–style information rather than by a grand jury indictment, at least now faces a trial jury of twelve "*honest and lawful men*," said Hamilton, reaching his peroration. "In your justice lies our safety," he told the jurors—whom he had artfully transformed, remarked William Smith, Jr., in his *History*, into "triers of their rulers rather than Zenger." Should they acquit Zenger, Hamilton concluded, "every man who prefers freedom to a life of slavery will bless and honor you as men who have baffled the attempt of tyranny." For the law they vindicate, as one colonist praised their swift not-guilty verdict, is natural law—what "ought to be law, and will always be law wherever justice prevails."[29]

James Alexander's 1736 *Brief Narrative* of the Zenger trial—one of the first of those pamphlets that John Adams thought sowed the Revolution—carried to every corner of British America Hamilton's virtuoso appeal to the historical liberties of the British constitution, to natural rights, and to abstract justice, and the colonists were to invoke all of them in various permutations for the next forty years.[30] "The trial of Zenger in 1735 was the germ of American freedom, the morning star of that liberty which subsequently revolutionized America," Gouverneur Morris, Chief Justice Morris's great-grandson and author of the final draft of the U.S. Constitution, pronounced decades later.[31] To London, Alexander's pamphlet brought news that Americans believed they had certain ironclad rights that they would not give up without a fight.

While serving as Alexander's and Smith's clerk, William Livingston also had more youthful concerns. Two years into his apprenticeship with Alexander, he fell in love at first sight with Susanna French, a young woman "above panygerick," he wrote, "uniting the Saint and Lady in one." She soon agreed to marriage, though apprenticeship rules required waiting until Livingston's clerkship would end two years later. Before then, however, Livingston had been fired and had transferred to Smith's office, extending the wait.

And then, Susanna (more lady than saint, it seems) got pregnant.[32]

The couple snuck off to New Jersey, where a friendly minister broke every rule and secretly married them in March 1747. They tried to hide their misadventure all their lives—though with imperfect success, since during the Revolution a Tory newspaper denounced Livingston, then governor, as "a most notorious fornicator."[33] Childbirth in May or June left Susanna ill and weak, and just after she recovered, her baby son died in September. Of twelve more babies, seven survived to adulthood, and after almost forty years of marriage Livingston wrote his wife, "If I was to live to the age of Methusaleh, I believe I should not forget a certain flower that I once saw in a certain garden; and however that flower may have since faded, towards the evening of that day, I shall always remember how it bloomed in the morning, nor shall I ever love it the less."[34]

Not just love but also poetry filled young Livingston's fancy. Shortly after his baby's birth, he published a skillful imitation of Pope's heroic couplets, *Philosophic Solitude*, in conventional praise of the simple, rural life, lived

Far from the painted belle, and white-gloved beau,
The lawless masquerade, and midnight show.

Immensely popular, the poem went through more than a dozen editions over the next forty years and still appeared in anthologies in the mid-1790s, after its author's death.[35]

One passage, for all its conventionality, makes you wonder if Livingston's lifelong scorn for pretentiousness, snobbery, and even injustice sprang from his judgment of his own rich and powerful father and grandfather:

Oft on the vilest[,] riches are bestow'd,
To show their meanness in the sight of God.
High from a dunghill, see a Dives rise,
And Titan-like insult the avenging skies:
The crowd in adulation calls him lord,
By thousands courted, flatter'd, and adored:
In riot plunged, and drunk with earthly joys,
No higher thought his grovelling soul employs;

The poor he scourges with an iron rod,
And from his bosom banishes his God.

The indulgent William Smith forgave Livingston for flouting the rule that apprentices can't marry, and the newlywed rejoined his fellow clerks, increasingly his close friends and allies—the boss's son (and future historian) William Smith, Jr., and John Morin Scott, both Yale graduates related to Livingston by marriage. All three were Presbyterians, too, once Livingston left the Dutch Reformed Church in search of sermons in English. The three clerks formed a discussion club that New York's Tories branded a seditious "republican cabel," thanks to the sponsorship of the elder Smith and James Alexander, the two Zenger-case Whig notables. Nonsense, Livingston replied in print; they were high-minded, philosophizing literati, not tavern-haunting snobs like their critics. But the three young men had already gained notoriety as the radical "triumvirate."[36]

In October 1748, Livingston joined the New York Bar, earning just under £100 a year doing wills and deeds for family and friends, when the big house he rented for the next two decades on busy Water Street cost £65 annually. Still struggling three years later, he wrote:

> *Avoid, avoid, the inextricable Snare*
> *Nor madly venture to approach the Bar;*
> *But instant clipping vain Ambition's Wing*
> *Turn* Carman, Cobbler, Fiddler, *any Thing.*

But just then, business took off, and by 1754 he was earning £450 a year and counted as one of New York's top lawyers.[37] Once so lank that he disparaged his "spindle shanks," along with his "long-nosed, long-chin'd ugly looking appearance," he ripened into a "dignified corpulence," thanks to his love of oysters, lobsters, and only the best wine, "at any Price."[38]

Still, his heart lay with literature, and early in 1749 the triumvirate of ex-clerks, along with another friend, met to plan a weekly magazine on the model of Addison and Steele's *Spectator*, "for correcting the taste and improving the Minds of our fellow Citizens," Livingston wrote. They'd launch their journal once they had written 150 articles in advance, so they'd never run out of material. Nearly three years later, with only twenty stories in the bank, Livingston, now twenty-nine, could wait no longer, and he launched the journal, ultimately writing thirty-three of the fifty-four essays, and part of four others.[39]

When the first issue of the *Independent Reflector* appeared on November 30, 1752, it looked like Addison and Steele's journal but sounded like Trenchard and Gordon's. As in *Cato's Letters*, politics, not taste, was the keynote. The magazine, Livingston wrote, wouldn't shrink "from vindicating the *civil and religious RIGHTS* of my Fellow Creatures: From exposing the peculiar Deformity of publick *Vice*, and *Corruption*: and displaying the amiable Charms of *Liberty*, with the detestable Nature of *Slavery* and *Oppression*."[40] Nor would he hesitate to point fingers, he promised, echoing Pope's *Epilogue to the Satires*, because "the obdurate Criminal, who fears not GOD himself, is seized with a Panic, at the Apprehensions of having his Actions publickly exposed."[41]

In the tenth issue, his corruption probe hit a nerve and sparked an uproar: city councilors, he reported, had schemed to sell their relatives city-owned East River lots at prices amounting to a £6,000 theft of public funds.[42] Magazine sales soared, and, in a New York whose squalid eighteenth-century politics often turned on the business and personal feuds of the Livingston and De Lancey clans, William Livingston also enjoyed shaming the De Lanceyite villains in this case.

His next campaign roused more furor—and boosted sales higher. The ruckus began with his defense of the Moravians, German pietists whose quirky beliefs troubled their neighbors. Their religious principles were nobody's business, Livingston wrote. After all, "Every Man is *orthodox* to himself, and *heretical* to all the World besides." All that concerns the civil authorities is conduct, and the Moravians "are a plain, open, honest inoffensive People," the *Reflector* observed, "irreprehensible in their Lives and Conversations." However much a "Pulpit-Scold" might dislike their worshipping without the "Bows

THE

INDEPENDENT REFLECTOR.

NUMBER XXX.

Thursday, June 21, 1753.

The Multiplicity of OATHS, *and the Levity and Indecorum wherewith they are administred and taken, pernicious to Society.*

Thou shalt not take the Name of the Lord thy God in Vain. MOSES.

AN Oath is a religious Asseveration, by which we renounce the Divine Clemency, or imprecate the Divine Vengeance, in Case we speak false. When, therefore, a Being, Omniscient and Omnipotent, is invoked, as a Witness to the Truth of our Testimony, it creates the strongest Presumption in favour of our Evidence; it being utterly improbable, that any Man should be so abandoned, and consummately impious, as seriously to defy almighty Vengeance, and deliberately to irritate a Being of uncontroulable Power. Hence an Oath is justly esteemed the firmest Bond of Society; without a due Regard to which, in the present degenerate Circumstances of Human Nature, no Government could long well subsist. Accordingly, all the Nations of the Earth have paid the greatest Credit to what was delivered on Oath, and expressed the deepest Horror at the Guilt of Perjury. *Our Ancestors,* says CICERO, *could never find any Thing stronger than an Oath, to bind us to the faithful Discharge of our Engagements.* The Historian DIODORUS SICULUS, reports of the ancient *Egyptians, That, by their Laws, Persons, who had forsworn themselves, were adjudged to capital Punishments, as guilty of the two greatest Crimes; in violating that Piety which they owed to God; and in destroying Faith from amongst Men, the strongest Pillar of human Society.* PLUTARCH carries the Matter so far, as to insist on the Performance of a Promise on Oath, tho' made to an Enemy. *He who deceives his Enemy,* says he, *by an Oath, confesses, that he fears him, but despises God.* Nay, the Ancients had so great a Dread of Perjury, as to imagine, it would be punished on the Posterity of the Criminal. Hence VIRGIL observes, that the *Romans* were sufficiently punished for the Perjury of the *Trojans,* from whom they claimed their Origin, by a beautiful Allusion to the fabulous Account of LAOMEDON'S Perfidy to APOLLO and NEPTUNE.

---Satis jam pridem sanguine nostro,
Laomedonteæ luimus perjuria Trojæ.

So sensible were the sage Legislators of Antiquity, of the Importance of Oaths, to the Well-being of the Community, that they never suffered them to be taken, but on very necessary Occasions, nor even then, without the utmost Solemnity. They were convinced, that every Thing, tending to abate the Awe, which Mankind naturally have for an Oath, ought to be discouraged; and on the contrary, whatever conduced to create or preserve a Veneration for that solemn Act of Religion, to be countenanced and promoted.

'And

The "Independent Reflector" *Collection of the Author*

and Capers" of established orthodoxy, they are entitled to "the undisturbed Enjoyment of their civil and religious Liberties."[43] In response, some of those pulpit-scolds demanded, loudly but in vain, that a grand jury indict the implacably anticlerical Livingston for libel.[44]

This skirmish proved but a prologue to the *Reflector*'s main battle, making the province of New York "a scene of confusion, of uproar, of disorder," as a Tory exile grumpily recorded, and leading Livingston, like so many seventeenth- and eighteenth-century English and American thinkers, from a defense of religious liberty to explicit political radicalism.[45] The fight concerned the founding of King's College, later Columbia, which New York's Anglicans wanted to set up as a sectarian institution with a royal charter.[46] Their plan tore open an old wound: in a colony only 10 percent Anglican, and in a city with two Dutch Reformed churches, and one each Presbyterian, Lutheran, German Reformed, and Anglican—plus a Friends meetinghouse and a synagogue—only the Dutch churches and the Anglican Trinity Church had royal-charter protection. More gallingly, Trinity alone received *all* the money from a 1693 tax imposed to support Protestant ministers, not specifically Anglican ones. Now the Anglicans (including the De Lanceys, who long ago had left the Huguenot church for Trinity in a huff) wanted to set up their own college with money raised from lotteries the Assembly had licensed for the general "Advancement of Learning," with an Anglican faculty to be paid from the colony-wide excise tax.[47] The "Money hitherto collected is public Money," the *Reflector* objected. "When the Community is taxed, it ought to be for the Defence, or Emolument of the Whole: Can it, therefore, be supposed, that all shall contribute for the Uses, the ignominious Uses of a few?"[48]

Moreover, as Livingston surveyed the colonial colleges, most looked like the Yale he remembered, places less of enlightenment than of indoctrination—literally, for they were training prospective clergymen in the doctrines of their sects. Any college has to be about forming as well as informing students' adolescent minds, of course, so much college teaching is bound to be indoctrination, with powerful consequences.[49] "The Principles or Doctrines implanted in the Minds of Youth," Livingston wrote, "pass from the Memory and Understanding to the Heart, and at length become a second Nature." In time they "appear on the Bench, at the Bar, in the Pulpit, and in the Senate, and unavoidably affect our civil and religious Principles."[50] So instead of indoctrinating students with narrow, sectarian dogma, why not infuse them with "public Spirit and Love of their Country" that will "make them more extensively serviceable to the Common-Wealth?"[51]

Because the college will shape New York's future as its graduates move into government, why not have it publicly chartered, funded, and controlled by the people's elected representatives in the Assembly, to allay fears that any one sect will gain control and impose a single viewpoint, based on "Doctrines destructive of the Privileges of human Nature"?[52] A rich multiplicity of competing opinions will surely foster deeper and freer thought than an enforced, intellectually stultifying, possibly false and possibly objectionable orthodoxy. Madison later echoed Livingston's contention that "the Variety of Sects in the Nation, are a Guard against the Tyranny and Usurpation of one over another" in his celebrated *Federalist* 10, which argued that a big republic is better than a small one, because the clash among "the variety of sects dispersed over the entire face" of it will ensure that no sect, faction, or interest group can control the rest.[53]

Of all possible sectarian colleges (and Livingston imagined only Protestant ones possible in America), an Anglican one would be the worst, he believed. It wasn't just that the Church of England retained "too many popish relicks"; more important, its High Church faction had never accepted the Glorious Revolution of 1688, with its strictly limited monarchy and Bill of Rights. Instead, High Churchmen clung to their belief in the divine right of kings, and they begrudged the 1689 Toleration Act that granted freedom of worship to Protestants who didn't belong to the official, established Anglican church headed by the monarch.[54] Given the chance, they'd restore the oppression of Dissenters that prevailed in England before that law—oppression, Livingston reminded his non-Anglican readers, that "drove your Ancestors to this Country, then a dreary Waste and a barren Desert." Never forget, he exhorted, "the countless Sufferings of your pious Predecessors, for Liberty of Conscience, and the Right of private Judgment. What Afflictions did they not endure, what fiery Trials did they not encounter, before they found in this remote Corner of the Earth, that Sanctuary and Requiem which their native Soil inhumanly deny'd them? . . . And will you entail on your Posterity that Bondage, to escape which they brav'd the raging Deep, and penetrated the howling Wilderness!"[55]

Despite Livingston's campaign, the college opened as an Anglican institution in July 1754, with seven students meeting in the Trinity Church vestry. A 1756 deal split the lottery money between the college and a quarantine center for crewmen of infected ships—"between the two pest houses," William Smith, Sr., scoffed—and the college didn't shake off the stigma the *Reflector* had placed on it until after the Revolution.[56]

The political issues at the heart of the college battle—taxation and freedom of thought and conscience—led Livingston to set forth his deepest political beliefs, the first public exposition of Lockean social-contract theory in the colonies.[57] Journalistic and unsystematic, his half-dozen issues on the subject nevertheless add up to a coherent argument that provided the Revolution's key justification. Untangled, Livingston's case runs like this—and it's worth hearing it in his own words, because they resounded in the colonists' ears for the next forty years as loudly as *life, liberty, and the pursuit of happiness* echo in ours.

Before there was any government, nature created men free, and endowed them with equal rights. But in that primitive "State of Nature," where physical strength carried all before it, "the Weak were a perpetual Prey to the Powerful." In order to "preserve to every Individual, the undisturbed Enjoyment of his Acquisitions, and the Security of his Person," men established society and chose rulers to keep the peace and settle disputes, by force if need be.[58]

This was a choice of the lesser of two evils, for "Government, at best, is a Burden, tho' a necessary one. Had Man been wise from his Creation, he . . . might have enjoyed the gifts of a liberal Nature, unmolested, unrestrained. It is the Depravity of Mankind that has necessarily introduced Government; and so great is this Depravity, that without it, we could scarcely subsist," wrote Livingston, more strongly influenced than Locke was by Thomas Hobbes's vision of the state of nature as a brutish war of all against all. Every political theory rests, explicitly or implicitly, on a psychology—on a theory about the raw material of human nature that politics has to work with—and Livingston accepted Hobbes's emphasis on man's instinctive predatory aggressiveness. To guard against our inborn tendency to invade each other's "Person or Fortune," Livingston wrote, we "have ceded a Part of our original Freedom, to secure to us the rest."[59]

For him, the point of this tale of government's birth was that it clearly marked the limits of royal power. "Communities were formed not for the Advantage of one Man," he stressed, "but for the Good of the whole Body."[60] Since subjects gave their king power only to defend them "in the peaceable Possession of their Rights, by punishing the Invader," only "what is injurious to the Society, or some particular Member of it, can be the proper Object of civil Punishment; because, nothing else falls within the Design of forming the Society."[61]

Yet all history shows that rulers thirst to overstep the limits of their legitimate authority because of the same all-too-human depravity that made the social contract necessary. Rulers have abused their power at least since Nero and Caligula, because "men being naturally ambitious, and aspiring after illimitable Dominion, are too apt to measure the Extent of justifiable Authority, by their insatiable Appetite for an unbounded Licentiousness."[62] So "a People should be careful of yielding too much of their original Power, even to the most just Ruler, and [they] always retain the Privilege of degrading him whenever he acts in Contradiction to the Design of his Institution."[63] As Thomas Jefferson later put it with his matchless pithiness, "kings are the servants, not the proprietors of the people," and they can be fired.[64]

Citizens should further hedge the limited power they give their ruler with checks and balances, just as the British constitution so ingeniously pits the lords and the commons against the king, Livingston wrote—though the Framers of the American Constitution later puzzled mightily over how to re-create that equipoise, anxiously searching for a counterpart to the House of Lords in a senate of the wise, good, and rich, until James Madison came up with an alternate mechanism in the Livingstonian balance of interest against interest.[65] Yet even "the best devised civil Constitution, is subject to Corruption and Decay, thro' the Pride, Ambition, and Avarice of those in whose Care it is lodged," Livingston warned. And when oppression grows too bitter, "Men of true Principles would rather return to a State of primitive Freedom, in which every Man has a Right to be his own Carver, than be the Slaves of the greatest Monarch, or even suffer under the most unlimited Democracy in the Universe."[66]

It was hard enough for Tories to hear that royal authority rests on so flimsy a foundation as the consent of the people rather than on divine right, harder still for them to hear that the people can legitimately depose their king. From such Whig radicalism, they thought, it was one short step to republicanism, and they condemned the *Reflector*'s authors as "noisy Scribblers" seeking "to mimick *Trenchard*" and the magazine itself as subversively antimonarchist.[67] It wasn't, but Livingston pulled no punches. A subject's "Person and Property are guarded by Laws, which the Sovereign himself cannot infringe," he insisted, and if "the Magistrate exercises Force unauthorized by Law, the Violence he offers must be considered as the Violence of a private Person, which the People have an undoubted Right to repel."[68] And repel it Britons have done, as recently as 1688, when they replaced James II with William and Mary, or when "Charles I paid his Head" in 1649 to show that "a Crown can never rescue its iniquitous Possessor from that Punishment which his Crimes may justly demerit."[69] It is the tyrant—not the rebel—who is the criminal. But his Anglican critics, Livingston lamented, clearly believed "that mankind was born with yokes and fetters; and that the original equality and independence of the species, was a chimera in politics, and blasphemy in religion."[70]

Where are the limits of royal power? Above all, no ruler can invade a citizen's property, which men hold by a right bestowed by nature, not by government. "It is a standing Maxim of *English Liberty*, 'that no Man shall be taxed, but with his own Consent,'" the *Reflector* therefore declared. In fact, a "Tax ought to be considered as the voluntary Gift of the People, to be applied to such Uses, as they, by their Representatives shall think expedient."[71] This statement appeared, remember, a dozen years before the Stamp Act turned *taxation without representation is tyranny* into a revolutionary catchphrase, and it prepared the colonists almost instinctively to recognize and resist that abuse of power when they saw it.

Second, since it is an "Absurdity to suppose, that Government was ever designed to *enslave* the *Consciences of Men*," the *Reflector* held, "the civil Power hath no Jurisdiction over the Sentiments or Opinions of the Subject, till such Opinions break out into Actions prejudicial to the Community, and then it is not the Opinion, but the Action that is the Object of the Punishment."[72] So no government can prescribe religious belief, and no monarch may "reduce a Man's Body to Ashes for the Illumination of his Understanding."[73]

More broadly, because the "Advancement of Learning depends on the free Exercise of Thought; it is . . . absurd to suppose that it should thrive under a Government that makes it Treason even for a Man to think."[74] Everyone is free to dissent, not just in religion but in all else, and Livingston urged everyone to think, question, examine, and criticize as widely and iconoclastically as he could. For him, thinking for yourself was a duty as well as a right. However commonplace that idea may sound today, it was radical in its time; though even in our own age, orthodoxies of received opinion serve as barriers to thought, since we assume we already know the truth about a host of issues that we therefore needn't analyze for ourselves. Livingston championed a characteristically American intellectual empiricism—"that sort of

Knowledge which is built upon the Observation of human Life" and that tests our "most darling Tenets . . . by the Rules of cool deliberate Reason."[75] Such knowledge yields powerful practical results, making a nation "free, enterprizing and dauntless."[76]

Free thought is key to political freedom, because it pierces the mystique of power, swathed in as many layers of superstition and mummery as the ritualistic religion Livingston so despised. Imprisoned in the mental dungeon of such absurd orthodoxies as the divine right of kings or the deference supposedly due to noble birth, men can't so much as glimpse the freedom and equality of rights that is their birthright. "Almost all the mischiefs which Mankind groan under, arise from their suffering themselves to be led by the Nose, without a proper Freedom of Thought and Examination," the *Independent Reflector* warned. "Upon this[,] Priestcraft has erected its stupendous Babel, and Tyranny reared her horrible Domination."[77] If people had the habit of free thought and critical reason, they'd see through the humbug that holds them in thrall, the first step toward liberty. And when citizens elect their own representatives in the Assembly or the city council, Livingston cautioned—unknowingly preparing his readers for the elective republic that lay in the future—they must be even more vigilant independent reflectors, always on guard against candidates' schemes "to enfeeble or bind them in the Fetters of Credulity," so that they'll "abandon their *Reason*, and . . . follow their Leaders with an implicit Faith," akin to the religious hysteria Livingston saw sweep over Yale.[78]

That's why a free press is a vital bulwark of liberty, allowing a patriotic editor to "diffuse his salutary Principles thro' the Breasts of his Countrymen, . . . warn them against approaching Danger, unite them against the Arm of despotic Power, and perhaps . . . save the State from impending Destruction."[79] On the same principle, Livingston's *Reflector* triumvirate helped found the New York Society Library in April 1754, modeled on the public-subscription Library Company of Philadelphia that Benjamin Franklin had organized in 1731. Filled with the classics of republican history and political theory, the sixty such libraries established before the Revolution, Franklin remarked, made American tradesmen and farmers as well informed and thoughtful as well-born foreigners, and nurtured the seeds of rebellion.[80] Though unable to foresee the ultimate consequences of his midcentury crusading, Livingston was explicitly trying to bring about in his countrymen that change in worldview that John Adams later identified as the real American Revolution.

As for Livingston's own freedom of the press: on November 22, 1753, after fifty-two issues, the *Reflector*'s printer suspended publication, without a word of warning. James De Lancey, now also serving as lieutenant governor while the royal governor was living in London, had told the printer he'd get no more government contracts if he kept putting out the anti–De Lancey, anti-Anglican magazine. To "be barbarously murdered is enough to make a spirit grumble, even in the *Elysian* fields," Livingston sighed.[81]

But in 1760, Livingston began to lead the colonists in framing the second great justification for rebellion—that Crown officials threatened not only the abstract Lockean social contract but also the concrete safeguards of the British constitution. In New York, De Lancey's successor as lieutenant governor, Cadwallader Colden, was doing just that. At seventy-three, the learned but brittle and self-important bureaucrat, hidebound from half a century in government, had decided he wanted no more insubordination from New York's turbulent lawyers and "all the chicanerie of the Law." To control them, he wanted judges he could dominate—judges who weren't members of the province's powerful clans, and judges he could fire, because he planned to give them commissions "during his Majesties pleasure" rather than the commissions for life that they had finally wrested from the government in 1750. De Lancey's death gave him the chance to name a new chief justice, and the death of George II three months later required all colonial judges to get their commissions renewed, so Colden could change the terms of their tenure—even at the cost of raking up all the bitterness of the Zenger trial of a quarter century earlier, which had begun with a challenge to Chief Justice De Lancey's commission during pleasure.[82]

Of course Colden was taking special aim at lawyers like Livingston, but Livingston, beside his personal irritation, was also touchy about Colden's affront to the legal fraternity, for he had worked hard to professionalize it, as he ever more profoundly grasped that the law, the courts, and those who man them are the shield of liberty. In 1752, he and William Smith, Jr., had codified the province's laws for the first time ever. Their volume sold out instantly, as did the supplement they published in 1760. Livingston's effort would culminate in 1770 with the triumvirate's founding of the Moot, weekly seminars in which such legendary lawyers as John Jay, Chancellor Robert R. Livingston, and Gouverneur Morris dissected cases, analyzed policy, and upgraded training for clerks.[83] So he countered Colden's attack by persuading the Assembly, which the Livingston clan then controlled, to legislate lifetime judicial tenure, a bill the lieutenant governor vetoed. And when Colden named a Bostonian as New York's chief justice, Livingston joined the rest of the bar in quickly driving him to resign.[84]

In December 1761, London turned the local crisis into a colonies-wide one by decreeing that *every* colonial judge henceforward would receive his commission at the king's pleasure. Livingston thundered in the press that this move subverted the colonists' "*undoubted Right*, of having the Judges of our Courts on a Constitutional Basis." For the next fifteen years, colonists loudly objected that the edict ended judicial independence and was "dangerous to the liberty and property of the subject," as a 1774 South Carolina pamphlet put it.[85]

Once the executive had blurred the separation of powers by appointing judges "who depended on the smiles of the crown for their daily bread," as the South Carolinia pamphlet protested, one last-ditch judicial-branch protection remained—the jury of one's peers.[86] At a frighteningly fast pace, Colden and the London ministry began undermining this bastion of liberty in 1764, and Livingston led the resistance.

In April, the Sugar Act empowered nonjury vice-admiralty courts to try smugglers and tax evaders. In October, the New York Assembly asked Livingston to write its protest to the House of Lords. The "amazing powers" of the vice-admiralty courts, he charged, denied colonists the protection of a jury trial that is "one of the most essential Privileges of Englishmen."[87]

Just then, Colden sharpened the threat. After a jury found a New Yorker named Cunningham guilty of stabbing a fellow townsman named Forsey, Forsey successfully sued his assailant for damages. Cunningham appealed the civil verdict to the lieutenant governor (whose office gave him the power to act as an appellate judge), asking him not just to look for legal errors but also to review the jury's finding of the facts. In November 1764, Colden agreed and demanded the trial transcript, noting that juries had after all reached "false and iniquitous verdicts" before, perhaps a peevish dig at Zenger's jury. Chief Justice Daniel Horsmanden's reply, written with the triumvirate's help and published at Livingston's expense to stir up public ire, rejected Colden's order to produce the transcript as illegal and a threat to liberty. After all, *juries* decide matters of fact; appellate judges can examine only matters of law. Once appeals judges can reverse jury verdicts about the facts, juries don't count.[88]

Colden then asked the Privy Council in London to hear Cunningham's appeal. While New Yorkers anxiously awaited the reply, Livingston began explaining the British constitution to them in a newspaper column, the "Sentinel," that ran for most of 1765 in the *New-York Gazette* and breathed the spirit of Commonwealth and Whig writers from Algernon Sidney to Trenchard and Gordon.[89]

The British constitution "is a constitution matured by ages," Livingston wrote, "repeatedly defended against lawless encroachments by oceans of blood, meliorated by the experience of centuries, alike salutary to prince and people, and guarded by the most awful sanctions."[90] How ancient is it? According to an influential tradition of thought, summed up in the eighteenth century by Paul de Rapin, whom Livingston lauded in the *Reflector* as the best historian of England, it is in fact the Gothic constitution of the Anglo-Saxons, who brought to England the free institutions of their German ancestors that Roman historian Tacitus had so glowingly described in the first century. Their constitution enshrined a privilege that "is one of the greatest a Nation can enjoy," Rapin noted: that "all Persons accused of any Crime were to be tried by their Peers." Sadly, William the Conqueror, "surnamed the *Bastard*," replaced the Anglo-Saxon constitution with his foreign feudal system, Rapin wrote; but time and again, from *Magna Carta* onward, Britons have violently thrown off the oppressive Norman yoke and forced the restoration of their ancient rights.[91]

Who could dream, the "Sentinel" marveled, that this long-cherished constitution was "now to be altered or abolished, by—the dash of a pen?"—as would happen if Colden really succeeded in depriving New Yorkers "of all the benefits of a trial by their peers," Livingston warned. "From such a system, the *Star Chamber* would be a redemption." For without the protection of a jury as the ultimate arbiter of the facts in any trial, the people would be treated "as so many beasts of burden."[92]

The British ministry's response was not reassuring. In April 1765, news of the Stamp Act, imposing a tax to which the colonists had not consented, reached America. In October, word came that the Privy Council, while declining to hear Cunningham's appeal itself, nevertheless had authorized Colden and his council to do so—a decision, one colonist contended, that enraged his countrymen even more than the Stamp Act.[93]

HOWEVER, BY 1766, when the London government backpedaled, repealing the Stamp Act and reaffirming that appeals courts could consider only legal errors, not facts, Livingston was a chastened man.[94] He had known theoretically about the depravity of human nature, but he had now had some up-close experiences of man's capacity for violence that shocked him. Demonstrations against the Stamp Act by New York's Sons of Liberty—artisans, tradesmen, sailors, stevedores, and blacks, led by a couple of sea captains—grew ever more threatening, and on November 1, 1765, they broke out into full-scale urban rioting.

A drunken mob hanged Colden in effigy, burned his treasured coach, and sacked the richly furnished house of British major Thomas James, despoiling it with the same wild ferocity a Boston mob had shown in tearing to pieces the magnificent house of Massachusetts lieutenant governor Thomas Hutchinson ten weeks earlier. In the spring, tenant uprisings—also sparked, Livingston heard, by the demotic Sons of Liberty—convulsed the huge Hudson Valley estates. In June, two hundred armed tenants on Livingston Manor itself marched on the great house and threatened to kill Judge Robert Livingston, the current lord of the manor, unless he lowered their rents. Some forty loyal tenants fought them off, and British troops arrested the ringleaders. But now William Livingston had seen his own family's tenants "turn Levellers," as one observer put it, and he had to wonder if the equality and rights he had so long championed really included "the common run of the species," who "seldom examine things with attention," he wrote, but "take all upon Trust" and can turn liberty into an exercise of "lawless power."[95] Were *they* free and equal too?

They certainly thought so. Livingston and his followers, our foremost historian of colonial thought Bernard Bailyn notes, set off a "contagion of liberty" that over the next decades and the next century spread far beyond the landless workers seeking rent cuts who so frightened Livingston (though the Livingston Manor tenant farmers were hardly the radical-egalitarian, anti-private-property Levellers of the mid-seventeenth-century English Civil War).[96] In time, the contagion's ever-widening circles touched even those who thought that a democracy with universal suffrage and no property qualifications for voting would not be the horror Livingston had imagined—quite the reverse. Were not all entitled to the principles the Founders extolled? If taxation without representation was tyranny, asked Continental Congressman Richard Henry Lee's unconventional, strong-minded sister, Hannah Corbin, as early as 1778, were not property-owning, taxpaying widows like herself entitled to vote, regardless of their sex? Perhaps, temporized her brother; but did she not think it "rather out of character for women to press into those tumultuous assemblages of men where the business of choosing representatives is conducted?"[97]

And if liberty was so precious and slavery so heinous, what about the "Grate Number of Blackes . . . held in a state of Slavery within the bowels of a free and christian Country?" asked a group of Massachusetts slaves in a 1774 petition. Do we not "have in common with all other men a naturel right to our freedoms?" What about the "grat number of us sencear . . . members of the Church of Christ how can the master and the slave be said to fulfil that command Live in love let Brotherly Love contuner and abound Beare yea onenothers Bordenes How can the master be said to Beare my Borden when he Beares me down whith the Have chanes [heavy chains] of slavery and operson [oppression] against my will?"[98] However little the Founders intended to make a social revolution, they sowed the seeds of a future, ever-broader one.

Livingston lost focus. Still sore over the King's College battle, he flushed with anger in 1768 when its second president, Myles Cooper, nursed dreams of setting up an Anglican bishop in America and turning the Anglican college into an "American University" that would "Prevent the Growth of Republican Principles, which already too much prevail in the Colonies."[99] In a new newspaper column, named the *American Whig* after the *Independent Whig*, another Trenchard and Gordon journal, he denounced the idea of a bishop as "more terrible" than the "so greatly and deservedly obnoxious stamp act."[100] In 1720, when Trenchard and Gordon wrote that "priestcraft and tyranny are ever inseparable, and go hand-in-hand," such a fear made sense; in New York, after the clear and present danger of the Stamp Act, it didn't.[101]

By 1772, Livingston craved peace and quiet. Since 1760, he'd been buying land on the edge of Elizabethtown, New Jersey, an easy sail down the harbor from New York and up the Elizabeth River. By 1768, he had 115 acres and had begun planting a garden, which blossomed

LIBERTY HALL
Residence of Governor Livingston,—Elizabethtown, N. J.

Print Collection, Miriam and Ira D. Wallach Division of Art, Prints and Photographs, The New York Public Library, Astor, Lenox and Tilden Foundations

into a passion for horticulture and ended with sixty-two kinds of pear trees and twenty-seven of plums, many imported from abroad. In 1771, he began building Liberty Hall, an elegantly restrained wooden house that he moved into in 1773, just as he was turning fifty. Retired from his law practice, with a comfortable income from a fortune of £6,000 to £8,500 and the 15,000 to 20,000 acres he'd inherited from his parents, he looked forward to the life of a country squire that he'd imagined poetically in *Philosophic Solitude* some three decades earlier.[102]

With famously pretty daughters, he didn't have much solitude, however, as Alexander Hamilton, John Jay, and Gouverneur Morris frequently came courting across the bay—and Jay married Livingston's daughter Sarah in Liberty Hall's long parlor in April 1774. Nor could philosophy displace politics. Before he had moved into his new house, Livingston had joined the town corporation and the county Committee of Correspondence, one of many formed across the colonies to synchronize resistance to George III's tightening squeeze of American liberty. As a delegate to the First Continental Congress in the fall of 1774, he hoped to patch up the colonists' differences with England, much to the disgust of John Adams, who later recalled the Congress's various efforts at conciliation as "children's play at marbles or push-pin," instigated by the conservative "privileged order" led by John Dickinson, "Billy, *alias* Governor Livingston, and his son-in-law, Mr. Jay." For his part, Livingston felt shock at the "designing Junto" of implacable New Englanders, hell-bent on independence, which the delegates "all professed to deprecate," though "the hearts of many of us gave our Invocation the lie."[103]

Even when he saw that independence was inevitable, he fussed about the timing, worried that the army was too green and that the French hadn't yet vowed support. Less than two weeks before the Declaration of Independence, his constituents recalled him, naming delegates keen to break with England. The rebuke stung, but on August 31, New Jersey elected him its governor, and, as British invaders drove him and his legislature across the state for years as they stalked Washington's army there, and as Patriots and Loyalists vied for the hearts of New Jerseyites as the American insurgency raged, he did much to keep the spirit of liberty alive, never doubting America's right "to renounce our Allegiance to a King, who in my Opinion had forfeited it, by his manifest Design to deprive us of our Liberty." He was proud that the British had put a price on his head and had sent freelance gangs of thugs to try to kill him.[104]

When the war ended seven years later, he and his family, dispersed to safer havens while hostilities raged, reunited in a much-vandalized Liberty Hall. The mahogany bannister still bears angry slashes from an enemy sword, and a later occupation by Continental troops did much more damage. "It is as in the time of Pharoah," wrote Livingston's daughter Kitty; "what the Canker worm dont eat the Locusts destroy."[105] Slowly the governor put the estate right and nursed his ruined gardens back to luxuriance, though his daughter Sarah imagined him "with his pruning-knife in his hand . . . almost at a loss where to begin his operations," given the shock of seeing "all the effects of his former care effaced by the wilderness that had sprung up in his absence."[106] He rejoiced in Sarah's weekend visits with her husband, John Jay, and his greatest pleasure was taking their son Peter to fish in the trout pond or the river. Still serving as governor, he died at sixty-six on July 25, 1790, having lived long enough to sign the Constitution and see the government he helped frame get under way with George Washington's inauguration a year before, on the balcony of the same building in which the Zenger trial's drama had unfolded more than half a century earlier.[107]

THE FATE OF Liberty Hall would have bemused him. He built what his imagination had conjured up in *Philosophic Solitude*:

> *On banks array'd with ever blooming flowers,*
> *Near beauteous landscapes, or by roseate bowers;*
> *My neat, but simple mansion I would raise,*
> *Unlike the sumptuous domes of modern days;*
> *Devoid of pomp, with rural plainness form'd. . . .*

Unpretentious but stylish, Liberty Hall had a two-story center section, three windows wide, above a raised basement for a kitchen, and two one-story wings on each side. It sported quoins carved to look like masonry at the corners of the central block, inspired by British colonel Roger Morris's fine house in Harlem (now the Morris-Jumel house-museum). A long parlor with two fireplaces, flanked by a library and a dining room, filled most of the ground floor, while five bedrooms crowded into the second story. In 1789, Livingston added a bedroom atop one wing for Martha Washington to stay in on her way to her husband's inauguration. It was an elegantly simple Georgian villa, filled with light streaming in through its generous windows and nestled in Livingston's lovingly tended gardens. Official visitors often found the governor in his gardening clothes.[108]

When he died, a year after his wife's death, his children, all with houses of their own by then, sold Liberty Hall out of the family and drew lots for the furniture, not a stick of which remains in place. But in 1811, Livingston's niece, Susan, bought the house. She had married a Continental Congressman from South Carolina, John Kean (pronounced cane), the first cashier of Alexander Hamilton's Bank of the United States, and their children and descendants lived in Liberty Hall until 1995. A dozen years later, the family sold it to Kean University, part of the state college system.

By then the house had swollen to fifty rooms, added between 1847 and the mid-1890s and overflowing with the rich furnishings of six generations of prosperous and powerful New Jerseyites who raised families there, including two U.S. senators, a ten-term congressman, another New Jersey governor, and a major political donor, whom many Republican candidates, including presidents, wooed in Liberty Hall. The house had originally looked over the Elizabeth River, where visitors moored their boats, but its front door migrated to the landward side after a dam shrank the once-navigable river to a little stream in the 1850s. Brightening that new front of the house, some of William Livingston's plantings still flourish, along with a horse chestnut his daughter planted and the remains of his niece's garden and lawns. On the other side, glass-and-metal college and office-park buildings loom out of the tarmac like stranded flying saucers, bordered by rows of cookie-cutter New Jersey condos. Inside the house, even Livingston's plain wooden parlor chimneypieces have given way to opulent English eighteenth-century marble ones, bought by an antique-collecting Kean in the 1920s and more in keeping with the "sumptuous domes" Livingston shunned than his "neat, but simple mansion."

Making a virtue of necessity, the enthusiastic young staff of the Liberty Hall Museum lead thousands of fourth- and fifth-graders through the house every year, making the tour a time-travel through

American history, from 1780 until 1940. Each guide, dressed in the clothes of the era of a given room's furnishings, explains the evolution of lighting, of transportation, of education to rapt schoolchildren, using such historical objects as an oil lamp or a schoolroom slate or one guide's cumbrous Victorian hoopskirt to bring home the concrete reality of the past. The children ask where the bathrooms were and what games the Livingston and Kean kids played, and they are fascinated to learn of chamber pots, metal bathtubs filled by servants with pitchers, and pre-video-game childhoods. The girls, in particular, find the transformation in the role of American women flabbergasting, which brings home to them all the more vividly that the world wasn't always the way it is today—the beginning of historical understanding, especially worth cultivating in a country where only 12 percent of high school seniors score at the proficient level in the most trusted national American history test.[109]

The guides stage a mock debate, pitting the Patriot governor William Livingston against the last royal governor of New Jersey, Benjamin Franklin's illegitimate son, William, and also against a spokesman for eighteenth-century New Jersey's many antiwar, anti-oath Quakers, who insisted on neutrality as the Revolution ravaged their hotly contested state. At the end, the guides ask the children to sign, in quill pen and ink, their choice among two loyalty oaths and a declaration of neutrality. Recently, most school groups have split equally among the three choices. Those opting for neutrality explain that it's "just easier" and that "people have no reason to hate you." But the Patriot child who declared, "I want to fight for freedom!" would have warmed William Livingston's ardent (if briefly cautious), liberty-loving heart.[110]

2

Conservative Revolutionaries: The Lees of Stratford Hall

Halfway along the flat, damp Northern Neck of Virginia, which stretches down to Chesapeake Bay between the Potomac and Rappahannock Rivers, stands one of America's most extraordinary houses, Stratford Hall. With its two rooftop triumphal arches piercing the sky, Stratford would be remarkable for its architecture alone, unique in the nation—and uniquely handsome. But its chief distinction lies in its having been home to four brothers who became revolutionary leaders—two Continental Congressmen who signed the Declaration of Independence and two diplomats—as well as to their cousin, one of the Revolution's most dashing war heroes. John Adams described these five Lees of Stratford as "that band of brothers, intrepid and unchangeable, who, like the Greeks at Thermopylae, stood in the gap, in the defense of their country, from the first glimmering of the Revolution in the horizon, through all its rising light, to its perfect day."[1]

From the sharp-tongued Adams, that's high praise indeed, in prose unusually florid for him. All five Lees merit it, but three of them deserve our special attention: Adams's close ally, Richard Henry Lee, one of the earliest revolutionary firebrands, whose motion in the Continental Congress that "these United Colonies are, and of right ought to be, free and independent States" led to the Declaration of Independence; his brother, diplomat Arthur Lee, who negotiated the first secret loans from France and Spain to support the Continental Army and made the first big deals for foreign arms to supply it; and their intrepid cousin, General "Light-Horse Harry" Lee, who, long after his revolutionary exploits, marked the end of the Founding by giving Congress's eulogy for George Washington, with its famous praise of his revered commander as "first in war, first in peace, and first in the hearts of his countrymen."[2]

This trio—and their remarkable Virginia forebears—provide a luminous vantage point onto the workings of the British Empire in the New World, how it rose and why it exploded. They became, paradoxically, conservative revolutionaries, indignantly fighting to preserve long-cherished British values and British liberties from British despoilment. Moreover, Light-Horse Harry's saga jumps the story forward, with unexpected twists, into the administration of his Princeton classmate James Madison—and it even points beyond thc confines of this book: for Harry's son, born at Stratford, became General Robert E. Lee.

From their arrival in America through the Revolution, the Lees operated as a multinational family firm, like proto-Rothschilds. In 1639, when their widowed mother died in the English Midlands, three young Lee boys became wards of their uncle, a prosperous Worcester cloth merchant. Dreaming big transatlantic dreams, he sent two of the youths to open a mercantile house in London and dispatched his middle nephew, Richard, to represent the firm in Virginia, raw Indian country, alive with wolves and cougars, and with hardly more than five thousand British settlers.[3] An enterprising genius, as a great-grandson rightly called him, the twenty-one-year-old immigrant started out as secretary to two successive royal governors, a grand-sounding title for the chiefs of a pioneer band, but he soon set up a thriving trading post on Virginia's most backwoods frontier, swapping British manufactures with the Indians for valuable furs and hides to send to his London brothers.[4] By midcentury, now owner of three plantations and part of a ship—and having narrowly escaped an Indian massacre that killed three hundred settlers—Richard Lee exported mainly tobacco and ran a flourishing salesroom for the European goods his brothers sent him. In his ship, he also transported Britons seeking work as indentured servants in the New World, for which he received grants of land called "headrights," Britain's incentive for getting the wilderness peopled and cultivated by Englishmen.[5] He traded in African slaves as well, three hundred of whom were in Virginia by 1649.[6]

But the fortunes of Richard's uncle and brothers dwindled under Cromwell's dictatorship, so, now married and with young children, he returned to England at the Restoration to recharge his vital transatlantic connection, starting a new London trading house and grooming his son Francis to run it. Like so many British imperialists for the next two centuries, he aimed to retire as a country gentleman back "home" and bought a big estate at Stratford-Langton, outside London, suitable for very different guests from the Wicomico and Chicacoan Indian chiefs he'd entertained as the first European settler of the Northern Neck. But on one of his periodic trips to Virginia in 1664, as death stole up on him at only forty-five, he foresaw what was far from obvious: that the future lay in the still untamed New World, not the Old. He wrote his wife to sell Stratford-Langton and bring the children (except for Francis) back to Virginia, where he was among the biggest and richest landowners.[7]

Dutifully, his Oxford-educated son, Richard, Jr., dubbed "the Scholar," gave up the future his teachers had predicted of "rising to the highest dignities" in the English church and moved from the pinnacle of European intellectual refinement to its opposite—one of his father's wilderness properties named, with unintentional mockery, Paradise. When his older brother's death in 1673 left him head of the family, he took a wife and moved to his father's Northern Neck headquarters, Machodoc Plantation, far from the more settled York River precincts of Virginia's Jamestown capital. It was an uncivilized place, meagerly furnished with a Spanish table, seven leather chairs, sixteen quarts of hominy, some books, a saddle, a pistol, sixteen shovels, and two frying pans. There, Richard the Scholar ran the family business conscientiously, but with frequent retreats into the civilized refuge of his own fine library. He followed his father in becoming first a member of the House of Burgesses (the elected lower house of Virginia's legislative Assembly) and then of the Council of State (the Crown appointed upper house, made up of the colony's half dozen or so top military and civil officials), and a pillar of the establishment.[8]

So much so, that when an upstart immigrant planter named Nathaniel Bacon received a Council seat in 1676 and stirred up his followers to slaughter Indians and change the terms of the fur trade, from which he claimed that Richard the Scholar and his fellow dignitaries had wrongfully excluded "the commons of Virginia," the starchily conservative Richard went to jail rather than bow to the multitude. He stayed there until dysentery fortuitously carried off Bacon two months later—not, however, before the full-scale rebellion Bacon had sparked among small farmers, laborers, and indentured servants had put Jamestown, the only town in an already class-ridden colony of isolated plantations and pioneer shacks, to the torch.[9]

Two decades later, the Scholar's establishment instincts made him swallow hard when the Glorious Revolution deposed the Stuarts; but authority being authority and the only bulwark against Bacon-style leveling and anarchy, he led his reluctant neighbors in recognizing William and Mary's legitimacy. As a reward, he became revenue collector for the Southern District of the Potomac, pocketing a cut of the tax on every ship that came into that bustling commercial hub and every hogshead of tobacco or bale of furs that went out of it. Tellingly, Virginia's royal governor praised him a few years before his death in 1715 for his "unexceptionable loyalty." By then, like his father, he too had put his sons into the family business, the younger ones in Virginia and the eldest in the London branch.[10]

He made sure as well that his second son, Thomas, got his lucrative revenue collector's job, which the young man's uncle, Thomas Corbin, a partner in the London branch of the firm, helped supplement with

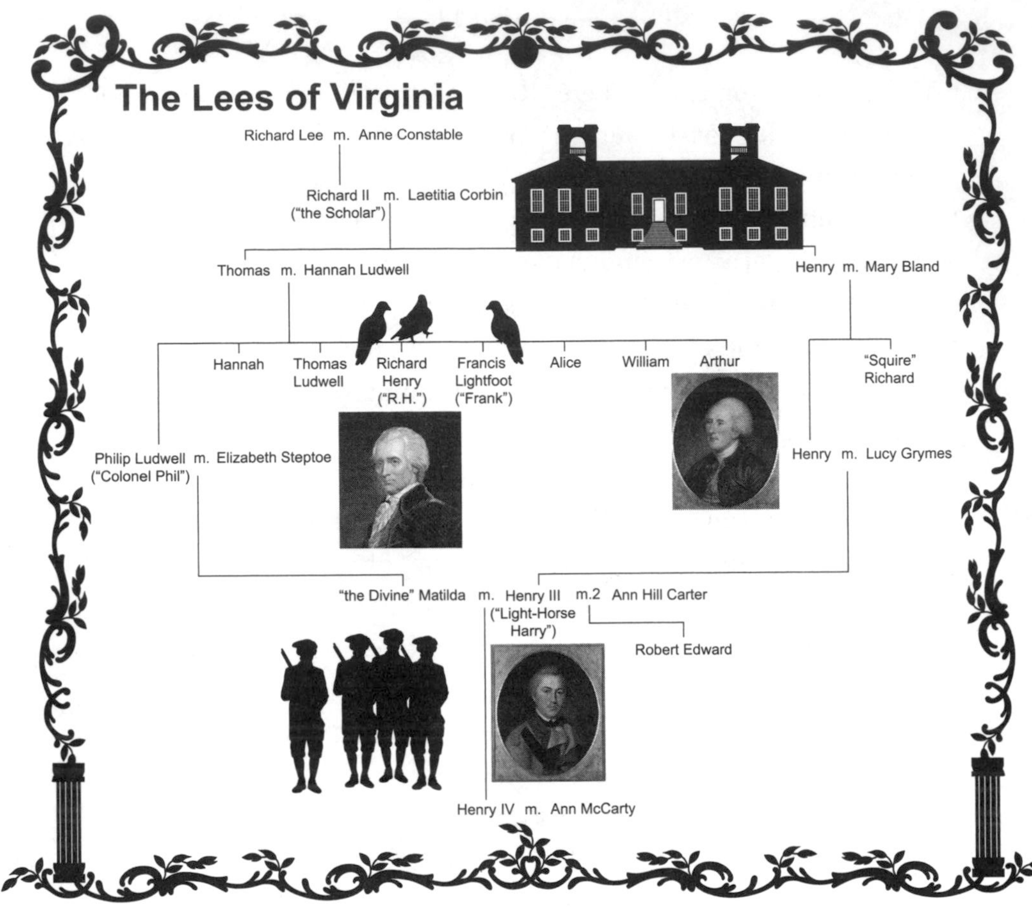

Two Branches of the Lee Family Tree *Alberto Mena*

an even richer job that led to the building of Stratford. Uncle Corbin kindly hinted to his friend Lady Fairfax that her million Northern Neck acres overseas seemed to be yielding paltry rents and that his go-getter nephew on the spot could boost them. Once young Thomas had coolly informed Lady Fairfax's former agent—Virginia's richest and most powerful man, Robert "King" Carter—that he was replacing him, he set about making good on Uncle Corbin's promise. As he crisscrossed the immense Fairfax domain doing so, he came upon a spot whose majestic white cliffs rising from the Potomac, seven shimmering miles wide at that point, took his breath away. He wanted the 1,443-acre property desperately enough to sail to England to seal the deal with its owner in 1718.[11]

It was twenty years before Thomas began to build Stratford on that beautiful land. Meanwhile, believing that "the first fall and ruin of families and estates was mostly occasioned by imprudent matches to embeggar families and to beget a race of beggars," he married heiress Hannah Ludwell, as strong-willed and overbearing as he. Entrepreneurial and visionary like his grandfather, Thomas believed that America would burst out westward, that the backwoods would teem with industrious settlers and blossom into prosperous farms, and that the Potomac, navigable even without improvement for about a hundred miles, would be a main transport artery into the profitable future.[12]

To cash in on that future, he began buying up as much land as he could along the river, especially 16,000 acres around the rocky falls where navigation ended, fifteen miles upstream of where Washington now stands.[13] He also was a key negotiator of the land-grabbing 1744 Treaty of Lancaster, acquiring from the Six Nations of the Iroquois all their territory to "the setting sun," which the Virginians interpreted far more expansively than their Indian counterparties to mean most of the Ohio basin. To settle that vast real estate, Thomas led fellow speculators in setting up the Ohio Company, which in 1749 received a Crown grant of half a million acres. To underscore the immensity of Virginia's claims, Thomas, the Ohio Company's first president and the colony's acting governor, reminded the Privy Council in London a year later that Virginia's 1609 charter had granted it all the land "to the South Sea to the West including California."[14]

As a justice of the peace, Thomas was always a hard-liner with lawbreakers, so revenge was the presumed motive for the robbery and torching of his house in 1729, which killed a servant girl, carried off his grandfather's silver and thousands of pounds in cash, and burned his father's cherished library. For a decade thereafter, he and Hannah lived in makeshift quarters, until they began building Stratford around 1739.[15] The ninety-foot-long house, on an H-plan, with two north-south wings joined by an east-west one, so as to multiply the number of bright corner rooms, was worth waiting for. It is what architecture

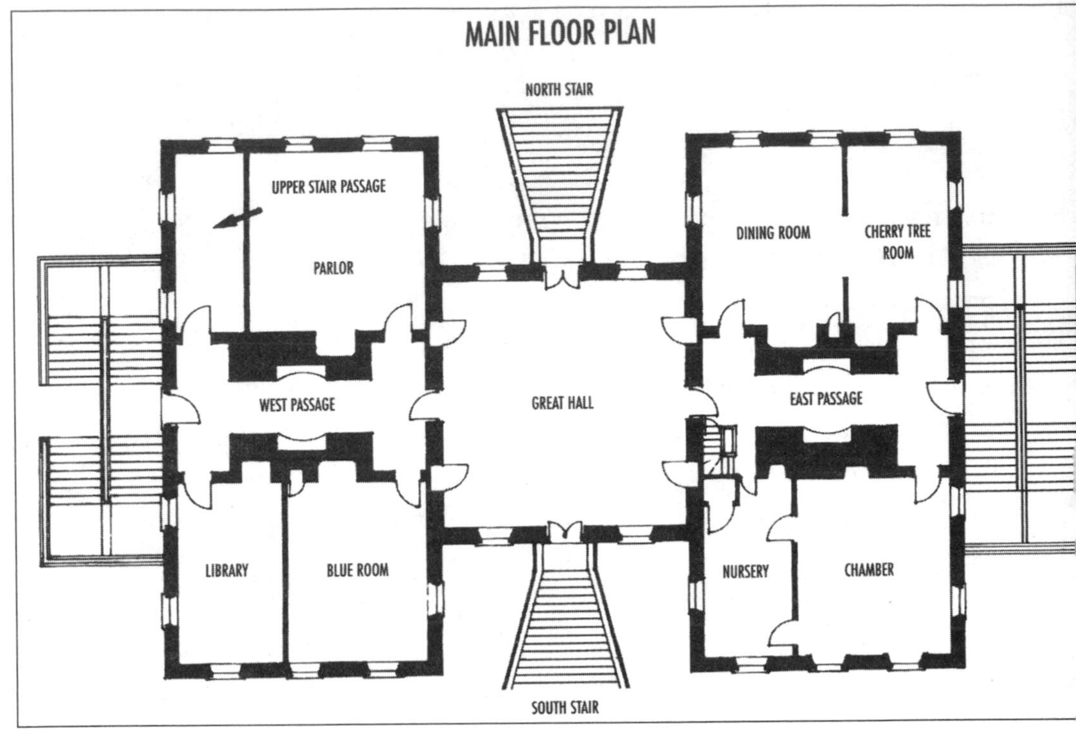

Stratford Hall Main Floor *Courtesy of Stratford Hall*

critics would call a "swagger" house: rich, stylish, handsome, proud almost to insolence, and strong.

It is in effect a one-story house—a single *piano nobile* above a raised basement. But what keeps it from looking merely long and low are the main floor's tall windows (sixteen panes over sixteen), the broad stone front staircase that climbs steeply to the imposingly elevated front door, and above all the two clusters of four huge chimneys, brilliantly conceived as a pair of triumphal arches springing from the roofs of each wing and leading the eye skyward. For colonial America, says the noted historian of English architecture John Summerson, Stratford is a "remarkable performance" that he would more readily believe the work of such great royal architects as Nicholas Hawksmoor or Sir John Vanbrugh than some local.[16] But the house's inspired designer, who worked closely with Hannah Lee, was most probably Virginia-born William Walker.[17]

The great houses of early Virginia—Berkeley or Shirley Plantations on the James, say—display beautiful brickwork, but Stratford is a fanfare in brick, flaunting every one of the refinements that London artisans had developed in the late seventeenth century. The craftsmen, mostly slaves, laid the bricks in "Flemish" bond—header, stretcher, header, and so on—but they distinguished the lower story by firing the ends of the headers hot enough to burn and turn them glassy, producing a checkerboard pattern of shiny dark bricks alternating with ordinary lighter-colored ones. The *piano nobile*, which a beautifully cut molding separates from the basement story, is by contrast all the same color and texture of brick. Rounded arches cap the lower-story windows, while flat arches crown the upper ones, all made of bricks rubbed smooth to produce a slightly different color and texture, as are the bricks defining the corners of the house and flanking the door and the upper windows. The vaunting chimneys, with viewing platforms at their bases, return to the checkerwork pattern of the lower story. Part of the pleasure of Stratford is figuring out what ingeniously different treatments of the same material, made from clay dug at Stratford and mortared with lime from Potomac oyster shells, produced such subtle but rich variations in effect.

THE BUILDING of Stratford, begun exactly a century after the first Richard Lee set foot in the New World, marks an inflection point in the history of British America. With no help from England other than royal charters saying they could claim land and create a social order, pioneers like the Lees had built a new civilization in the wilderness, and it was now pouring forth wealth. The prime minister at that time, Sir Robert Walpole, 280 pounds of wily competence, was continuing by wisdom the policy that seventeenth-century Britain had begun by weakness: "salutary neglect," as Edmund Burke later called it, meaning that colonies that enriched England by supplying raw materials and markets for its manufactures should be left alone to do what they were doing so well. As Walpole's long, benign rule drew to a close in 1742, and as Stratford neared completion, the colonial wealth-producing machine went into high gear.[18]

The rich got richer, and, as the American population exploded—and as English and Scottish investment capital poured into Virginia—everyone else prospered too.[19] At Stratford, the twenty-nine-foot-square great hall, still one of America's most beautiful rooms, acquired a cut-glass British chandelier to hang from its seventeen-foot-high ceiling, glittering even in the daylight flooding in from the doors and windows to the north and south. Someone went so far as to gild one of the refined Corinthian pilasters on the paneled gray walls before having second thoughts and painting it over, either as too gaudy or too flaunting even for those palmy days.

While Thomas Lee filled his lofty rooms with walnut and mahogany, silver and china, paintings and musical instruments, Americans everywhere, in what historians call the eighteenth-century consumer revolution, started taking luxuries for granted, including matched tea sets from Chinese (and later English) potteries.[20] Benjamin Franklin reported coming to breakfast one morning to find his pewter spoon and earthenware bowl gone, his wife having decided that "her Husband deserved a Silver Spoon & China Bowl as well as any of his Neighbours."[21] By the 1760s, Thomas Jefferson's father-in-law, John Wayles, observed that while he'd seen few fancy rugs in his youth, "Now nothing are so common as Turkey and Wilton Carpetts."[22] By then, too, British-American trade had doubled since the 1740s, with nearly half of all English shipping engaged in it—and with Virginia tobacco accounting for 40 percent of all American exports.[23]

THOMAS AND Hannah Lee moved seven of their brood of eight, ranging from toddlers to teens, into Stratford's grand surroundings sometime in the 1740s—all but Philip, the eldest, already at Eton. The children had the customary tutors and dancing masters who oversaw privileged Virginia childhoods, and, along with the social graces and some Greek and Latin, the boys also mastered horses and boats, since Chesapeake Bay and Virginia's four great rivers formed the colony's main highways for visiting as well as for trade. As Stratford, like the handful of other great houses of the Virginia tobacco magnates, was the outward emblem of social preeminence and political power, Thomas liked to strut its drop-dead splendor with the days-long house parties fashionable among the Virginia gentry as sociable respites from life on isolated plantations.[24] They politicked, courted each other, and gossiped in this spectacular setting, while boating on the Potomac and playing cards, dancing, and feasting in the magnificent rooms, with plenty of wine, a regular topic in the Lee family correspondence. Thomas had become a suaver host in the years since he had anxiously fussed over every detail of his first big party, given as a suitor to impress Hannah's family; back then he had even taken a cram tutorial in Latin and Greek phrases, so he could seem learned.[25]

When Thomas and Hannah died within ten months of each other in 1750, Philip, studying law at the Inner Temple, returned from London to become Stratford's master. Under his regime, the plantation soared to its apogee of wealth and opulence.[26] Colonel Phil, as his five brothers and two sisters called him, turned Stratford into a major tobacco-shipping operation. He upgraded its wharf and shipyard to handle oceangoing vessels, built a big warehouse that collected fees from the surrounding planters for the required inspection of tobacco, and bought the ninety-ton *Mary* to transport the tobacco abroad for a further fee. A tannery, barrel-making shop, mill, and import warehouse sprang up, too, along with housing for workers that turned the whole area into a little village called Stratford Landing.[27] Philip even brought prize stallions from England and went into the horse-breeding business. Over time, he increased the 4,800 acres he had inherited at Stratford to 6,595.[28]

The new wealth made entertainment at Stratford Hall even grander. The colonel loved music and filled the house with it. Musicians played from the observation platforms between the chimneys; music, not the standard gong or bell, announced dinner; trumpeters atop Philip's carriage heralded his comings and goings. Getting the latest printed scores from London for his musicians and his harpsichord-playing daughters, who had a live-in music teacher, preoccupied him. And his taste was good: he was thrilled to snag the newly published selection of Scarlatti's keyboard sonatas.[29]

As the executor of his father's will and guardian of his minor siblings, however, the "arrogant, hauty" Philip, in a contemporary's words, was less openhanded. The will called for distribution of the estate once Thomas's debts had been settled, so the colonel simply delayed paying the debts and distributed pittances. Since he couldn't escape the will's education bequest for the younger boys, he dutifully sent Arthur, the youngest, to Eton—directing, however, that he get "as little pocket money as ever any boy had at your school and rather less." After all, he explained, Arthur "has not an estate to support him as a gentleman without a profession. So the more he minds his studies, the less time he will have to spend money."[30] Tightfistedness turned meaner when young Richard Henry, fresh out of school in Yorkshire, proposed marriage to a highly suitable English girl. Philip refused consent, writing to the girl's father that such a match "must be very bad for her, as his Brother's fortune [would] only maintain him alone."[31]

Little wonder that in 1754 Philip's siblings sued to make him pay up. Though the suit dragged on for years and fizzled out, the four minor children at least did manage to get their guardian changed. The colonel released the real-estate bequests in 1758, but he held tight to the money until he died seventeen years later.[32]

Nevertheless, when Richard Henry Lee finally got possession of his Prince William County property, he didn't want to live there. He wanted to stay on at Stratford, even though he was now married, having wed nineteen-year-old Anne Aylett the year before. The reason was political: at twenty-five, he had just won election to represent Westmoreland County in the House of Burgesses and needed to stay in the county to keep his seat. So he rented out his inherited land, leased five hundred acres of the Stratford Hall plantation from Philip, and, still living under his childhood roof, began planning his own house three miles down the river. By 1763 he, Anne, and their two baby boys moved into their gracious new wooden villa, called Chantilly, with a big bay window commanding an Elysian view from a high bluff over the Potomac. It was no Stratford Hall, but in its twenty- by twenty-four-foot dining room, he entertained like a Lee.[33]

The Lees by then had formed their own faction in the House of Burgesses: R.H., as his siblings nicknamed him, took office the same year as his cousin Squire Richard Lee; his cousin Henry Lee was already a burgess. The next year, his brothers Francis Lightfoot (Frank) and Thomas settled into their inherited estates in different counties and also became burgesses, while Philip served on the Council of State. During the next fifteen years, R.H. became part of an oligarchy within Virginia's tiny ruling oligarchy, one of only seven men who chaired the house's standing committees during that entire time.[34]

But R.H. didn't start out in the inner circle. The reason was temperament. Before he had set out for school in England, his father had come upon him—frail, asthmatic, and epileptic—boxing with a "stout negro boy." Angrily, his father asked, "What pleasure can you find in such rough sport?" R.H. replied that he practiced like this every day, because "I shall shortly have to box with the English boys, and I do not wish to be beaten by them."[35] That pugilistic spirit never left him.

He certainly showed it in his maiden speech as a burgess in 1759. Despite the stage fright that plagued him until the eve of the Revolution, he rose to support a motion to tax the slave trade so heavily as to end it, and he delivered one of eighteenth-century America's most forthright, stinging denunciations of slavery itself. Slavery is wrong as a matter of policy, he began. Just look at how the free colonies, settled later than Virginia and with no richer soil than hers, have outstripped her economically, because "*with their whites they import arts and agriculture, whilst we, with our blacks, exclude both.*" Worse, the resentment that burns in slaves every minute that they see the luxury and liberty their masters enjoy, "whilst they and their posterity are subjected for ever to the most abject and mortifying slavery," must make them "natural enemies to society, and their increase consequently dangerous." Only consider the slave rebellions of Greece and Rome, which laid the Greek colonies of Sicily waste, for example, and brutalized the Romans into passing laws to govern slaves "so severe, that the bare relation of them is shocking to human nature."

But beyond these practical considerations is the moral evil. How can slave owners believe that "our *fellow-creatures* . . . are no longer to be considered as created in the image of God as well as ourselves, and equally entitled to liberty and freedom by the great law of nature?" Those who profess Christianity ought to live up to its precepts. It's time, he concluded, to "convince the world that we know and practise our true interests, and that we pay a proper regard to the dictates of justice and humanity."[36] This, remember, was more than a century before the Civil War.

If this wasn't enough to rile up his fellow burgesses, he then attacked their popular and powerful longtime speaker, John Robinson, also the colony's treasurer. Beyond the fact that Robinson had no legal right to hold both these offices at once, the real problem, R.H. charged, was that he seemed to be cooking the colony's books. Beginning in 1760, R.H. demanded annual audits, which by 1763 turned up a troubling discrepancy. But only when Robinson died in 1765 did the whole truth emerge. Though as treasurer he was supposed to burn the old paper currency turned in for new notes, he simply lent out the old money to friends—£100,000 worth to assorted oligarchs. Robinson's illicit expansion of the money supply explained the mystery R.H. had been trying to solve: Why was inflation skyrocketing? But by the time he got his answer, Parliament had responded to Robinson's debasement of the currency by barring the colonies from issuing paper money, hamstringing the American economy.[37]

By then, however, a vast geopolitical upheaval had remade the world—an upheaval that began with Thomas Lee's forming the Ohio Company in 1749 and that led, after a remarkable rippling outward of events in the Old World and the New, to American independence. The French had their own designs on the vast territory that the Virginians claimed, and in direct response to the Ohio Company's charter, they sent soldiers from Canada into the Ohio Valley to plant lead plaques warning that this land was their land. In 1753, Virginia's governor dispatched twenty-one-year-old George Washington (born four and a half miles up the road from Stratford at idyllic Pope's Creek) to find out what the French were doing and to tell them that the region was "so notoriously known to be the property of the crown of Great Britain" that they should clear out. When Washington reported back home that, *au contraire*, the French planned to fortify the whole valley, the governor sent troops to build his own fort where the Allegheny and Monongahela merge to form the Ohio at present-day Pittsburgh, but the French drove them off and made the strategic fort their own. Sent to evict them in 1754, Washington fought two skirmishes, one a mistake and one a defeat—and ignited the French and Indian War, the first true world war.[38]

It began with a string of British losses, led by a full-scale British army attempt to retake the fort that ended in a rout. Then the French launched their own ferocious countercampaign. In 1756 they took Fort Oswego, on Lake Ontario; in 1757 Fort William Henry on Lake George, pushing British America's western frontier as far east as Albany. Even worse, on the European front, they defeated King George II's son the Duke of Cumberland in Germany and forced Britain to cede the king's beloved Hanover.[39]

With the war at its darkest, Secretary of State William Pitt the Elder told his cabinet colleagues, "I can save this country, and nobody else can." After a couple of false starts, the watchful, melancholy-eyed fifty-year-old piled victory upon victory. In 1758, the skilled young officers he had named to top army commands, backed up by the huge navy he was enlarging daily, took the great Canadian fortress of Louisbourg, retook Fort Oswego and the fort at Pittsburgh, and by miraculous heroism seized Quebec, the hub of French might in America. By 1759, when the British took Montreal and the sugar islands of the West Indies, they had ended French power in the New World—and, pronounced nineteenth-century naval historian A. T. Mahan, the "kingdom of Great Britain had become the British Empire."[40]

And then in 1760, after a thirty-three-year reign, King George

II died, and his twenty-two-year-old grandson, the pigheaded martinet George III, pushed aside the victory-crowned Pitt, and pushed aside as well Pitt's Walpolean vision of a free, fast-growing British America—already with a third the population of Britain—pouring out a cornucopia of riches on the Mother Country. George III had other ideas: after the war ended in 1763, he was determined to make the colonists help pay for the army that Britain had decided to leave in the colonies. Trouble was, now that Pitt had ended the French threat in North America, the colonists no longer needed Britain's protection, and they certainly didn't want to pay for it.[41]

THE NEW KING'S POLICY sparked all Richard Henry Lee's pugnacity. He instantly grasped how opposed it was to the Walpole-Pitt vision of an empire based on entrepreneurship and freedom. When Parliament began putting the new policy into effect in 1764, tightening enforcement of Britain's sugar and molasses tax in the colonies (ruinous to New England's rum industry), R.H. wrote that Britain seemed resolved to deprive Americans of such "essential principles of the British constitution [as] the free possession of property, the right to be governed by laws made by our representatives, and the illegality of taxation without consent."

Perhaps people who had done Britain some great injury might deserve such treatment, but certainly not "brave adventurous Britons, who originally conquered and settled these countries, through great dangers to themselves and benefit to the mother country." The result was bound to be war, R.H. saw eleven years before the Revolution broke out. "Poverty and oppression, among those whose minds are filled with ideas of British liberty," he wrote, in time "may produce a fatal resentment of parental care being converted into tyrannical usurpation."[42]

It's hard to imagine a more orthodox conservative radicalism than this. It is, as R.H. put it succinctly to the pro-America Lord Shelburne a few years later, merely the "manly assertion, of social privileges founded in reason, guaranteed by the English constitution, and

George III forcing tea down the throat of America by Paul Revere
Private Collection / Peter Newark Pictures / The Bridgeman Art Library

rendered sacred by a possession of near two hundred years."[43] It is the assertion, he wrote a neighbor in 1765, of "the most palpable privileges of human nature, the legal rights of America, and the constitutional freedom of British Subjects."[44] After all, he explained in an article at that time, the colonists' ancestors received an additional legal guarantee of their constitutional rights when they came to America: the king, "knowing what great benefit it would be to England, to settle this country, and what great dangers the first settlers must meet with, did give them . . . a charter, that they and their children, and all who came after them, should hold their liberty and property, as the people of England did."[45]

This is the radicalism of a British-educated British subject, steeped in the culture of British constitutional liberty, asserting that, even in the colonies, Britons never will be slaves, as the then-new song put it. But now Britain threatened to reduce the colonists to "Egyptian bondage," R.H. protests in letter after letter, "deprived of every glorious distinction that marks the Man from the Brute."[46]

It is not surprising that a man who'd thought deeply about the differences between slavery and freedom would be among the first to abhor the tendency of the new policy, as would a man proud that his tough and determined ancestors had forged out of a wilderness a mighty engine of trade and wealth for the British Empire. More personally, who would be quicker to feel "a fatal resentment of parental care being converted into tyrannical usurpation" than a man whose brother had wrongly deprived him and his siblings of what their father had bequeathed them?

I WISH I COULD report that Richard Henry never lapsed from this clear-sightedness. He did, though—badly. Six months after he condemned the 1764 Sugar Act, he wrote a London acquaintance that if Parliament passed its proposed Stamp Act, he'd like the job of collecting the tax in Virginia. By the time someone else got the post, he realized how wrong he'd been to seek it. But his application, which came back to bite him, was part of his continual, anxious search for extra money. He liked good wine and "Havana segars," but he had the income of a younger son. He augmented the rent from his lands and the produce of his Chantilly plantation by working as an agent for his brother Philip's tobacco warehouse and later for his older brother William's London-based shipping business, which he once even suggested should deal in slaves before he dropped the idea as unprofitable.[47] Always strapped, he sent his sons to college in England, because, at £30 a year, it was a lot cheaper than the £100 Princeton or Harvard charged. (William and Mary, cheaper even than England, was out of the question, because "there, so little attention is paid either to the learning, or the morals of the boys.")[48]

But this lapse aside, R.H. stepped to the front rank of Patriot leaders, and in his doings and reflections you can watch the inexorable unfolding of the Revolution with vivid clarity. When the Stamp Act took effect in March 1765, he spearheaded Virginia's opposition, part of a wave of protest and mob violence that swept the colonies. Heading an angry demonstration and penning a fierce denunciation, he pushed the tax collector to resign, though not before that officer disclosed R.H.'s earlier application for the job, prompting a red-faced public explanation.[49] In February 1766, R.H. organized the Westmoreland Association to punish anyone who tried to administer or obey the act, since it "does absolutely direct the property of the people to be taken from them, without their consent." And he led an obstreperous mob threatening to pillory and jail a neighbor who had promised compliance with the act. The affrighted neighbor recanted and apologized.[50]

In response to the upheaval, Parliament repealed the Stamp Act that same month, while reasserting, however, in a Declaratory Act, its right to legislate for the colonies "in all cases whatsoever," since they "are, and of right ought to be, subordinate unto, and dependent upon the imperial crown and parliament of Great Britain"—fighting words that R.H. flung back at Britain a decade later.

While things were exploding in the public arena, they were exploding in R.H.'s private life too. He was out shooting swans one wintry day in 1768—they still abound in the Elysian inlets around Stratford, among hundreds of noisy geese and, overhead, the occasional bald eagle—when his gun blew up, blowing the four fingers off his left hand. Ever after, he wore a specially made black silk glove to cover his disfigurement. In time, he practiced gesturing dramatically with it, which, with his Roman nose, high forehead, tall, gaunt frame, aristocratic bearing, and fluent eloquence graced with classical allusions, added to his command as an orator. Shortly after the accident, his wife caught pneumonia and died very suddenly, at only thirty, leaving him with four young children.[51] "I have been so covered with affliction this past winter," he wrote his brother Arthur, "that I have thought but little of any thing but my own unhappiness."[52]

A year later, however, he remarried. His new wife, Anne Pinkard, herself recently widowed, proved "a most tender, attentive, and fond mother" to his children, he wrote, and between 1770 and 1782 he had five more babies with her.[53] After the first, he wrote with grim jocularity to his brother William of his money worries, "oppressed as I am with a numerous family. Five—children already, another far advanced on the stocks, with a teeming little Wife, are circumstances sufficiently alarming."[54] But he was a kind and loving parent, happy at his "prattling fireside," where "I have heared every little story and settled all points."[55] His letters vibrate with concern for his boys studying in England and anxious inquiries about buying annuities to protect his girls.[56]

His was a characteristically American style of reasoning, spare-the-rod child-rearing, common in Virginia even then, and aimed at raising self-governing citizens. "The power of his rebuke, and the influence of his parental authority and affection," his grandson relates, were enough to make his children behave. After a gentle paternal reprimand, one of his sons "went into the house crying, and when asked by his mother, 'what was the matter,' he replied, 'My father has been talking to me about consequences.'"[57] As R.H. wrote much later, "Force and opinion seem to be the two ways alone, by which men can be governed[;] the latter appears the most proper, for a free people"—a precept as applicable to children as to grown-ups.[58]

As THE CRISIS with Britain unfolded, R.H. took the lead in uniting the colonies in their opposition, to forestall Britain's Machiavellian strategy of "*conquest, by division*," he explained.[59] So when Parliament imposed the 1765 Quartering Act on New York, for example, it assumed that the other colonies, relieved to have escaped the expense and danger of a standing army in their midst, would keep silent. But "a prudent man," R.H. writes, "should lend his assistance to extinguish the flames, which had invaded the house of his next door neighbour, and not coldly wait, until the flames had reached his own."[60] He was the first to suggest, writing in 1768 to Philadelphia lawyer and pamphleteer John Dickinson, that the colonies should form committees of correspondence to inform and support one another, and that individual members should keep in touch privately, too.[61]

In this spirit, after Bostonians rioted in the wake of the new Townshend Act duties on glass, lead, paint, paper, and tea, and Britain sent in troops to overawe the town later in 1768, R.H. wrote Dickinson again, more sharply. Why, he wanted to know, was Pennsylvania standing by "silent, when the Liberty of America is thus dangerously invaded . . . and when a Union of the whole must infallibly establish the public freedom and security?" Our silence, he warned, will be "deemed a tacit giving up of our Rights, and an acknowledgement that the British Parliament may at pleasure tax the unrepresented Americans."[62] He himself organized a Virginia boycott of British imports, one of a number in the colonies that within a year slashed sales by up to two-thirds.[63] By the time Parliament repealed the Townshend duties in April 1770, except for the tax on tea, R.H. scoffed at the move as too little, too late.[64]

John Adams was right to say that the "Revolution was in the minds and hearts of the people," but now the idea began to turn into reality. As Britain threatened to subvert the basic constitutional right to trial by a jury of one's peers, R.H. added Bostonian Samuel Adams to his circle of conspirators-by-correspondence. In early 1773, apologizing for writing to a stranger, he hoped that "to be firmly attached to the cause of liberty . . . renders proper, the most easy communication of sentiment" among those whom tyrants aim to oppress. The Sugar Act had already proposed to try customs-evasion cases in nonjury vice-admiralty courts, but now something worse seemed in store. When a particularly obnoxious British revenue schooner, the *Gaspée*, ran aground on a Narragansett Bay sandbar, Rhode Islanders had rowed out and burned her to the waterline while wounding her captain. Royal authorities, rumor had it, planned to send the suspects to England for trial, where by definition they could have no jury of their peers. Was this true? R.H. asked Adams. If so, "I hope it will never be permitted to take place, while a spark of virtue, or one manly sentiment remains in America"—just the kind of warlike murmuring that was spreading fast.[65]

Bostonians displayed manly sentiment aplenty at the end of 1773 by dumping into their harbor a shipload of tea not just unconstitutionally taxed but now also under an onerous monopoly. As Bostonians braced for retaliation, R.H. asked Samuel Adams to alert the Virginia legislature when the blow fell, so we can all be "cool, firm, and united," especially necessary since R.H.'s younger brother Arthur had just reported from London that "There is a persuasion here, that America will see, without interposition, the ruin of Boston. It is of the last importance to the general cause, that your conduct should prove this opinion erroneous. If once it is perceived that you may be attacked and destroyed, by piecemeal, *actum est*, every part will, in its turn, feel the vengeance which it would not unite to repel, and a general slavery or ruin must ensue."[66]

The retaliation, in the 1774 Coercive Acts, was fierce, closing Boston Harbor and imposing quasi-martial law. The British commanding general became also governor of Massachusetts, empowered to appoint legislators and judges and take over public buildings as barracks. "No shock of Electricity could more suddenly and universally move," Richard Henry wrote Arthur of the legislature's response that June. "Astonishment, indignation, and concern seized on all." He got the legislators to declare a day of fasting and prayer in protest—the kind of tactic that changed minds and hearts—and he called for an expansion of the trade embargo to include exports as well as imports, now that "the dirty Ministerial Stomach is daily ejecting its foul contents upon us." He also began to agitate for a colonies-wide congress.[67]

In September the First Continental Congress gathered in Philadelphia. As the leading radical firebrands, R.H., his brother Frank, and their fellow Virginian Patrick Henry, along with the Boston cousins Samuel and John Adams, stoked defiance. They convinced Congress to endorse the just-issued Resolves of Suffolk County in Massachusetts, whose impassioned language invokes the Pilgrims in recalling how the British "of old persecuted, scourged, and exiled our fugitive parents" and also echoes Locke in recalling that the colonists owe the Crown allegiance only because of a "compact," which, by implication, the king is breaking. The incendiary Resolves call on the county—which includes Boston—to ignore the Coercive Acts and to pay no attention to the new, unconstitutional courts but instead to settle disputes by arbitration, to treat anyone who accepts office in the new, illegitimate legislature as an enemy, to take a British hostage for every Patriot leader the army arrests, and to set up a militia that trains every week, captained by "inflexible friends to the rights of the people."[68]

R.H.'s call to go a step further and form a national militia, while demanding British withdrawal from Boston, failed however, since, as Silas Deane of Connecticut objected, it would be a declaration of war. But Congress did impose a colonies-wide trade embargo and form the Continental Association—devised by R.H.'s committee—which urged local groups to police the boycott, as part of a fast-spreading grassroots network that was forming a shadow government throughout the colonies.[69] That winter, too, Colonel Philip Lee died, leaving R.H. executor of his estate and, until Philip's two-year-old heir grew up, master of Stratford.[70]

A few months later, by the time the Second Continental Congress convened in May 1775, Paul Revere had already ridden his midnight ride, the shots at Lexington and Concord had crackled out, and colonial troops had besieged the British in Boston. In June, the British drove the besiegers from their fortified Bunker Hill position. Sure that their trained regulars would make short work of the rebellious rabble, the British gasped at the 40 percent casualties the colonists' guerrilla tactics inflicted. "What an unfair method of carrying on a war!" a British survivor whimpered.[71] In Philadelphia, Congress now established an army, with George Washington at its head, and R.H. boasted that Virginia could produce 6,000 frontiersmen with amazing "dexterity . . . in the use of the Rifle Gun. There is not one of these Men who wish a distance of less than 200 yards or a larger object than an Orange—Every shot is fatal."[72]

As a last-ditch reconciliation effort, in early July the congressmen sent the king an *Olive Branch Petition*, asserting loyalty and asking him to restore the former harmony of Britain's pre-1764 colonial policy. More realistically, however, the same week they published a *Declara-*

tion of the Causes and Necessity of Taking up Arms, explaining to potential foreign allies and lenders how royal policy, not colonial rebelliousness, had ignited the fighting. The king almost instantly replied that the colonists were in open revolt, aimed, he told Parliament in October, at "establishing an independent Empire." In December 1775, Parliament passed the American Prohibitory Act, blockading the colonies and declaring all ships bringing goods to America liable to seizure and confiscation, "as if the same were the ships . . . of open enemies."[73]

The king was right, of course. R.H., like many other Patriot leaders, was busily stockpiling gunpowder and, on behalf of Congress, buying ships to form a navy. But the royal statements and the Prohibitory Act swept away all his congressional colleagues' hesitations about the real state of affairs. The law has "dissolved our government . . . and placed us on the high road to Anarchy," R.H. wrote Patrick Henry. "This proves the indispensable necessity of our taking up government immediately, for the preservation of Society." How else could Americans secure the foreign trade and alliances they needed to survive?[74]

Accordingly, on June 7, 1776, acting on instructions from a Virginia legislature led by his brother and one of his uncles, R.H. moved in Congress "That these United Colonies are, and of right ought to be, free and independent States, that they are absolved from all allegiance to the British Crown, and that all political connection between them and the State of Great Britain is, and ought to be, totally dissolved."[75] Congress also empowered each colony to form its own government, and R.H., summoned by George Mason's plea that "we cannot do without you" (words later carved on his gravestone), rushed home to help write a constitution—a very democratic one, he made sure—leaving Thomas Jefferson to write the Declaration that made his motion for independence a reality.[76] In August, R.H. and Frank joined fifty-four other congressmen in signing the great document, after R.H. politely commiserated with Jefferson over Congress's having "mangled" the Declaration by editing out Jefferson's blaming of Britain for introducing slavery into America. "However," R.H. assured the crestfallen author, "the *Thing* is in its nature so good, that no Cookery can spoil the Dish for the palates of Freemen."[77]

THE LEES ACTED as a transatlantic family firm in revolution as in business, with family members abroad working to advance the family enterprise at home. The most luminous expatriate Lee was R.H.'s youngest brother, Arthur, who served as a key American agent in Britain and France. His saga is material for a thriller, as a youth from the fringe of the empire becomes first a radical wheeler-dealer at the center of British affairs, intimate with a vivid array of the eighteenth century's celebrities, and then a spy. After a few post-Eton years back at Stratford, Arthur returned to England in 1760 to study medicine, heading to Edinburgh on Samuel Johnson's advice that it had Britain's best medical school. There he became close friends with his classmate James Boswell, later Johnson's incomparable biographer, and he graduated with the gold medal as top student. Thanks to Benjamin Franklin, Pennsylvania's London lobbyist and a nurturer of talented Americans, Arthur got elected to the prestigious Royal Society, and he formed a lifelong friendship with Lord Shelburne, who later became prime minister (and whose dining room, where Arthur hobnobbed, you can visit in New York's Metropolitan Museum).[78]

Laden with honors, Arthur returned to Virginia in 1766 to practice medicine, presuming on his brand-new expertise to hector R.H., fruitlessly, to quit smoking his beloved cigars. But after the glitter of London, Williamsburg palled—as did doctoring, compared to the excitements of politics, once the Townshend Acts radicalized Arthur in 1767. With a series of articles, bylined "Monitor," in a Virginia paper, he began a long career as a crusading polemicist for justice and liberty for America. "I cannot Conceive of the Necessity of becoming a Slave," he wrote, in terms that R.H. would approve, "while there remains a Ditch in which one may die free."[79]

In the autumn of 1768, just after Arthur finished writing the "Liberty Song"—which became an American Revolutionary anthem, with its lines "By uniting we stand/By dividing we fall"—he headed back to London, aiming to turn British public opinion against George III's American policy. Changing professions as well as countries, he entered the Middle Temple to study law in 1770, happy with his rooms overlooking the Temple garden and the Thames, and with his visits to the Royal Society, the theaters, the opera, and the concert halls, especially when Johann Christian Bach performed. And of course he politicked. "In the field of politics," he boasted, "from the politician in the cider-cellar to the peer in his palace, I had access and influence."[80]

He was closest to one politician in particular, John Wilkes, a radical, pro-American member of Parliament and later lord mayor of London, who championed Britain's ancient constitutional liberties, including a restoration of (perhaps legendary) Saxon annual parliaments.[81] He was also a libertine, famously quick and sharp of tongue. When fellow rake Lord Sandwich—berating him for a squalid practical joke he had played at the Hellfire Club—told him he would die either on the gallows or of the pox, Wilkes shot back, "That depends on whether I embrace your Lordship's principles or your mistress."[82] He had become a popular hero—specializing, in Caroline Robbins's astute phrase, in "highclass rabble-rousing"—when the government foolishly charged him first with seditious libel for accusing George III of having "sunk even to prostitution" for his embrace of Lord Bute's ministry and then with blasphemous obscenity for a wildly pornographic parody of Alexander Pope.[83] The authorities jailed him and threw him out of Parliament. Middlesex voters, chanting "Wilkes and Liberty," kept reelecting him, until finally the government gave in and seated him.[84]

Arthur Lee—a leader of Wilkes's political party, the Bill of Rights Society—made the cause of American liberty integral to British radicalism. Who knows, Wilkes reportedly prophesied in 1773, whether "in a few years the independent Americans may not celebrate the glorious era of the revolution of 1775, as we do that of 1688?"[85] The colonists for their part hung on every turn of Wilkes's fate. His exclusion from Parliament as the people's legitimately elected representative convinced many Americans that the assault on their own freedom was not accidental but rather the result of what R.H. Lee called deep-laid, malevolent "designs for destroying our constitutional liberties."[86]

Arthur became a propagandist, writing—"with a pen dipped in the gall of asps," one royal official complained—tracts and seventy-five widely read newspaper articles between 1769 and 1776 on Britain's injustices in the colonies. In 1774, now Massachusetts' official London agent, he wrote that Britain couldn't win an American war. When the fighting started at Concord and Lexington, Arthur got the news by fast schooner from Salem and could spread the pro-American version of the story uncontested for two weeks before official accounts reached the British government. Anybody who didn't believe him, he wrote, could see the signed affidavits of American eyewitnesses, on display at his friend the lord mayor's Mansion House.[87]

Using Wilkes's political machine, Arthur had gotten his elder brother William, Stratford Hall's business agent abroad and a prosperous London merchant, elected co-sheriff of London in 1773 and an alderman two years later. With such credentials, William, despite his American origins, emerged as the London merchants' radical spokesman, and in 1775 he organized a pro-American petition from them, complaining that the colonists' embargo was ruining them, and Parliament should give in to American demands. Petitions from Britain's other commercial cities soon followed.[88]

While R.H. was buying gunpowder and ships, Arthur was making his own equally essential war preparations. At the Mansion House, he had met another celebrity-to-be, Pierre-Augustin Caron, first a brilliant watchmaker whose innovations made timepieces smaller and more accurate, then harp teacher to Louis XV's daughters, and later—having added "de Beaumarchais" to his name—the immortal playwright of *The Barber of Seville* and *The Marriage of Figaro*. At that moment he was a French secret agent and arms dealer, through whom Arthur arranged for a clandestine loan to Congress of a million livres from officially neutral France, as well as an additional loan from

Spain. He also made a deal with Beaumarchais to supply Congress with desperately needed arms and provisions in the French agent's forty-ship fleet.[89]

Commissioned Congress's spy in London after independence, Arthur sent a flood of intelligence about transatlantic troop movements and British political developments. In December 1776, Congress made him one of its three secret commissioners to France, to negotiate loans, buy arms and supplies, and above all to get France to join America's war against Britain. William crossed the Channel soon after him to serve as America's commercial agent in France.[90]

And now Arthur's troubles began. He discovered that his fellow commissioner, ex–Connecticut congressman Silas Deane, was war-profiteering, accepting kickbacks and loading the blockade-running supply ships not just with needed materiel for Congress but also with scarce and valuable commodities for Philadelphia financier Robert Morris to sell privately. Virginians including the Lees, Patrick Henry, and George Mason believed that republican virtue was indispensable to political freedom, so Arthur was scandalized, the more so after smoldering under his brother Philip's swindles and finagles for so many years. He was equally outraged that the third commissioner, Benjamin Franklin, seemed not to care, perhaps because he believed that when in France, do as the Frenchmen do, perhaps because he knew Robert Morris well, perhaps because his grandnephew was part of Deane's operation.[91]

But there was worse. Arthur began charging that Deane's office was a nest of spies and traitors. Deane angrily countered that Arthur was quarrelsome and paranoid, an image of him that has stuck to this day. Franklin wrote that he had a "sick mind, which is forever tormenting itself with jealousies, suspicions, and fancies that others mean you ill. . . . [I]t will end in insanity."[92]

But Arthur was right. Deane's secretary, an American doctor named Edward Bancroft, was indeed a spy—the "supreme spy of his century," one historian judges.[93] The Foreign Office paid the doctor handsomely to copy the American commissioners' correspondence in invisible ink and hide it in a hollow tree in the Tuilleries garden for British agents to speed to two British secretaries of state. After the great American victory at Saratoga persuaded the French to join the war against Britain, Bancroft had the Franco-American treaty at the Foreign Office less than two days after its signing on February 6, 1778.[94]

The brouhaha among the diplomats prompted Congress, led by R.H., to recall Deane to explain his behavior, including his promiscuous handing out of commissions to French officers wishing to serve in Washington's army. He had no receipts to show for his purchases of materiel and little to say beyond bluster. Instead he wrote a scathing article, reprinted in English and French newspapers, falsely accusing Arthur Lee and his brothers of double-crossing France by seeking a separate peace with Britain, and claiming that Arthur achieved nothing by his diplomacy but "universal disgust." Congress, after much bitter wrangling, publicly vindicated Arthur; but as Deane and Franklin had discredited him with the French government, his diplomatic career was as dead as Deane's, and he returned to America for good in 1780.[95]

Though Arthur was probably wrong to claim that Deane was Bancroft's knowing accomplice as a British spy, his accusation turned out in time to be sadly prophetic, for Deane, broke and disgraced, ended up a traitor and a British tool, hired to write a series of letters arguing that independence was a mistake and that prodigal America should crawl back to the Mother Country—letters intercepted by prearrangement and published in a New York Loyalist newspaper. As payment for trying to persuade "the provinces to offer to return to their allegiance on the former foot," George III wrote his prime minister, Lord North, in 1780, "I think it perfectly right that Mr. Deane should so far be trusted as to have £3000 in goods for America." Deane died suddenly in 1789—poisoned, some historians think, by Dr. Bancroft.[96] Arthur Lee went on to be a Virginia assemblyman, a congressman, and one of the three directors of the Board of Treasury until Alexander Hamilton took it over. "Unprejudiced posterity," summed up Samuel Adams, "will acknowledge that Arthur

Lee has borne a great share in defending and establishing the liberties of America."[97]

ARTHUR RETURNED to America to find R.H. and Frank out of Congress. Worn down, they had gone home to Virginia in May 1779, Frank for permanent, tranquil retirement. The acrimonious battle over the Deane affair had dispirited them: it was bad enough to fight the enemy, but life in Congress, which served as the executive branch and the bureaucracy as well as the legislature, seemed an endless struggle against their own people, trying to get the individual states to provide troops and supplies, trying to stop war profiteers who seemed to be everywhere, trying to smooth over the squabbling among generals, trying, in R.H.'s case, to convince the delegates of the need for a navy and get it built.[98]

For three years, as a member or chairman of every military and naval committee, R.H. had poured out torrents of correspondence, ordering 40,000 uniforms from France and reminding the commissioners "that they should be generally for Men of stouter make than those of France"; diplomatically assuring the factious and egotistical General Charles Lee (no relation) that of course he is "conscious of the thousand occasions in which the service must suffer immensely if Commanders at a distance are not to accommodate conduct to circumstances," but even so, it's a good idea to follow orders and get congressional permission when possible; joyfully telling Samuel Adams that Virginia will ratify the Articles of Confederation; bursting out to Patrick Henry about the difficulty of recruiting soldiers: "O for 10, or 12 thousand Americans to sweep these vermin from our land!"[99]

And all this under wartime conditions. "Mr. Lee's fortune not being very ample & having a large family to support, he was obliged to live on the pay^{ts} from the State of V^{a}.," someone wrote long ago in the corner of one of R.H.'s letters. "To be of as little expence as possible, to his Constituents, at a time when every Dollar was needed for their preservation, he Marketed for himself. For two months during Nov & Dec^{r} '77 which were unusually cold, he lived upon wild pigeons," which "were sold for a few cents p^{r} Dozen & afforded but a scanty fare."[100] Only a few months earlier, R.H. had not been reelected to Congress because his enemies had spread a false rumor—one of many—that he was purposely trying to devalue Virginia's currency. He had to vindicate himself to the House of Delegates before being allowed to go back to Philadelphia and eat pigeons in a cold room.[101] "My eyes fail me fast," he wrote Patrick Henry that year, "and I believe my understanding must soon follow this incessant toil."[102]

He was a changed man when he returned to Chantilly in 1779. Loyal Virginian that he was, he had become an American. He dreamed of ending his days in the "wise and free republic in Massachusetts Bay," he wrote John Adams, since he had come to prefer it to "the hasty, unpersevering, aristocratic genius of the south"—sentiments already latent in his antislavery speech twenty years before.[103] And in the same vein he had changed his views about the future he wanted for his sons. He always wanted Ludwell to be a lawyer, but now he'd like him to learn soldiering, too, to be ready for anything "the service of his Country might point out." For Thom, his eldest, he no longer wanted a career as a clergyman but rather as an international businessman. Virginia may have strayed from its entrepreneurial roots, but he'd like the Lees to return to theirs.[104]

After the fighting ended at Yorktown in 1781 and the Treaty of Paris restored peace in 1783, R.H. returned to Congress in 1784, and his colleagues elected him to a one-year term as their president, the chief executive of the United States. Now R.H. made up for the cold and the pigeons with presidential opulence. "If for the good of my country I must be a Beau, why I shall be a Beau," he sighed archly—and put on "the very best black silk [as befits] my station." When Congress moved to New York in January 1785 and began paying the presidential expenses, a nephew reported that R.H. was living "in a palace [and] does the honors of it with as much ease and dignity as if he had been always crowned with a royal diadem." The Lee style of entertaining was back in force, as "crowds of obedient domestics run to his call, [and] Champagne, Claret, Madeira, and Muscat [wash down] a profusion of the delicacies and luxuries of good living" at thrice-weekly dinners for twenty-five.[105]

Pomp aside, R.H. led Congress in passing two crucial democratic measures, the Land Ordinance of 1785 and the Northwest Ordinance of 1787, which laid out America's western territory in parcels that ordinary citizens could buy and provided for the West's organization into new states with the same political rights as the old ones—and without slavery (as Lincoln stressed in denouncing the pro-slavery Kansas-Nebraska Act much later).[106] It was built into British America's democratic DNA from the start that, as new settlements sprang up, they sent representatives to the colonial legislatures as a matter of course. Before the Ordinances could pass, Virginia had to give up its vast western claims, which R.H. energetically urged, rendering worthless his family's shares in the Ohio Company, which had triggered so many years of upheaval.[107] He saw Congress's sale of the lands as a quick way of paying off the Revolutionary War debt, though Alexander Hamilton, like an alchemist, later transmuted that debt into something magical.[108]

R.H.'s PASSION for democracy, wildly opposed to his ancestor Richard the Scholar's worldview, sparked his last public drama over the new Constitution. He had declined appointment to the Constitutional Convention, because, as a congressman charged with revising the new document, he thought it a conflict of interest to help write it. He was aghast, therefore, when the Convention decided to send its work directly to the states for ratification rather than let Congress tinker with it first, as the Articles of Confederation demanded.[109] And, though he thought the Constitution sound, it needed fine-tuning, as did any system of government that, from "Moses to Montesquieu, the greatest geniuses" have produced, he wrote Governor Edmund Randolph in October 1787.[110]

He complained that the new Constitution provided for insufficient separation of powers. Concentrating too much power in the president and the Senate, with the House of Representatives being "a mere shred or rag of representation," it was "most highly and dangerously oligarchic" and could produce an "elective despotism." Worse, it lacked a bill of rights. "The corrupting nature of power and its insatiable appetite for increase, has proved the necessity . . . of the strongest and most express declarations of that *residuum* of natural rights, which is not intended to be given up to society," he wrote Samuel Adams. It's no good hoping that the new legislature will cure this defect: it may or may not.[111] These reasonable objections helped impel the Constitution's supporters to vow to add a bill of rights by amendment, and R.H. accepted election as the first senator from Virginia in 1788 in order to support that change.[112]

Crippled by gout and having injured his one good hand so he could no longer write, he retired to Chantilly permanently in 1792. There he was often "of a gay and cheerful disposition," his nephew recalled, "and very fond of promoting mirth." He died two years later, aged sixty-one.[113] A British warship shelled Chantilly to ruins in the War of 1812; in the Depression, scavengers carried off the last bricks of its hearth.[114]

In the last famous master of Stratford Hall, his cousin General Henry Lee III, R.H.'s dream of renewed Lee family entrepreneurship turned into a nightmare and ended in a peculiarly American self-made tragedy. As a daring Revolutionary War hero, the perfect incarnation of a Virginia cavalier, a shining favorite of his superiors, George Washington and Nathanael Greene, Henry was a virtuoso of the lightning raid that captured British prisoners, horses, and supplies with no losses of his own. In 1778, he won command of an independent partisan corps of light dragoons operating outside the normal chain of command (hence his nickname, "Light-Horse Harry"). After the twenty-three-year-old major's breathtakingly audacious 1779 capture of a British fort at Paulus Hook (now Jersey City), New Jersey, Congress promoted him to colonel, gave him its highest medal, and expanded his corps into Lee's Legion, with infantry as well as cavalry.[115]

With its courage, esprit de corps, fine uniforms, and splendid horses that could always outrun the enemy, the Legion quickly gained a mystique. These were self-consciously elite troops, and, though Harry maintained rigid discipline (to the scandalous extreme, once, of setting up the head of an executed deserter on a pike to deter others), he took solicitous care of his men, keeping them well fed and healthy, and never endangering them needlessly. He led them in gloriously daring exploits, but only after meticulous calculation, preparation, and sometimes rehearsal. "A soldier is always in danger," he emphasized, "when his conviction of security leads him to dispense with the most vigilant precautions." He molded the Legion into "a band of brothers," one observer wrote, "having entire confidence in each other, and all having equal confidence in, and personal esteem for, their commander, Lee." Unlike other Continental Army soldiers, who signed up for a limited hitch, Harry's men volunteered for the duration of the war. As for Harry himself, this was, he said, "a command I most sincerely love."[116]

But the raids that were the Legion's specialty don't win wars. "To win a victory [is] but the first step in the actions of a great captain," Harry wrote, in censure of the British commander, General Howe. "To improve it is as essential; and unless the first is followed by the second, the conqueror ill requites those brave companions of his toils and perils, . . . and basely neglects his duty to his country."[117] Did Harry never wonder if this shoe fit him? Certainly he heard other carping, since the favoritism of his superiors, and the arrogance that stares out at you from Charles Willson Peale's portrait of him as a young officer, sowed resentment and enmity all around him. The result was two trumped-up courts-martial, which acquitted Harry with honor but left him embittered, a resentment that grew with later, and more justified, criticism that his absence from his assigned positions at the Battles of Guilford Court House and Eutaw Springs cost his comrades clear-cut victories.[118]

What he took to be slights, "ill natured insinuations," and neglect of his merit gnawed at him, prompting his mentor, General Greene, to remind him sharply that "I have run every risk in favor of your operations," and "jealousies and discontents have not been wanting in the Army at the opportunities afforded you to the prejudice of others."[119] Nevertheless, Harry decided to quit the service in February 1782, six months after the last great battle at Yorktown, citing ill health, grief, misery, "the persecution of my foes"—some force majeure from outside rather than his own free decision.[120]

One reason he gave for leaving was undeniably true: he was getting married in April. His bride was his second cousin, the "Divine Matilda" Lee, the nineteen-year-old harpsichord-playing daughter of Colonel Phil, a shrewd and funny "fine lady with a fine fortune [and a] fine figure."[121] The pair lived at Stratford, which, because Philip's toddler heir had tumbled headlong down its steep stone grand stairway to his death, now belonged to Matilda's mother. When she remarried and moved away, she left Harry and Matilda in charge. When she died in 1789, Stratford became Matilda's in fact.[122] Harry put his stamp on it, enlarging and updating its drawing room with a stylish federal mantelpiece, wainscoting, and door and window frames, and turning the basement story, hitherto storage and servants' quarters, into more bedrooms.

Harry had grown up with great expectations. His father was a Potomac grandee; his mother, even richer, a famous beauty whom George Washington had courted unsuccessfully. And because his uncle, Squire Richard Lee, was rich and unmarried, everyone expected him to make Harry, his favorite nephew, the heir of his 10,000 acres. The squire was not wifeless for lack of trying: his brother had tirelessly pitched a succession of eligible widows at him, and he himself had proposed to a parade of unsuitable young women who humiliatingly turned him down. In amorous matters, the Falstaffian squire was a "barbarian," "lewdly indulgent" with his slaves, Bab and Henny. "If he ever marries," a friend predicted, "you may depend upon it, . . . it will be with some mop-squeezer who can satiate his filthy amours in his own way." But around the time of Harry's marriage, the squire, now past sixty, wed a beautiful sixteen-year-old cousin, with whom he fathered four heirs by the time he died at sixty-nine.[123]

Harry, then, would have to make his immense expectations a reality by his own efforts. He would be even more heroic an entrepreneur than he was a soldier and would win the full-throated hosannas he craved. He saw like a shining vision the same American Dream his great-uncle Thomas Lee had dreamed half a century earlier, of settlers thronging into the continent's rich undeveloped lands, planting farms lush with ripening fields and fat cattle, and turning the Potomac into a river of gold. Now that America had won independence and the Northwest Ordinance had set the terms for new settlements, all this was bound to come to pass, supercharged by a flood of immigrants and foreign investment.[124]

AND so, while Harry had a seemingly normal official life as a statesman—at the Continental Congress from 1785 to 1789, Virginia governor from 1791 to 1794, commanding general who put down the Whiskey Rebellion in 1794, U.S. congressman from 1799 to 1801—he had another life that seemed more real and much more exciting to him.[125] He bought land, compulsively—well over a million acres of it, from the Great Falls of the Potomac into the Northwest Territory; in Kentucky, in North Carolina, in Georgia. He bought mines and mineral rights. He bought shares in the Potowmack Company, which George Washington had first conceived before the war to build canals to float barges around the Potomac falls and ultimately create a trade artery linking to—who knows?—maybe Lake Erie. As Washington himself told Madison, "It opens up a field almost too extensive for imagination." Harry began to talk in a promoter's get-rich-quick language: "the value of the spot is above present calculation," "the most convenient & productive iron estate in our country," and so on.[126]

Harry's vision was right, of course. It all came true. Even the canal materialized, though more modestly than Harry figured. It's just that he was way too early, he way overpaid, and he was way overleveraged. European investors, making a killing (in more ways than one) by financing Napoleon's wars, kept their capital in Europe, and in 1795 the American real-estate bubble began to deflate, even as speculators were frenziedly buying warrants for land neither they, the sellers, nor any surveyor had ever seen. It exploded in 1797, when Robert Morris's six-million-acre North American Land Company went bust, vaporizing $40,000 that Morris owed Harry. But Harry kept on buying.[127]

At first Harry had spent—"invested"—his own money and his wife's. A few days before Matilda died in childbirth at only twenty-seven in 1790, she cannily put Stratford in trust for their three children, but Harry chipped away at their inheritances as much as he could get away with.[128] In 1793, he married Ann Hill Carter, twenty, of Shirley Plantation and spent her grand fortune too. When the cash ran low, he began borrowing, mortgaging existing properties to buy new ones, and constructing, with gravity-defying leverage, a pyramid of debt. Ann's father took Harry's measure accurately, and, "apprehensive [that] they may be destined to come to want," he left his property solely to Ann and her children. After her father died in 1806, Ann begged Harry to come to his senses, since "your afflicted, fatherless wife can now only look to you to smooth her rugged path through life, and soften her bed of death!"[129]

But nothing stopped him, not even as creditors dunned him in the governor's mansion; not even as the acreage around Stratford shrank, the best furnishings went out the door, the house itself grew shabby; not even as he gave Washington a bad check, by no means the only one he passed. "No event of my life has given me more anguish," he wrote his lifelong friend and hero. As creditors closed in and threatened lawsuits, he sold off land to two different buyers, land that was still mortgaged, land he didn't own, and reportedly even a friend's horse and slave.[130] He made promises, asked for more time, grew vague. He begged his Princeton classmate and friend Secretary of State Madison to send him abroad as a consul—to escape the duns. But they cornered him. Because the laws then gave creditors the right to take all a bankrupt's property, Harry, trying to save something for his family, refused to take the oath of insolvency. He took the other choice instead: starting in April 1809, he served eleven months in jail for debt.[131]

When he came out from behind bars for the brief and violent finale of his tragedy, he turned Stratford over to his and Matilda's twenty-three-year-old son, Henry Lee IV, to settle a debt, and he, Ann, and their children decamped to a small row house in Alexandria.[132] As the family was boarding the boat for the trip up the Potomac, legend has it, no one could find Harry's three-year-old son, Robert E. Lee, who turned up in the nursery next to the room in Stratford where he was born, saying a tearful good-bye to the winged cherubs cast into the iron fireback of the little fireplace there. Arriving at the new house, the first thing Harry did was spread out his papers, soaked in the voyage, to dry—especially the first chapters of his memoirs of the Revolution, which he had begun in jail. Though the vivid book never made money, as he'd hoped, it became a standard reference work on the war.[133]

Harry claimed it was to find a publisher for the memoirs that he went to Baltimore in July 1812. He also claimed he'd gone there to play whist. He claimed, implausibly, that he did not go there looking for trouble—but trouble is certainly what he found.[134]

Baltimore was a Republican town filled with England-hating Irish and French immigrants who full-throatedly supported the War of 1812 against Britain, declared the month before. Harry was a staunch Federalist—like most ex–Continental Army officers, whom the wartime failures of the Continental Congress had made supporters of strong central government—and he opposed this new war as a useless waste of soldiers' lives. Two days after the war started, a mob had chased Federalist newspaper editor Alexander Hanson out of Baltimore and had wrecked his office for his antiwar stance. Hanson quietly returned to town on July 26, distributing the next day a new issue of his paper, which charged the mayor and governor with letting the June riot rage unrestrained and never punishing its leaders for political reasons. He then locked himself in his house with a gang of tough young Federalists who'd come from southern Maryland intent on "wresting Baltimore from the tyranny of the mob" and vindicating "the liberty of the Press." Harry happened to drop in that Monday evening and suggested that the group be "fully prepared to resist an attack." Famous for holding off and then driving away seventy to two hundred British soldiers—accounts varied—who'd tried to surprise and capture him and seven companions in a house during the Revolution, Harry became leader by popular acclaim.[135]

For all his talk of driving off the mob with "the vigorous use of the bayonet," when night fell and the mob swelled, Harry counseled keeping the house dark and quiet. Rejecting his advice, the Federalists fired over the heads of the crowd, and when the mob, throwing rocks and shooting guns, swarmed in—and a gun held to Harry's head misfired—Harry, who "wished above all things, to avoid the effusion of blood," recommended surrendering to the militia and going to jail. Over Hanson's sharp warnings not to count on the protection of the authorities, the Federalist defenders took Harry's advice.[136]

A mistake. When darkness fell the next night, the mob overran the undefended jail, beating, kicking, and knifing the Federalists, with special animus toward those "damned old tories," Lee and his fellow ex–Continental Army officer James Lingan. When Lingan pulled open his shirt to display the wounds he'd suffered freeing the country when his attackers were still—he sneered—"in the bogs of Ireland," the rioters killed him. As Harry told the "base villains" that "they disgraced the country in which they had found an asylum," they beat him senseless, slitting his nose and trying to gouge out his eyes. Only when they thought all their victims were dead did the rioters depart. Lingan, however, proved the sole fatality.[137]

"Black as a negro" from his bruises, "covered with blood from tip to toe," Harry, sewed up and bandaged all over, never really recovered. In May 1813, permanently scarred, "absorbed in misery & tortured with pain," he sailed for the Caribbean, wandering from island to island for five years, trying different doctors, and treatment after treatment, looking for relief he never found. He wrote letters of advice, encouragement, and love to the abandoned Ann and her five children, who, as the bank twice reduced the interest on the annuity her father left her, grew poorer and poorer. Finally, as what sounds like bladder cancer ate away at him and he knew he was dying, he booked passage for home, so ill that he never made it. He had to be put ashore at Cumberland Island, Georgia, where Nathanael Greene's daughter lived, "to die in the house and in the arms of the daughter of my old friend and compatriot." With officers from the nearby bases sitting with him in shifts, he died in agony two weeks later, on March 25, 1818, aged sixty-two. He was buried on the island, the flagship of the nearby naval base firing its minute gun until the earth closed over him.[138]

The Stratford story has a coda, brief, scandalous, and tragic. Not that sexual irregularity necessarily made the Lees squirm. When the young husband of R.H.'s strong-minded sister Hannah Corbin died, for instance, leaving a will that would force her out of their beautiful house if she remarried, she had her new lover move in without marriage, and gave the son she had with him her first husband's surname. Family and friends took it in stride and didn't shun her.[139]

But nobody forgave the transgression of Harry's son, Henry Lee IV. Conventionally enough, Henry married the orphaned heiress next door, Ann McCarty of Pope's Creek, whose 2,000 acres bordered Stratford. Ann spruced up threadbare Stratford munificently, bore a daughter Henry modestly allowed was "said to be beautiful," and brought along her younger sister Betsy, whose guardian Henry became. But at a high-spirited family party, Henry's beautiful two-year-old plunged down Stratford's steep front steps to her death, just as Colonel Phil's son had done forty years earlier.[140]

Ann, inconsolable, found solace in morphine—and died of it alone in a Paris garret at age forty-three. Henry found solace in Betsy, who believed he had made her pregnant, though no one knows if that part of the story was true. Betsy complained, and a public scandal ensued. Henry didn't see what was such a big deal. Couldn't a moment of "unguarded intimacy . . . surprise" anyone into sex with his twenty-year-old sister-in-law and ward? He couldn't understand why "recent events here have shattered my amicable and social relations." It was totally unfair: "for one transgression, one fatality rather, I am left in total darkness." But there were two transgressions: Henry had also squandered Betsy's fortune, of which he was guardian, and to pay her back he had to sell Stratford in 1822. When the buyer died six years later, the house went on the auction block. The new owner, for $11,000: Henry D. Storke and his wife—Henry Lee IV's ward Betsy McCarty, who presided as mistress of Stratford for half a century, until she died in 1879.[141]

By THEN, of course, Light-Horse Harry's fifth son, General Robert E. Lee, whom Harry had abandoned when he was six, had broken up the union his forebears had toiled to create, had won his amazing string of victories from Second Bull Run to Chancellorsville in 1862 and 1863, had stood on the field at Gettysburg apologizing to the few bloodied survivors who made it back from Pickett's doomed and foolhardy charge that he had ordered, had surrendered, in resplendent full-dress uniform, to the muddy and bedraggled General Grant at Appomattox, and had been buried in the chapel at Virginia's Washington College (later Washington and Lee), where he had dutifully toiled as president to support his wife and four spinster daughters.[142] Eight months into the Civil War, before all these great and tragic events unfolded, he wrote to his wife, "I wish I could purchase 'Stratford.' That is the only other place that I could go to, now accessible to us, that would inspire me with feelings of pleasure and local love. You and the girls could remain there in quiet. It is a poor place, but we could make enough cornbread and bacon for our support, and the girls could weave us clothes."[143]

As if life at Stratford had ever been uneventful.

PART II

The Federalists

3

George Washington: In Pursuit of Fame

For we who believe that great men, not impersonal forces, make history, George Washington is Exhibit A. As the Revolution's commander in chief, president of the Constitutional Convention, and first president of the United States, he was luminously the Founding's indispensable man, in biographer James Flexner's pitch-perfect phrase. A pragmatic visionary—that familiar American combination—he conceived from his hard-won experience in the French and Indian War the central Founding ideas of an American union under a strong executive three decades before the Constitutional Convention, and his hardships in the Revolution led him to forge that vision into a plan. An ambitious entrepreneur, he shared the "spirit of commerce" he knew was America's ruling passion, and he eagerly foresaw a nation where industry and trade, not just farming, would provide opportunity for all and would generate the wealth he thought key to national power and security, a vision he fulfilled in his two terms as president. He had a born leader's knack of attracting brilliant, like-minded young men to work with him to fill in the details and make his dream a reality. They were visionaries together, but he was the visionary in chief.

He was indispensable, too, for the force of his character along with his accomplishments as general, lawgiver, and statesman. He inspired, reassured, and steadied his subordinates and his countrymen at every critical moment from the first stirrings of revolt in the 1760s until he stepped down as chief executive in 1797. He embodied the spirit of the nation, before the nation existed except as an idea, and for three decades, the power of his example emboldened Patriots to make that idea come true.

Part of what makes his life story so gripping is that he shaped himself into the world-historical figure he became, in the quintessentially American tradition of men who spring, as F. Scott Fitzgerald famously wrote, from their own Platonic conception of themselves. But his self-conception was extraordinary: it began as a worthy ideal and evolved into a magnificent one. In his fiercely ambitious youth, he sought to win acclaim for his heroism and savoir faire. In his maturity, he strove to be, in his own conscience even more than in the eyes of others, virtuous, public-spirited, and (though his ethic wouldn't allow him to claim the word) noble. He did hope, however, that posterity would recognize and honor the purity of his motives; and Americans, who owe him so much, do him but justice in understanding not only what he did for them but also what greatness of soul he achieved to do it.

THOUGH SELF-CREATED, Washington was not self-made in the sense of raising himself from "poverty and obscurity" to "affluence" and "celebrity," as Benjamin Franklin boasted of doing.[1] His father, Augustine Washington—a genial, powerfully built six-footer whose seafaring English grandfather had run aground on the Virginia coast in 1656 and decided to stay—had inherited 1,100 acres along the Potomac, then married 1,750 more with his first wife. He prospered both as a planter and as part owner and manager of an ironworks across the river in Alexandria. But Augustine died young, at forty-nine, when Washington was eleven, and as a third son, George inherited only the 260-acre Ferry Farm opposite Alexandria, a few lots of land, and ten slaves, enough to set him up as a modest planter. It wasn't enough to let him follow his two elder brothers to their fine English boarding school, and all his life he felt shame at his "defective education," whose details no one knows.[2]

"My father died when I was only 10 years old," Washington wrote when he had become world famous; and that he remembered himself as younger than he was suggests how vulnerable and bereft he had felt.[3] With good reason: from every indication, his mother, Augustine's second wife, was unloving and exploitative at best, mentally unbalanced at worst, a potentially soul-destroying burden for a fatherless boy—or a spur to assert his worth all the more forcefully. "Of the mother," recalled one of Washington's playmates, "I was more afraid than of my own parents"—though he also acknowledged her kindness.[4]

Washington's later dealings with her, from which we have to infer the past, display frostily correct dutifulness on his part, belittling, ungrateful complaint on hers. Having twice tried to thwart his military career, she dismissed his martial exploits by saying, "Ah, George had better have stayed at home and cultivated his farm."[5] In 1772, after letting her have Ferry Farm rent-free for three decades, he bought her a pretty house in Fredericksburg, lent her money she never repaid, and gave her an allowance. Nevertheless, in 1781, as the Revolutionary War was ending, she asked the Virginia Assembly for a pension, saying she was "in great want," a move that Assembly speaker Benjamin Harrison knew would so mortify Washington that he sent the general a warning letter, so he could quash the scheme.[6] After years of such antics, Washington wrote to remind her how generously he had treated her, to assure her that "whilst I have a shilling left you shall have part, if it is wanted, whatever my own distresses may be," and to reproach her for causing him to be "viewed as a delinquent, & considered perhaps by the world as [an] unjust and undutiful Son."[7] When told that Fredericksburg had planned a ball to honor Washington and his French allies for their victory at Yorktown and that "His Excellency" had agreed to come, Mrs. Washington sneered, "His Excellency! What nonsense!" After her death in 1789, her son the president left her grave unmarked.[8]

But when his father died, the eleven-year-old luckily found refuge in an alternative, exemplary world. His idolized half brother, Lawrence, fourteen years older and resplendent in the uniform of an army captain with a royal commission, had inherited most of his father's 10,000-acre estate, including a house overlooking the Potomac that Lawrence renamed Mount Vernon and made his home. Three months after his father's death, Lawrence married the girl next door—though next door was Belvoir, a grand brick mansion shimmering on the water four miles downstream, and the girl was Ann Fairfax, daughter of Colonel William Fairfax, who as agent for his cousin Lord Fairfax's 5-million-acre Virginia holdings was himself a powerful grandee.[9] So Washington, who often stayed at Mount Vernon, also became a frequent visitor at Belvoir; he was a favorite of Colonel Fairfax, who saw his rare worth, and a close friend of his shy son, George William Fairfax, eight years older. From a home where his mother could barely spell—"My dear Georg I was truly unesy by Not being at hom," she once wrote, "it was a onlucky thing"—he was translated as if by Scheherazade's magic carpet to the world of the British aristocracy, with its stately rooms and its polished silver, mahogany, mirrors, and manners.[10] "I considered," he wrote nearly forty years later, "that the happiest moments of my life had been spent there."[11]

He set about acquiring some polish himself, absorbing through the essays and plays of Addison and Steele, and the novels of Fielding and Smollett, the eighteenth-century's ideal of the English gentleman, with good breeding, good sense, and a good heart.[12] At fifteen, he copied out a translation of a 1595 French etiquette guide, which counseled readers to speak concisely and to the point, to "bedew no mans face with your Spittle," to let everyone speak without interruption or constant contradiction, to cultivate a "Grave Settled" manner, to hide their feelings, and to show social superiors unrepublican deference.[13] Most of these precepts stuck with him, especially those regarding economy of speech and gravitas of manner, and his own intense concern with appearances soon blossomed into a lifelong passion for clothes: at seventeen or eighteen he wrote down his first of many meticulously detailed designs, this one for a "Long Waisted" frock coat with lapels "5 or 6 Inches wide" sporting "six Button Holes" each—and on and on for a hundred more words.[14]

Belvoir offered a more concrete route to self-improvement too. Washington advised Jack, one of his four younger siblings, to "live in Harmony and good fellowship with the family at Belvoir, as it is in their power to be very serviceable upon many occasion's to us young beginner's"—as he knew from experience.[15] When he was fourteen, his brother Lawrence and Colonel Fairfax tried to land him a coveted berth as a Royal Navy midshipman, but his mother dashed the plan on the lip of success. So, in an infant colony where land was wealth, and with a head for figures sharpened by hundreds of pages of exercises in geometry, compound interest, and weight and measure problems, Washington took his father's kit of surveying instruments and apprenticed himself to a surveyor, earning his first fee at fifteen. When the fabled Baron Fairfax crossed the ocean to view his colonial principality firsthand, the rich landscape kindled both his foxhunting and his property-development ardor, and he resolved to build a hunting lodge in the Shenandoah Valley and start selling his beautiful acreage there. His cousin the colonel recommended the sixteen-year-old Washington to survey the lots and his own son as the agent to sell them, and in March 1748 the two friends mounted their steeds and sallied forth across the Blue Ridge.[16]

The monthlong adventure that Washington recounts in his vivid journal made a frontiersman of him. Even sleeping involved drama. The first Tuesday night, he undressed in the dark and got into bed, to find himself on loose straw under "only one Thread Bear blanket with double its Weight of Vermin such as Lice Fleas &c." He learned to sleep in his clothes. Straw bedding, he learned another night, burns fast; a servant luckily awoke to douse the blaze before it broiled him. The explorers shot wild turkeys, saw a "Rattled Snake," and met a party of sad Indians coming home from war with but one scalp, whom they comforted with liquor, which "put them in the Humour of Dauncing

. . . in a most comicle Manner" to the music of a deerskin drum and a gourd rattle. A group of Dutch settlers struck him "as Ignorant a Set of People as the Indians," since they spoke Dutch, not English. His appraising eye, however, didn't miss the lush groves of sugar maples, and it lingered over a stretch of "Land exceeding Rich & Fertile" that "produces abundance of Grain Hemp Tobacco &c."[17]

The next year Lord Fairfax had him appointed Culpeper County's official surveyor, Virginia's youngest ever—a striking testament to the baron's faith in his seventeen-year-old protégé's genius, which he saw as clearly as the colonel, though he also valued Washington's flair for foxhunting. But laying out plots on Fairfax's Shenandoah domain took up most of the young surveyor's time and paid him so well that in 1750 he bought 1,500 Shenandoah acres himself, which tenants farmed for their eighteen-year-old landlord. With 2,315 acres by the time he was twenty, he was on his way as a high-rolling land speculator.[18]

No one can explain how Shakespeare, say, captured truth and beauty with such clarity that it enlightens us every time we ponder it; or how Mozart or Handel did what Salieri or Schütz did, but with such an ineffable intensification as to move us to tears. There's a similar mystery with Washington. We can describe how he developed those inborn gifts of character and charisma, as the sociologists call a genius for leadership that inspires confidence, but no one can say where he got them. Washington would credit Providence, and I can't do better.

Whatever the spark was that the Fairfax cousins saw in Washington—some mix of will, focus, courage, and honor—Lieutenant Governor Robert Dinwiddie, the Crown's highest resident official in Virginia, saw too when the young surveyor called on him in Williamsburg in January 1752, bearing letters of recommendation that gained him an invitation to dinner and then an appointment as major in the Virginia militia a couple of weeks before his twenty-first birthday, February 22, 1753. Certainly he looked the part: "Six feet high & proportionably made," he wrote to his London tailor, "rather Slender than thick . . . with pretty long arms & thighs," narrow shoulders and chest compared with his wide hips, big hands, piercing gray-blue eyes above a long, straight nose, powdered brown hair tied in a queue, a firm mouth clenched ever tighter as age decayed his teeth, and with "a Constitution hardy enough to encounter and undergo the most severe tryals, and I flatter myself resolution to Face what any Man durst," he boasted to Dinwiddie.[19] As strong as his father, he was also, as Jefferson later marveled, "the best horseman of his age and the most graceful figure that could ever be seen on horseback."[20]

Late that fall, the neophyte major put his hardihood and wilderness experience to the test by volunteering for a mission that "I believe few or none would have undertaken," he wrote, and that set earthshaking events in motion. British and French imperial ambitions were on a collision course in the Ohio Valley when France made plans to build a string of forts there to enforce its claim to the territory, and the British responded with plans for outposts of their own, along with an ultimatum demanding the French troops' peaceable departure from the region. Washington's mission: to deliver the ultimatum.[21]

As he recounts in a gripping pamphlet that made him famous on two continents after its publication, he set out on October 31, 1753, and by mid-November, when the diplomatic party reached western Maryland and began to make its way into uninhabited country, winter had blown into the wilderness, and "the face of the Earth was covered with snow and the waters covered with Ice."[22] By November 22, he had reached the Forks of the Ohio, where Pittsburgh later rose, and two days later he arrived at an Indian settlement twenty miles farther northwest. While waiting for a Seneca chieftain called the Half King, to request an escort to the French headquarters just below Lake Erie, Washington learned from four French deserters that a chain of French forts stretched from New Orleans to the Great Lakes, and two of the planned Ohio Valley forts had already been built, tightening the noose southeastward around land Britain claimed.[23]

The Half King arrived with plenty to report. His enmity for the French, whom he accused of eating his father, was at a full boil, for a

French commander had just stingingly insulted him. The Half King had reminded the officer of the French promise to stay off Indian land, he told Washington. "I saw that Land sooner than you did," the Frenchman contemptuously retorted; "it is my land, & I will have it." The Half King's views didn't interest him. "I will not hear you: I am not afraid of Flies or Musquito's; for the Indians are such as those," he said. "I have Forces sufficient to . . . tread under my Feet all that stand in Opposition." So Washington—on whom the Half King officially bestowed the prophetic, long-remembered Indian name "Connotaucarious," the Town Taker—knew what the French and at least some of the Indian tribes had in mind.[24]

The next day, with the aplomb of a practiced diplomat, the twenty-one-year-old major assured an Indian council of the esteem "your Brother the Governor of Virginia" held for such good friends and allies as they, and he asked their help in getting to the French. The Half King pledged "a Guard of Mingoes, Shawnesse, & Delawar's," though in the end only he and three shamans accompanied the party. On December 4, seventy miles later, they reached a French outpost, whose three officers told them that the commander of the next fort was the proper recipient of their message. The Frenchmen invited Washington to dinner, and, having "dos'd themselves pretty plentifully with" wine, which "gave license to their Tongues," they told him just what the Half King had heard: "it was their absolute Design to take Possession of the Ohio, & by G— they wou'd do it," for they had "an undoubted right to the river from a Discovery made by one La Sol [La Salle] 60 Years ago."[25]

On December 7, Washington's party set off, but "excessive rain, Snows, & bad traveling, through many Mires & Swamps" kept it from reaching the commander's fort until the twelfth. While waiting there for the Frenchman to ponder the ultimatum, the ever-observant Washington gauged the fort's strength and drew Dinwiddie a detailed plan. As the snowstorm worsened and his horses weakened, the young major sent the animals homeward, while the French stalled, got his escort drunk, and promised them guns—"plot[ting] every Scheme that the Devil & Man cou'd invent, to set our Indians at Variance with us" and "get the Half King won to their Interest."

Finally prying his Indians loose, the young envoy caught up with his horses 130 miles down the road on Christmas Eve. But by the day after Christmas, the poor beasts were so feeble, the cold so biting, and the frozen, snow-clogged roads so much worse, that Washington wrapped himself and an interpreter in Indian fur coats, stuffed his supplies and papers in a backpack, and set off with his gun to speed his report to Dinwiddie, leaving the others to follow slowly with the horses.[26] He knew what the letter he was bearing said, for the French commander had told him, "As to the summons you send me to retire, I do not think myself obliged to obey it."[27]

The trek grew harder. On December 27, a band of French-allied Indians ambushed him and his interpreter, with one firing at them from "not 15 Steps, but fortunately missed." As their attackers melted into the woods, the two envoys pressed on all night until dark the next day, so the Indians couldn't find them again. But then they met another hindrance: a river they expected to be frozen hard enough to walk across was churning with ice floes. Already exhausted, they spent the whole next day building a raft with their one worn-out hatchet. Halfway across, they got stuck in the ice, and Washington, struggling to pole the raft free, got "Jirk'd . . . into 10 Feet [of] Water, but I fortunately saved my Self by catching hold of one of the Raft Logs." They couldn't budge the raft but managed to wade to an island and spent the night in cold "so extream severe" that it gave the interpreter frostbite and froze the river solid enough to walk across in the morning. On New Year's Day 1754, they reached the interpreter's house, after passing an Indian war party fearful of being blamed for killing settlers they'd found already scalped and half-eaten by pigs.

The next day, Washington bought a horse, reached Belvoir on January 11 for a day's rest, and presented Dinwiddie with the French commander's letter in Williamsburg on the sixteenth. It's easy to see how his published report, with its exotic account of savage Indians, daring wilderness adventure, and haughty French defiance, made the twenty-two-year-old an instant celebrity. In London, the *Gentleman's Magazine* praised him as "a youth of great sobriety, diligence, and fidelity," and Dinwiddie jumped him to lieutenant colonel.[28]

No applause greeted his next wilderness exploit, however. Instead, as London's great gossip Horace Walpole quipped, "a young Virginian in the backwoods of America set the world on fire," and it took until 1763 for the Seven Years' War that Washington ignited to blaze not just through the New World but through Europe and even India and Africa before it burned itself out.[29]

The flash point was a spot at the Forks of the Ohio that after his last mission Washington had recommended as perfect for a fort, which a small British force had started to build. Hearing that the French were probing the strategic site, Dinwiddie ordered his new lieutenant colonel to "restrain all such offenders" or "kill and destroy them." On April 2, 1754, Washington and his militiamen marched into the forest, but with fifty miles still to go, their scouts reported that a thousand French soldiers had occupied the half-finished stockade, renaming it Fort Duquesne. Washington camped at what seemed a defensible spot called Great Meadows (near present-day Uniontown, Pennsylvania) and called for reinforcements.[30]

Meanwhile, he heard from the Half King, encamped nearby, that French troops were skulking around his position. Washington leapt into action—disastrously. The Indians led him and forty men to "a very obscure place surrounded with Rocks," where on May 28 they attacked, capturing twenty-one French soldiers and killing ten, including wounded men whom Washington saw the Indians "knock . . . on the head and bereave them of their scalps." Among the dead: a thirty-five-year-old nobleman, the Sieur de Jumonville, who, like Washington on his earlier wilderness assignment, was an envoy bearing an ultimatum to the British to clear out of the Ohio Valley, as the captured French officers indignantly insisted.[31]

At first, Washington didn't want to believe he'd made so gross an error as to attack a diplomatic mission. The French officers, he blustered in his dispatch to Dinwiddie, were "bold Enterprising" men "of gt subtilty and cunning," and "the absurdity of this pretext is too glaring as your Honour will see." Later that day, as worry that he had blundered ate at him, Washington wrote Dinwiddie again, warning with defensive sarcasm that the captured French officers surely "will endeavour to amuse your Honour with many smooth Story's," such as that "they calld to us not to Fire," and doubtless "they will have the assurance of asking the Priviledges due to an Embassy, when in strict Justice they ought to be hang'd for Spyes of the worst sort."[32] To his brother Jack, by contrast, Washington boasted of a victory, in which "I heard Bulletts whistle and believe me there was something charming in the sound." When the *London Magazine* printed the letter, the battle-hardened George II scoffed, "He would not say so, if he had been used to hear many."[33]

The French, Washington knew, wouldn't let the incident pass unavenged, so he strengthened his camp, now mordantly dubbed Fort Necessity, though his Indian allies deemed the exposed position hopeless and abandoned him in mid-June, urging him to retreat too. Rightly so. At 9 AM on July 3, with "Shouts, and dismal Indian yells," almost 800 French and 400 Indians swooped in, commanded by Jumonville's enraged elder brother, and "from every little rising, tree, stump, Stone, and bush kept up a constant galding fire upon us; which was returned by us in the best manner we could till late in the Afternn. when their fell the most tremendous rain," soaking his soldiers' powder and making further resistance impossible. As dusk fell, with a third of his 300 men dead or wounded, Washington signed the surrender that the elder Jumonville offered, proud to be able to march away with drums beating and flags flying. What he hadn't realized is that he had signed a document, in a language he didn't understand, that admitted his "assassination" of young Jumonville, a propaganda coup for the French. Now they could claim that the war crime of a trigger-happy backwoods officer had forced conflict upon an innocent France.[34]

Though the French banged that drum hard, Washington's reputation in England and America soon bounced back; people deemed his stand at Fort Necessity a gallant defiance of overwhelming odds.[35] Yet he himself was simmering with discontent. Why, he wrote Dinwiddie from the forest depths even before he killed Jumonville—why should London treat colonial officers such as himself as inferior? Why should British officers with royal commissions "have almost double our pay," while "we must undergo double their hardship"? Instead of "serv[ing] upon such ignoble terms" and "slaving dangerously for the shadow of pay, through woods, rocks, mountains—I would rather prefer the great toil of a daily laborer, and dig for a maintenance."[36] His next letter reports Jumonville's death only after pages of complaints about his "trifling pay," though the money bothered him less than the disrespect. The "motives that lead me here were pure and Noble," he protested; "I had no view of acquisition but that of Honour, by serving faithfully my King and Country."[37] To his meritocratic mind, it was a question of his *worth*.

So imagine his outrage when, in October 1754, London decided to split the Virginia regiment into ten parts, each headed by a captain—meaning Lieutenant Colonel Washington would be demoted. Equally galling, officers with royal commissions would now outrank colonial officers of the same nominal rank. Washington fumed that he could never have "any real satisfaction, or enjoyment in a Corps, where I once did, or thought I had a right to, command," especially when "every Captain, bearing the King's Commission . . . would rank before me," including "many who have acted as my inferior Officers."[38] As he recalled bitterly more than thirty years later, writing of himself in the third person, "This was too degrading for G. W. to submit to; accordingly, he resigned his Military employment."[39]

He knew he'd be back, though; and in March 1755, when General Edward Braddock, impressed with his repute as a crack frontier fighter, invited him to become his aide-de-camp for an assault on Fort Duquesne, he signed on as an unpaid volunteer, to finesse the status issue.[40] But Braddock, with a British officer's characteristic arrogant condescension, couldn't hear advice from any mere colonial. Shortly after the general's arrival in America, Benjamin Franklin gingerly tried to warn him against "ambuscades of Indians." So "dextrous" are they, Franklin hinted, that Braddock might find his long line of troops "attacked by surprize" and "cut like a thread in several pieces." Braddock, Franklin reported, "smiled at my ignorance and replied, 'These savages may indeed be a formidable enemy to your raw American militia; but upon the King's regular and disciplined troops, sir, it is impossible they should make any impression.' "[41]

Washington's counsel had no more effect. As the army lumbered into the woods in early June, he urged Braddock to travel lightly and prepare for Indian attack tactics—a lesson he had learned bitterly at Fort Necessity. But "so prepossessed were they in favr. of *regularity* and *discipline* and in such absolute contempt were *these people held*, that the admonition was suggested in vain," Washington wrote. Woolen-clad redcoats fainted and died from the heat as they cut a road for their heavy wagons. When Braddock finally took his young aide-de-camp's advice and sent a lighter detachment on ahead, he ordered Washington, now desperately ill with the dysentery sweeping through the army, to travel lying in a wagon back with the baggage, promising he could come forward when the fighting seemed about to start. Accordingly, on July 9, "tho' much reduced and very weak," Washington "mounted his horse on cushions," to ease his dysentery-inflamed hemorrhoids, and took his place at Braddock's side.[42]

At 10 AM, a few miles short of the fort, the French and Indians attacked, firing hidden behind trees and rocks. The "Hallooing and whooping of the enemy, whom they could not see," Washington recalled, so panicked the British regulars, marching in serried ranks, that they "broke & run as Sheep before the Hounds," exposing "all those who were inclin'd to do their duty, to almost certain Death." By contrast, the "Virginians behavd like Men, and died like Soldier's." Washington offered to lead the survivors in fighting the enemy in their own guerrilla style, but Braddock's assent came too late. Nevertheless, with steely courage, Washington galloped all over the battlefield, trying to turn chaos into orderly retreat, his tall figure so conspicuous that he "had 4 Bullets through my Coat, and two Horses shot under and yet escaped unhurt," a miracle that he ascribed to Providence.[43] Fifteen years later, an Indian chief told him he had reached the same conclusion: that the Great Spirit must have a brilliant future in store for the young officer whom his braves couldn't kill even though he had repeatedly ordered them to shoot him down.[44]

No such spirit watched over Braddock. A bullet pierced his lung. Washington laid him in a cart and, as his only unwounded aide-de-camp, relayed his orders. Braddock wanted him to bring the rear detachment forward to cover the retreat; so, after twelve adrenaline-fueled hours on horseback, Washington set off on an all-night, forty-mile ordeal, as he groped his way through the darkness of the thick woods, while the cries of the wounded and dying—"enough to pierce a heart of adamant"—rang in his ears and still echoed in his mind thirty years later. By the time the two units joined and made it to safety, 1,000 of the original 3,000-man force lay dead or wounded, two-thirds of whom, he estimated, "receiv'd their shott from our own cowardly dogs of Soldier's." There, Braddock—bewilderedly muttering "Who would have thought it?"—breathed his last, and Washington buried him with full honors, before driving wagons back and forth to obscure his grave so that the Indians couldn't dig up his body for a "savage triumph" over a man his aide-de-camp judged "brave even to a fault and in regular service would have done honor to his profession." Braddock left him a red silk sash and brace of pistols, which Washington cherished.[45]

"If wisdom is not to be acquired from experience," Washington liked to ask, "where is it to be found?"[46] Certainly his hard-earned experience of the summer of 1755 taught him priceless lessons. The first had to do with military tactics. "The folly and consequence of opposing compact bodies to the sparse manner of Indian fighting, in woods, which had in a manner been predicted, was now so clearly verified that henceforward another mode obtained in all future operations," he noted.[47] Second, the folly was Braddock's and the other British officers', not his—and, accompanied as it was by such an arrogant contempt for the experience of others, it seemed to be irremediable. "The whole transaction," as Benjamin Franklin summed up the Braddock debacle with his usual wryness, "gave us Americans the first suspicion that our exalted ideas of the prowess of British regulars had not been well founded."[48]

After years of such defeats, British arms, under Secretary of State William Pitt's brilliant new commanders, finally—and gloriously—won the French and Indian War (the American part of the Seven Years' War), ending French power in North America. Washington's part in the conflict proved frustratingly inglorious, though. However thrilled he was when Dinwiddie named him colonel and commander in chief of the Virginia regiment in August 1755, his was the impossible task of "protect[ing] from the cruel Incursions of a Crafty Savage Enemy a line of Inhabitants of more than 350 Miles Extent with a force inadequate to the taske."[49] He couldn't prevent the constant murders of the Shenandoah Valley settlers and their wives and babies. The hopelessness tore his heart out. "But what can I do?" he wrote Dinwiddie. "I *see* their situation, *know* their danger, and participate [in] their *Sufferings*; without having it in my power to give them further relief, than uncertain promises. . . . The supplicating tears of the women; and moving petitions from the men, melt me into such deadly sorrow, that I solemnly declare, if I know my own mind—I could offer myself a willing Sacrifice to the butchering Enemy, provided that would contribute to the peoples ease."[50] But it wouldn't.

Those three hard years patrolling the frontier turned Washington from a cocky prodigy into a mature commander. For all the heartache—indeed, because of it—he came away with three convictions that stayed at the core of his worldview. Three weeks after Jumonville's death in 1754, with a French war clearly looming, representatives of seven of the thirteen colonies met at Albany, New York, to discuss "a plan for a union of all the Colonies under one government, so far as might be necessary for defence and other important general purposes," as Benjamin Franklin, the plan's author, described it. Neither the colonial assemblies nor the London authorities approved the scheme for a Crown-appointed executive and a grand council chosen by the colonial assemblies; but the idea of an American union was very much in the air from then on, and Washington's experience trying to hold off the Indian allies of a European power with nothing but a Virginia regiment made him a true believer. "Nothing I more sincerely wish," he wrote the governor of Pennsylvania in 1756, twenty years before the Articles of Confederation, "than a union to the Colonys in this time of Eminent danger."[51]

Similarly, more than thirty years before the Constitutional Convention, he was already calling for energy in the executive. You can't "govern, and keep up a proper spirit of Discipline, with[ou]t Laws" and "a person invested with full power to exert his Authority" to carry them out, he wrote Dinwiddie from the frontier in October 1755. It is amazing, he observed, in terms that *The Federalist* echoed a generation later, "that we alone shou'd be so tenacious of Liberty as not to invest a power, where Interest, and Politicks so unanswerably demand it." The very people whose lives and property he was trying to defend—whose self-interest was identical to the public interest—wouldn't recognize his authority to requisition supplies from them, he complained: "no orders are obey'd but what a Party of Soldier's or my own drawn Sword Enforces; without this a single horse for the most urgent occasions cannot be had." This was a hard way to supply an army, he grumbled, but he'd keep on doing it, "unless they execute what they threaten i, e, 'to blow out my brains.'"[52] Someone has to be able to wield the force on which governmental authority ultimately rests, he understood, and he was willing to go far to do so. He wrote a fellow officer in July 1757 that out of 400 recently enlisted soldiers, 114 had already deserted. "I have a Gallows near 40 feet high erected (which has terrified the *rest* exceedingly:) and I am determined," he wrote, "to hang two or three on it, as an example to others."[53]

But such a measure, he well knew, was only the last resort in a grave crisis. As he told the Continental Army on New Year's Day 1776, shortly after he became its commander, his "first wish [was] to have the business of the Army conducted without punishment," and therefore, as far as it was in his power, he would "reward such as particularly distinguish themselves."[54] Behind that declaration lies an important eighteenth-century theory of human behavior that Washington took as a bedrock assumption all his life—and that intellectual historians have called the "love of fame" or "emulation" theory.[55] According to such writers as La Rochefoucauld, Bernard Mandeville, Adam Smith, and Edmund Burke, people don't behave virtuously or heroically because they have an inborn love of virtue or of their fellow men. But they *are* born with a craving for distinction, for the good opinion, admiration, and applause of others. This craving, which Washington's contemporaries called "pride" or "emulation," isn't in itself moral or public-spirited (and indeed may be the opposite), but its effects tend to be the same as those that virtue or conscience or magnanimity would produce: in order to win the approval, praise, and honor you want, you have to behave in praiseworthy, socially approved, publicly beneficial ways.

Washington could not have been clearer about feeling such passions himself. He described himself in 1758 as "a person who would gladly be distinguished in some measure from the *common run* of provincial Officers," and twenty years later he was still avowing that "to stand well in the good opinion of my Countrymen constitutes my chiefest happiness."[56] Later still, in thanking Benjamin Franklin's daughter for sending him some praise from her father, he wrote that "nothing in human life, can afford a liberal Mind, more rational and exquisite satisfaction, than the approbation of a Wise, a great and virtuous Man."[57] He knew, too, that such feelings impelled his troops, no less than himself, to deeds of bravery and endurance. He told the Continental Army that he hoped "a laudable Spirit of emulation"—the ambition to excel—would pervade it, for "without such a Spirit, few

Officers have ever arrived to any degree of Reputation, nor did any Army ever become formidable."[58]

So the third great conviction he formed in the French and Indian War was that he would never get the honor his merit deserved from Britain—that the Mother Country ("our unnatural Parent," as this son of a withholding mother later called it) would always treat him and his fellow Virginia officers as second-class citizens.[59] "We cant conceive, that being Americans should deprive us of the benefits of British Subjects; nor lessen our claim to preferment," he wrote Governor Dinwiddie in 1757. After all, "it is the service done, not the Service engag'd in, that merits reward," so surely royal commissions should be granted as readily "for three years hard & bloody Service, as for 10 spent at St James's &ca where real Service, or a field of Battle never was seen." The top brass should realize, he concluded, that "the disregarding the faithful services of any Body of His Majesty's Subjects; tends to discourage Merit and lessen that generous Emulation, spirit, and laudable ambition so necessary to prevail in an Army and which Contributes so much to the Success of Enterprize."[60]

He was becoming dispirited himself, but he stayed for one more push to retake Fort Duquesne in November 1758. The expedition proved anticlimactic, except for one frightful moment when two Virginia detachments, mistaking each other for the enemy, began killing one another; Washington galloped in to push up their gun barrels with his sword and "never was in more imminent danger."[61] Hearing that a huge force was approaching, the small French garrison blew up the fort and fled, leaving only a smoking ruin behind.[62] Shortly thereafter, thanking his officers—"for if I have acquired any reputation, it is from you I derive it"—he quit forever the service of His Britannic Majesty.[63]

He "exchanged the rugged and dangerous field of Mars for the soft and pleasurable bed of Venus," as he once put it, marrying a rich, warmhearted widow named Martha Dandridge Custis in January 1759 and a month later, on his twenty-seventh birthday, taking his seat in

Virginia's House of Burgesses.[64] To understand how different his life now became from fighting in the backwoods only weeks before, let's quickly double back in time. For a run of unlikely strokes of fortune befell him—smacking more of the picaresque world of *Tom Jones* or *Candide* than of real life—and, with a strange mix of grief and good luck, they changed everything.

Ten years earlier, while Washington was surveying Lord Fairfax's lands, his half brother Lawrence contracted tuberculosis. Neither London doctors nor Virginia hot springs helped; so, because his wife had to stay home with their new baby, Lawrence asked Washington to take him to Barbados, then thought healthy for consumptives. Two weeks after they arrived in November 1751, Washington caught smallpox—his first lucky calamity, for his light case of the dread disease made him immune to the eighteenth-century military's greatest scourge. Lawrence's lungs got worse, however, and he died at Mount Vernon in July 1752, aged thirty-four. Death carried off his little girl two years later, and his widow, Ann, soon remarried and moved away. Since Lawrence's will decreed that if he died with no surviving child, Mount Vernon and his fortune would go to his favorite half brother after Ann's death, Ann gladly leased her life interest in the now-vacant 2,126-acre estate for a hefty rent to its heir. When she died at thirty-three in 1761, Washington became Mount Vernon's outright owner. Already rich as master of his wife's inheritance, as husbands were by eighteenth-century law, he now became very rich.[65]

Nevertheless, he spent more than his income. In the army, he had signaled his thirst for distinction through his regiment's showy uniforms, like Scott Fitzgerald's Gatsby, who in displaying his drawerful of custom-made shirts paradoxically tried to show through his outer trappings the inner specialness and refinement he craved. For his officers, Washington prescribed a blue coat, faced and cuffed with scarlet and trimmed with silver; a scarlet waistcoat; and a silver-laced hat, "of a Fashionable size."[66] He had already outfitted himself with gold: gilt buttons, gold shoulder knot, gold lace on his hat.[67] Even late in life, he was still designing uniforms for himself, puzzling over whether to have embroidery or not, slash cuffs or not—but needing for sure "tasty Cockades (but not whimsically foolish)," incorporating silver eagles, for his hat.[68]

But now Mount Vernon became the outer emblem of his inner worth, showing him as perfect an English country gentleman as any officer with a royal commission who had ever condescended to him. It became his self-created embodiment of his own ideal life, continually evolving as his view of himself and the world deepened. It was his mental escape hatch from the battlefield: no matter where he was or what privations he suffered, he could conjure up in his mind's eye, with a surveyor's precision, every inch of the house, every outbuilding, tree, and field, and he daydreamed about improving, extending, planting, beautifying. The work of art he spent thirty years perfecting, Mount Vernon represented all that he was fighting for.

The minute Washington had leased the estate, prior to owning it outright after Ann's death, he started planning, deep in the Indian-thronged woods, to enlarge Lawrence's story-and-a-half wooden house, with four rooms on a floor, that their father had built on a Potomac bluff around 1740. Content simply to build upon the past, he raised the roof and added a story in 1757, in preparation for his marriage to Martha, so he now had five good second-floor bedrooms, plus an attic. Acting, like so many eighteenth-century gentlemen, as his own architect, with a stack of English pattern books to consult, he slathered on the ornament between 1757 and 1760, enriching the exterior with a cornice modeled on the Roman Pantheon, a pedimented front door, and wooden siding beveled and finished with a mix of sand and buff paint to look like blocks of stone.

More ambitiously, he turned the interior into a jewel box of mid-century classicism, though each room's corner fireplace, relatively small size, and modest ceiling height ensured snug coziness rather than grandeur. The wide center hall, its east and west doors open to river breezes in hot weather, he embellished with paneling, a cornice echoing the one outside, pedimented doorways, and a rich new walnut staircase. A pair of pottery British lions, each with a paw on a globe, stood guard on brackets over the riverside door. With no compunction about the faux, he later had the walls and doors grained to look like mahogany.

The west parlor got the full Palladian treatment: an ornately pedimented door case with Ionic pilasters went in, along with raised paneling and a finely carved rococo chimneypiece and overmantel adapted from *The British Architect* and incorporating a marble fireplace surround and a "neat landskip" from England.[69] Carved in a scrolled pediment crowning the overmantel were Washington's coat of arms and flying-griffin crest in which he took great pride, though he had never heard of the ancestral Washington home—sixteenth-century Sulgrave Manor in Northamptonshire—or of his great-great-grandfather Lawrence, a fellow of Brasenose College, Oxford, persecuted by the Cromwellians. All he could tell the master of the Royal College of Arms, who sent him genealogical queries when he was president, was that, "I have often heard others of the family, older than myself, say that our ancestors . . . came from some one of the Northern Counties of England," but which one "I do not precisely remember."[70]

Nevertheless, the arms and crest, cyphers of distinction, went on everything, from the silverware he had made for his wedding, to the coach he ordered from London "in the newest taste, handsome, genteel, & light," to the brass-mounted harnesses for his horses, the bookplates for his library, the gilt mirror between his windows, and the gold head on his stick. From London, too, he ordered a mahogany bed for his newly paneled downstairs bedroom, a dozen mahogany chairs, damask table linens, china, wallpaper: everything to be "fashionable—neat—and good." And starting with the purchase of 500 additional acres in 1757, he added land to the estate, too, which totaled 8,000 acres when he was done.[71] By 1763, all this "swallowed up before I well knew where I was, all the money I got by Marriage nay more."[72]

When Washington died, his wife burned most of the personal letters written between her and her "Old Man," as she called him, so we can't hear firsthand the tone of their marriage; but we can catch it in the advice the president, then married thirty-five years, gave his step-granddaughter Betsy Custis when she pondered wedlock. "Do not," he counseled, "look for perfect felicity," and remember that "love is too dainty a food to live on *alone*." While "a necessary ingredient for . . . matrimonial happiness," it is less important "than that the object on whom it is placed, should possess good sense [and] good dispositions"—which "cannot fail to attract (after marriage) your esteem and regard, into wch. or into disgust, sooner or later, love naturally resolves itself." After all, "all our enjoyments fall short of our expectations," none more so than "the gratification of the passions."[73]

Esteem and regard, good sense, and a good disposition: a very precise description of the foundation of the Washingtons' marriage. A British observer thought Washington "a more respectful than a tender husband," but those who knew the couple well saw the devoted affection under the respect. "Mrs. Washington is excessive fond of the General and he of her," General Nathanael Greene remarked during the Revolution. "They are happy in each other." With the romantic hyperbole of a young Frenchman, the Marquis de Lafayette concluded that the then-matronly Mrs. Washington "loves her husband madly."[74] As Washington himself told her when he left to take command of the Continental Army, "I should enjoy more real happiness and felicity in one month with you, at home, than I have the most distant prospect of reaping abroad, if my stay was to be Seven times Seven years."[75]

Though the pair had no children, Washington doted on Patsy, Martha's daughter from her first marriage, and he was almost as inconsolable as his wife when, after their years of worried visits with doctors about her worsening epilepsy, the "Sweet Innocent Girl" died suddenly at seventeen, "without uttering a Word, a groan, or scarce a Sigh," her stepfather wrote.[76] When Martha's son Jacky died at twenty-six, the Washingtons took in his two youngest children, as they did Martha's motherless niece and the three orphaned children of Washington's brother Samuel.[77] Fussing over a houseful of children seemed Mrs. Washington's natural element.

One other piece of matrimonial advice, to step-granddaughter

Nelly Custis, shines a different light on this part of Washington's life. "Love is said to be an involuntary passion," he wrote. But everyone has seen that, once a woman beautiful and accomplished enough to have "set the circle in which she moves on fire" gets married, the "madness *ceases* and all is quiet again, . . . because there is an end of hope. Hence it follows, that love may and therefore ought to be under the guidance of reason."[78]

Easy to say, but there's a world of self-mastery there, among Washington's many classical virtues of self-mastery. When Sarah Fairfax, wife of his friend and wilderness companion George William Fairfax, wrote to congratulate him on his engagement to Martha, he replied with an oblique revelation of whom he really loved. "Tis true, I profess myself a Votary to Love—I acknowledge that a Lady is in the Case"—a lady "known to you . . . , as well as she is to one who is too sensible of her Charms to deny the Power, whose Influence he feels and must ever Submit to. I feel the force of her amiable beauties in the recollection of a thousand tender passages," confided Washington. "I have drawn myself, into an honest confession of a Simple Fact—misconstrue not my meaning—'tis obvious—doubt it not, nor expose it—the World has no business to know the object of my Love, declard in this manner to—you when I wanted to conceal it—One thing, above all things in this World I wish to know, and only one person of your Acquaintance can solve me that, or guess my meaning."[79] But he would never ask Sarah directly if she loved him back. When the Fairfaxes moved permanently to England and had the contents of Belvoir auctioned, Washington bought more than half, from mahogany furniture to a bust of Shakespeare, all fraught with layers of sentiment for him.[80]

Except for his passionate foxhunting—out before dawn three times a week in a blue riding coat and gold-trimmed red waistcoat, with his "Turkish"-costumed, turban-wearing slave, Billy Lee, an equally fearless horseman, at his side—Washington was too much an entrepreneur to be an ordinary country squire at Mount Vernon. He restlessly experimented with sixty-odd crops before giving up soil-depleting tobacco in 1766 for more profitable wheat and corn. He built a high-tech gristmill and exported flour and cornmeal to the West Indies, England, and Portugal. The Potomac at his door was beautiful, yes, but surely it had a *use* too. He bought fishing boats, and by 1772 he was salting and exporting a million herring a year, plus sturgeon and shad. He started a distillery, ultimately America's biggest, pumping out 11,000 gallons of rye and bourbon a year.[81] He operated with a methodical precision that Ben Franklin would have approved, and he favored such *Poor Richard*–like aphorisms as "System in all things is the soul of business," or "many mickles make a muckle," an "old Scotch" adage recommending attention to detail.[82]

Slaves did most of Mount Vernon's work, and at this stage of his life, Washington's feeling toward them was chiefly annoyance. They ran away, and he advertised rewards for them, with closely observed descriptions, from Jack's scar-decorated face ("being his Country Marks") and large feet ("for he requires a great Shoe") to Cupid's coarse skin, "inclined to be pimpley," and his "unintelligible *English*," since a slave ship had brought him only two years earlier. They stole. They sometimes so misbehaved that he sold them to the West Indies, where slaves' lives were especially nasty, brutish, and short.[83] And—in a remarkable failure of sympathy on his part—he couldn't understand why people robbed of their liberty had no work ethic. He denounced the slave carpenters of his buildings as an "idle set of rascals," and, standing over them with his pocket watch in his hand, he drove them to quadruple their output of boards. He complained that his slave seamstresses turned out nine shirts a week when Mrs. Washington was at Mount Vernon, but only six when she wasn't. "There are few Negroes who will work unless there be a constant eye on them," he grumbled, as if such passive resistance were a moral failing.[84]

Much of his entrepreneurial zeal surged into real-estate speculation. How were the colony's greatest fortunes made? he asked a neighbor rhetorically in 1767. "Was it not by taking up & purchasing at very low rates the rich back Lands which were thought nothing of in those days, but are now the most valuable Lands we possess?" And opportunity still abounded: "an enterprizing Man with very little Money may lay the foundation of a Noble Estate in the New Settlemts upon Monongahela for himself and posterity."[85]

Enterprise might mean cutting the odd legal or moral corner, though, which didn't faze the devil-take-the-hindmost Washington of this era. True, Britain had outlawed land sales west of the Alleghenies, he wrote one of his ex-officers living there; but surely, in an expanding country surging with entrepreneurial vim, the ban could only be "a temporary expedient to quiet the Minds of the Indians & must fall of course in a few years." Therefore, anyone "who neglects the present oppertunity of hunting out good Lands & in some measure Marking & distinguishing them for their own (in order to keep others from settling them) will never regain it." Washington proposed a deal: if his ex-comrade would pick out prime lots in huge quantity, Washington would pay to survey and register the claims as soon as it became legal, with a fair cut for his accomplice. "I would recommend to you to keep this whole matter a profound Secret," Washington counseled, so as not to "give the alarm to others," who might try to horn in. You might carry out the scheme, he suggested, "under the pretence of hunting other Game."[86]

In 1770, he drafted his brother Charles into a stealthier scheme. Because of a tangle of competing land claims on top of the 1763 British settlement ban, who knew when—or if—the government would honor its promise of land grants to French and Indian War officers? But it might. So though he "would hardly give any Officer a button for his Right," Washington wrote Charles, he nevertheless heard that one lieutenant sold his rights to 2,000 acres for £10. "Now, coud I purchase 12 or 15,000 Acres upon the same terms, I woud do it, considering of it as a Lottery only," for if it worked out, it "woud form a Tract of . . . great dignity." So "if you woud (in a joking way, rather than in earnest at first) see what value they seem to set upon their Lands," and if they ask £5 to £7 per thousand acres, buy them, "in your own name; for reason's I shall give you when we meet" and settle up. But "do not let it be known that I have any concern therein."[87]

Meanwhile, conflict of interest notwithstanding, Washington the burgess lobbied the authorities to keep their promise of land for ex-officers, himself included, and he scoured the Ohio country by horse and canoe in 1770 to scout out prime sites firsthand. When the government finally awarded the pledged land in 1772, Washington owned, by grant and purchase, over 30,000 rich acres, including forty miles along the Great Kanawha, much more than rules about riverfront property allowed.[88] And with his surveyor's mind able to visualize the continental terrain as if from a satellite, he began planning yet another entrepreneurial use for the Potomac. With dredging, locks, and portages, privately financed like an English turnpike company, it might become the profitable "Channel of conveyance of the extensive & valuable Trade of a rising Empire" in the West, where he was a major landholder.[89]

Once again, heartbreak had a silver lining for him. When his teenaged stepdaughter Patsy died in 1773, her inheritance—one-third of her father's fortune—went to Martha, doubling her wealth. Washington paid off his debts and decided to double the size of Mount Vernon, too, creating a preeminent mansion for a preeminent landowner. He designed extensions at each end, and planned to embellish the west front with a pediment and the east front with a deliciously cozy, two-story-high, Tuscan-pillared piazza—his most influential innovation—framing the sparkling river view and catching the breeze in the afternoon shade. A cupola for light and ventilation would crown the red-painted roof, and curved, open arcades revealing glimpses of the river, another innovation, would connect the main house to the service wings, their roofs originally painted blue. Bucolic drives meandering through informal, Capability Brown–style plantings would replace the straight approach road and symmetrical gardens to the west, while toward the river Washington planned to sculpt the earth itself to improve the view and provide a grassy podium for the piazza.[90]

In 1774, he started to build, adding on to Mount Vernon's south

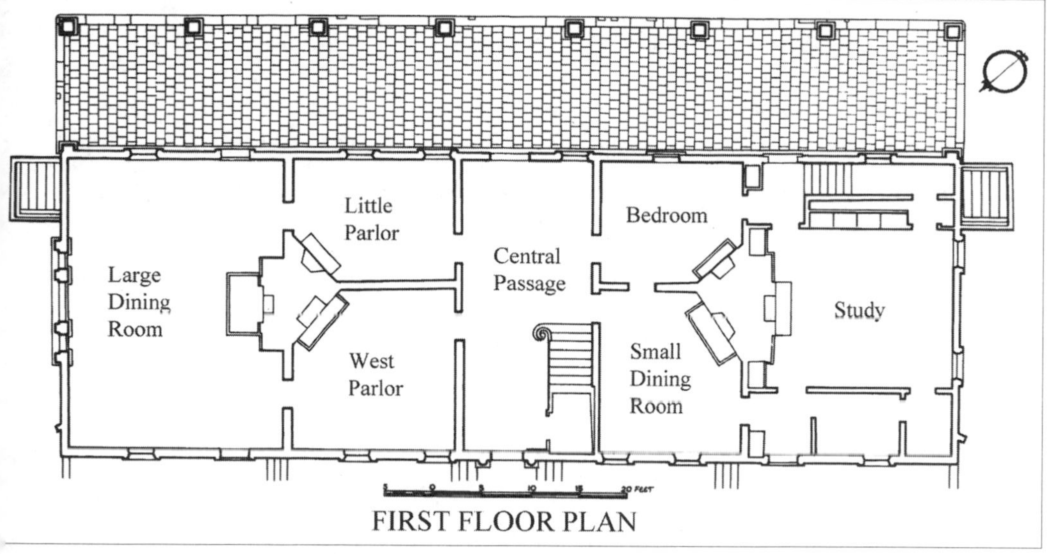

Courtesy of the Mount Vernon Ladies' Association

end a spacious study for himself with a master bedroom above. Anterooms buffering this addition from the rest of the house, plus a separate staircase and entrance from outside, created a private sanctum "that none entered without orders," recalled Martha's grandson.[91] In 1776, work began on the north extension, a grand, two-story-high dining room lit by a magnificent Venetian triple window and, when finished, one of America's most stately and beautiful rooms. But it was a long time finishing—for in the spring of 1775, its architect left to fight the Revolution. The work advanced glacially in his absence: the piazza rose in 1777 and the cupola in 1778, all constructed according to directions Washington sent from the battlefield.

When he next saw the house in 1781—briefly, after six years—he was a changed man. And a certain ambivalence in the design of the house foreshadows the change. Yes, it is ambitious. But compared to an English country mansion, it is surprisingly modest. While the lofty dining room wouldn't be out of place in an English grandee's manor, the rest of the house breathes cozy domesticity, especially since no two interior doors line up to reveal the expanded building's full length. Nor does Mount Vernon's main façade achieve the dignified classical symmetry of such splendid eighteenth-century Virginia houses as Stratford Hall down the Potomac or Shirley Plantation on the James—or even George Mason's much smaller but perfect Gunston Hall just down the road (which visitors to Mount Vernon should also tour). For all its efforts at balance, Mount Vernon is lopsided: the pediment embraces two windows to the left of the front door but only one to the right; the cupola is ten inches off center. The ends too are asymmetrical, with a humble cellar door elbowing the grand Venetian window to the north, and the doorway to Washington's study marring the symmetry of the south.

These defects lie at the heart of Mount Vernon's meaning. The house embodies the temperament of a conservative revolutionary. Just as Edmund Burke described how improvement in government ought to proceed—gradually, organically, and with deep respect for time-tested institutions—so Mount Vernon evolved in stages over decades, as Washington embellished, modernized, and extended its asymmetrical core, rather than razing it in order to rebuild from scratch, according to some abstract, rational blueprint, as the French revolutionaries did. A 1773 pencil sketch he made shows that he thought about regularizing the windows during the new enlargement, as he easily could have done. But that would have changed the harmonious balance of the rooms within, and he didn't want to meddle with what already worked so well, even while he was hugely altering the existing structure. Architect Allan Greenberg, a leading modern neoclassicist, suggests a related explanation for Mount Vernon's irregularities: he guesses that Washington wanted both a manor house and a vernacular farmhouse and tried to combine the two. For all his ambition, he built the house of a citizen, not a seigneur, and the endearingly homey Mount Vernon turned out to be a large but undoubted example of what Greenberg calls America's architecture of democracy.[92]

Washington already chafed under a sense of slighted merit when he left the king's service for marriage just before Britain won the French and Indian War in 1763, and his resentment of the English, increasingly rubbed raw during these years as a planter, set him on the

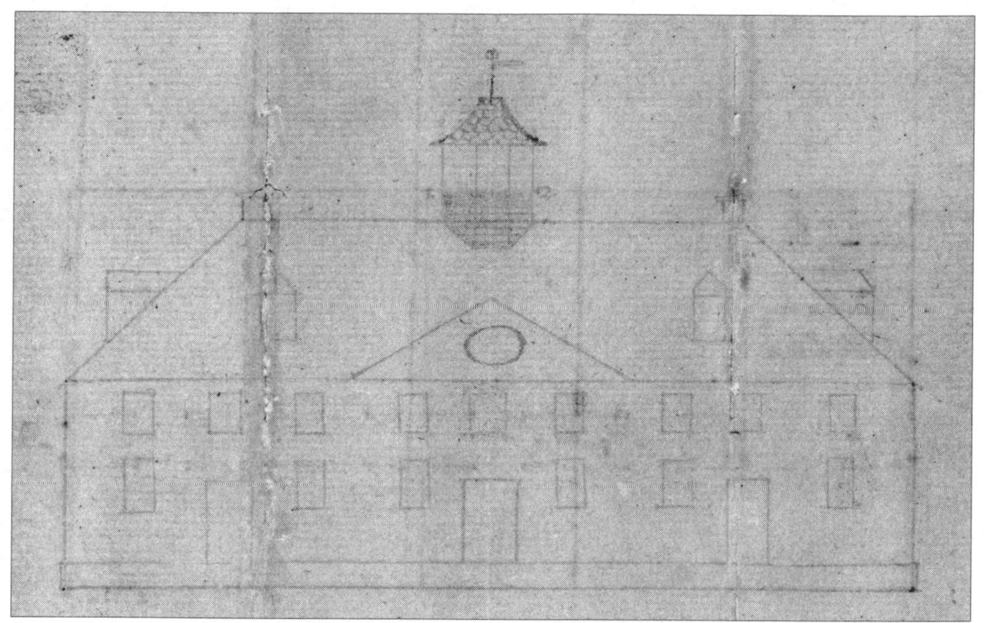

Washington's sketch of an ideally symmetrical Mount Vernon
Courtesy of the Mount Vernon Ladies' Association

road to revolution. When Britain had forbidden settlement west of the Alleghenies to protect its Indian fur trade, Washington saw his land-speculation schemes blocked. Then London barred the colonies from printing paper money, whose rapid depreciation harmed British merchants trading with America, so his cash-strapped tenants and other debtors couldn't pay him. With cash now scarce in the colonies, the stamp tax that Britain imposed on Americans in 1765 to make them defray the debt for a war they thought they'd fully paid for in blood and treasure sparked outrage that in Washington's case was especially personal, since he thought Britain owed *him* for the war, not vice versa.

At first, he took out his ire on Cary & Co., the London agents through whom he sold his produce and bought much of the finery that bedecked himself, his family, and Mount Vernon. The firm had had the gall to send him a dunning letter in 1764. "Mischances rather than Misconduct," he replied in the clear, round, powerful penmanship that made his written battlefield orders impossible to mistake, explain why "a corrispondant so steady, & constant as I have proovd" is late in paying his bill. Crops have been poor, he said; when they've been "tolerable," Cary has sold them for "little or nothing." And because of the London-made cash crunch, bills of exchange from his debtors that Washington sent in as payment bounced.[93]

A year later—just after the Stamp Act—he was flaming with anger over having to suffer passively the British merchant's and the British government's malign role in every part of his economic life. He sends "none but Sweetscented Tobacco," carefully packed, he thundered to Cary, and Cary gets him lower prices for it than his neighbors' poorer product commands—and lower than a Liverpool agent got for worse stuff. Plus Cary sends wrong or shoddy goods from London, overcharges for them, and blithely says to send them back next year and meanwhile do without clothes and household necessities. Since "the selling of our Tobacco's well, & purchasing of Our Goods upon the best Terms, are matters of the utmost consequence to our well doing," if Cary doesn't perform better, they're fired. As for the Stamp Act, which "the speculative part of the Colonists" consider "a direful attack upon their Liberties": loading Americans with taxes will leave them less money to buy British goods, and they are learning "that many of the Luxuries which we have heretofore lavished our Substance to Great Britain for can well be dispensed with," to Britain's detriment. And since the act requires payment in hard money for the stamps required on legal documents and the like, and the colonies have so little of it, the law courts will have to shut—so good luck trying to sue to collect your debts.[94]

Britain repealed the Stamp Act in 1766. But when it imposed its new Townshend taxes in 1767 and sent two regiments in 1768 to scare Bostonians out of their boycott of British goods, Washington knew that war was likely. Since "our lordly Masters in Great Britain will be satisfied with nothing less than the deprivation of . . . the liberty which we have derived from our Ancestors," he wrote his neighbor George Mason in April 1769, "no man shou'd scruple, or hesitate a moment to use a—ms in defence of so valuable a blessing, on which all the good and evil of life depends." Of course the colonists should try everything else first. But they had already "proved the inefficacy" of petitions to king and Parliament, so now only "starving their Trade & manufactures, remains to be tried."

Naturally, "selfish designing men" will try to evade a boycott, and they "ought to be stigmatized, and made the objects of publick reproach," since (as he well knew) the opinion of one's fellows powerfully shapes behavior. But a boycott might also have unforeseen advantages for the compliant, he mused, drifting off into the personal. "The extravagant & expensive man . . . is thereby furnished with a pretext to live within bounds." Surely "prudence dictated œconomy to him before, but his resolution was too weak," he wrote; "for how can I, *says he*, who have lived in such & such a manner change my method? . . . [S]uch an alteration in the System of my living, will create suspicions of a decay in my fortune, & such a thought the world must not harbour."[95] That's the emulative Washington speaking, spending beyond his ample means to win admiration—except he's beginning to imagine a larger and loftier ideal.

Hitherto a lightweight in the House of Burgesses, he threw himself into its work and emerged a leader. He approved the May 1769 Virginia Resolves declaring that only Virginians could tax themselves. When the new governor, Lord Botetourt, punished such effrontery by dissolving the House, Washington successfully presented George Mason's nonimportation plan to his colleagues, gathered extra-legally—as so often during this tumultuous period—at Williamsburg's Raleigh Tavern.[96] In March 1773 he voted to start a Virginia Committee of Correspondence, part of a colonies-wide network created to harmonize the colonies' response to British encroachment and to convene a meeting of colonial representatives.[97]

When Britain savagely retaliated for the December 1773 Boston Tea Party with the 1774 Intolerable Acts, closing the town's port and suspending the colony's charter, Washington understood, he wrote in June 1774, that "the cause of Boston . . . ever will be considered as the cause of America," for the English were "endeavouring by every piece of Art and despotism to fix the Shakles of Slavry upon us."[98] After all, he wrote a friend on July 4, "Does it not appear, as clear as the sun in its meridian brightness, that there is a regular, systematic plan formed to fix the right and practice of taxation upon us," and "that the administration is determined to stick at nothing to carry its point?"[99]

On July 17, George Mason came to Mount Vernon with a draft of his Fairfax Resolves, and, as the two friends wrote a final version together, Washington got a crash course in political theory, from natural rights to legitimacy to constitutions. The next day, with Washington in the chair, the Fairfax County constituents whom he represented in the House of Burgesses approved the radical Lockean Resolves, which declared that the Americans' ancestors had established the colonies at their own expense, not the Crown's, and that they had formed a compact with Britain, confirmed by charters, promising them all the rights guaranteed by the British constitution, particularly the right of "being governed by no Laws, to which they have not given their Consent, by Representatives freely chosen by themselves"—meaning our "own Provincial Assemblys or Parliaments." Since "Taxation and Representation are in their Nature inseperable," it follows that "the Powers over the People of America now claimed by the British House of Commons, in whose Election we have no Share," are "totally incompatible with the Privileges of a free People, and the natural Rights of Mankind," and "must if continued, establish the most grievous and intollerable Species of Tyranny and Oppression, that ever was inflicted upon Mankind."[100]

Two days later, Washington put it in simpler terms in a letter to a friend: "I think the Parliament of Great Britain hath no more Right to put their hands into my Pocket, without my consent, than I have to put my hands into your's, for money." Indeed, my "Nature . . . recoil[s] at the thought of Submitting to Measures which I think Subversive of every thing that I ought to hold dear and valuable"—and "the voice of Mankind is with me."[101]

In August, the Virginia burgesses, locked out of their chamber again, renamed themselves the Virginia Convention and adopted many of the Fairfax Resolves, including Washington and Mason's plan for an ever-harsher trade boycott. They chose Washington and six others as delegates to the First Continental Congress. The veteran soldier saw war looming. "I could wish, I own, that the dispute had been left to Posterity to determine," he wrote later that month, "but the Crisis is arrivd where we must assert our Rights, or Submit to every imposition that can be heap'd upon us."[102]

Mrs. Washington, too, sensed what was in store: when her husband set off from Mount Vernon for the Congress in Philadelphia with fellow delegates Patrick Henry and Edmund Pendleton on August 31, 1774, she "talked like a Spartan mother to her son on going to battle," Pendleton recalled. " 'I hope you will stand firm—I know George will,' she said."[103]

While Washington politicked with notables of the other colonies, George Mason, also filled with foreboding, set up a Fairfax County militia that, along with four nearby county militias, elected Washington its commander and started "arming, equipping, and training for the worst event," Washington noted approvingly. On October 9, shortly before the Congress adjourned, Washington wrote that without doubt "more blood will be spilt on this occasion (if the Ministry are determind to push matters to extremity) than history has ever yet furnished instances of in the annals of North America; and such a vital wound given to the peace of this great Country, as time itself cannot cure or eradicate the remembrance of."[104] In preparation, before he left Philadelphia, he outfitted himself with a new silk sash, a gorget, and epaulettes.[105]

The March 1775 meeting of the Virginia Convention—where Patrick Henry cried, "Give me liberty or give me death!"—elected Washington as one of Virginia's seven delegates to the Second Continental Congress. The next month, when the shots rang out at Lexington and Concord, Washington knew that the war had begun. "Unhappy it is," he wrote, "that a Brother's Sword has been sheathed in a Brother's breast, and that, the once happy and peaceful plains of America are either to be drenched with Blood, or Inhabited by Slaves. Sad alternative! But can a virtuous Man hesitate in his choice?"[106] Not he: he arrived at the Congress in May in his uniform. On June 15, his fellow delegates unanimously elected him commander in chief of the American armies and toasted him at a midnight supper. Moved by the honor, he rose to thank them; and they, moved by the enormity of what they were doing, rose with him, and drank standing in solemn silence.[107]

As the vastness of his task sank in over the next few days, Washington had two conflicting feelings that recurred at his life's turning points. Of course he worried he might fail—he was going up against the world's greatest military. "I am now embarked on a tempestuous Ocean from whence, perhaps, no friendly harbour is to be found," he wrote. "It is an honour I wished to avoid . . . from a thorough conviction of my own Incapacity & want of experience in the conduct of so momentous a concern." He hoped, however, to come through it "with some good to the common cause & without Injury (from want of knowledge) to my own reputation." But "as reputation derives its principal support from success, . . . it will be remembered I hope that no desire, or insinuation, of mine placed me in this situation."[108] To his familiar love of fame, he now adds a new concern: Will people recognize that his inner motives are pure, that he values the public good more than his own repute—and certainly more than his own fortune, for he had refused a salary for his service? There are times when you can see a culture's moral life revising itself, Lionel Trilling once said: here, the arbiter of honor is migrating from the outer world to the inner conscience.[109] George Washington now began to live as examined a life as Hamlet—except that he could act, with a vengeance.

But along with his fear of inadequacy went a remarkable self-assurance, tied to his public spirit, that shines out from the moving letter he wrote his wife from Philadelphia, telling her he was off to war. Despite "my unwillingness to part with you and the Family," he writes, "it was utterly out of my power to refuse this appointment without exposing my Character to such censures as would have reflected dishonour upon myself, and . . . could not, and ought not to be pleasing to you, & must have lessend me considerably in my own esteem." But clearly he had been pondering why such amazing strokes of good fortune had befallen him, preserving his life in lethal firefights and, through the unlikeliest chain of circumstance, making him rich, and he had reached the same conclusion as the Indian chief who had tried so unsuccessfully to kill him: some great fate must await him. "[A]s it has been a kind of destiny that has thrown me upon this Service, I shall hope that my undertaking of it, is designd to answer some good purpose," he writes. "I shall rely therefore, confidently, on that Providence which has heretofore preservd, & been bountiful to me, not doubting but I shall return safe to you in the fall." Like any good soldier, however, he made his will and sent it with the letter.[110]

4

General Washington

WASHINGTON LOVED THEATER—Shakespeare, Sheridan, and above all Addison's patriotic Roman tragedy *Cato*—and a good thing, too: for running the war, and all his later career, required adroit stagecraft. He became a virtuoso of appearance, a paragon of role playing, who could move an audience to passion, to tears, and to action. And of course he loved dressing for a role.

The Battle of Bunker Hill had blazed up as he headed toward Boston to take command of the army. The British had marched 2,300 redcoats straight up the hill on June 17, 1775, intending to overawe the Americans by showing "that trained troops are invincible against any numbers or any position of undisciplined rabble," as General John Burgoyne had brayed. The shock and awe were on the other side, though, because the Americans, whom Colonel William Prescott had ordered not to "fire until you can see the whites of their eyes," didn't retreat until they had killed or wounded almost half the British, including 90 officers, compared to 430 American casualties, out of nearly 2,000 men.[1] It was a "dear bought victory," mourned General Sir Henry Clinton; "another such would have ruined us."[2]

When Washington arrived in Massachusetts on July 2, the Continental Army had taken control both of Dorchester Neck, between Boston and the rest of Massachusetts, and Cambridge, across the Charles River to the north, bottling up the sobered redcoats. Trouble was, the Americans had no ammunition for "Months together, with what will scarce be believed—not 30 rounds of Musket Cartridges a Man," Washington wrote.[3] Not only to make the British believe they were in his power but also to keep his own men confident, the General had to pretend—convincingly, twenty-four hours a day, despite his own fear and frustration—that all was well, while he waited, like Mr. Micawber, for something to turn up. "I know that without Men, without Arms, without Ammunition, without any thing that is fit for the accomodation of a Soldier that little is to be done—and, which is mortifying; I know, that I cannot stand justified to the World without exposing my own Weakness & injuring the cause by declaring my wants," he wrote. "[M]y Situation has been such that I have been obligd to use art to conceal it from my own Officers."[4] All this "produces many an uneasy hour when all around me are wrapped in Sleep. . . . I have often thought, how much happier I should have been, if . . . I had taken my Musket upon my Shoulder & enterd the Ranks, or . . . had retir'd to the back Country, & lived in a Wig wam—If I should be able to rise superior to these, and many other difficulties, . . . I shall most religiously believe that the finger of Providence is in it, to blind the Eyes of our Enemys."[5]

Nor was this all. For the first years of the war, Washington endured what his biographer Ron Chernow calls the Sisyphean nightmare of having his whole army evaporate on December 31, when the troops' one-year hitches ended. By late November 1775, only 3,500 soldiers agreed to stay past their terms, and by year-end a paltry 9,650 untrained new recruits had signed on, half the number needed.[6] "It takes you two or three Months to bring New men to any tolerable degree acquainted with their duty," and even longer to bring independent-minded Americans to "such a subordinate way of thinking as is necessary for a Soldier," Washington lamented. Then, as the end of their terms approaches, you must "relax your discipline, in order as it were to curry favour with them," to cajole them to stay longer—meaning that "the latter part of your time is employed in undoing what the first was accomplishing."[7]

Nevertheless, Washington crowed afterward, during those months "we have disbanded one Army & recruited another, within Musket Shot of two and Twenty Regimts, the Flower of the British Army."[8]

Meanwhile, Congress had written new roles for him and his army, and Washington had to establish them credibly in the eyes of the enemy, including General Thomas Gage, the British commander in chief and royal governor of Massachusetts, who had served with him under General Edward Braddock in the French and Indian War twenty years earlier. A few weeks after taking command, Washington wrote Gage that he had heard that American soldiers captured at Bunker Hill, even "those of the most respectable Rank, when languishing with Wounds and Sickness," have been "thrown indiscriminately, into a common Gaol appropriated for Felons." Please know, he wrote, that the Continental Army will treat British POWs just as the redcoats treat Americans. It was for Gage to choose: either "Severity, & Hardship" or "Kindness & Humanity."[9] Gage replied that of course he mixed up officers and enlisted men promiscuously, "for I acknowledge no rank not derived from the king."[10] This was the wrong response, especially to a general who had once resented having to defer to officers with less merit than he but with royal commissions.

"You affect, Sir, to despise all Rank not derived from the same Source with your own," Washington thundered back, asserting a new, democratic understanding of legitimacy and worth. "I cannot conceive any more honourable, than that which flows from the uncorrupted Choice of a brave and free People—The purest Source & original Fountain of all Power." Furthermore, Gage claims to have shown clemency by not hanging American soldiers as rebels. But it remains to be seen "whether our virtuous Citizens whom the Hand of Tyranny has forced into Arms, to defend their Wives, their Children, & their Property; or the mercenary Instruments of lawless Domination, Avarice, and Revenge best deserve the Appellation of Rebels." A higher authority than Gage would decide. "May that God to whom you then appealed, judge between America & you!"[11]

Lord North, the prime minister, got the point: "the war is now grown to such a height," he noted, "that it must be treated as a foreign war."[12] Others were slower on the uptake, and Washington had to assert his new character sharply at least once more. When Admiral Lord Howe, the British naval commander, and his brother General William Howe, who had led the assault up Bunker Hill and then replaced Gage as commander in chief, wanted to negotiate with Washington in New York in July 1776, they sent an envoy with an invitation addressed to "George Washington Esq., etc. etc." Washington's aides wouldn't take the letter, saying that "there was no such person in the Army," and indeed "all the world knew who Genl Washington was." Some days later, the Howes sent another message addressed to "His Excellency, General Washington," asking him to meet their envoy to discuss a parlay. But when the emissary arrived at the meeting with the original, provocatively misaddressed letter, Washington refused it with frigid politeness, emphasized by inviting the ambassador "to partake of a small collation" before he left.[13] "I would not upon any occasion sacrifice Essentials to Punctilio," Washington reported to John Hancock, president of Congress, "but in this Instance . . . I deemed It a duty to my Country and my appointment to insist upon . . . respect."[14]

Good fortune as 1776 dawned finally gave Washington the means to stage a spectacular coup de théâtre in Boston. A month before Bunker Hill, Connecticut militia captain Benedict Arnold, along with Ethan Allen and his Green Mountain Boys, had rowed across Lake Champlain to the New York side and seized the lightly manned British Fort Ticonderoga, with its rich cache of arms and ammunition. In an almost superhuman feat, Colonel Henry Knox, a towering, 300-pound, stentorian-voiced Boston bookseller who had taught himself gunnery from his shop's stock of artillery manuals, had gone to

Ticonderoga on Washington's orders and hauled fifty-five mortars and cannon on ox-drawn sleds across 300 miles of snowy mountains and frozen rivers, presenting them to Washington on January 17. He happily discovered that Washington had acquired 2,000 muskets and two tons of ammunition, separately captured in the meantime.[15]

Washington crowned Knox's feat with a suitably dramatic finale. Across a narrow strip of Boston Harbor, and looking down upon the city from the south, towered Dorchester Heights—sheer cliffs over a hundred feet high (though now leveled and part of South Boston). The British had carelessly failed to occupy this territory, and if Washington could get Knox's guns up there, he would command Boston in a military checkmate. But how to do it without the British overpowering him in the process?

Out of tree trunks, poles, baskets of earth, and hay bales, Washington built portable fortifications, like a stage set. On the night of March 2, he began a deafening cannonade of Boston from sites away from Dorchester Heights, and this diversion continued incessantly through the night of the fourth, when—as a bright moon shone on the Heights but unusual warmth swathed harbor and city in fog—oxen dragged the heavy weapons and prefabricated fortifications on straw-muffled wheels up a slope frozen firm, while the diversionary bombardment masked what little noise the operation made. When the British awoke on the morning of the fifth, they found themselves pinned down under the guns of a fortress instantly conjured up, it seemed to one British officer, by "the Genii belonging to Aladdin's Wonderful Lamp."[16]

Both Washington and General Howe wanted to attack at once, but a fierce rainstorm and prudent second thoughts held them back. Seeing his position now untenable, Howe resolved to leave the city. He too tried the theatrics of a diversionary cannonade, but Washington glimpsed the hurried confusion of his preparations, and he gloated that when the British sailed away on March 17, they left behind an estimated £30,000 to £40,000 worth of cannon and provisions, along with a wilderness of destroyed baggage wagons and gun carriages drifting in the harbor. The town itself "has shared a much better Fate than was expected," and Washington was pleased to write Hancock that his house had "receiv'd no damage worth mentioning," and "the family pictures are all left entire and untouch'd." As for the Boston Loyalists: "no Electric Shock—no sudden Clap of thunder—in a word the last Trump could not have Struck them with greater Consternation" than the thought of facing "their offended Countrymen." Many fled by any vessel they could find; one or two committed suicide.[17]

Those countrymen had universal praise for Washington's miraculous, morale-boosting achievement. To one who called him "the savior of your country," the theatrical General replied by paraphrasing his favorite line from Addison's *Cato*: "To obtain the applause of deserving men is a heartfelt satisfaction, to merit it is my highest wish."[18] Here is the love of fame at its most refined: we seek the praise of the discerning, not of the mob, and they confer it only for authentic merit and virtue, not appearance.

Correctly guessing that the British had sailed away to New York aiming to seize control of the Hudson River and cut off New England from the rest of the colonies, Washington hurried his army there. He had already sent his second-ranking general, Charles Lee—the beanpole-thin, warily hunched son of a British officer who had bought him the royal commission Washington had never obtained—to get the city ready. A radical who had espoused the American cause and a loner who preferred his many dogs to human company—and whom Washington had disliked when they served together under Braddock—Lee had started fortifying New York and accurately assessed the military challenge: "What to do with the city, I own puzzles me; it is so encircl'd with deep navigable water, that whoever commands the sea must command the town."[19]

The Royal Navy, long the city's shield, began sailing into the harbor as its invader in late June 1776, and by late August half of all Britain's warships and two-thirds of its army had arrived. It was an arrogant military, and rightly so; for, despite its by-the-book rigidity, its successes had made it feared around the world. Though its officers were aristocrats who had bought their commissions, they had risen in rank by battlefield achievement; most weren't upper-class blunderers like the later Crimean War generals. The Howe brothers—their mother was an illegitimate daughter of George I, and they had grown up at court with their cousin and friend George III—were a case in point. The elder, Richard—"Black Dick" to his admiring sailors—became England's youngest admiral and invented ship-to-ship signaling by flag hoists, a communications revolution. William, the younger—"as brave and cool as Julius Caesar," his enemies said—rose to the army's command by his heroism in the final Canadian victories of the French and Indian War and then at Bunker Hill, though after the strange fortune of that battle he became silent, overly cautious, and passionately addicted to games of chance by night. The brothers had long sat in Parliament as prominent Whigs. They loudly opposed the king's American policy to his face and went to America reluctantly and only because the king had asked them to, while hinting that they might solve the conflict by peaceful negotiation—a hope that colonial secretary Lord George Germain soon dashed.[20]

Charles Lee was right, of course: New York *was* indefensible, especially against the world's mightiest navy. But Washington worried about how it would look to Congress and his fellow Americans—and to the French whose support Congress wooed—if he just gave up a major city without a shot.[21] He knew how crucial morale and public opinion were: citizens had to believe that their cause was just and their army resolute.

Thomas Paine had given a boost to the first in January 1776 with his best-selling *Common Sense*, forcefully arguing that while the constitution of England was admirable for the benighted times that produced it, "it is the republican and not the monarchical part of [it] which Englishmen glory in"—and that since George III has proved such a "hardened, sullen-tempered Pharaoh" who can "composedly sleep with [his American subjects'] blood upon his soul," he has dispelled the last wisp of monarchy's mystique of legitimacy, and has made American independence inevitable.[22] In July, as the British fleet crowded into New York Harbor, the Declaration of Independence fulfilled Paine's prophecy and justified the American cause in Jefferson's eloquent, indignant prose. Washington, who had called *Common Sense* "sound doctrine" and had foreseen independence ever since Bunker Hill, had the Declaration read to his men on July 9, and told them that each man was "now in the service of a State, possessed of sufficient power to reward his merit, and advance him to the highest Honors of a free Country."[23]

As for proving the army determined, that was his job, and he set about strengthening the defenses Charles Lee had begun, putting barricades at the water's edge, placing cannon, sinking wrecks in the rivers to obstruct British warships, and building twin forts facing each other on either side of the Hudson—Fort Washington and Fort Lee—to bar the Royal Navy from control of the river. But on July 12, to show the futility of these flimsy shields, two warships—the *Phoenix* and the *Rose*—blew through them effortlessly before "a brisk Wind & strong tide," Washington reported, strafing the city for two hours with ceaseless cannon fire. As round shot rocketed down the smoke-filled streets and smashed through houses, New Yorkers panicked. The "Shrieks and Cries of these poor creatures running every way was truly distressing and I fear will have an unhappy effect on the Ears and Minds of our young and inexperienced Soldiery," the General soberly wrote. Almost untouched by the American return fire—a British sailor tauntingly sat at one masthead the entire time—the two ships then anchored in the Tappan Zee, beyond American cannon range.[24]

Now followed three months of cat and mouse all around New York, as the British stalked and pounced, and the Americans scurried wildly just out of reach (for the most part). On August 22, General Howe's troops came ashore at Brooklyn's Gravesend Bay, at the southwestern tip of Long Island, whose farm produce the British needed. Wrongly judging the maneuver a feint and expecting the main thrust against Manhattan, Washington countered the combined 22,000-

man force of British regulars and Hessian mercenaries with 6,000 of his 19,000-man army, whom he stationed along Brooklyn Heights, at Long Island's northwestern tip. When he realized his mistake, the novice commander in chief sent only 3,000 more men to Brooklyn, whom his subordinates ordered to hold the Heights of Guana (Gowanus Heights), a ridge farther south.

Splitting their army into three parts, the British sent two north and the third, about 10,000 strong, on a long flanking loop to the northeast through the negligently unguarded Jamaica Pass. Surrounding the Americans on the ridge on August 27, the redcoats put them to flight when they burst out of the woods seemingly from everywhere, killing the rebels in cold blood and spitting some to trees with their bayonets. Four out of five Americans managed to sprint to Brooklyn Heights, though. With the rebels now squeezed up against the East River, and the Royal Navy poised to sail up behind them, General Howe thought the battle as good as won and, with what became habitual hesitation, decided to start tightening his siege in the morning and pluck his prize.[25]

But as Howe dug his trenches closer, the weather changed. The wind backed to the northeast, barring his brother the admiral from sailing into position behind the Americans. A cold rain began on the night of the twenty-eighth, soaking the soldiers to the skin and spreading illness to one American in four. Worried that dividing his force had imprudently left his 10,000 men in Manhattan also vulnerable, Washington decided to act fast. On the twenty-ninth, as the storm, now a fierce nor'easter, howled down the river, he moved to get his men out of Brooklyn, in secret and silence.[26]

The Continental Army had some vividly colorful units. There were the Baltimore Independent Cadets, "composed of gentlemen of honour, family and fortune" (their commander wrote), who dressed themselves in "the most macaroni cocked hat" and scarlet coat with buff facings and gold buttons, but stripped down to fringed Indian hunting shirts when it came time to fight. There were the Philadelphia Associators, a quintessentially American, purely voluntary, self-financed militia, which Franklin had organized in 1747 to finesse Quaker Pennsylvania's religious objection to an official military force. Mustered only in wartime and composed of all classes, they voted a uniform costing no more than ten shillings, to "level all distinctions," and chose their officers by secret ballot, electing one of Philadelphia's richest merchants, Colonel John Cadwalader, their commander, and painter Charles Willson Peale a company captain. But perhaps the most memorable unit of all was the Fourteenth Massachusetts, a regiment of oilskin-clad Marblehead fishermen and seamen—some of them Indians, some blacks (who ultimately composed 5 percent of the army). Under the taut command of their ship-owning colonel, John Glover, it was they who got Washington's men to safety.[27]

With Washington, on horseback, directing every moment of the embarkation, the troops mustered in strict silence on the Brooklyn shore after nightfall, communicating by hand signals as they filed into a motley fleet of boats gathered under pretense to preserve secrecy. Myriad campfires blazed on Brooklyn Heights, a piece of theater aimed at making the army appear settled in for the night. With craft laden almost to the gunwales, Glover's mariners struggled with muffled oars against the tricky currents and strong wind, making up to a dozen crossings each of the river, some two-thirds of a mile wide at that point. As dawn neared on the thirtieth, "a very dense fog began to rise," one officer recalled, so thick you could "scarcely discern a man at six yards' distance"—a "providential occurrence," the New Englanders concluded, shrouding the operation in invisibility until Washington stepped into the last boat and followed his 9,000 men to the safety of Manhattan. So ended the Battle of Long Island, the first battle he had fought in fourteen months as commander.[28]

Two weeks later, Howe invaded Manhattan, sending 4,000 British and Hessians ashore at Kip's Bay on the low East River shore, intending to cut the island in half. A thunderous hour-long cannonade terrified the few hundred green American defenders, who fled before the enemy advance—or tried to surrender, only to be shot in the head and, in one case, decapitated, his head impaled on a pike. Seeing the battle smoke from his hilltop headquarters in what's now the Morris-Jumel house-museum in Harlem, Washington leapt into the saddle and galloped downtown with his aides, shouting at the retreating soldiers furiously and cutting at them with his riding whip to stop their "most Shameful and disgraceful" flight, to no avail. "Good God!" he cried. "Have I got such troops as these?" Stunned with rage and vexation, he stood like an equestrian statue alone on the battlefield as fifty redcoats ran toward him, leveling their muskets, until one of his aghast aides grabbed his reins and galloped him away. But as Howe unaccountably failed to cut the island in half, Washington got most of his men back up toward Harlem. The next day, when 1,000 Americans bravely engaged the British in the Battle of Harlem Heights near present-day Columbia University, fought them back, and almost caught them in a trap, even as the redcoats taunted them with the hunting-horn call that means the fox is fleeing before the hounds, Washington's spirits and his army's morale rose again.[29]

But he didn't grasp how much danger he was in. Howe could trap him on Royal Navy–ringed Manhattan Island by seizing King's Bridge, linking its northern end to the mainland. On October 12, four weeks after the Kip's Bay invasion, Howe set out to do that, landing a force behind the Americans on Throg's Neck on the mainland (now in the Bronx), just where the East River opens out into Long Island Sound. A marshy quasi island, it was useless as a landing place, Howe found, but a storm stranded his men there for a week before they could seek a better one. Luckily, General Charles Lee returned to New York from defeating a bungled British invasion of Charleston, South Carolina, in the nick of time, saw at once the peril Washington faced, and implored him to rush his army off Manhattan before Howe could take the bridge. Washington moved out on the eighteenth, while Colonel Glover's doughty Massachusetts salts delayed the British with withering fire as they struggled ashore on a firmer beachhead.[30]

Five days and twenty miles later, the Continentals reached White Plains in Westchester and waited for Howe on a well-chosen ridge high above the Bronx River. When Howe appeared on October 28, he threateningly displayed the fearsome might of his 13,000 British and Hessians in serried ranks and smart uniforms, the sun glittering on their bayonets, in a golden autumnal wheat field. Truly as fierce as they looked, his troops loosed a murderous artillery barrage and then clambered straight up the seemingly impregnable sixty yard-high rock cliff. Both sides fought resolutely, until the Hessians found a weak spot and began pushing the no-longer-green defenders back. Washington retreated to safety; Howe hesitated, as usual; a cold fall storm blew in, and when it passed on November 1, the Americans had vanished.[31]

Except 3,000 men still held Fort Washington, in northern Manhattan, which General Washington had wanted to abandon as impotent against Lord Howe's warships, but had been persuaded to hold by Nathanael Greene—a tall, limping, hardworking, brilliantly blue-eyed Rhode Island Quaker who had learned military tactics from manuals he bought from Henry Knox's bookshop before becoming Washington's youngest (and favorite) general at thirty-three.[32] The commandant, Colonel Robert Magaw, blustered that his fort was impregnable, that he would defend his post "to the last extremity" and could easily escape across the Hudson if the unthinkable happened. All wrong. Washington watched through his telescope from Fort Lee, on the opposite shore, as Howe's 13,000 troops battered the citadel with artillery from all sides on November 16. Surrounding the fort with cannon, they called on Magaw to surrender. For all his bravado, the colonel saw he had no chance and filed out with his men to captivity in Britain's pestilential prison ships. Washington turned his back and wept "with the tenderness of a child."[33]

Not long after his miraculous retreat from Brooklyn, Washington began to realize that "on our side the War should be defensive"—a "War of posts," he called it, in which "we should on all occasions avoid a general Action or put anything to the risque unless compelled by a necessity into which we ought never to be drawn."[34] By the time he began his long retreat down New Jersey after the fall of Fort Washington and abandonment of Fort Lee, he fully understood that he was leading an insurgency and that he didn't so much have to win the war as not lose it, while harassing, exhausting, and frustrating the British until the London authorities had had enough. "[T]ime, caution, and worrying the enemy . . . was the plan for us," he summed it up many years later.[35] His army could lose cities and melt into the interior, to emerge and fight again. "It is our arms, not defenseless towns, they have to subdue," he wrote.[36] Executing such a strategy meant that he first had to subdue his own impulses, since he preferred activity, initiative, glory.

Though New Jersey had its share of Loyalists, for the most part Washington fought among (and for) sympathetic countrymen, and he knew he depended on "the spirit and willingness of the people" for support, intelligence, and supplies. He stopped at nothing to win hearts and minds. When a court-martial found three members of his own elite guard guilty of looting valuables from a New Jersey civilian's house, Washington pointedly endorsed the death sentences it imposed, as "examples which will deter the boldest and most harden'd offenders" from "horrible villainies of this nature."[37] Moreover, he expected "that humanity and tenderness to women and children will distinguish brave Americans, contending for liberty, from infamous mercenary ravagers, whether British or Hessian."[38] When he chose Valley Forge as his winter quarters in 1777, he explained to his troops that he had purposely avoided anyplace to which the "virtuous citizens" of Philadelphia had fled from the British, "sacrificing their all," so as not to compete with them for supplies. "To their distresses humanity forbids us to add."[39]

The Howes planned to fight a counterinsurgency, one colony at a time, starting by wooing New Jersey rebels by granting pardons to any who would swear allegiance to the king. And they would romance the Loyalists. "You are deceived if you suppose there are not many loyal and peaceable subjects in that country," General Howe wrote. "I may safely assert that the insurgents are very few, in comparison of the whole people." He too executed soldiers who mistreated civilians and stole or destroyed their property, and he condemned the terror tactics of his colleagues who earlier had torched the Massachusetts towns of Charlestown and Falmouth (later renamed Portland, Maine).[40]

But he had a much harder task than Washington. His men saw the Americans as low-life rebels, not as countrymen, and treated them as such from the moment they came off Lord Howe's ships onto New York's Staten Island. As one aristocratic British captain there notoriously joked, "The fair nymphs of this isle are in wonderful tribulation, as the fresh meat that our men have got here has made them as riotous as satyrs. A girl cannot step into the bushes to pluck a rose without running the most imminent risk of being ravished, and they are so little accustomed to these vigorous methods that they don't bear them with the proper resignation, and of consequence we have the most entertaining courts-martial every day."[41] As for Britain's Hessian allies: theirs was entirely a for-profit enterprise, and plunder was of its essence. Hearts and minds were the last thing these career mercenaries cared to win.[42]

New Jerseyites hedged their bets. Wanting to be in the winner's good graces, many signed the British loyalty oath, however glumly, as they watched Howe's commander in the New Jersey campaign, Lord Cornwallis—an experienced officer with Whig sympathies, who had amazed his aristocratic family by marrying for love—chase Washington's cold and shrinking army across the bleak winter landscape for two weeks. The Continentals' summer clothes turned to rags; they wrapped themselves in blankets. Their shoes disintegrated, and they trudged barefoot or tied rawhide to their feet. "No nation ever saw such a set of tatterdemalions," a British officer scoffed; though the sick and hungry "Raggamuffins," as Lord Howe's secretary derided them, kept the pursuing enemy at a respectful distance by rearguard actions of spirited ferocity, with Washington always near them, a calming presence closest to the pursuers.[43]

By the time they reached the Delaware River north of Trenton and began to cross into Pennsylvania on December 2, they seemed spectral wraiths out of Dante. Charles Willson Peale's painterly eye glimpsed "the most hellish scene I ever beheld. All the shores were lighted up with large fires, boats continually passing and repassing, full of men, horses, artillery." As if what he's describing sounds incredible even to himself, he repeats it: "The Hollowing of hundreds of men in their difficulties of getting Horses and artillery out of the boats, made it rather the appearance of Hell than any earthly scene." As the soldiers trudged by, "a man staggered out of line and came toward me. He had lost all his clothes. He was in an old dirty blanket jacket, his beard long and his face full of sores . . . which so disfigured him that he was not known by me on first sight. Only when he spoke did I recognize my brother James."[44]

Once he'd crossed the river, here was Washington's plight. His oft-defeated army, from illness, desertion, capture at Fort Washington, and some enlistments that ended on December 1, was down to fewer than 3,000 men. General Charles Lee, who had dawdled over bringing in reinforcements, had fallen into enemy hands, ignominiously captured at an inn, away from his army. Washington, who by mistake had just opened a letter of his filled with criticism of the commander in chief's "fatal indecision of mind which in war is a much greater disqualification than stupidity or even want of personal courage," took the loss of so disloyal and insubordinate an officer with equanimity.[45] Lee's strictures perhaps stung all the more because Washington had made every mistake in the book in the New York campaign. He had misread the enemy's intentions; he had divided his forces in the face of superior numbers; he had provided no cavalry; he had hesitated almost fatally to get his army out of Manhattan once he grasped the folly of keeping it there; he had allowed Greene to persuade him against his better judgment to keep men in Fort Washington; he had allowed a wealth of precious tents, flour, ordnance, and ammunition at Forts Washington and Lee to fall into enemy hands. And now, on December 17, he had two weeks before the enlistments for most of the rest of his army expired. "Our only dependance now, is upon the Speedy Inlistment of a New Army," he wrote Lund Washington, his cousin and trusted manager at Mount Vernon; "if this fails us, I think the game will be pretty well up, as from disaffection, and want of spirit & fortitude, the Inhabitants instead of resistance, are offering Submission, and taking protections from Genl Howe in Jersey."[46]

At such a moment of crisis, his thoughts turned, as usual, to Mount Vernon for solace. Could Lund please plant holly trees—or, if unavailable, pines—on the riverbank, and maybe some sycamores or honey locusts? Certainly locusts should go in from the New Garden to the Spinning House, fifteen or sixteen feet apart—close "enough for the limbs to Interlock when the Trees are grown."[47] Similarly, after the Battle of Harlem Heights he had fretted to Lund from the Morris-Jumel house that "such is my situation that if I were to wish the bitterest curse to an enemy on this side of the grave, I should put him in my stead with my feelings," for "I never was in such an unhappy, divided state since I was born," and then he immediately comforted himself by adding directions to make his new dining room an embodiment of the balance, harmony, and perfection that seemed so out of reach. "The chimney in the new room should be exactly in the middle of it—the doors and every thing else to be exactly answerable and uniform—in short I would have the whole executed in a masterly manner."[48] And a few days later he wrote his brother Jack, quoting his favorite biblical verse, that he craved nothing so much as "the peaceable enjoymt of my own vine, & fig Tree"—for Mount Vernon was his healing vision of the soldier's earthly paradise, where, as the prophet Micah promised, men "shall beat their swords into plowshares, and their spears into pruninghooks: nation shall not lift up a sword against nation, neither shall they learn war any more. But they shall sit every man under his vine and under his fig tree; and none shall make them afraid."[49]

AND NOW CAME one of history's miraculous turning points, in which a handful of men transformed failure into triumph. Tom Paine heralded it with his magniloquent article, *The American Crisis*, which he wrote on a drumhead by campfire light, retreating with the Philadelphia Associators, and which the troops huddled together to read aloud just days after it came out in the *Pennsylvania Journal* on December 19.[50] "These are the times that try men's souls," Paine passionately proclaimed, telling his exhausted fellow troopers just what they hungered to hear. "The summer soldier and the sunshine patriot will, in this crisis, shrink from the service of their country; but he that stands it *now*, deserves the love and thanks of man and woman." Let there be no talk about "peace in my day," but think instead that "If there must be trouble, let it be in my day, that my child may have peace." As for General Washington, he is one of those men who never appear "to full advantage but in difficulties and in action," Paine assured them. "There is a natural firmness in some minds which cannot be unlocked by trifles, but which, when unlocked, discovers a cabinet of fortitude," wrote Paine, a former corset-stay maker and tax collector, who had arrived from England at age thirty-seven in 1774 with a letter from Benjamin Franklin recommending him as a likely clerk or assistant tutor—though he soon found his true calling. The General, he wrote, is blessed with "a mind that can even flourish upon care."[51]

And so it proved. In crossing to Pennsylvania, Washington had the foresight to gather every boat for sixty miles up and down the river, so that the British couldn't follow, and he had them stashed in creeks and inlets on the Pennsylvania bank—just in case. But General Howe didn't try to follow. He left Hessian regiments to guard the Delaware's east bank, including three to hold Trenton, while he eased into a cozy New York winter, planning to take Philadelphia when the spring fighting season opened. Washington, his dwindling troops disheartened, and their enlistments nearly up, saw that without a "lucky blow," he could never "rouse the spirits of the people, which are quite sunk by our misfortunes." So when Charles Lee's reinforcements finally turned up with some militia units on December 22, momentarily boosting Washington's strength to 7,600 men—still too few to fill Madison Square Garden even halfway—he knew he had to act at once, before his army melted away. He would cross the Delaware on Christmas Day to attack Trenton—a plan of such imaginative, unconventional audacity that no by-the-book English officer could ever dream it up.[52]

Could the men get across the river in just one night, as he planned, since it had taken five days to cross the other way? his staff worried at the Christmas Eve planning dinner. They were "not to be troubled about that," Colonel Glover imperturbably pledged, "as his boys could manage it." On horseback and out front, as usual, Washington would lead the main force of 2,400, which would split into two columns on the opposite shore. Two other detachments would cross elsewhere, to multiply the chances of success. The revealingly desperate password for the operation: "Victory or Death."[53]

Once again, as at Brooklyn, Washington marshaled his men at the river's edge in silence and secrecy on Christmas afternoon, only this time their bare feet left bloody tracks in the snow. Once again, rain and sleet lashed them, which during the night turned to snow and became "a perfect hurricane," one Boston fifer recalled. Washington crossed first, to take charge if the enemy appeared, and in groups of forty the men squeezed onto flat-bottomed freight scows to cross the churning, ice-clogged river, while Glover's mariners ferried horses and 400 tons of cannon across too. The storm slowed them down, so Washington feared he had lost the surprise of reaching Trenton before dawn, and it stymied the other two detachments altogether, so they didn't cross. Even so, wrote Washington, "as I was certain there was no making a Retreat without being discovered, and harassed on repassing the River, I determined to push on at all Events."[54]

It was 3 AM on December 26 when the last man safely reached the Jersey side, 4 AM before the line of march formed up and set off, straight into driving snow and hail, with Washington galloping back and forth, exhorting and encouraging them, "in a deep & Solemn voice," one soldier recalled, to "Press on, boys!" and marveling at how "they seemed to vie with the other" in doing what he asked, in a way that "reflects the highest honor upon them." When the sky lightened at 6 AM, they'd gone only half the nine miles south to Trenton, and the storm had soaked their powder, leaving them to fight with bayonets alone. That they would catch the enemy sleeping off a Christmas drunk is a legend; the 1,500 Hessians, whose foraging parties American patrols constantly harried and whom Loyalist spies kept informed, had slept on their arms for three nights and were on rigid alert, even though most viewed American prowess with wry contempt and felt certain that the storm made an attack that day unlikely.[55]

Before the Continentals reached Trenton shortly after 8 AM, the wind had shifted, blowing the snow and hail into the Hessians' faces, so that the Americans really did surprise them, coming at them from three directions, with Washington leading the main charge. Henry Knox fired his artillery straight down the town's two streets with murderous effect, satisfied, he remarked with sober awe, that the resultant "hurry, fright, and confusion of the enemy" resembled "that which will be when the last trump shall sound." When the Hessian commander tried to rally his troops to charge Washington, the General galloped to a group of Americans, cried "March on, my brave fellows, after me!" and headed off the commander and his men, wounding him

Battlefield sketch of the victory at Trenton by John Trumbull
Charles Allen Munn Collection, Fordham University Library

mortally. In an hour, the Americans had won, killing or wounding 105 Hessians and taking almost 900 captive, as against two Continentals killed, plus four or five frozen to death on the march. "This is a glorious day for our country!" Washington congratulated his men, before turning to speak a word of comfort to the dying Hessian commander. But had these 2,400 failed, their Revolution might well have died with them, obliterated in the Jersey snow. "It may be doubted," summed up the eminent Whig statesman and historian Sir G. O. Trevelyan, "whether so small a number of men ever employed so short a space of time with greater and more lasting effects upon the history of the world."[56]

Sixty sleepless hours after they set out, Washington's men had recrossed the river with their prisoners and trove of captured supplies and arms. "The General," Washington told them on the morning of the twenty-seventh, rewarding them with cash and an extra tot of rum, "with the utmost sincerity and affection, thanks the officers and soldiers for their spirited and gallant behavior." But that afternoon, he learned that they'd have to go back. Colonel Cadwalader and his 1,800 Philadelphia Associators, unable to negotiate the ice-treacherous river on Christmas, had finally made it across and, with their usual democracy, had voted to stay and fight. Washington would not leave the determined Pennsylvanians prey to the 8,000 British troops in south Jersey. He ordered his force across the river on December 29 in two groups. With the temperature plummeting, the first found the Delaware frozen enough to tiptoe gingerly across, though not enough to bear their artillery and tents; the second, with Washington at its head, had to wait until the thirtieth, and the guns couldn't cross until New Year's Eve.[57]

Now what? Most of the troops' enlistments would end when midnight tolled, and even Glover's tars burned to get home to make their fortunes serving their country as privateers. The merchant-officers of the Philadelphia Associators told Washington that they had chipped in to offer a $10 bonus in hard money to any of their men who would stay on, and it had worked. Impressed, the General called his troops together and made them the same offer, with no idea where he'd get the money. "The drums beat for volunteers," one soldier recounted, "but not a man turned out." Washington, as a sergeant never forgot, "wheeled his horse about, rode in front of the regiment," and said: "My brave fellows, you have done all I asked you to do, and more than could be reasonably expected; but your country is at stake, your wives, your houses, and all that you hold dear. You have worn yourselves out with the fatigues and hardships, but we know not how to spare you. If you will consent to stay one month longer, you will render that service to the cause of liberty, and to your country, which you probably can never do under any other circumstances."[58]

The drummers drummed; the men spoke low to one another; a few stepped forward, and then nearly all did. The choice cost almost half of them their lives. An officer asked if he should enroll them in writing. No need, Washington replied. In his new ethic, a man with the merit of a gentleman *was* a gentleman, and his word of honor was enough.[59] These were men whom sixteen months earlier Washington had described as "exceeding dirty & nasty people."[60] Now he knew them better. "A people unused to restraint," he wrote a couple of weeks later, "must be led; they will not be drove."[61] And he had used the magic American word with them: *consent*.

With the vengeful enemy barreling toward him—the enraged Hessians had orders to take no prisoners—Washington remembered a high knoll south of Assunpink Creek in Trenton, ideal for defense, and he ranged his army there, with artillery aimed at the bridge and possible fords. When the British thundered into Trenton toward dusk on January 2, 1777, the American advance guard struggled to get back over the bridge before the enemy cut them down. Washington raced to the stone span with a troop to protect them. One private, squeezed against Washington's horse and boot during the skirmish, left an oft-quoted evocation of the quasi-mythical stature the General was now acquiring in his soldiers' eyes: "The noble horse of Gen. Washington stood with his breast pressed close against the end of the west rail of the bridge, and the firm, composed, and majestic countenance of the General inspired confidence and assurance in a moment so important and critical. . . . The horse stood as firm as the rider, and seemed to understand that he was not to quit his post and station." The British tried bravely three times to force their way across the bridge, until it "looked red as blood, with their killed and wounded and red coats," a sergeant wrote. The enemy corpses, perhaps 365 in all (as against 50 Americans), "lay thicker and closer together," another soldier recalled, "than I ever beheld sheaves of wheat lying in a field which the reapers had just passed."[62]

Still, the British outnumbered the Continentals by more than five to four. "We've got the Old Fox safe now," Earl Cornwallis assured his staff as they met that night. "We'll go over and bag him in the morning."[63]

Washington could figure the odds too, and he knew that his position, though strong, had vulnerabilities that Cornwallis's greater numbers could exploit by getting to his rear, a peril insurgencies shun. He wanted to get his men to safety without damping "popular opinion." The army's morale was soaring, and Jerseyites now flocked to the militia and harassed the British continually, so whatever he did had to "give reputation to our arms," maintaining the initiative and pressing on. By an inspiration of genius, he gave vent to his inner Washington, all boldness and enterprise, and turned a withdrawal into an attack. Seizing on information that Colonel Cadwalader had heard from "a very intelligent young gentleman" just come from Princeton that no sentries guarded the wide-open east end of the little college town, Washington decided to strike there. "One thing I was sure of," he recalled, "was that it would avoid the appearance of a retreat, which was of consequence."[64]

By now he had the theatrics down pat. Cloth muffled the wagon wheels, watch fires sparkled with brighter-than-usual cheer, trenching tools crunched as noisily as if hundreds were auditioning for the grave digger in *Hamlet*. So silently did Washington slip away after midnight that "many of his own sentinels never missed him," an officer chuckled. Roads that the British had labored along "halfleg deep" in mud had now frozen hard and smooth as the exhausted Americans virtually sleepwalked the sixteen-mile byroad to Princeton, leaving it "literally marked with the blood of soldiers feet," a sergeant noticed. In the ice-bright dawn, two British regiments galloping to Cornwallis's aid in Trenton ran smack into the Americans and "were as much astonished as if an army had dropped perpendicularly down upon them," General Knox quipped.[65]

No less astonished by the ferocity of the immediate British charge, the Americans fell back in panic. Just then, Washington materialized among the Associators, waving his tricorne. "Parade with us, my brave fellows!" he urged. "There is but a handful of the enemy, and we will have them directly." The General led his men straight into the British fire with such defiant courage that one of his aides clenched his eyes shut, unable to watch his commander's all-but-certain death. "Away, my dear colonel, and bring up the troops," Washington said to him when the smoke cleared. "The day is our own!" A couple of hundred British took cover in the college's Nassau Hall, only to be cannonaded into surrender by artillery commander Alexander Hamilton, just about to turn twenty-two. "The achievements of Washington and his little band of compatriots between the 25th of December and the 4th of January, a space of 10 days," pronounced one of the era's foremost generals, Frederick the Great, "were the most brilliant of any recorded in the annals of military achievements."[66]

In retrospect, that was the turning point of the war, when Washington proved to himself, his troops, and the world his inspirational brilliance as a leader, and when a shocked Britain saw it could lose its American empire. But experience as you live it never feels the way it looks in retrospect, and, despite all the merit and achievement in the world, nobody reaches such an eminence without Nemesis raining down spite. "[W]hy should I expect to be exempt from censure; the unfailing lot of elevated station?" Washington sighed philosophically. "Merits and talents, with which I can have no pretensions of rivalship, have ever been subject to it."[67]

It was long after the 1777 fighting season opened—eighteenth-century commanders really thought in such terms—that the chastened Howes roused themselves, sailing out of New York Harbor in late July for Chesapeake Bay, from which they would march north and attack Philadelphia at last. Washington hurried his 12,000 troops there from their camp in Morristown, New Jersey, staging a morale-boosting parade through the threatened city, each soldier with a sprig of green in his hat signifying victory, all commanded, as the song says, to mind the music and the step, and with their commander in chief playing his role of national hero with swagger, out front on his slapping charger. He headed off the British at Brandywine Creek southwest of town on September 11, but, in a replay of the Heights of Guana debacle two years earlier, they turned his flank through a negligently unguarded ford, inflicting 700 casualties and capturing 400 Americans. Ten nights later they barbarously bayoneted hundreds more Continentals as they lay sleeping in the woods.[68]

After Howe and Cornwallis marched into Philadelphia on September 26—Congress having fled "like a covey of partridges," John Adams harrumphed—Washington, wanting "to remind the English that an American army still existed" and to avenge the bayonet murders, attacked two British regiments camped at Germantown, northwest of the city (and today absorbed into it) on October 4. As his army charged in the misty dawn, the enemy torched the sere autumnal fields, and in the blinding smoke and fog, "a bloody day" unfolded, Washington wrote, with American casualties more than double British losses—and with the bodies lying "as thick as the stones in a stony plowfield," one rebel soldier grieved—but with both armies awed by the Continentals' spunk in attacking so soon after a defeat. Also impressed was French foreign minister Charles Gravier, Comte de Vergennes, who moved closer to upgrading his secret financial support for America to a formal alliance, key to the Revolution's success.[69]

Yet to Washington's disadvantage, it wasn't he who won the big victory that prompted Vergennes to sign the vital treaty in February

1778. It was General Horatio Gates, who took British general John Burgoyne and his army prisoner after two blood-soaked battles at Saratoga, New York, on September 19 and October 7, 1777, just when Washington was suffering his Pennsylvania defeats. Following three previous victories that sent the king rushing into his wife's room, crying, "I have beat all the Americans!" Burgoyne, his supply lines now stretched to breaking, was lumbering south from Canada, seeking to join his redcoats with Howe's in New York, to accomplish what the British had long intended: to seize control of the Hudson Valley and split the colonies in two. He learned too late that the Howes had scrapped that strategy and gone to Philadelphia.

Gates won thanks to General Benedict Arnold's gross insubordination in seizing battlefield control and wielding it with skill, and Colonel Daniel Morgan's lethal Virginia sharpshooters, who killed over forty British officers with rifles that famously could hit an orange at 200 paces, unlike the British army's quicker-to-load but inaccurate unrifled muskets. But Granny Gates, as his men called the short, stout general, predictably chose to claim all the credit himself, and he decided that after such a triumph he deserved to be commander in chief.[70] Unlike Washington, after all, he had once held a royal commission, bought for him by the Duke of Leeds, whose housekeeper his mother was—though with neither the money nor the successes to rise higher in the British army after his service in the Braddock expedition, the republican-minded Gates settled in Virginia and joined the rebels.[71]

Gates had earlier disparaged Washington's leadership to Congress, and now he dawdled almost a month before personally telling the commander in chief of his victory, a slight that Washington understood signaled a struggle for preeminence. To inform Congress directly, Gates sent a voluble young aide-de-camp, who by chance met an aide to one of Washington's loyal generals on the way and told him with theatrical flair what contempt Gates felt for his superior. To heighten the anti-Washington drama, the young man displayed a toadying letter that General Thomas Conway had sent Gates, belittling the commander in chief by writing that "Heaven has been

Photo by Eileen Tweedy / The Art Archive at Art Resource, NY

THE FOUNDATIONS OF AMERICAN LIBERTY

Above: *Departure of the Puritans from Delft Harbor to Join the Mayflower* by Adam Van Breen (1620); *below*: *John Locke*, the Founders' favorite political theorist, by Godfrey Kneller (1697)

bpk, Berlin / Hermitage / Roman Beniaminson / Art Resource, NY

Overleaf: *William Livingston* by John Wollaston (1750s)
Courtesy of Fraunces Tavern Museum

Above: Stratford Hall; *below:* the great hall of Stratford Hall, with portraits of the first Richard Lee (left), his son Richard the Scholar (right), and Hannah Ludwell Lee (center), who with her husband, Thomas, built Stratford

Overleaf: Stratford Hall, south front
Photo by Christopher Cunningham, courtesy of Stratford Hall

Independence National Historic Park

Richard Henry Lee by Charles Willson Peale (1785)

Arthur Lee
by Charles Willson Peale (1785)

Independence National Historic Park

Henry (Light-Horse Harry) Lee
by Charles Willson Peale (1782)

Below: *Signing the Declaration of Independence* by John Trumbull

Signing the Declaration of Independence, July 4th, 1776 (oil on canvas), Trumbull, John (1756–1843) / Capitol Collection, Washington, USA / The Bridgeman Art Library

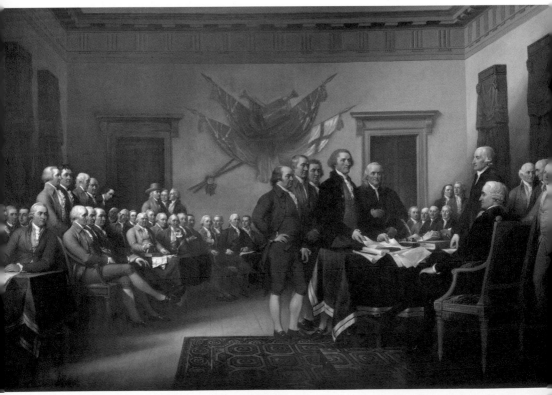

Opposite: George Washington at Princeton by Charles Willson Peale (1779

Courtesy of the Pennsylvania Academy of the Fine Arts, Philadelphia. Gift of Maria McKean Alle and Phebe Warren Downes through the bequest of their mother, Elizabeth Wharton McKea

General Henry Knox
by Gilbert Stuart (1805)

Brigadier General John Glover
by John Trumbull (1794)

The John Cadwalader Family
by Charles Willson Peale (1772)

Baron Frederick William von Steuben
by Charles Willson Peale (1780)

Marquis de Lafayette at age eighteen by Louis Leopold Boilly (1788)

Washington Crossing the Delaware River by Emanuel Leutze (1851)

Washington Crossing the Delaware River, 25th December 1776, 1851 (oil on canvas) (copy of an original painted in 1848) / Metropolitan Museum of Art, New York, USA / The Bridgeman Art Library

Brown University Library, Providence, Rhode Island, USA / The Bridgeman Art Library

General Sir William Howe, after Richard Purcell (1777)

Admiral Lord Howe by John Singleton Copley (1794)

RIGHTS OF MAN
Engrav'd from a Picture by Peel of Philadelphia in the Possession of TB Hollis Esq.
THOMAS PAINE ESQ.R
Late Secretary for Foreign Affairs to the American Congress;
Author of
The Rights of Man, Common Sense, &c.

The Granger Collection, New York

Below: George Washington Presiding at the Constitutional Convention in 1787
by Junius Brutus Stearns (1856) The Granger Collection, New York

FEDERAL HALL
The Seat of CONGRESS
Printed & Sold by A Doolittle New-Haven 1790

The Inauguration of George Washington as First President of the United States
by Amos Doolittle (1790)

The Washington Family by Edward Savage (1789–96)

The Granger Collection, New York

Mount Vernon

Courtesy of the Mount Vernon Ladies' Association

View of Mount Vernon with the Washington Family on the Portico
by Benjamin Henry Latrobe (1796)

Courtesy of the Mount Vernon Ladies' Association

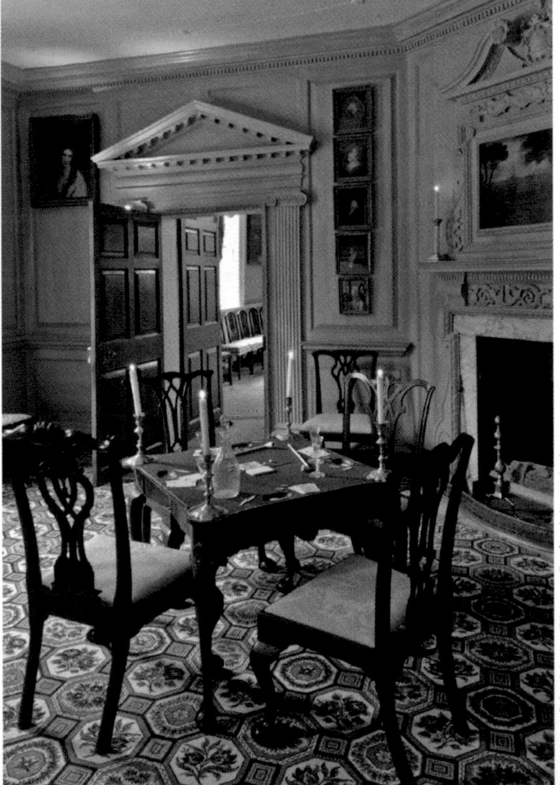

Courtesy of the Mount Vernon Ladies' Association

Above: Mount Vernon, West Front

Courtesy of the Mount Vernon Ladies' Association

Left: Mount Vernon, West Parlor

Opposite: Mount Vernon, "New" Dining Room

Courtesy of the Mount Vernon Ladies' Association

Courtesy of the Mount Vernon Ladies' Association

Above: Mount Vernon, "New" Dining Room; *below*: *Palmy Days at Mount Vernon* by Thomas Prichard Rossiter (1866), showing George Washington with, from right to left, James Madison, Alexander Hamilton, Patrick Henry, and Martha Washington

Courtesy of the Mount Vernon Ladies' Association

determined to save your Country; or a weak General and bad Counsellors would have ruined it." Washington's loyal friend immediately informed him of such "wicked duplicity of conduct."[72]

So Washington knew that treacherous undercurrents swirled beneath a rumor he'd heard that Congress planned to bypass worthier generals for promotion to major general and instead anoint Conway—an Irish-born professional soldier who'd made colonel in the French army before joining the Continentals as his next career move. Washington wasn't having it. To make Conway a major general, he told Congress's president, Richard Henry Lee, "will be as unfortunate a measure as ever was adopted," for "General Conway's merit . . . exists more in his own imagination than in reality." If Congress jumped Conway over more senior generals, they would quit, said Washington, and so would he. "I have been a Slave to the service," he wrote, "but it will be impossible for me to be of further service, if such insuperable difficulties are thrown in my way."[73] Taking up the challenge for preeminence, Washington tersely informed Gates and Conway that he'd heard the line about "a weak General."[74]

Still, their shadowy machinations—the so-called "Conway Cabal," aimed at goading Washington to resign, to make way for Gates—got preliminary results. Congress named Gates president of a strengthened Board of War, with some authority over the commander in chief. The board in turn appointed Conway to the new post of inspector general, with the promotion to major general Washington had opposed—which he learned when Conway arrived in his camp just after Christmas 1777 to exert his new powers. He could do no such thing until Congress sent official notification of his appointment, Washington told him, with frigid correctness. Henry Laurens, the new president of Congress, wrote Washington that Conway had complained of his cool reception. Surely, Washington pointedly replied, no one would expect him to welcome warmly a "man I deem my Enemy." Forced to make a choice of whether Washington really was commander in chief or not, Congress backtracked, assigning Conway elsewhere, over his noisy objections and threats to resign.[75]

Gates rose to command the army's southern department and suffered a career-ending defeat at Camden, South Carolina, in August 1780, running from the battlefield for 180 miles before he stopped. "One hundred and eighty miles in three days and a half," Alexander Hamilton snickered. "It does admirable credit to the activity of a man at his time of life." General Conway threatened to quit once too often, and Congress took him up on it. He also publicly denigrated Washington once too often, and Philadelphia Associators commander Cadwalader challenged him to a duel, shooting him in the face and snapping, "I have stopped the damned rascal's lying anyway." But Conway didn't die; he painfully recovered and went back to France. And in his brush with death, he clearly reexamined his own life. "I find myself just able to hold the pen during a few minutes, and take this opportunity of expressing my sincere grief for having done, written, or said anything disagreeable to Your Excellency," he wrote Washington on the eve of his departure. "You are, in my eyes, the great and the good man. May you long enjoy the love, veneration, and esteem of these states whose liberties you have asserted by your virtues."[76]

THE THEORY OF an insurgency is simple: hold off the enemy, harry him, outlast him. The practice is brutal. Endurance and fortitude may seem passive virtues, but they take a huge effort of active will. Just before Christmas 1777, Washington led his troops into winter quarters at Valley Forge, Pennsylvania, twenty miles northwest of Philadelphia. And then, for the next three years, he and his men plumbed the meaning of waiting out the enemy.

He had planned to spread his winter quarters widely, for better forage and sanitation, but Congress wanted the army pressed close to Philadelphia as a buffer against the British, who were occupying that city in comfort and even luxury: local Loyalists gave balls and dinners for wellborn British officers, and their daughters flirted with them, while General Howe dallied with his "flashing blonde" mistress, wife of an extra-loyal Loyalist.[77] So Washington had his soldiers build a village of more than 2,000 earthen-floored log huts, each fourteen feet by sixteen and sleeping a dozen men in bunks three tiers high. To his volunteer aide-de-camp, the Marquis de Lafayette, the hovels seemed "scarcely gayer than dungeon cells."[78]

Life there was no gayer. "For some days past, there has been little less, than a famine in camp," Washington wrote in February 1778. "A part of the army has been a week without any kind of flesh, and the rest three or four days."[79] They dined, one soldier said, on "a leg of nothing," and they sang a song that went, "No bread, no soldier."[80] Two months later, Washington could only marvel at their fortitude. "To see Men without Cloathes to cover their nakedness, without Blankets to lay on, without Shoes, by which their Marches might be traced by the Blood from their feet, and almost as often without Provisions as with; Marching through frost and Snow, and at Christmas taking up their Winter Quarters within a day's march of the enemy, without a House or Hutt to cover them till they could be built and submitting to it without a murmer, is a mark of patience and obedience which in my opinion can scarce be parallel'd."[81]

Without clothes, shoes, or socks, the men froze on watch; "feet and legs turned black with frostbite, and often had to be amputated," Lafayette reported.[82] Without soap, they suffered constantly from a rash they called "the itch" or "the scab."[83] Without blankets, many must "set up all Night by fires, instead of taking comfortable rest in a natural way," Washington wrote.[84] And as typhus, dysentery, and pneumonia raged through camp, they died and died—one man in seven, versus one in thirty slain fighting in the Battle of the Bulge.[85] Some probably lie in the vast mass grave under Philadelphia's Washington Square, where a monument reads, most truly, "Beneath this stone rests a soldier of Washington's army who died to give you liberty."

The three years of waiting had their ups as well as downs, though the ups meant less bad, never good. However grimly February 1778 began, though, it ended on an upswing. Lady Washington, as the soldiers called Martha, arrived to spend the winter in camp—as she did the following winters—brightening her husband's mood and inspiriting the troops by her tireless care, as she led officers' wives in knitting them socks and making them clothes, visiting the sick, and "giving all the comforts to them in her power," one observer reported—making her rounds through camp with the quiet resolution "of the Roman matrons of whom I had read so much," another remarked. Later that month, food started trickling in, too, and by spring Washington felt relieved enough to let his junior officers stage a play—Addison's *Cato*, of course.[86]

At the end of February, an amazing apparition materialized at Valley Forge and turned waiting into a whirlwind of activity. Magnificently theatrical in a golden waistcoat and gold-lapelled coat shimmering with stars and medals, a greyhound at his heels, Baron Friedrich Wilhelm von Steuben, a humbly born Prussian infantryman who had risen to captain, served on Frederick the Great's staff, and won the title *freiherr* from an impecunious princeling, now seized America's opportunity to reinvent oneself and presented himself to Washington, perhaps merely through a mistranslation, as a lieutenant general. He straightaway fell to training the troops and improving sanitation, starting by moving latrines and dead horses away from cooking areas. Whatever might have been fake about the baron, his military know-how was real, and, despite his rudimentary English—which at first extended not much further than "Goddamn!"—he fascinated, entertained, and inspired the men, who enthusiastically performed endless drills and learned his state-of-the-art techniques and maneuvers. With the "trappings of his horse, the enormous holsters of his pistols, his large size, and strikingly martial aspect," one of his soldier-pupils wrote, he "seemed to me a perfect personification of Mars." And Steuben, once he got over his shock at the nakedness of the soldiers and even officers, and had begun to clean up the filth and disorder, began to appreciate with an equally fascinated affection the "genius of this nation" compared with Europe. In Europe, he wrote, "You say to your soldier, 'Do this,' and he doeth it, but I am obliged to say, 'This is the reason you ought to do that,' and then he does it."[87]

During that same pivotal February, American diplomats Benjamin Franklin, Arthur Lee, and Silas Deane concluded an alliance with France, which recognized the independence of the United States. When Washington heard of the epochal pact in late April, he declared May 5 a day of thanksgiving to "the Almighty ruler of the Universe" for "raising us up a powerful Friend among the Princes of the Earth to establish our liberty and Independence up[on] lasting foundations." Human ingenuity conjured up wine, spirits, and meat, and 1,500 officers and their wives sat down at outdoor tables and gave thanks indeed.[88]

At that moment, what the army was waiting *for* also began to change. Until then, Washington had watched to see what the redcoats would do. He soon got a dramatic answer. Lord North, the prime minister, fired William Howe as commander in chief—someone had to take the blame for Saratoga—and replaced him with the reluctant Sir Henry Clinton, who'd lived in New York as a boy when his aristocrat father was royal governor, and who repeatedly begged the king to let him come home to his "motherless babes," after his beloved wife had died giving birth to the fifth.[89] Instead, Clinton was to move the army from Philadelphia to New York, a British diplomat's Patriot laundress told Washington. But Washington didn't grasp that the new Franco-American alliance had sparked a radical strategic shift in London that prompted Clinton's northward march. The ministry, viewing the raw materials of the West Indies and the southern states as Britain's principal transatlantic interests, gave up on New England and the mid-Atlantic and envisioned an American empire that would extend from Canada down the trans-Appalachian West—which British-allied Indians would control—through the southern states and then to the sugar isles, now under French naval threat. So the war would move south, where Clinton would redeploy a third of his troops once he got them to New York. And Washington would now wait to see what France would do.[90]

But he wasn't letting the redcoats leave Philadelphia scot-free. He led his Steuben-honed army after Clinton's 10,000 men and caught them near a crossroads called Monmouth Court House (now Freehold, New Jersey) on June 27. He ordered Charles Lee, just back from British captivity, to attack with 5,000 troops in the morning, while Lafayette would lead another thousand, and he himself 6,000 more. When he arrived around noon on a day so hot that his men had peeled off their shirts and his beautiful white horse finally dropped dead beneath him, he found Lee's men in headlong retreat after a bungled attack, and Lee himself riding after them, his dogs panting behind. Furious, Washington swore as no one had heard him swear before or since. "What is the meaning of this, sir?" the General demanded. A flustered Lee blamed the troops. "You damned poltroon, you never tried them," Washington raged.

Ordering General Anthony Wayne to hold off the approaching British main force, Washington galloped after the fleeing Americans to rally them by dauntless charisma. His whole "bearing," his "calm and deportment," inspired "the highest degree of enthusiasm," Lafayette marveled. Quelling the panic by his "coolness and firmness," said Hamilton, Washington asked the men if they'd stand and fight. Three thunderous cheers said they would, and they followed him back into ferocious battle beneath the blazing sun, maneuvering with disciplined professionalism against an entire British army, while Washington "directed the whole with the skill of a master workman," according to Hamilton. The British retreated as the merciless sun began to sink, and Washington resolved to follow them in the morning. Taking a leaf from his playbook, however, Generals Clinton and Cornwallis showily ignited sparkling campfires as they slunk away in the night, ending the war's last full-scale battle in the North. Washington boasted about fighting the king's army to a draw and driving it off, but in his heart he had yearned for a decisive rout.[91]

As Washington watched and waited, he also thought and talked, trying to make sense of the world-changing whirlwind he struggled to direct. In his 1778–79 winter camp in Middlebrook, New Jersey—

where, learning from Valley Forge, he had dispersed his troops, decreed healthier barracks, imposed Steuben's Prussian hygiene, and issued warm, French-supplied uniforms—his soldiers still stayed hungry in the midst of bountiful farmland. As at Valley Forge, American farmers sold produce to the British for hard money rather than to their own countrymen for ever-depreciating paper.

Coolly realistic, Washington understood why. People "may talk of patriotism; they may draw a few examples from ancient story, of great achievements performed by its influence; but whoever builds upon it, as a sufficient Basis for conducting a long and bloody War, will find themselves deceived in the end," he wrote. "We must take the passions of Men as Nature has given them," and though "I do not mean to exclude altogether the Idea of Patriotism," nevertheless it "must be aided by a prospect of Interest or some reward."[92] Since suppliers want to profit from their labors and need to be paid in money that's worth something, he warned on the way to Middlebrook, the army can't keep fighting if inflation vaporizes the value of America's currency.[93]

All through 1779, the inflation worsened: in January, you could exchange eight paper Continental dollars, which Congress had begun to print in 1775, for a dollar of specie; in October, it took thirty; in December, forty-two.[94] Washington grasped personally why no one wanted dollars, as opposed to British pounds. In August 1779, he wrote his cousin Lund how heartsick he felt when people who owed him money offered to pay in paper dollars worth only sixpence or a shilling instead of £1. Someone who bought six hundred acres from him "in the most valuable part of Virginia, that ought to have been pd. for before the money began to depreciate; nay years before the War," Washington complained, now wants to pay the debt in currency that today is worth no more than a year's salary for "a *common* Miller." Would Lund please "consult Men of honor, honesty, and firm attachment to the cause" as to what they think is the proper course? If "sacrificing my whole Estate would effect any valuable purpose I would not hesitate one moment in doing it. [B]ut my submitting to matters of this kind unless it is done so by others, is no more than a drop in the bucket, in fact it is not serving the public but enriching individuals and countenancing dishonesty." Already, the "fear of injuring by any example of mine the credit of our paper currency if I attempted to discriminate between the real and nominal value of Paper money" has cost dearly—and there's a limit.[95]

Worried that victory would turn on "whose Finances (theirs or ours) is most likely to fail," he had traveled to Philadelphia just before Christmas 1778 to prod Congress to solve the country's most "momentous concerns"—"a great and accumulated debt; ruined finances, depreciated money, and want of credit (which in their consequences is the want of every thing)."[96] What he saw horrified him. Profiteers who bought up goods to sell when the scarcity they helped create boosted prices were running the country—along with crooks who sold contraband, spoiled, or adulterated goods. "Speculation, peculation, and an insatiable thirst for riches seems to have got the better of every other consideration" in the minds of legislators sunk in "idleness, dissipation and extravagance." Congressmen struck him as a flock of second-raters who cared less about the common weal than about high living at extravagant parties, costing £300 or even £400 and hosted by swindling war profiteers bent on wheedling more government business from their gullible guests—and all this "while a great part of the Officers of [the] Army from absolute necessity are quitting the Service and the more virtuous few rather than do this are sinking by sure degrees into beggery and want." Washington earnestly wished that the states would send their ablest, most energetic citizens—by compulsion, if need be—to replace such lightweight legislators, so "that public abuses should be corrected, and an entire reformation worked."[97] Otherwise, as the British often jeer, "we shall be our own conquerers."[98]

That's how Washington interpreted the enemy's passivity during the 1779 fighting season: while American troops took the British forts at Stony Point on the Hudson and Paulus Hook (now Jersey City), and slaughtered Britain's Indian allies, the British stood by, apparently "placing their whole dependance in the depreciation of our money, and the wretched management of our finances."[99] With ample reason.

Soon after the Americans went into winter quarters at Morristown, New Jersey, at the end of 1779, conditions sank to a Valley Forge depth of desperation. Inflation grew so severe that "a waggon load of money will scarcely purchase a waggon load of provision," Washington wrote, and with money worthless, many farmers, still unpaid for what they'd already supplied, had grown only what their families could eat.[100] Those who did have something to sell couldn't get to Washington's camp, buried in drifts twelve feet deep after a four-day blizzard in January 1780 and twenty-seven more snowstorms thereafter, while that winter's freakish cold froze New York Harbor hard enough to bear cannon.[101] Soldiers would go "five or Six days together without Bread, then as many without Meat, and once or twice, two or three without either," Washington wrote.[102] They ate dogs, tree bark, and ruined shoes (roasted). Mourned Nathanael Greene: "A Country, once overflowing with plenty, are now suffering an Army employed for the defense of every thing that is dear and valuable, to perish for want of food."[103]

During these three long winters, Washington pondered the army's plight with such brilliant aides as Alexander Hamilton and the Marquis de Lafayette, fatherless youths who had joined his military "family" in 1777 and whom the childless commander loved; John Laurens (son of president of Congress Henry Laurens); and Tench Tilghman, who all lived crammed together in tight quarters next to their chief, dining with him every midday—in the worst of times off a single tin plate, and waited on, Washington wrote, by a servant "indecently and most shamefully naked."[104] The talk, at least, was nourishing; and from these high-powered seminars, as well as from "long thinking, close application, and strict observation," Washington refined into a sophisticated political and economic worldview the conclusions he'd drawn from his French and Indian War experience, when he'd requisitioned supplies at swordpoint and yearned for a colonial union and a strong executive.[105]

America was bursting with resources, he knew, but Congress lacked the power to mobilize them to supply the army. The nation would have to "give more energy to Government" by making Congress "the supreme controuling power of the united States," fully vested with powers to levy taxes and contract loans. Sure, Americans will resist new taxes, for "a commercial and free people, little accustomed to heavy burthens, pressed by impositions of a new and odious kind, . . . may imagine, they have only exchanged one tyranny for another"—but needs must. And loans will be easy to repay: Congress can sell America's vast tracts of valuable state-owned land, he wrote, and "the advantages of every kind we possess for commerce, insure to this country a rapid advancement in population and prosperity." By repaying its debts and keeping its currency sound, Washington believed, America would keep its credit strong.[106]

Amid the Morristown snows, Washington weighed how the counterpoise of financial power might play out in the Revolution. "In modern wars," he wrote, "the longest purse must chiefly determine the event." Here France and Spain (which was helping America secretly with money and joined France in the war in 1779) might seem to have the edge—but not for long. If the war kept on, Versailles would have to tax beyond the level the French could endure, and then "France makes war on ruinous terms," Washington wrote prophetically: for to raise revenue to pay France's huge war debts in 1789, Louis XVI had to convene the Estates-General for the first time in 175 years, lighting the fuse that detonated the French Revolution. Spain, Washington cautioned, famously "derives great wealth from her mines" in South America, but it was less than people thought, and waning. More important, what really constitutes the wealth of nations? "Commerce and industry are the best mines of a nation; both of which are wanting to her," concluded Washington, whose economic thought had, like Hamilton's, outgrown both mercantilism and agricultural sentimentality. Commercial Britain, by contrast, should be America's model, Washington thought; it was a rich and prospering country, with a sound system of public credit that made it mighty in war.[107]

Making matters worse for America, the national belief that a standing army is dangerous to liberty results in a military system that only an Eastern Nabob could afford. Raising a new army every year costs ten times as much as a permanent force, since new arrivals and veterans about to leave can't fight but still need to be fed. Nor can such an army ever be as efficient a fighting force as "a permanent body of Men, under good organization and military discipline." Perhaps prejudice against a standing army might make sense in peacetime, especially in countries that hire mercenaries. But to reject a permanent army in wartime, when the soldiers "are Citizens having all the Ties, and interests of Citizens," makes no sense.[108]

During the war, in other words, Washington thought his way to federalism, long before a Federalist Party existed. He believed in a strong central government, supreme over the states; a strong financial system on the British model, with taxes to fund its debt; a flourishing commerce to create prosperity (and to train seamen for a powerful navy, which would in turn protect shipping); and a strong military. And most officers came out of the experience of the Revolution with the same views.[109]

As he waited for the French to act, Washington became a proto-Federalist in foreign policy too. "[H]atred of England may carry some into an excess of Confidence in France," he wrote, again prophetically, given the strife over revolutionary France that racked 1790s America; "but it is a maxim founded on the universal experience of mankind, that no nation is to be trusted farther than it is bound by its interest."[110] Certainly George Washington's personal experience bore out the maxim, since his French allies, over whom he was nominally supreme commander, treated him with a ceremonious politeness just short of satire, agreeing with him effusively though insincerely, while keeping him in the dark as to their intentions for months on end, and carrying out their own program on their own schedule. John Adams, then a minister to France, had the same experience. "We get nothing," he complained. "They communicate nothing."[111]

Of course dismay struck the French when their fleet arrived in American waters in July 1778 and they first saw the American army, poor, unprofessional, and small. "I have never seen a more laughable spectacle," a French officer sneered at what he took to be "tailors and apothecaries" playing soldier. "They were mounted on bad nags and looked like a flock of ducks in cross belts." The tough, battle-scarred Comte de Rochambeau, who arrived as commanding general of the French forces in America in July 1780, advised his government: "Do not depend on these people nor upon their means; they have neither money nor credit; their means of resistance are only momentary and called forth when they are attacked in their own houses."[112] And the Americans felt their penury with shame. "A Military Man has the same turn to sociability as a person in Civil life; he conceives himself equally called upon to live up to his rank; and his pride is hurt when circumstans. restrain him," the emulative Washington wrote late in the war. "Only conceive then, the mortification they (even the Genl. Officers) must suffer when they cannot invite a French Officer . . . to a better repast than stinking Whiskey (and not always that) and a bit of Beef without Vegitables."[113]

Because Washington nursed dreams of retaking the New York he had lost—dreams that the French, though they humored him, thought delusory—he was much slower than they to see that the war had moved to the South, even though Britain had inaugurated its new southern strategy by taking a laughably ill-defended Savannah at the very end of 1778.[114] Rochambeau stepped ashore in America just weeks after Clinton and Cornwallis had brought that strategy to a full boil by capturing Charleston in May 1780 after a textbook siege. American general Benjamin Lincoln, who'd watched as if spellbound as his many opportunities for escape vanished one by one, had to surrender his army humiliatingly into captivity in the worst American defeat of the war.[115]

In August 1780, a month after the French commander arrived, Horatio Gates, the hero of Saratoga, whom Congress had sent south to halt Cornwallis in his blood-drenched conquest of the rest of the Carolinas, believed that by energy and dispatch he could defeat the divided British forces one by one; but unfortunately, thinking he was attacking only a small detachment, he bit into the tail of the whole

British lion. Cornwallis turned snarlingly and pounced upon him, sending Gates's green troops, and Gates himself, fleeing in terror, though some weren't fast enough to outrun "Bloody" Colonel Banastre Tarleton's dragoons, who inflicted their trademark "rout and slaughter" upon them, young Tarleton bragged.[116]

Yet Washington dreamed of New York even as a savage guerrilla civil war between largely Anglican Loyalist bands and back-country Presbyterian Patriots convulsed the Carolinas; as the giant backwoods general Daniel Morgan, sciatica-plagued at forty-four, crushed Tarleton at the brilliantly executed Battle of Cowpens in January 1781, in which his soldiers terrified the enemy with their "Indian halloo" that became the Civil War's rebel yell; and as Nathanael Greene, now commander of America's southern division, inflicted such grievous casualties on Cornwallis at the Battle of Guilford Court House near Greensboro, North Carolina, in March that he rightly pronounced that the "Enemy got the ground . . . but we the victory."[117]

Washington even yearned for New York when the British began marauding in Virginia, and their sloop *Savage* anchored off Mount Vernon in April 1781 to free his slaves and demand provisions, which his cousin Lund, who went aboard bearing refreshments, agreed to provide if they'd leave the estate and the slaves alone. To "commune with a parcel of plundering Scoundrels; and request a favor by asking the surrender of my Negroes, was exceedingly ill-judged," Washington rebuked him. "It would have been a less painful circumstance to me, to have heard, that in consequence of your non-compliance with their request, they had burnt my House, and laid the Plantation in ruins. You ought to have considered yourself as my representative, and should have reflected on the bad example of communicating with the enemy, and making a voluntary offer of refreshments to them with a view to prevent a conflagration." Strong words about his beloved Mount Vernon: and he went on to say that he expected the enemy's "plundering plan" to end "in the loss of all my Negroes, and the destruction of my Houses; but I am prepared for the event"—for him, very nearly the ultimate sacrifice.[118]

Even though the southern war had grown hard to ignore, Washington, Rochambeau fretted, still "did not conceive the affairs of the south to be [of] such urgency."[119] Both Cornwallis and Greene had followed Guilford Court House by striking out on their own enterprising courses. Cornwallis, the man who had defied convention by marrying for love, disobeyed Commander in Chief Clinton's orders to hold the Carolinas fast and instead headed to Virginia, where he aimed to disrupt rebel supply lines to the lower South. There he might bring the Americans to a decisive battle, unlikely in the militarily dispersed Carolinas. Greene, seeing the field clear, turned back to liberate South Carolina, which he brilliantly accomplished in ninety days, pushing the British back into their last redoubt of Charleston.[120]

Cornwallis, after his burst of un-English initiative, had second thoughts: bureaucratic self-protection now seemed more urgent than making war. In mid-May, he met a British force whose commander had died just after Clinton had ordered him to set up a Virginia naval base. Cornwallis made the troops and the orders his own. For the base, he chose Yorktown. On a bluff where the York River narrows enough to afford a good escape route to the far bank, it was, he judged, a "safe defensive" site. He wrote to tell Clinton what he'd done, adding that if the commander in chief wanted to wage "offensive War," he should come to Virginia, "the only Province, in which it can be carried on."

Outraged by Cornwallis's insubordination, Clinton ordered him to send half his men to New York, where he believed Britain's last chance of a climactic battle lay, now that its counterinsurgency had failed "to gain the hearts and subdue the minds of America." The other half should stay put—Clinton's own stab at bureaucratic self-protection, since London wanted troops in Virginia. Fine, Cornwallis agreed, in a dispatch that now self-protectively belittled Yorktown as only a few "Acres of an unhealthy swamp" that "cannot have the smallest influence on the War" and is "ever liable to become prey to a foreign" navy.[121] And there he remained, a sitting duck.

With the South in ferment, Rochambeau and Washington met on

May 21 to plan the 1781 campaign. Their conference was, as always, a charade. With Washington pushing for an attack on New York and the sharp-faced Rochambeau favoring Virginia—sometimes suavely, sometimes "with all the ungraciousness and all the unpleasantness possible," a French participant said—the generals determined, as Washington recorded, either "to commence an operation against New York . . . or to extend our views to the Southward as circumstances and a Naval superiority might render more necessary and eligable."[122] Rochambeau was only pretending to agree with Washington that New York was primary, however; in fact, he directed the French admiral, Comte de Grasse, to bring his giant fleet from the Caribbean to the Chesapeake, not to New York.[123]

Just before the French army, in their formfitting white uniforms and black cocked hats, marched into the American camp near White Plains on July 6, Rochambeau had informed Washington that de Grasse was sailing northward and had asked what his destination should be. The American, tantalizingly within striking distance of New York, vacillated, hoping he could muster needed reinforcements to pounce.[124] But he couldn't; and when news came that Cornwallis had trapped himself on the Yorktown peninsula, where the allies might squeeze him between their troops and de Grasse's armada, Washington couldn't help but give the answer Rochambeau wanted, and the two armies set off for Virginia on August 19, 1781.

Rochambeau came south by boat, and when he reached Delaware, he saw, with amazement, "General Washington standing on the shore and waving his hat and white handkerchief joyfully." When the count docked, the staid Washington hugged him and poured out the news that de Grasse (who at six foot two liked to call the six-foot Washington "*mon cher petit générale*") had entered the Chesapeake and sent marines ashore to help a Lafayette-led American troop pin Cornwallis in place. Since the admiral couldn't stay in Virginia beyond October, the allies stepped up their pace—though Washington couldn't resist a flying detour with Rochambeau and his aides to Mount Vernon, his first visit in over six years and his first glimpse of his still-unfinished new dining room, which perhaps he inaugurated with a strategy-planning dinner with the French dignitaries amid the building materials.[125]

As the troops marched, de Grasse's twenty-eight giant warships poured out of Chesapeake Bay to trounce the Royal Navy's smaller but faster copper-bottomed squadron, which had sought to bar a second French flotilla from bringing in essential siege guns from its Rhode Island base. This bloody and critical Battle of the Virginia Capes not only made the Yorktown siege possible but also weakened any hope that Clinton might reinforce or evacuate Cornwallis by sea. When the two allied armies, swollen by volunteer reinforcements to 19,000, arrived at Yorktown in late September and surveyed the by-the-book defenses of earthworks, artillery batteries, and redoubts that Cornwallis's 9,000 troops had built, the experienced Rochambeau took charge of what would unfold as a textbook siege, all "reducible to calculation," he told Washington with cool professionalism—though the textbook fails to calculate the misery the besieged suffer.[126]

On the night of October 5, Washington swung a pick into the Yorktown earth so history could record that he broke ground for the siege's first offensive parallel, two miles long, four feet wide, and four deep. "Not a word or a whisper was uttered—nothing but silent work" during the long, dark night, so as not to alert enemy sharpshooters, whom French infantrymen distracted with a diversionary attack while the utterly exposed sappers dug for dear life, one wrote. The British, Washington recorded, were "totally ignorant of our labor till the light of the Morning discovered it to them," by which time "the trenches were in such forwardness as to cover the Men from the enemys fire."[127]

After the 1,500 sappers had toiled for four nights, digging and then easing the cannons into place, General Washington put the match to the first gun, a soldier wrote, "and Earl Cornwallis . . . received his first salutation" on the afternoon of October 9.[128] The ball, rumor had it, crashed into an officers' mess and hit the man at the head of the table.[129] By October 10, almost a hundred allied cannon, double

Cornwallis's number, thundered away, hurling 150 balls an hour into the little fortified village by day and by night, when the projectiles streaked across the sky "like fiery meteors with blazing tails, most beautifully brilliant," a Continental soldier exclaimed. The sappers zigzagged inexorably closer, until by October 14 they had dug enough of the second parallel so guns from there could methodically smash Yorktown into tangled rubble laced with body parts, with suffocating dust settling on dead and dying men and horses, while the living huddled in cellars or trenches, wondering if the inevitable defeat would find them alive or dead, whole or maimed.[130]

A moment for old-fashioned military glory arrived that evening, and Alexander Hamilton, who had begged Washington for just such a chance, got the nod. To extend their second parallel fully, the allies had to capture Britain's two remaining redoubts, sheltering artillery and marksmen close enough to be lethal. The French got the harder job of overrunning Redoubt Nine, and its 120 defenders killed almost a quarter of the 400 attackers before giving up. Hamilton's 400 attackers, who like the French fought only with axes and bayonets so as not to shoot each other in the hand-to-hand fighting, poured into Redoubt Ten with an Indian yell and lost only a tenth of their number in the struggle against only 45 British defenders.[131] Washington, who watched the victory from so exposed a position that he had to silence an anxiously fussing aide by telling him, "if you are afraid, you have the liberty to step back," recorded with satisfaction that "The bravery of the attacking troops was emulous and praiseworthy"—his highest accolade.[132]

As short-range howitzers from the second parallel lobbed shells over Yorktown's walls, making the whole peninsula shake as they hammered the town with a new intensity of destruction, and as the smell of rotting horses shot for lack of fodder and thrown into the river fouled the already fetid air, Cornwallis, for bureaucratic form's sake, made two symbolic but useless efforts from his subterranean bunker to strike back and escape.[133] The face-saving seemed to work for the earl, though: he later went on to serve as governor-general of India and lord lieutenant of Ireland. But his career in this war was over.

At ten in the morning of October 17, 1781, Cornwallis raised a white flag over his ruined fortress, and as the "thundering of our infernal machines" died away into "solemn stillness," wrote two American soldiers, a red-coated officer emerged with a drummer beating the signal to parlay. Led blindfolded to Washington's tent, across a battlefield strewn with corpses—including those of smallpox-infected blacks whom the British had sent out in a prototype of germ warfare—the officer presented a letter from Cornwallis proposing a twenty-four-hour cease-fire to settle terms for surrender. Washington asked for a written sketch of Cornwallis's proposed terms, which, when it arrived two hours later, he and Rochambeau deemed a reasonable starting point for talks.[134]

But the October 18 session deadlocked when Cornwallis's negotiators refused to turn over the American deserters and Loyalists in their camp, or the slaves who had joined the British army, and Washington's envoys insisted on subjecting the vanquished redcoats to the same ritual humiliation that the British had inflicted on the defeated American army at Charleston. Cornwallis knew he had lost and wanted quick care for his sick and wounded; Washington didn't want victory to evaporate through some accident of weather or British reinforcements, which, after weeks of irresolution and incompetence, set sail from New York Harbor the next day. Each commander therefore told his negotiators that night to be fast and flexible. It took them but an hour the next morning to agree to each other's fixed positions.[135]

That afternoon—six and a half years to the day since the Battles of Lexington and Concord had begun the war—more than 8,000 sullen redcoats and Hessians filed out into captivity, their drums muffled in black, looking only toward the French, and flinging down their weapons hard, to try to break them. With an equal lack of grace, Cornwallis had claimed indisposition and sent his second in command to yield his sword—to Rochambeau. The allied officers told him to surrender to Commander in Chief Washington, who, with the same punctiliousness he had shown when refusing a letter addressed to "George Washington Esq., etc. etc." in 1776, signaled his second in command to take the sword from the weeping Briton. One war legend worthy of being true is that the British band played a march called "The World Turned Upside Down." What is certain is that Lafayette told the American band to blast out "Yankee Doodle," forcing the sour redcoats to look their way.[136]

THE WAR WAS OVER, but neither George Washington nor George III knew it, so different does lived experience look from history crystallized in books. Almost two more years passed before the Paris peace treaty was signed in September 1783. Meanwhile, the king burned to step up the war effort—even though his prime minister groaned, "Oh God! It's all over!"—and Washington, knowing his adversary, felt sure that "the King will push the war as long as the nation will find men or money," so Americans shouldn't let Yorktown lull them into letting their guard down.[137]

Far from over was the army's hardship; and as the soldiers waited uncertainly in their cold, needy camp in Newburgh, New York, they fell into discontent, not relaxation. By October 1782, Washington sensed that "the patience, the fortitude, the long and great sufferings of this Army is unexampled in History; but there is an end to all things and I fear we are very near one to this." He planned "to stick very close to the Troops this Winter and to try like a careful physician to prevent if possible the disorders getting to an incurable height."[138]

He had seen what such discontent could do—and not just when by chance he foiled the treason of the once-heroic Benedict Arnold, who, seething with resentment at what he thought shabby treatment after crippling wounds sidelined his career, nearly succeeded in betraying West Point to the British and helping them kidnap Washington himself for £6,000 and a royal commission in September 1780.[139] Three months later, 1,300 Pennsylvania soldiers mutinied, killing and wounding the officers who tried to stop them from storming Congress to protest "the total want of pay for nearly twelve Months, [the] want of cloathing, at a severe season, and not unfrequently the want of provisions," reported Washington, who understood their distress but also viewed their crime with horror and sent Anthony Wayne with troops to catch them. Wayne stopped them near Trenton, agreeing to discharge some of the men and furlough others, but insisting that a firing squad of mutineers execute a dozen of their ringleaders, at such close range that the powder flashes set their blindfolds alight. When 200 New Jersey soldiers mutinied less than two weeks later, Washington sent troops after them with orders not to negotiate. As before, a firing squad of vanquished mutineers had to shoot the ringleaders.[140]

So as the *officers* at Newburgh grew restive over the back pay and pensions owed them—especially after the British abandoned Charleston in December 1782 and rumors of a peace deal spread in early 1783—Washington could not but worry when on March 10 a handbill went round the camp, calling officers to a protest meeting the next day. A second broadside warned officers to "assume a bolder Tone" than their previous pleas to Congress: they should appeal not to government's "Justice" but to its "fears," if they didn't want to be discharged without pay and "grow old in poverty, wretchedness, and Contempt," now that peace was at hand. And they should distrust anyone counseling moderation and forbearance—meaning Washington. The author: General Gates's aide, John Armstrong, one of American history's great wreckers, who in his later career as secretary of war pigheadedly disobeyed President Madison's order to defend Washington, D.C., against the British attackers who torched it unopposed in the War of 1812.[141]

Washington—though he sympathized with the officers' unease and, he wrote Hamilton, feared that many faced debtors' prison "if they are turned loose without liquidation of accts. and an assurance of that justice to which they are so worthily entitled"—forbade the meeting, which he thought could end with the officers "plunging themselves into a gulph of Civil horror from which there might be no receding." He called an assembly of his own for March 15 in an echoing hall dubbed the Temple of Virtue.[142] "Sensibly agitated," one observer wrote, the General mounted the stage and beseeched his officers to pause for cool deliberation before letting an anonymous provocateur lure them into making demands of Congress at gunpoint, as

Armstrong had insinuated. Surely officers don't want to "tarnish the reputation of an Army which is celebrated thro' all Europe, for its fortitude and Patriotism." And surely, Washington implored, as "I have never left your side for one moment, but when called . . . on public duty" and "have ever considered my own Military reputation as inseparably connected with that of the Army"—surely "it can *scarcely be supposed* . . . that I am indifferent to its interests." He would do all in his power, he promised, to make sure Congress dispensed "compleat justice for all your toils and dangers."[143]

Sensing he hadn't carried his point, he reached into his pocket to read a congressman's letter reaffirming the official promises. But he couldn't see the script and drew out a pair of spectacles that none but his closest aides had ever known him to wear. "Gentlemen, you must pardon me," the fifty-one-year-old, visibly aged commander said, putting them on. "I have grown gray in your service and now find myself growing blind." That homely gesture brought the human reality straight to the officers' hearts, and tears stung many eyes. He read them the letter and left the Temple, and they unanimously voted to tell him that they "reciprocated his affectionate expressions with the greatest sincerity of which the human heart is capable." The danger passed—and Congress did make good on its promise, to the extent of five years' full pay in lieu of half pay for life.[144] But even so, Washington the realist also knew that many officers—who "have been *obliged* to dress, and appear in character" and therefore "to anticipate their pay"—would consequently have debts that "will compell them to part with" the government bonds they will receive as their pensions for whatever they might fetch from "unfeeling, avaricious speculators," such as he had been when he bought up officers' land claims after the French and Indian War.[145]

On the eighteenth of April in '83, eight years to the day after Paul Revere's midnight ride, Washington announced to his troops the official end of hostilities. The war—in which one American soldier in four had died, compared with one in five in the Civil War and one in forty in World War II—was really over, and all soldiers should be proud of "the dignifyed part they have been called to act . . . on the stage of human affairs" in "erecting this stupendous *fabrick* of *Freedom* and *Empire* . . . and establishing an Asylum for the poor and oppressed of all nations and religions," he told them in his favorite imagery. "Nothing now remains but for the actors of this mighty Scene . . . to close the Drama with applause; and retire from the Military Theatre."[146]

When the signed peace treaty reached America in November, the General wrote a *Farewell Address* to his army, taking "leave of those he holds most dear" and thanking them for their "unparalleled perseverence . . . through almost every possible suffering and discouragement for . . . eight long years"—a feat "little short of a standing miracle." In his first General Orders as commander in July 1776, hoping to make the army America's first truly national institution, he had urged his men to lay aside "all Distinctions of Colonies" to serve "the great and common cause in which we are all engaged." Now he marveled at how well they succeeded. "Who, that was not a witness, could imagine that the most violent local prejudices would cease so soon, and that Men who came from the different parts of the Continent . . . would instantly become but one patriotic band of Brothers," he told them, echoing *Henry V*. As so often, he closed with a benediction: "May the choicest of heaven's favours, both here and hereafter, attend those who, under the devine auspices, have secured innumerable blessings for others."[147]

On December 4 he said good-bye to some thirty of his officers at a buffet at Black Sam Fraunces's Tavern, still standing (much altered) on Pearl Street at Manhattan's southern tip. He toasted them with a trembling hand and "a heart filled with love and gratitude," he said, and his face streamed with tears as each of them, beginning with Knox and Steuben—also "suffused in tears," a colonel wrote—came up to be hugged and kissed. And then he walked across the room, waved his hand, and was gone.[148]

On his way home to Virginia, he fulfilled another promise he had made when he took command. "When we assumed the Soldier," he said just after Bunker Hill, "we did not lay aside the Citizen."[149] On December 23, he appeared before Congress and, his hand trembling again, surrendered the parchment commission he had received eight and a half years earlier to the civil authorities who had granted it, dramatizing the subordination of the military to the civil power. "Having now finished the work assigned me," he said in a voice thick with emotion, "I retire from the great theatre of Action." When George III heard that he intended to return like Cincinnatus to his farm, he exclaimed with amazement, "If he does that, he will be the greatest man in the world!" On Christmas Eve 1783, private citizen Washington dismounted his horse at his beloved Mount Vernon's welcoming door.[150]

5

President Washington

A MONTH AFTER WASHINGTON RETURNED home to Mount Vernon, he wrote Lafayette how happy he was to be "under the shadow of my own Vine & my own Fig tree, free from the bustle of a camp & the busy scenes of public life." Unlike "the Soldier who is ever in pursuit of Fame," he wrote, "I am retireing within myself," content to "move gently down the stream of life, until I sleep with my Fathers."[1] To Lafayette's wife, he wrote to invite the whole family to visit him in his "small Villa, with the implements of Husbandry and Lambkins around me," where she will "see the plain manner in which we live, & meet the rustic civility, & . . . taste the simplicity of rural life."[2]

Balderdash, of course. There was nothing sentimentally pastoral about his busy Virginia life, and even on the banks of the Potomac he remained a public figure: Mount Vernon thronged with dignitaries and curiosity seekers, up to thirty a day, whom the rules of hospitality required him to entertain handsomely, as well as provide for their servants and horses. On June 30, 1785, a year and a half after his return home, he noted in his diary that he "dined with only Mrs. Washington, which I believe is the first instance of it since my retirement from public life."[3]

Plus he had an ambitious house to finish, and it took two frustrating years just to find the needed workmen. He was willing to take them from anywhere, he wrote Tench Tilghman. "If they are good workmen, they may be of Assia, Africa, or Europe. They may be Mahometans, Jews, or Christians of any Sect—or they may be Atheists—I would however prefer middle aged, to young men."[4] As he searched, his merchant friend Samuel Vaughan sent him an Italian mantelpiece he claimed he had no place for. Washington hesitated to accept it, judging from its ten huge crates that it was sure to be "too elegant & costly by far . . . for my own room, and republican stile of living." But he couldn't resist installing it, in what he always called the "New Room," and it did indeed have swains, shepherdesses, milkmaids, plowboys, oxen, and—yes—lambs, beautifully carved upon its sumptuous creamy marble surface, between two Ionic columns of even more gorgeous golden stone.

When he finally found skilled craftsmen early in 1786, he had them follow the mantel's lead and incorporate in the new dining room's exquisitely delicate and restrained plasterwork such instruments of husbandry as scythes, sickles, and rakes, and he finished the room, with its rich but plain verdigris wallpaper, with the same chaste refinement.[5] The pastoral imagery adorning a lofty, formal, neoclassical room, in the style that Robert Adam had made all the rage in English aristocratic mansions, nicely embodied the tensions in Washington's life at this time. Unlike the cozy domesticity of the rest of Mount Vernon, the imposing New Room was a stage set for public functions—even down to the damask-draped boards on trestles in lieu of a dining table, easy to remove, stretch, or shrink, depending on the scene being played.

He also needed, from two continents, such basic materials as flagstones to floor his ninety-two-foot-long piazza, he wrote in 1784, and he hoped he could get some "with a rich polished face" in "common Irish Marble (black and white)" or even in "the very cheap kind of Marble, good in quality," that he had heard was for sale in Flanders.[6] He needed glass for the grand Venetian window in the dining room, boarded up until now. The piazza floor and the New Room weren't finished until Washington was away at the Constitutional Convention in 1787, and at that crowning moment of the Founding, fittingly, the weathervane, which Washington had a Philadelphia carpenter fashion as a dove of peace with an olive branch in her mouth, went up on top of the cupola of the victorious warrior's house, where the swords and spears seemed to have been stuccoed into plowshares and pruning hooks.[7]

When he had written to the Marquise de Lafayette, not only did his "Cottage," as he coyly called it, stand unfinished, but even the lambkins were a work in progress: two years later he was trying to buy a couple of hundred, his stock of sheep having dwindled during his absence.[8] Wishing to improve his five farms at Mount Vernon, he leapt at British agronomist Arthur Young's 1786 offer to send him his farming journal as well as seeds and tools from England. "Agriculture has ever been amongst the most favourite amusements of my life, though I never possessed much skill in the art," Washington confided to his new correspondent, and what skill he had had withered after "nine years total inattention." But he did know that Virginia's farming methods were "unproductive" and "ruinous," so he was thrilled to have Young's scientific guidance, and he asked for bushels and pounds of top-quality seeds, two of "the simplest, & best constructed Plows," and perhaps even a "good Plowman at low wages."[9]

His "greatest pride is now to be thought the first farmer in America," a visitor reported, and Washington worked hard at it, riding round on daily inspections, always ready to get off his horse and work beside his slaves and hired hands when needed—though, when he had his hounds with him, he would just as quickly jump back in the saddle and gallop after them if they scented a fox. "It's astonishing with what niceness he directs everything in the building way," his visitor noted, "condescending even to measure the things himself, that all may be perfectly uniform."[10] As Washington wrote when he was president, "I shall begrudge no reasonable expense that will contribute to the improvement and neatness of my Farms; for nothing pleases me better than to see them in good order, and every thing trim, handsome, and thriving about them."[11]

His chief claim to agricultural fame is, oddly . . . the mule. The king of Spain had promised (without irony) to send him two prize jackasses "as a mark of his esteem," only one of which made it safely to Mount Vernon in 1786. Washington set out to breed the creature, whom he named Royal Gift, with American mares, to produce a hybrid, hardier and stronger than a horse, and cheaper to feed. Royal Gift, disappointingly, could scarcely perform "his labours—for labour it appears to be"—"seldomer, or with more majestic solemnity," Washington reported. "However, I am not without hope that when he becomes a little better acquainted with republican enjoyments, he will amend his manners, and fall into a better & more expeditious mode of doing business."[12] He fortunately did, and the fifty-seven mules that Mount Vernon produced proved the worth of these animals to American farmers and earned Washington—not Royal Gift—the title of "Father of the American Mule."[13]

Even as "a private citizen on the banks of the Potomac," as he liked to call himself, Washington kept trying to shape public affairs, and his words and actions disprove the myth that in politics he became but a stately figurehead for the views of Madison and Hamilton. Not at all. Well before he left the army, the idea of a constitutional convention took root in his mind. On March 4, 1783, he wrote Hamilton from his Newburgh camp that congressmen must fire up their constituents to fix "the great defects of their Constitution" by giving Congress adequate power. Otherwise, "the blood we have spilt in the course of an Eight years war, will avail us nothing."[14] In June, he stressed the need for an "indissoluble Union of the States under one Federal Head."[15] By July, he was calling for "a Convention of the People" to make the states as subordinate to the federal government as the counties are to the state governments. How can anyone fear this step? he exclaimed. "For Heavens sake who are Congress? are they not the Creatures of the People, amenable to them for their Conduct, and dependant from day to day on their breath? Where then can be the danger of giving them such Powers as are adequate to the great ends of Government?"[16] The need for an energetic central government is "as plain as any problem in Euclid," he wrote from Mount Vernon in 1784.[17] Too bad the people weren't as quick to understand their rational self-interest and pursue it, he sighed in May 1786. "It is one of the evils of democratical governments that the people, not always seeing and frequently mislead, must often feel before they can act right."[18]

From early on, too, he mocked the Jeffersonian fear of commerce. Why waste time speculating "whether the luxury, effeminacy, & corruption which are introduced by it, are counterballanced by the conveniencies and wealth of which it is productive," he wrote acidly in October 1785, since by now "the spirit of Trade which pervades these States is not to be restrained"? The only worthwhile question is how to regulate trade justly among the states—and, in indolent Virginia, to "*force* this spirit" before the state falls behind its neighbors. He did his part by hosting a conference at Mount Vernon of Virginia and Maryland dignitaries in March 1785, trying to make a reality of his cherished Potomac canal idea to encourage the industry of the West and knit the country into a commercial unity, with Virginia a key entrepôt.[19]

The gravest danger of the existing ineffectual government of thirteen sovereign states pulling in different directions and canceling each other out, he warned, was anarchy. "Liberty, when it degenerates into licentiousness, begets confusion, and frequently ends in Tyranny," he wrote in 1783. Three years later, in August 1786, he saw (or thought he saw) that prediction come horrifyingly true in Shays's Rebellion, a violent aftershock of Britain's postwar closure of its West Indian ports to American ships, as being no longer British. That move nearly halved U.S. exports and sparked a depression, nowhere harsher than in mercantile New England. Thousands of desperate, pitchfork-wielding young farmers in western Massachusetts tried to wrest weapons from the Springfield armory to close the courts before judges could seize their farms for tax delinquency or allow creditors to foreclose. Henry Knox, sent to quell the revolt, reported that the rebels' "creed is, that the property of the United States has been protected from confiscation of Britain by the joint exertions of *all*, and therefore ought to be the *common property* of all," Washington wrote Madison in November, adding his own incredulous italics. Further, Knox reported, "They are determined to anihilate all debts public & private." Washington—who had spent two months on his western lands in the fall of 1784 trying to evict squatters and collect rents from his deadbeat legitimate tenants, and two more years in lawsuits to vindicate his property claims—drew his own conclusions about the breakdown of the Lockean social compact: "What stronger evidence can be given of the want of energy in our governments than these disorders? If there exists not a power to check them, what security has a man of life, liberty, or property?"[20]

THE CONFERENCE he called at Mount Vernon to discuss chartering a Potomac canal company proved as fateful as the fluttering of a butterfly's wings that proverbially changes the climate on the other side of the world. It led to a further meeting of five states on national issues in Annapolis in September 1786, that, pushed by delegates Hamilton and Madison, scheduled a constitutional convention for May 1787 in Philadelphia. Just after Christmas 1786, Madison and other Virginia notables asked Washington to head the state's delegation, "as a mark of the earnestness of Virginia," wrote Madison, and an enticement "to the most select characters of every part of the Confederacy" to come.[21] General Knox weighed in, with shrewd insight into what made his old chief tick, telling him that, as he was sure to be named the convention's president, its success would be "highly honorable to your fame . . . and doubly entitle you to the glorious republican epithet 'The Father of Your Country.'"[22] Given Washington's longtime support for such a step—"to avoid, if possible, civil discord, or other impending evils," as he put it—he knew he had to go.[23] He performed what became his characteristic hard-to-get dance, but he went, aiming to achieve "no temporizing expedient" but "radical cures," he wrote Madison, that "will stamp wisdom and dignity on the proceedings."[24]

But just as with a problem in Euclid, Washington could calculate the angles: accepting this appointment, he ruefully told Virginia governor Edmund Randolph, "will, I fear, have a tendency to sweep me back into the tide of public affairs."[25] The fame he had already won conferred the aura of his prestige on the Convention, and that prestige would be essential to legitimate whatever the Convention brought forth. Deeply aware of his symbolic role, he wore his military uniform when he accepted the meeting's presidency on May 25, 1787, and he presided with the firm and quiet dignity of a judge, speaking rarely and keeping delegates in line.[26] That Olympian reserve, heightening the mystique of his prestige, influenced the delegates in their shaping of the executive branch: Pierce Butler of South Carolina opined that they would not have made it so strong "had not many members cast their eyes toward General Washington as president and shaped their ideas of the powers to a president by their opinion of his virtue."[27]

On September 17, 1787, the delegates signed the document, and, the Convention's "business being thus closed, the Members adjourned to the City Tavern, dined together and took a cordial leave of each other," Washington recorded.[28] The outcome, which gave form to the energetic government he had long favored (and which largely followed the blueprint he and his fellow Virginia delegates had helped Madison sketch out just before the Convention opened, as Chapter Nine recounts), elated him. He sent Congress the document that same day, with a cover note invoking classical social-contract theory. Just as "[i]ndividuals entering into society, must give up a share of liberty to preserve the rest," he wrote, so the states agreed to cede some "rights of independent sovereignty to . . . provide for the interest and safety of all," in a "spirit of . . . mutual deference and concession" that was indispensable—and that, in light of the states' wide cultural and economic differences, he told Lafayette later, seemed to him "little short of a miracle."[29] The Constitution, he wrote an Irish baronet, "approached nearer to perfection than any government hitherto instituted among Men."[30]

He followed the ratification debates avidly. A "greater Drama is now acting on this Theatre than has heretofore been brought on the American Stage, or any other in the World," he told his Dublin correspondent, inflating his favorite imagery to the hyperbole of a playhouse handbill—"the Novel and astonishing Spectacle of a whole People deliberating calmly on what form of government will be the most conducive to their happiness."[31] Thanking Hamilton for sending him *The Federalist*, he pronounced it an instant classic and boasted that he'd read everything on the ratification question. Much later, as president, he proudly asserted his expertise when he dismissed a congressional demand as unconstitutional. As a framer of the Constitution, he knew firsthand its animating principles, he said, and he also had at his fingertips the arguments of all the state ratifying conventions. Anybody who doubted him could consult "the plain letter of the Constitution itself," along with "the Journals of the General Convention, which I have deposited in the office of the department of State," he tartly concluded, with an uncharacteristic emphasis on the personal pronoun.[32]

But with all his enthusiasm for the Constitution, Washington never saw it as a self-activating machine, sufficient on its own to ensure American freedom. Any constitution can be subverted, "if the spirit and letter of the expression is disregarded," he knew.[33] True, an unprecedented array of checks and balances made this one unlikely to degenerate into a despotism, "so long as there shall remain any virtue in the body of the People." But in future ages, if that virtue should give way to "corruption of morals, profligacy of manners, and listlessness for the preservation of the natural and unalienable rights of mankind," then tyranny that no lawgiver's prudence can prevent might sweep away liberty, for no "mound of parchmt can be so formed as to stand against the sweeping torrent of boundless ambition on the one side, aided by the sapping current of corrupted morals on the other."[34]

In other words, the Constitution is the letter; its animating spirit is what we would call a culture of liberty, though Washington used the eighteenth-century language of morals and manners to mean the same thing. That's what he had in mind when he noted that "the information and morals of our Citizens appear to be peculiarly favourable for the introduction of such a plan of government," where "due energy will not be incompatible with the unalienable rights of freemen."[35] That's why he insisted in his First Inaugural Address on the "indissoluble union between virtue and happiness, between duty and advantage."[36] And it's why, in his first annual message to Congress—the first State of the Union—he dwelt on the critical importance, for the "security of a free Constitution," of "teaching the people themselves to know and to value their own rights; to discern and provide against invasions of them; to distinguish between oppression and the necessary exercise of lawful authority; . . . to discriminate the spirit of liberty from that of licentiousness," and to unite "a speedy, but temperate vigilence against encroachments, with an inviolable respect to the laws."[37]

As clearly as such anti-federalists as George Mason, Washington knew from his own experience that, while some men will follow what they see as their rational self-interest and sell supplies to British occupiers rather than to Patriot insurgents, no free country can exist unless many of their brothers have what he called "the sacred fire of liberty" burning within, sufficient to resist tyranny—some even to the point of marching barefoot through the snow to attack its armies, their lives on the line.[38]

Washington understood that not everyone would see the subtle distinction between the constitutional machinery and the particulars of the American culture that animated it. "I expect, that many blessings will be attributed to our new government, which are now taking their rise from that industry and frugality into the practice of which the people have been forced from necessity," he wrote Lafayette as the Virginia Ratifying Convention met. But culture and Constitution would reinforce each other in a virtuous circle, he foresaw. "When the people shall find themselves secure under an energetic government, . . . when the seeds of happiness which are sown here shall begin to expand themselves, and when every one (under his own vine and fig-tree) shall begin to taste the fruits of freedom, then all these blessings (for all these blessings will come) will be referred to the fostering influence of the new government. Whereas many causes will have conspired to produce them."[39] Though Washington didn't have the clunky term, he well understood how the character of the people and the spirit of the laws interact dialectically to shape a society.

Perhaps he was so sensitive to the question of virtue because, as the Constitutional Convention neared—and especially as he saw, with "a kind of gloom upon my mind," that he would have to serve as the nation's president—his concern with appearances turned inward, and he scrutinized ever more self-consciously the content of his own character.[40] This note first sounded in his letters early in 1785, when, at his prompting, the Virginia Assembly voted to charter canal companies on the Potomac and the James, and, as thanks for his conceiving the project, to award him some shares. Rarely can an intended honor have caused such consternation. He wanted to be "at liberty," he wrote Governor Benjamin Harrison (the master of Berkeley Plantation and father of the ninth president), "to suggest what may occur to me, under the fullest conviction, that . . . there will be no suspicion that sinister motives had the smallest influence"—that "every individual who may hear that it was a favorite plan of mine, may know also that I had no other motive" than the public good and certainly no thought of personal gain.[41] It took him seven months to agonize over what he saw as a dilemma, since "I am aware that my non-acceptance of these shares will have various motives ascribed to it, among which an ostentatious display of disinterestedness—perhaps the charge of disrespect or slight of the favors of my Country, may lead the van." In the end, he came up with the Solomonic solution of accepting the gift but using it to endow two charity schools.[42]

"An ostentatious display of disinterestedness"—can anyone ever have burrowed more anxiously into the convoluted strata of outer appearance and inner psychological reality than this? Driven by the love of fame, he had become the world's most famous man, and now he sought something more. He sought sincerity; he sought virtue; he sought inner wholeness; but, since appearances still haunted him, he worried that people might think he counterfeited these qualities as one more way of winning fame. Paradoxically, as his countrymen were about to give him the highest honor the new nation could bestow, he felt riven. He could scarcely even speak of the prospect, "without betraying, in my Judgment, some impropriety of conduct, or without feeling an apprehension that a premature display of anxiety, might be construed into a vainglorious desire of pushing myself into notice as a Candidate," he wrote Hamilton.[43] To General Benjamin Lincoln, on the other hand, he confided with tortured ambivalence that he'd accept the job only from "a *conviction* that the partiality of my Countrymen had made my services absolutely necessary, joined to a *fear* that my refusal might induce a belief that I preferred the conservation of my own reputation & private ease to the good of my Country."[44]

As he jotted pages of notes for an Inaugural Address after his unanimous election on February 4, 1789, he all but turned himself inside out. "I solemnly assert and appeal to the searcher of hearts to witness the truth of it, that my leaving home to take upon myself the execution of this Office was the greatest personal sacrifice I have ever . . . been called upon to make," he agonized in his orderly, businesslike study at Mount Vernon, with his large world globe beside him. "And, from the bottom of my Soul, I know, that my motives on no former occasion were more innocent than in the present instance."[45]

But realizing that the Constitution was just an abstract framework, inert until someone breathed the spirit of life into it and fleshed it out, he also recognized that it mattered who would do the job. He had asked Hamilton "whether there does not exist a probability that the government would be just as happily and effectually carried into execution, without my aid, as with it," and he concluded that the answer was no.[46] His fame, his moral authority, made him indispensable. "Whenever a government is to be instituted or changed by the Consent of the people," he mused, "confidence in the person placed at the head of it, is, perhaps, more peculiarly necessary."[47] So he took the job out of "an absolute conviction of duty," he wrote the celebrated English Whig historian Catharine Macaulay Graham (who had visited him at Mount Vernon), especially since the "establishment of our new Government seemed to be the last great experiment, for promoting human happiness, by reasonable compact, in civil Society."[48] Even so, he told Henry Knox a month before the inauguration, "my movements to the chair of Government will be accompanied by feelings not unlike those of a culprit who is going to the place of his execution."[49]

After he took the oath of office in a trembling voice on the balcony of New York's old city hall on April 30, 1789, his hand on a Bible hastily borrowed from a nearby Masonic lodge, he began his Inaugural Address by confessing his "anxieties" over "the magnitude and difficulty of the trust" he was assuming.[50] This wasn't just formulaic modesty. After all, as he explained to Graham a few months later, "Few . . . can realise the difficult and delicate part which a man in my situation had to act"—a part for which no one had written the script. There had never been such a thing as the president of the United States before, or a president of any modern republic. There was no State of the Union address, no "Hail to the Chief," no cabinet, no White House, no chief of protocol. There was so much he had to make up as he went along, out of his own judgment, experience, and instinct, and he had to bring his audience along with him by force of character. "Much was to be done by *prudence*, much by *conciliation*, much by *firmness*," he wrote Graham. "I walk on untrodden ground. There is scarcely any action, whose motives may not be subject to double interpretation. There is scarcely any part of my conduct wch may not hereafter be drawn into precedent."[51]

So those precedents needed to be right. In all he did in inventing the presidency, he believed, he ought to "maintain the dignity of office, without subjecting himself to the imputation of supercilious-ness or unnecessary reserve" and "without partaking of the follies of luxury and ostentation."[52] A republican chief executive who symbolically embodied a nation of freemen had to navigate the tensions between superiority and equality inherent in his role; a president who valued a culture of freedom needed to set the right tone of republican manners, which would dramatize every day the new nation's ideal of the relations between the people and their elected magistrate—and, more broadly, between citizen and citizen.

Would it be acceptable for him to visit his friends privately, he anxiously asked Adams, or would such visits "be construed into visits from the President of the United States?" What kind of parties should he give? Could he have legislators to dinner in small groups, or must he invite them all at once?[53] As for his title, he rejected Adams's grandiloquent suggestion of "His Highness, the President of the United States of America, and Protector of their Liberties"—which the vice president suggested not because he wanted a king but rather because he sought, through titles, "parade," and "ceremony," to harness that "passion for distinction" or love of fame that, like Washington, he believed to be the strongest motive for virtuous behavior.[54] Nevertheless, Washington modestly chose "the President of the United States."

Of course he was right to predict that the motives behind every choice would draw scrutiny and suspicion. At Hamilton's suggestion, he held "levees"—a term with unfortunate royal connotations, as his enemies later objected—every Tuesday at 3 PM, stiff, men-only receptions, at which he struggled to exchange a few decorous words with each guest, bowing instead of shaking hands, to the great disgust of the more egalitarian dignitaries, who complained that his bow wasn't even a very gracious bow. "Would it not have been better to have thrown the veil of charity over them, ascribing their stiffness to the effects of age" rather than to "pride"? the fifty-eight-year-old president, his hearing failing and his painful false teeth freezing his smile, plaintively wondered. He was only doing what he and those he consulted thought was right, he told Jefferson later, and if he "could but know what the sense of the public was," he would "most cheerfully conform to it."[55]

"ALL SEE, and most admire, the glare which hovers round the external trappings of elevated Office," he told Graham. "To me, there is nothing in it, beyond the lustre which may be reflected from its connection with a power of promoting human felicity."[56] Yes and no: he hadn't lost his taste for display, but he began to realize the toll that presidential pomp would take on his personal life. Soon after his inauguration, he was writing to Gouverneur Morris in France, asking him to buy a "neat and fashionable but not expensive" mirror-finish plateau for the center of his dinner table, which Morris found in Paris, and a set of wine coolers, which the faithful emissary had a London silversmith make in Sheffield plate—at Washington's expense, on top of the £5,671 that Congress had already spent redecorating and finishing the dignified, neoclassical presidential mansion it had rented at 3 Cherry Street near the East River, just north of today's Brooklyn Bridge. As Morris wrote him, it was the president's task "to fix the Taste of our Country properly," making sure everything was "substantially good and majestically plain; made to endure"—though Washington privately grumbled that the price of the wine buckets "far exceeds the utmost bounds of my calculation." When the French Revolution broke out and Paris recalled its minister, Washington was happy to rent the diplomat's bigger and grander house at 39-41 Broadway, and he used his own funds to buy much of the minister's elegant French furniture before moving in February 1790.[57]

Though land-rich but often cash-poor—he had had to borrow £500 to pay his Virginia taxes and travel to his own inauguration—Washington entertained lavishly out of duty, inclination, and the vow of Black Sam Fraunces, who had given up tavern keeping to run the chief executive's household, that "while he is President of the United States and I have the honor to be his steward, his establishment shall be supplied with the very best of everything that the whole country can afford." The heaps of oysters, lobsters, and other delicacies made visitors gape and made the $25,000 annual presidential salary dwindle relentlessly. Washington made up the difference out of his own pocket, and he paid as well for such luxurious gewgaws as the scarlet-trimmed white liveries of the presidential household's twenty servants and slaves.[58]

What the "external trappings of elevated Office" were to be first became clear as barges elaborate enough for Cleopatra, with thirteen white-clad sailors at the oars, rowed him across rivers as he traveled to New York for his inauguration, and choirs of white-robed virgins and matrons mellifluously hymned his praises as the defender of mothers and daughters, scattering petals before him as he rode, with tear-streaming eyes, under triumphal arches of flowers.[59] The petals and virgins became routine. When the first congressional session closed in late September 1789 after the Bill of Rights passed, and after the president had proclaimed the first Thanksgiving on November 26, Washington set off on a tour of New England—the first of several national peregrinations "to see with my own eyes the situation of the country" and take the people's pulse. By then he could perform the role of hero like an old trouper. Just before reaching the next town, he would climb out of his gleaming white chariot with liveried coachman, footmen, and postilion, heave himself up in the stirrup of his huge white charger—who the night before had been rubbed with glistening white pomade, wrapped in clean sheets, and bedded in fresh straw, after having his hooves blackened and his teeth brushed—and settle onto his pigskin saddle atop a gold-trimmed leopard-skin saddle blanket, sometimes (one imagines) with a weary grunt, just before the local cavalry honor guard appeared in a cloud of dust to escort him to the hymning ladies, the bowers, the balls, the dinners, and the throngs of admiring citizens, who still sometimes brought tears to his eyes.[60]

But by the time he made his 1,800-mile circuit of the South in the spring of 1791, his patience for going through the same performance over and over had begun to wear thin. Sometimes he would announce the wrong time for his intended departure and sneak off hours earlier, or leave in the rain, to skip the hoopla.[61] No backslapping politician, but rather a commander and Virginia gentleman with studied reserve and self-restraint (beginning with his 1595 etiquette book), he lacked the gift of small talk and jollity with strangers, and the obligatory dinners and receptions could bore him as much as others. Chronically grumpy Pennsylvania senator William Maclay described the president drumming distractedly on the table with his fork at "the most solemn dinner ever I ate at," where "dead silence" reigned, though at a later dinner the solon grasped that Washington's deafness made him miss much of the conversation.[62]

Being the observed of all observers, as he had once wished to be, exacted a cost. During the war, he had worried that when peace arrived, because of the cares he'd borne and the suffering, folly, and evil he'd seen, "I may be incapable of . . . social enjoyments."[63] Now his august celebrity isolated him; the national icon he had made himself into and that the country needed—the grave and majestic role he had first yearned, and then consented, to play—obscured the man. His "presence generally chilled my young companions," Martha's granddaughter Nelly Custis wrote, "and his own near relatives feared to speak or laugh before him. This was occasioned by the awe and respect he inspired and not from his severity. When he entered a room where we were all mirth and in high conversation, all were instantly mute. He would sit a short time and then retire, quite provoked and disappointed, but they could not repress their feelings."[64] Martha summed up the couple's situation most succinctly: "I think I am more like a state prisoner than anything else," she wrote.[65]

However irksome the adulation, he preferred it to the criticism that grew louder and nastier with every year of his two terms. Though he proved brilliant at inventing the presidency, setting a standard of probity, wisdom, and dignity that still measures his successors and though his eight years in office yielded success upon success—his everyday experience as chief executive seethed with partisan bitterness that poisoned cabinet meetings, spewed out from a press as foul as today's most noxious blogs, and exasperated and baffled him. If he had expected something like the miraculous "spirit of amity" and "mutual deference and concession" he had seen at the Constitutional Convention, he got instead the suspicion, backbiting, and recrimination that seem the natural fertilizer of democratic politics, where interest jars with interest, worldview with worldview, and ambition with ambition.

Almost no success of the Washington administration went unpunished. The rumblings of opposition began as legislators considered the first part of Hamilton's 1790–91 financial plan, directing the federal government to pay the outstanding war debts of the states to help establish the credit of government paper, a measure odious to paid-up states (as Chapter Seven explains). Congress, Washington fretted, debated the issue "with a warmth & intemperence; with prolixity & threats; which it is to be feared has lessened the dignity of that body"; and in their letters home, individual congressmen ascribed "the worst motives for the conduct of their opponants; . . . by which means jealousies & distrusts are spread most impolitickly, far & wide."[66] The bill passed, after Congressman James Madison agreed to drop his opposition in exchange for Hamilton's promise to round up votes to move the national capital to Philadelphia for ten years before permanently housing it in a new federal city on the Potomac. But such rancor was to be a keynote of American politics.

When the next year Hamilton dropped the second shoe of his financial plan, a scheme for a national bank, the vituperation exploded. Madison objected, in an eloquent speech on the House floor in its new home in Philadelphia's State House, that the Constitution gave Congress no power to charter a bank. Secretary of State Thomas Jefferson, Washington reported to Hamilton, charged, more darkly, that the plan would empower "corrupt squadrons of paper dealers," who would seduce the legislature into changing America's republican government into a British-style monarchy. That Hamilton's sole speech in the Constitutional Convention had suggested a president for life, elected by the propertied but subject to impeachment, gave grounds enough for Jefferson's long-lived canard that Hamilton favored an elective monarchy.[67]

At first, Jefferson assumed that Washington's support for the new financial system blindly followed Hamilton's lead. "Unversed in financial projects and calculations and budgets, his approbation of them was bottomed on his confidence in the man," the secretary of state judged.[68] But just as Washington had contentedly looked on as the Constitutional Convention, under Madison's guidance, gave form to the energetic government he had long envisioned, so he ardently backed Hamilton as the Treasury secretary conjured into being the modern financial structure that the president knew from hard Revolutionary War experience was the basis of national power and prosperity. After dutifully weighing the arguments on both sides, he signed the bank bill in February 1791. And almost overnight, he reported in July 1791, "Our public credit stands on that ground which three years ago would have been considered as a species of madness to have foretold."[69]

So WHILE JEFFERSON, Madison, and their "levelling party" lambasted Hamilton as an antirepublican "monocrat" and "Angloman," they gradually included Washington in the indictment, pointing to his levees, his stiff bow, his coach and horses as damning evidence that justified their "continually sounding the alarm bell of aristocracy," Washington complained.[70] The charges shocked him. Shortly after Yorktown, when a colonel had written urging him to be king, he replied, "I must view with abhorrence, and reprehend with severety," a thought that "seems big with the greatest mischiefs that can befall my Country."[71] His notes for his Inaugural Address include the assurance that, as "the Divine Providence hath not seen fit, that my blood should be transmitted or my name perpetuated by the endearing, though some times seducing channel of immediate offspring," he had "no family to build in greatness upon my Country's ruins"—though the line didn't make the final cut.[72] And when, early in his presidency, a Philadelphia silversmith had asked permission to place the Washington coat of arms over his door and bill himself as "Silversmith to the President," like purveyors to British royalty, Washington refused the request as "very disagreeable."[73]

Even so, to rehash the litany of condemnation tirelessly, Jefferson hired angry third-rate poet Philip Freneau as a state department translator, a no-show job to support him while he ran an administration-bashing newspaper, the *National Gazette*, launched in October 1791. Typically, on July 4, 1792, Freneau printed a Page One piece denouncing Hamilton's financial system as a recipe for "changing a limited republican government into an unlimited hereditary one"—and, typically, he cheekily had three copies dumped at the door of Washington's rented house. A week later, when Jefferson visited, he found Washington fuming. Nobody planned to turn America into a monarchy, he exploded, as Jefferson recorded in his diary. "He considered [Freneau's] papers as attacking him directly," Jefferson reported him as spluttering. "That in condemning the admn of the govmt they condemned him, for if they thought there were measures pursued contrary to his sentiment, they must conceive him too careless to attend to them or too stupid to understand them."[74]

At first, Washington didn't know that his secretary of state and his congressman friend orchestrated these blasts. All he knew was that he wanted to go home to Mount Vernon when his term ended, and he had even sent Madison a sketch of a farewell address in May 1792, asking him to flesh it out.[75] Though Madison complied, he begged Washington to stay on for a second term, arguing, he recorded, "that in the great point of conciliating and uniting all parties under a Govt which had excited such violent controversies & divisions, it was well known that his services had been in a manner essential."[76] Jefferson repeated the plea a few days later. "North and south will hang together if they have you to hang on," he urged.[77]

In time, the president realized that much of the partisan bitterness sprang from the war between his secretaries of state and Treasury, and in late August he tried to make peace between them. "How unfortunate, and how much it is to be regretted, . . . that internal dissentions should be harrowing and tearing our vitals," he wrote Jefferson. If, "instead of laying our shoulders to the machine after measures are decided on, one pulls this way and another that, before the utility of the thing is fairly tried, it must inevitably be torn asunder—And, in my opinion the fairest prospect of happiness and prosperity that ever was presented to man, will be lost." Could there not be, he pleaded, "liberal allowances—mutual forbearances—and temporising yieldings on *all sides*"? To Hamilton he wondered a few days later why "Men of abilities—zealous patriots—having the same *general* objects in view, and the same upright intentions to prosecute them, will not exercise more charity in deciding on the opinions, & actions of one another." Otherwise, he lamented, "I do not see how the Reins of Government are to be managed."[78]

The truth was, no one but he could manage them, his irresistibly vivacious friend Elizabeth Powel wrote him in November, urging him to a second term by appealing with spot-on insight to every value he held most dear. Having won his countrymen's faith that he was "the only Man in America that dares to do right on all public Occasions," because he was immune to the seductions of power or flattery, how could he think of leaving half done a momentous task crucial not only to his fellow citizens but to posterity? "[You] have frequently demonstrated that you possess an Empire over yourself. For Gods sake do not yield that Empire to a Love of Ease, Retirement, rural Pursuits, or a false Diffidence of Abilities which those that best know you so justly appreciate," Powel wrote. "[C]onvince the World then that you are a practical Philosopher, and that your native Philanthropy has induced you to relinquish an Object so essential to your Happiness. . . . That you are not indifferent to the Plaudits of the World I must conclude when I believe that the love of honest Fame has and ever will be predominant in the best the noblest and most capable Natures. Nor is the Approbation of Mankind to be disregarded with Impunity even by you."[79]

Those arguments carried the day. He stood for reelection and again won unanimously on December 5. In an ostentatious display of republican modesty, he rode alone in his coach to his March 4, 1793, inauguration, delivered a no-frills 135-word address, and left "as he had come," the *Pennsylvania Gazette* reported, "without pomp or ceremony."[80] He dutifully soldiered on as one of the people's "public servants; for in this light I consider myself, whilst I am in this office," he wrote in July; "and, if they were to go further and call me their slave, (during this period) I would not dispute the point."[81]

BUT BY THEN the French Revolution had sharpened America's political acrimony to a razor edge, since the revolutionaries had guillotined Louis XVI in January 1793, just after Washington's reelection. Jefferson, Madison, and their followers—who now called themselves Republicans, to signal support for the new order in France as well as opposition to American "monocrats"—embraced the upheaval enthusiastically. They intensified their criticism of the Washingtonian "Federalists" as crypto-royalists and aristocrats for their dislike of the French regicides and refusal to join France in the war it had declared on the European monarchies in April 1792. In turn, the Federalists came to view the Republicans as leveling fomenters of violence, mobocracy, and anarchy—Shays's rebels on a geopolitical scale.

Right from the start, Washington foresaw with uncanny clarity the transatlantic horrors to come. In October 1789, only three months after the Paris mob stormed the Bastille, he wrote that "the revolution is of too great magnitude to be effected in so short a space, and with the loss of so little blood."[82] Six months after that, he wrote the Chevalier de la Luzerne, Versailles' former minister to the United States, that "nobody can wish more sincerely for the prosperity of the French Nation than I do," but he warned that the revolutionaries might be "making *more haste than good speed*, in their innovations. So much prudence, so much perseverance, so much disinterestedness & so much patriotism are necessary among the Leaders of a Nation, in order to promote the national felicity, that sometimes my fears nearly preponderate over my expectations."[83]

His fears had a more personal aspect too. He worried about Lafayette. Dubbed "le Vassington français" for his American exploits, he had stepped forth as a key leader of the moderate, constitutional-monarchy stage of the revolution, writing the *Declaration of the Rights of Man and of the Citizen* in August 1789, with editorial help from Jefferson, just then winding up his four years as American minister in Paris. A few days later, as commander of the Paris National Guard, the marquis ordered the razing of the Bastille shortly after its capture, sending the huge key to "that fortress of despotism" to "my adoptive father," along with a sketch he made of the ruins, both of which still hang in Mount Vernon's central hall.[84] Washington thanked him for "the token of victory gained by Liberty over Despotism," which brought the distant uprising to his hand in cold iron, but he emphasized that the revolution had many dangers to navigate before it could boast of success.[85]

A year later, as the revolution turned more radical, Washington wrote the marquis of his worry about his protégé's safety and cautioned him against the Paris mob. "The tumultuous populace of large cities are ever to be dreaded," he wrote. "Their indiscriminate violence prostrates for a time all public authority, and its consequences are sometimes extensive and terrible," especially when "wicked and designing men, whose element is confusion," agitate them.[86] Another year on, shortly before the Paris Commune imprisoned the king and queen and abolished the monarchy, he again warned his young friend that "cool reason, which can alone establish a permanent and equal government, is as little to be expected in the tumults of popular commotion, as an attention to the liberties of the people is to be found in the dark Divan of a despotic tyrant."[87]

Lafayette's fate confirmed Washington's fears: condemned as a counterrevolutionary traitor for his resistance to fanaticism, he fled France just before the September 1792 massacres—in which, among other outrages in its five-day murder spree of 1,500 innocents, the drunken Paris mob speared the Princesse de Lamballe for refusing to disavow the king and queen, ripped her beating heart from her chest, and ate it.[88] Lafayette escaped only to be imprisoned in Austrian and Prussian dungeons for five years as a dangerous revolutionary. Washington shrank from sparking an international incident by demanding his release—or even welcoming his fourteen-year-old son into his household instead of fobbing him off on Hamilton for months before taking him in—but Gouverneur Morris's quiet diplomacy in Paris managed to keep the marquise from following her mother, sister, and grandmother to the National Razor in the blood-drenched frenzy of 1793 and 1794.[89]

A JOLT OF French revolutionary anarchy galvanized America in April 1793 in the fiery-haired, flamingly radical person of Edmond Genêt, thirty, Paris's militantly undiplomatic new ambassador, who had begun his foreign-service career as an eighteen-year-old language prodigy, while his father was the ancien régime foreign ministry's chief clerk. As Genêt landed in Charleston and made his slow, incendiary way to Philadelphia to present his credentials to the president, Washington learned that France, which had declared war on Austria in April 1792 in order to export *liberté*, *égalité*, and *fraternité* at the barrel of a gun, had also declared war on Britain in February 1793. The murder of Louis XVI had annulled America's 1778 treaty with royalist France, Washington judged, and the United States could only lose by getting embroiled in European wars. Moreover, he saw that Britain was and would stay America's chief trading partner. Accordingly, he issued a neutrality proclamation on April 22, declaring that the United States, out of "duty and interest," would "pursue a conduct friendly and impartial to the belligerent parties."[90]

But the antiauthoritarian Genêt paid no respect to such reactionary nonsense as he traveled northward. Defying Washington's edict, he commissioned American privateers to prey on British shipping, perhaps hoping to spark an Anglo-American war, whether Washington liked it or not. And he harangued huge crowds along his way, firing them up with revolutionary zeal, which over the next year blazed up in dozens of pro-French Democratic-Republican Societies—soon just "Democratic Societies"—whose members staged rallies and banquets, called each other "citizen" and "citizeness" in French revolutionary style, and wouldn't shrink, Washington believed, from "plunging this country in the horrors of disastrous war."[91]

Jefferson, Madison, and their Republicans didn't like the neutrality proclamation any more than Genêt did. Freneau blasted Washington's ingratitude in abandoning his Revolutionary War allies and treating "with cold indifference the struggles of those very friends to support their own liberties against an host of despots."[92] Madison, after sneering at "degenerate citizens . . . who hate our republican government, and the French revolution," as if the two sentiments were inseparable, went on to say that declaring neutrality is a legislative act like declaring war or ratifying a treaty, so for the executive to do such a thing is in theory "an absurdity—in practice a tyranny" (though late in life he apologized for his article's "intemperance of party" and its "perverted view of Presidt Washington's proclamation of neutrality").[93]

Even Jefferson had second thoughts after an emboldened Genêt arrived in Philadelphia in mid-May and went from excess to excess. That month, a French privateer had brought a captured British brigantine, the *Little Sarah*, into Philadelphia, and Genêt, deaf to the secretary of state's warning not to do so, had her fitted out as a fourteen-gun privateer and sent her to sea in July, renamed *La Petite Démocrate* and partly crewed by American sailors. He had threatened to appeal to the American people over the head of "*le vieux Washington*" to overturn the neutrality proclamation, and, true to his word, he stirred up angry mobs of armed French tars and Democratic Society zealots to picket the president's house. "The town is one continuous scene of riot," the British consul wrote. "Genet seems ready to raise the tricolor and proclaim himself proconsul." Much later, John Adams reminded Jefferson of "the terrorism excited by Genet in 1793 when ten thousand people in the streets of Philadelphia, day after day, threatened to drag Washington out of his house and effect a revolution in government or compel it to declare war in favor of the French Revolution against England."[94]

In August, amid all this commotion, Secretary of War Henry Knox brought to a cabinet meeting a broadside by Freneau, describing King Washington being guillotined. The president—who, portraitist Gilbert Stuart judged from long study of his face, normally kept under iron control "the strongest and most ungovernable passions," which, "had he been born in the forests," would have made him "the fiercest man among the savage tribes"—exploded.[95] He "got into one of those passions where he cannot command himself," Jefferson recorded; "ran on much on the personal abuse which has been bestowed on him; defied any man on earth to produce one single act of his since he had been in the government which was not done with the purest motives; . . . that *by God* he had rather be in his grave than in his present situation; that he had rather be on his farm than made *emperor of the world*; and yet here they were charging him with wanting to be a king."[96]

All the partisan strife had begun to change something within Washington. It drove him deeper into himself. Instead of caring so much about how others understood and praised his actions and motives, he began to realize that he was the best judge of his own worth. In September 1792, just after he had tried to make peace between Jefferson and Hamilton, he wrote one correspondent: "If nothing impeaching my honor, or honesty, is said, I care little for the rest. I have pursued one uniform course for three score years, and am happy in believing that the world have thought it a right one: of its being so, I am so well satisfied myself, that I shall not depart from it by turning either to the right or to the left, until I arrive at the end of my pilgrimage."[97] At the height of the Genêt Affair, he wrote his friend, Light-Horse Harry Lee, in a letter marked "Private," that, while "diabolical" men have been heaping abuse upon him, "as it respects myself, I care not; for I have a consolation within, that no earthly efforts can deprive me of, and that is, that neither ambitious nor interested motives have influenced my conduct. The arrows of malevolence, therefore, can never reach the most vulnerable part of me; though, whilst I am *up as a mark*, they will be continually aimed."[98]

By the fall of 1795, as his seventh year in office neared its close, this inner transformation was complete: he liked fame, but he loved virtue more, and the change gave him a new sense of inner wholeness and freedom, an austere and bleakly lonely self-possession, far deeper than the reserve he had learned from his childhood etiquette book. "Next to a conscientious discharge of my public duties, to carry along with me the approbation of my Constituents, would be the highest gratification my mind is susceptible of; but the latter being subordinate, I cannot make the former yield to it," he wrote Knox. If there existed a "standard of infallibility to political opinions," he wrote, no one "would resort to it with more eagerness than myself, so long as I remain a servant of the public. But as I have found no better guide hitherto than upright intentions, and close investigation, I shall adhere to these maxims while I keep the watch; leaving it to those who will come after me to explore new ways, if they like; or think them better."[99]

Almost twenty years earlier, he had declared that "to stand well in the good opinion of my Countrymen constitutes my chiefest happiness." Now he cared more about how he stood in his own opinion. Eliza Powel was right: he now possessed an empire over himself, in which he was an absolute monarch, in exact measure as he was, in his sovereign judgment, the public's most faithful slave. The emulative, convivial world of Fielding and Smollett, the anxiety about reputation, the worry about how his motives would appear—all that was largely behind him. He had had his own inner revolution, and for him, at least, the eighteenth century was over.

At the climax of the Genêt Affair, the French Revolution lurched leftward again; the Jacobin dictators recalled Citizen Genêt, doubtless to add him to Paris's mountain of headless corpses—for being *too moderate*. With the help (strangely enough) of Hamilton, he won refuge in America. Jefferson, worn out, retired from the cabinet at the end of 1793. And for a moment, calm returned.

To America, that is; but not to France, where the Terror reached its fever pitch of bloodlust and furnished an object lesson in what a revolution should not be, but can easily become. Everything Washington feared came to pass, and more. Perhaps even he could not have imagined over two hundred victims guillotined weekly for two years; people tied naked in groups and drowned in slowly sinking barges; children buried alive; victims flayed and their skin made into gloves, by brutal urban mobs agitated by artful and designing men like Maximilien Robespierre—a fanatic without a scintilla of Washington's disinterestedness, conciliation, or the prudence to know there is no "standard of infallibility to political opinions," so that not even someone as convinced as he of the purity of his motives has a right to sweep away everything that exists, in order to remake the world and human nature according to his vision of what is rational and just, killing everyone who doesn't want to be remade. "You have driven out the kings," Robespierre demanded, "but have you driven out those vices that their fatal domination bred within you?"[100] If not, off to the guillotine, in the spirit of "No man, no problem," as Stalin later put it. Washington had said again and again that mob anarchy ends in tyranny: and here was proof positive—terror indeed.

In the summer of 1794, all the volatile elements that for four years had spewed noxious vapors into American politics—Hamilton's financial system, the French Revolution, Genêt and his Democratic Societies—exploded into an uprising in western Pennsylvania that, Washington believed, threatened the very existence of the social order, just like the Paris mob.[101] To fund the government, Hamilton's 1790 financial plan included a liquor excise, galling to western farmers, who made their corn and grain into whiskey that didn't spoil and was cheap to ship to eastern markets. For two years, the government tried to explain, forbear, and accommodate local needs, Washington wrote—to no avail.[102]

In July 1794, armed Pennsylvanians torched a revenue agent's house and shot at a U.S. marshal trying to serve summonses on tax-dodging distillers, before forcing both officers to flee for their lives. Speakers whipped up a riotous mob of 6,000, one urging them to burn down Pittsburgh as God had incinerated Sodom, another recommending a Committee of Public Safety, just like Robespierre's.[103] French-style liberty poles sprang up, and talk ran high of condemning local officials to the guillotine. The leader of this so-called "Whiskey Rebellion": the vice president of the local Democratic Society.[104]

That did it for President Washington. These are "acts which . . . amount to treason, being overt acts of levying war against the United States," he thundered in his proclamation sending the militia into western Pennsylvania in August.[105] If "the laws are to be so trampled upon, with impunity, and a minority . . . is to dictate to the majority, there is an end put, at one stroke, to republican government," he wrote; "and nothing but anarchy and confusion is to be expected thereafter; . . . until all Laws are prostrate, and every one (the strongest I presume) will carve for himself."[106] And who was to blame? "I consider this insurrection as the first *formidable* fruit of the Democratic Societies," he told Harry Lee, "instituted by *artful* and *designing* members . . . primarily to sow the seeds of jealousy and distrust among the people, of the government, by destroying all confidence in the Administration of it."[107]

After a final warning to the rebels in late September, Washington, with Hamilton as chief of staff, sallied forth to Pennsylvania in October—in a coach, since the sixty-two-year-old had thrown his back out—to lead 13,000 militiamen to put down the rebellion. To negotiate a settlement, the frightened insurgents sent two emissaries, whom Washington told that only "unequivocal *proofs* of absolute submission" would avert bloodshed. The envoys' evident anxiety satisfied him that the rebels had lost heart, so he turned back to Philadelphia, leaving Hamilton to mop up. The militiamen took 150 rebels prisoner, and a court sentenced two leaders to death, though Washington later pardoned them.[108]

He did not pardon Madison, however. His dawning suspicion that his onetime confidant was mixed up with the Democratic Societies sharpened when Madison faulted him for blaming, in his November 1794 annual message to Congress, "certain self-created societies"—guess which—for having incited the Whiskey Rebels to "crimes, which reached the very existence of the social order." Such reproach, Madison told Congress, was out of line in republican government, where "the censorial power is in the people over the government, and not in the government over the people."[109] Washington, figuring that even a president had freedom of speech, was offering an opinion, not instigating a witch hunt, and when Madison's rebuke made his views about the Democratic Societies clear, Washington ended their friendship. A more decisive end to an era was Hamilton's resignation as Treasury secretary in January 1795, though Washington asked his advice at times of tension until the end of his presidency, and beyond.

It was one thing for Washington to proclaim neutrality in the European war but quite another to make it stick. While a wealth of international law existed on such matters, it was more theory than fact. Countries fighting for their lives did what they thought they had to; and Britain, seeing America's enthusiasm for Citizen Genêt's antics, concluded that its former colony intended war and responded accordingly. To starve the French, British warships began seizing American vessels trading with France or French colonies, and kidnapping American seamen, claiming that they were British nationals subject to conscription into a shorthanded Royal Navy. Nor would the British vacate their forts in the American Northwest, as the treaty ending the Revolution required, and, claiming the territory around them as their own, they incited their Indian allies to commit "murders of helpless women and innocent children along our frontiers," an outraged Washington wrote Chief Justice John Jay.[110] Misreading American intentions, Washington's plain words notwithstanding, London was doing everything it could to provoke a war it didn't want.

Angry as he was at Britain's "open and daring" provocations, the president resolved to make one last try to head off a war he thought inevitable otherwise.[111] He sent the chief justice, who had brilliantly negotiated the Treaty of Paris, which ended the Revolution, to London in April 1794 to see what he could do.

This time, Jay's hard bargaining (as the next chapter recounts) yielded seemingly meager results. In the Jay Treaty, signed in November, he got the British to give up their American forts, and he won compensation for seized U.S. ships and cargoes, couched in terms so diplomatic, though, that few could see how big a concession he'd wrested. In return, he promised that American courts would make U.S. debtors pay their British creditors. Debt-swamped southerners fumed, claiming that the Revolution had canceled what they owed to British merchants, and they further reviled Jay for not demanding payment for slaves that the redcoats had carried to freedom at the war's end. But what, they grumbled, could you expect from a man who as foreign secretary in 1784 had horrified them and westerners alike for briefly considering a treaty with Spain that would give up America's right to navigate the lower Mississippi for twenty-five years—a vital interest to southwestern pioneers—to gain trading rights benefiting northerners? Francophile Republicans also fumed. First Washington's neutrality proclamation had shrugged off America's treaty obligations to France, and now his envoy was making a treaty with *perfidious Albion*?

The Senate ratified the pact by the slimmest possible margin in June 1795. For all its apparent modesty, though, the Jay Treaty, like the neutrality proclamation, achieved Washington's goal of avoiding a ruinous war that America could lose. After all, the president wrote, explaining his rationale, it doesn't take a prophet to know "that if this country can remain in peace 20 years longer: and I devoutly pray it may do so to the end of time; such in all probability will be its population, riches, and resources, when combined with its peculiarly happy and remote Situation from the other quarters of the globe, as to bid defiance, in a just cause, to any earthly power whatsoever."[112] That's why his policy was "to be upon friendly terms with, but independent of, all the nations of the earth."[113]

As Washington's ex-friend Madison led a rancorous Republican-dominated Congress in drawn-out fussing over the Jay Treaty, the president announced a further pact, signed in October 1795: the Treaty of San Lorenzo, which gained Spain's agreement to let Americans navigate the lower Mississippi.[114] Despite the best efforts of "designing men . . . to excite a belief that there is a real difference of local interests and views" and "to misrepresent the opinions and aims of other Districts," Washington later summed up, this treaty gave westerners "a decisive proof how unfounded were the suspicions propagated among them of a policy of the General Government and in the Atlantic States unfriendly to their Interests in regard to the MISSISSIPPI." John Jay wasn't trying to harm any American's interest in 1784 any more than he was in 1794.[115]

Only later did Washington realize that Jefferson was chief among those "designing men" sowing strife, and in July 1796 he reproached his former secretary of state for "his insincerity," which he had never before suspected, as he gently put it. But now, he said, "it would neither be frank, candid, or friendly to conceal" that he had heard that Jefferson had spoken ill of him; and the more he wrote, the more he worked himself up. He could hardly believe it possible, he said, "that, while I was using my utmost exertions to establish a national character of our own, independent . . . of every nation of the earth; and wished, by steering a steady course, to preserve this Country from the horrors of a desolating war, . . . that every act of my administration would be tortured, and the grossest, most insidious mis-representations of them be made, . . . and that too in such exaggerated and indecent terms as could scarcely be applied to a Nero; a notorious defaulter; or even to a common pick-pocket."[116] A year later, Washington wouldn't refer to Jefferson by name but only as "*that man*." They never spoke again.[117]

BUT FOR ALL the rancor—irksome to him but mere static in the music of history—he had done what he set out to do. He had made the new government an established fact. Peace and prosperity reigned, thanks to the neutrality proclamation, the two foreign treaties, Hamilton's financial system, and the people's "industry," "frugality," and "spirit of commerce," which he had fostered, not squelched. With the Mississippi open, settlers poured into the Southwest—into the new states of Kentucky and Tennesee, and even farther south toward New Orleans. Others thronged into the Ohio country once the British had left their northwestern forts and Anthony Wayne had crushed the Indians whom they had spurred to war. Youngstown, Cleveland, and Dayton sprang up. On the banks of the Potomac, a new national capital slowly rose, whose site Washington had chosen, and whose planner and chief architects he had hired. The city, he predicted, would someday be "though not as large as London, yet of a magnitude inferior to few others in Europe."[118] Fittingly, it bore his name.

By the spring of 1796, he felt he had done his duty and could go home when his second term closed in March 1797, setting another precedent for (most) future presidents. "Before the curtain drops on my political life, . . . I expect for ever," though, he had a few more lines he wanted to deliver, and in May he sent Hamilton a *Farewell Address*, asking him to edit it, so it could appear before "the public in an honest; unaffected; simple garb."[119] The result, published on September 19, 1796, ranks with the wisest of the *Federalist Papers*, even as it highlights democracy's thorniest dilemma.

The Address developed more fully the idea of a culture of liberty that Washington had thought key to animating the Constitution. Like Edmund Burke, he took for granted that men act partly by reason but more often by tradition, by loyalties built up over time, by beliefs that gain authority through age, by unexamined cultural assumptions that take on the power of passions, because they are feelings of the heart as much as they are thoughts. That's why "time and habit are at least as necessary to fix the true character of Governments, as of other human institutions," he explained in the Address. "With me, a predominant motive has been to endeavour to gain time to our country to settle and mature its yet recent institutions," and to settle the "habits of thinking" crucial to a free country as well.[120]

In such a country, he noted, education was crucial, for when "a government gives force to public opinion, it is essential that public opinion should be enlightened."[121] But still more important: "Of all the dispositions and habits which lead to political prosperity, Religion and morality are indispensable supports," Washington counseled, in language that could have come from Burke's *Reflections*. "The mere politician, equally with the pious man ought to respect and to cherish them," because, quite apart from the question of their truth, they are "the firmest props of the duties of Men and citizens." Nor should anyone "indulge the supposition, that morality can be maintained without religion," for the majority act morally because they believe that an all-seeing judge watches their acts and thoughts, and dispenses rewards and punishments accordingly. A moment's reflection confirms religion's social utility: "Let it simply be asked where is the security for property, for reputation, for life, if the sense of religious obligation *desert* the oaths, which are the instruments of investigation in Courts of Justice?"[122] If you're an unbeliever, what's to stop you from lying when you put your hand on the Bible and swear to tell the truth *so help me God*?

As to what kind of religion could do the job, Washington was genially undoctrinaire. "It is now no more that toleration is spoken of, as if it was by the indulgence of one class of people, that another enjoyed the exercise of their inherent natural rights," the president had written the worried Newport, Rhode Island, Jewish congregation in 1790. "For happily the Government of the United States, which gives to bigotry no sanction, to persecution no assistance requires only that they who live under its protection should demean themselves as good citizens, in giving it on all occasions their effectual support." This is a land, he assured the "Children of the Stock of Abraham," in his favorite image of security, where "every one shall sit in safety under his own vine and figtree, and there shall be none to make him afraid."[123] Indeed, he liked the story of the Jews' deliverance from Egyptian bondage to the land God had promised Abraham well enough to mention several times that America would be to "the poor, the needy, & oppressed of the Earth . . . the second Land of promise," where they could "dwell in peace, fulfilling the first & great Commandment."[124]

His own belief was deep but similarly undoctrinaire: the world has meaning; God has a plan for it; "the allwise disposer of events has hitherto watched over my steps" and will continue to "mark the course so plainly, as that I cannot mistake the way," just as Providence protects the United States.[125] Indeed, surely "peculiar scenes of felicity are reserved for this country," he wrote, for "I do not believe, that Providence has done so much for nothing."[126] Though he belonged to the Episcopal Church, he attended irregularly, church-hopped from sect to sect when he wasn't at Mount Vernon, stood rather than knelt to pray, and didn't take communion. Though he had no clergyman attend his deathbed, he had a priest read the Episcopal burial service at his funeral, after which an aproned Freemason from the lodge he had joined as a young man conducted the rites of that brotherhood.[127] A latitudinarian in the broadest sense, he left no stone unturned.

Rousseau once wrote that a "good and sound constitution is one under which the law holds sway over the hearts of the citizens," and in the same spirit, Washington's Farewell Address urged Americans, now that they had so epically vindicated "the right of the people to make and to alter their Constitution," to cherish this "offspring of our own choice" as "sacredly obligatory upon all."[128] He counseled them to develop "a cordial, habitual and immovable attachment" to "the national Union" as "the Palladium of your political safety and prosperity," and he hoped they would feel more "pride of Patriotism" in being Americans than in being Virginians or Pennsylvanians. Along with "the love of liberty" itself, which Washington thought was "[i]nterwoven . . . with every ligament of your hearts," he considered these beliefs key to an American culture of liberty.[129]

Of course the Farewell Address is a document of an age, as well as for all time; and these last points show the scars of President Washington's political battles, when he thought that the Jefferson- and Madison-supported Democratic Societies had not only fomented government-destroying anarchy in the Whiskey Rebellion, but also had led Kentuckians to consider secession from the Union by their lie that John Jay had intentionally sold out western settlers in not pushing for Mississippi navigation rights.[130] Even after eight years in office, Washington feared that the greatest accomplishments of the Founding—the Union and the Constitution—might not be settled and matured enough to be permanent.

So in addition to urging cultural safeguards for that inheritance, he also condemned the forces threatening it. "Let me now . . . warn you in the most solemn manner against the baneful effects of the Spirit of Party," which, "unfortunately, is inseparable from our nature, having its root in the strongest passions of the human Mind"—especially in "that love of power, and the proneness to abuse it, which predominates in the human heart." That spirit "agitates the Community with ill founded jealousies and false alarms, kindles the animosity of one part against another, foments occasionally riot and insurrection." Parties can "become potent engines, by which cunning, ambitious and unprincipled men will be enabled to subvert the Power of the People, and to usurp for themselves the reins of Government," the president cautioned. "There is an opinion that parties in free countries are useful checks upon the Administration of the Government and serve to keep alive the spirit of Liberty. This within certain limits is probably true," Washington conceded, but, "there being constant danger of excess, the effort ought to be, by force of public opinion, to mitigate and assuage" that danger.[131]

But the democratic dilemma is: How? Even if most Americans became moral, religious, well educated, and imbued with Washington's culture of liberty, there is still no standard of infallibility to political opinions, to use Washington's own words—and there *can* be none, for opinion isn't fact.[132] There will always be disagreements and animosities, clashes of interests and worldviews, and struggles for power among the people themselves, who are the source of power. So while Washington's ideal was a government that would calmly frame "wholesome plans digested by common councils and modefied by mutual interests"—an ideal based on his experience of the Constitutional Convention and one that Madison had shared until the Convention rejected his vision of a senate of enlightened sages—the tone of American democratic government from 1790 onward has, perhaps unavoidably, been that of factional strife.[133]

If there are no standards of political infallibility, that doesn't mean there are no standards at all, of course, and Washington's call for habits of thinking that are temperate, judicious, informed, patriotic, and virtuous is a better recipe for good policy making than rancor, suspicion, utopianism, and demagoguery. Washington's Address proposed the surest standard: his legendary prudence. Is there a doubt whether a democratically reached policy is right? "Let experience solve it," the Address advised. Don't trust "mere speculation." Do "a fair and full experiment."[134] There may not be infallibility to opinions, but there *is* truth, and one can find it out after the fact if not before, and adjust course accordingly.

With the Republicans' infatuation with the French Revolution in mind, Washington urged the same prudence in foreign affairs. A rational calculation of national interest should govern dealings with other countries, as he had first written almost twenty years earlier.[135] Never, the Farewell Address counseled, should we form "permanent, inveterate antipathies against particular Nations and passionate attachments for others," for we will end up making decisions "contrary to the best calculations of policy," adopting "through passion what reason would reject." We should "steer clear of permanent Alliances," Washington concluded, trusting to "temporary alliances for extraordinary emergencies."[136]

In his first address to Congress (and often thereafter), Washington had stated his key foreign-policy principle—"To be prepared for war is one of the most effectual means of preserving peace"—and he recurred to that theme in the Farewell Address, noting that "timely disbursements to prepare for danger frequently prevent much greater disbursements to repel it."[137] And in his very last speech to the legislature, in December 1796, he added one further wrinkle. "To an active external Commerce, the protection of a Naval force is indispensable." As experience had taught him, a country can't otherwise "secure respect to a Neutral Flag." In fact, a strong navy "may even prevent the necessity of going to War, by discouraging" depredations that leave no other choice.[138] Following this advice might have prevented the War of 1812.

Washington had just turned sixty-five when he returned home in March 1797, and his time there proved cruelly short. Everywhere,

Mount Vernon showed "wounds . . . sustained by an absence and neglect of eight years," its owner wrote. "I find myself in the situation, nearly, of a young beginner; for although I have not houses to build . . . yet I have not one or scarcely anything else about me that does not require considerable repairs," he wrote after two weeks back. Even the floor of his new dining room sagged and needed strengthening. "I am already surrounded by Joiners, Masons, Painters &ca &ca. and . . . I have scarcely a room to put a friend into or to set in myself, without the Music of hammers, or the odoriferous smell of Paint." He fretted that "the expence of repairs almost as great, and the employment of attending to Workmen almost as much, as if I had commenced an entire new establishment."[139]

And he was worried about money. As a business venture, Mount Vernon was a flop. He now had twice as many slaves as he needed, so feeding and clothing them made the estate a break-even operation, at best. "To sell the overplus I cannot, because I am principled against this kind of traffic in the human species," he wrote in the last year of his life. "What then is to be done? Something must or I shall be ruined."[140]

As president, he had had so little success in converting his managers to profitable scientific-farming techniques that he had tried to lease out four of the estate's five farms to skilled English farmers, whom he asked agronomist Arthur Young to try to recruit, arming him with an enticing description of Mount Vernon that is as infused with love as Odysseus's depiction of his homeland of Ithaca, whose beauty in his eyes is bound up with its fertility and usefulness. "No estate in United America is more pleasantly situated than this," the president wrote. "It lyes in a high, dry and healthy Country. . . . Its margin is washed by more than ten miles of tide water; from the bed of which, and the enumerable coves, inlets, and small marshes with wch. it abounds, an inexhaustible fund of rich mud may be drawn as a manure. . . . This River . . . is well supplied with various kinds of fish at all Seasons of the year . . . ; the whole shore in short is one entire fishery."[141]

But he found no takers and planned to do the upgrading himself—which he never got to do. Meanwhile, still land-rich and cash-poor, he made ends meet by selling off $50,000 worth of his western property between 1794 and 1799.[142]

He needed money not only to support his expensive estate but also because he had so many relatives dependent upon him, including step-grandchildren, nieces, and nephews, whom Martha had raised and whom he had paid to educate.[143] When the ex-president moved back to Mount Vernon, the once-noisy household was quieter. Only Martha's witty, talented, and sharp-tongued granddaughter, Nelly Custis, whom Washington loved, came with them. Her grandmother had supervised the education of what she called the "wild little creature," sending her to boarding school, giving her painting and music lessons, and relentlessly making her practice the harpsichord. "The poor girl would play and cry, cry and play, for long hours, under the immediate eye of her grandmother, a rigid disciplinarian in all things," Nelly's brother recalled.[144] Washington had bought her an opulent, London-made harpsichord in 1793, and back at Mount Vernon, in the Little Parlor where it now stands, Nelly would enchant family and visitors alike with the spell she could conjure from its two keyboards.[145] For all Martha's strictness, she "has been ever more than a mother to me, and the president the most affectionate of fathers," Nelly wrote after they had died. "I love them more than anyone."[146]

In trying to rent his farms, Washington had hoped not only to assure himself an adequate, predictable income but also, as he told his secretary, Tobias Lear, "to liberate a certain species of property which I possess, very repugnantly to my own feelings; but which imperious necessity compels."[147] The deal, he hoped, would let him free his slaves, whom the English farmers would then hire as ordinary field hands.[148]

His motives were both principled and practical. Though in May 1786 he had gently pooh-poohed Lafayette's scheme for a South American colony of freed slaves, only four months later he had decided that "I never mean (unless some particular circumstances should compel me to it) to possess another slave by purchase; it being among my first wishes to see some plan adopted, by the legislature by which slavery in this Country may be abolished by slow, sure, & imperceptable degrees."[149] Nor would he sell or rent out his slaves, for that would mean breaking up slave families, to which "I have an aversion."[150] He once stingingly condemned overseers as a class, because "they seem to consider a Negro much in the same light as they do the brute beasts, on the farms; and often times treat them as inhumanly."[151]

But beside its evil, he thought that slavery was just not tenable. "I can clearly foresee that nothing but the rooting out of slavery can perpetuate the existence of our union, by consolidating it in a common bond of principle," Washington told one visitor. Moreover, he saw every day that while masters became "imperious and dissipated from the habit of commanding slaves and living in a measure without control," slaves were "growing more and more insolent and difficult to govern."[152] So even before federal government action, he wrote, "I wish from my soul that the Legislature of this State could see the policy of a gradual Abolition of Slavery; It would prevt. much future mischief."[153]

Washington the slave owner knew about slavery's dialectic of insolence and imperiousness from the inside. As his retirement neared, his wife's favorite maid, Oney Judge, whom he had let roam freely around Philadelphia, recoiled at the thought of returning to hardbound slavery in Virginia, especially when Martha let slip that she planned to bequeath the twenty-two-year-old to one of her granddaughters, whom Judge disliked. So she ran away to Portsmouth, New Hampshire. The Washingtons, unable to see that their affection didn't outweigh liberty in Judge's heart, assumed that only a rake (and probably a French one) could have seduced her away.

But when a friend of Nelly Custis's ran into Judge in Portsmouth, she learned that there had been no rake. Acknowledging how kindly the Washingtons had treated her, Judge explained herself: "I want to be free, misses; wanted to learn to read and write." Outraged at her maid's supposed ingratitude, Mrs. Washington pressed her husband to wield his power to bring her back. Far exceeding his legal authority, Washington asked Treasury secretary Oliver Wolcott to order a Portsmouth customs official to kidnap Oney and send her to Virginia. The official complied, but when he seized the girl, she unsettled him by saying that no one had seduced her but that "a thirst for complete freedom" had led her to flee. Out of her "great affection and reverence for her master and mistress," the now-hesitant official reported to Washington, she would willingly "return and serve with fidelity during the lives of the president and his lady, if she could be freed on their decease." Washington huffily rejected any such negotiation with a slave, and Judge stayed put. Three years later, Martha asked a nephew who was traveling to Portsmouth to try to get Judge back. Now married and a mother, Judge replied, "I am free now and choose to remain so." And she did.[154]

Washington revealed what was on his mind perhaps more than he intended when he explained his hard line to the customs man: "however well disposed I might be to a gradual abolition, or even an entire emancipation of that description of people," he wrote, freeing Judge now would be both unfair, for it would "reward *unfaithfulness*," and imprudent, sowing "discontent" in "the minds of all her fellow servants."[155] Two and a half years later, when he sat down to make a new will, he decreed just that emancipation, righting, as far as he was able, the great wrong he had taken part in all his life. He wanted to do right both for virtue's sake and, still nursing his lifelong love of fame, to ensure "that no reproach may attach to me when I have taken my departure for the land of the spirits."[156] So crucial did he think the matter that he wrote the will himself "over many of my leisure hours," with no lawyer's help, and though the deeply considered result might seem "crude and incorrect" as a piece of legal draftsmanship, he expected his intent would nevertheless be "plain, and explicit."[157]

After leaving his whole estate to Martha, he directed that, after her death, "all the Slaves which I hold in *my own right*, shall receive their freedom." The intrepid horseman Billy Lee, now old, crippled, and garrulous, would be free at once, however, with a $30-a-year pension, "as a testimony of my sense of his attachment to me, and for his faithful services during the Revolutionary War." The will set up a fund to feed and clothe those too old and infirm, or too young, to support themselves after emancipation—as it did until the last beneficiary died in 1833. Freed orphans were to be apprenticed to trades until they were twenty-five, and taught to read and write. And Washington "most pointedly, and solemnly enjoin[ed]" his executors "to see that this clause respecting Slaves, and every part thereof be religiously fulfilled . . . without evasion, neglect or delay."[158]

From his own ambivalence, he understood better than most the urge to evade and delay: only on his deathbed did he ask his wife to get two wills out of his desk and burn the one he'd written in 1775, suggesting that he finally opted for emancipation only on the brink of the grave.[159] But as a man who thought it wrong to break up enslaved families, he faced a special problem in freeing Mount Vernon's slaves: he owned only 124 of them, while the other 153, belonging to the estate of his wife's first husband, neither he nor Martha could free. So while liberating his own slaves upon his death, or even earlier, would accomplish justice and solve the economic problem of more slaves than he needed in one stroke, such a course, "though earnestly wished by me," presented "insuperable difficulties," he thought, because his and Martha's slaves were so intermixed by marriage that freeing one set without the other would "excite the most painful sensations, if not disagreeable consequences" from those remaining in slavery, while their own spouses or children went free.[160]

But on whom would those "disagreeable consequences" fall? They fell on the widowed Martha, whose demise would mean freedom for 124 souls. She "did not feel as though her life was safe in their hands," she told Abigail Adams, since "it was their interest to get rid of her." In short order, someone tried to burn down Mount Vernon, and a year after Washington's death, his frightened wife set his slaves free.[161]

Early in his retirement, Washington penned a whimsical account of a typical day back home: up at dawn, make sure "my hirelings are

. . . in their places," discover some new "wounds" in Mount Vernon, eat breakfast, "mount my horse and ride round my farms . . . until it is time to dress for dinner," then "a walk, and Tea, brings me within the dawn of Candlelight." Every day, "I resolve, that, as soon as the glimmering taper, supplies the place of the great luminary, I will retire to my writing Table and acknowledge the letters I have received; but when the lights are brought, I feel tired, and disinclined to engage in this work, conceiving that the next night will do as well." Notice, he added, "that in this detail no mention is made of any time allotted for reading. . . . I have not looked into a book since I came home, nor shall I be able to do it until . . . the nights grow longer; when possibly I may be looking in doomsday book."[162] Two years later, acknowledging the news of his last brother's death, he wrote, "[W]hen I shall be called upon to follow . . . is known only to the giver of life. When the summons comes I shall endeavour to obey it with a good grace."[163]

It came in less than three months. On December 12, 1799, he rode round his farms, as usual, but hail began to fall, and then snow. Not wanting to keep his guests waiting when he got back, he came to the dinner table without changing his wet clothes or drying his hair. The next day, with snow still falling and now with a sore throat, he walked down toward the river to mark trees for felling, still sculpting his estate. He woke in the middle of the night, his throat aflame; and though he felt ill enough to wake Martha, he wouldn't let her go get help for fear she'd catch cold. When morning came, he could hardly "utter a word intelligibly," wrote Tobias Lear, who sent for a doctor.[164]

Two more came in the course of the day, and the trio drained about half the blood from Washington's body and dosed him twice with a powerful laxative, orthodox but harmful steps. The youngest doctor, judging (probably correctly) that an acutely inflamed epiglottis was closing the patient's throat and suffocating him, suggested a tracheotomy to bypass the obstruction and allow him to breathe, but as the operation had been performed only some two dozen times since the year 1500, his seniors dismissed the possibly lifesaving idea. Struggling for breath, the sixty-seven-year-old Washington told Lear that he knew "the disorder would prove fatal," and to one of the physicians he said, "Doctor, I die hard, but I am not afraid to go." He was afraid, however, of being put in Mount Vernon's family vault while still alive, so he made Lear promise not to bury him for at least three days after he died. Holding back tears, Lear could say nothing, and Washington asked if he'd understood. The grief-stricken secretary raised his hand in assent. " 'Tis well," Washington said—and took his departure for the land of the spirits.[165]

His wife never slept in their bedroom again but moved to the plainest of plain little rooms in Mount Vernon's attic. For four days before the December 18 funeral, Washington lay in his New Room, under the light of its stately Venetian window, and as news of his death spread, church bells tolled and shops shuttered across the land.[166]

In the will he had so meticulously drafted, Washington had lovingly cataloged his landholdings—some 51,000 acres (not counting Mount Vernon), which he conservatively valued at $465,000, which with livestock, securities, and building lots in Alexandria and the federal city brought his total estate to $530,000. To defend those acres, and more, the old soldier left one of his swords to each of his six nephews, with "an injunction not to unsheath them for the purpose of shedding blood, except it be for self-defence, or in the defence of their Country, and its rights; and in the latter case to keep them unsheathed, and prefer falling with them in their hands, to the relinquishment thereof." And he urged his executors "not to be precipitate in disposing of the landed property, . . . experience having fully evinced, that the price of land" has "been progressively rising, and cannot be long checked in its increasing value."[167]

Such was his faith in the boundless future of the nation he had founded.

6

John Jay: America's Indispensable Diplomat

Few could fathom why fifty-five-year-old John Jay turned down President John Adams's nomination to rejoin the Supreme Court when his two terms as New York's governor ended in 1801. What would lead him, in the hale prime of life, to retire instead to the plain yellow house he'd just built on a hilltop at the remote northern edge of Westchester County, two-days' ride from Manhattan, where visitors were few and the mail and newspapers came but once a week? After twenty-seven years at the forge of the new nation's Founding, why would so lavishly talented a man give up his vital role on the world stage for the quiet life of a gentleman farmer?

But just that option—to enjoy the peace and domesticity that "gladden ye Heart, & in some Measure gild this iron cage with Streakes of Gold," as he wrote his father-in-law—is what he had labored more than a quarter century to bring about, and he felt he had achieved it.[1] As the first chief justice both of New York and of the United States, as president of Congress and governor of his state, as secretary for foreign affairs, and, most important, as the diplomat who stamped his vision on America's foreign policy for generations to come, he had striven to ensure for his countrymen the peace, order, and stability that had seemed to him fragile and elusive from the moment he was born.

Even from before he was born, in fact. When you visit his comfortably solid and serene Federal house, overflowing with the rich treasures and curiosities he and the four prosperous generations of his descendants who lived there accumulated, it comes as a shock to read his family history as he sketched it in old age. It is a record of oppression and violence. His Huguenot great-grandfather, a rich merchant in La Rochelle, had sent his eighteen-year-old son Auguste on a trading voyage to Africa (for slaves, no doubt, though Jay is silent) in 1683, two years before Louis XIV revoked the 1598 Edict of Nantes, which had granted Protestants civil liberty in Catholic France. Like so many Jews in Nazi Germany centuries later, the Huguenots should have seen "the fury of persecution" that was coming in 1685 and fled sooner, Jay remarks. "Such, however, is human nature."

Only after troops had leveled La Rochelle's Protestant church and occupied great-grandfather Pierre Jay's house did Pierre send his family to England and then clandestinely intercept one of his returning ships before it reached port, diverting it across the Channel to join them. Once sold, the ship and its cargo kept him in comfort ever after, though the French treasury swallowed up the fortune left behind. With no word of what had happened, young Auguste, Jay's grandfather, returned from Africa to find his family gone and his world turned upside down. Friends snuck him aboard a ship bound for South Carolina, whose miasmal climate soon drove him to New York.[2]

Hired by Frederick Philipse, one of the colony's richest merchants, Auguste—now Augustus—entered a world with its own brand of violence and instability, since among other ventures Philipse traded with Madagascar pirates for slaves.[3] On one voyage Augustus fell into the hands of Saint-Malo's dread privateers, from whose fortress he daringly escaped, though his shipmate didn't make it. Of grandfather Augustus's marriage to Anna Maria Bayard, all Jay reports is that one of her forebears was a Protestant theology professor in Paris, compelled to flee French anti-Protestant oppression for refuge in Holland.[4] Their son, Peter—Jay's father—grew up to marry Mary Van Cortlandt, granddaughter of Frederick Philipse, whose Protestant family had been driven by Catholic persecution from Bohemia to Holland and then to New York. Thus Jay, says his son and biographer William, could claim the distinction of having three "ancestors who chose to abandon their country rather than their religion."[5] Like the Plymouth Pilgrims and so many later immigrants to the New World, Jay and his family never forgot that they'd escaped to a unique refuge from the Old World's murderous tyranny.

A sense of life's fragility hung over Jay's childhood; at six, he was already grave and reserved, his father said, though "indowed with a very good capacity."[6] Before he was born, smallpox had blinded an elder brother and sister, for whom, Jay later wrote, "this World has not been a Paradize";[7] of his four other siblings, one was retarded and another emotionally disturbed. Shortly after John's birth on Manhattan's Pearl Street in 1745, Peter Jay moved his brood to a farm bordering Long Island Sound in Rye, an easier setting for his two blind children. (You can visit it today, rebuilt beyond recognition.) Though Peter had grown rich as a merchant, married an heiress, and counted most of the colony's Dutch and Huguenot establishment as his relatives, and though he and Mary were loving parents, Jay's childhood after he went to boarding school at age eight in the French-speaking Huguenot town of Nouvelle Rochelle had its share of privations. His eccentric schoolmaster treated his pupils "with little food and much scolding," Jay's son reports. The boy struggled to keep the snow off his bed by blocking up his broken window with scraps of wood.[8]

After entering six-year-old King's College (later Columbia) at fourteen and spending four happy years among his twenty-odd fellow collegians, Jay—six feet tall, stick-thin, round-shouldered, and fine-boned, with a sensitive mouth and thoughtful, melancholy eyes—began his law studies as a clerk for kindly, whimsical Benjamin Kissam, who perceived at once the young man's talent. Your "Whirl of Imagination," he wrote his clerk, "bespeaks the Grandeur . . . of the Intellectual Source from whence the Current flows."[9] Fellow clerk Lindley Murray, whose school grammars and readers later sold in the millions, remembered him as "remarkable for strong reasoning powers, comprehensive views, indefatigable application, and uncommon firmness of mind."[10] Right after Jay joined the bar in 1768, lameness temporarily sidelined the successful Kissam, and he unhesitatingly turned his cases over to Jay.

But Jay's placid interval was short-lived. In the first year of his four-year apprenticeship, Parliament passed the Stamp Act, and six months later the American Revolution had its prologue a few blocks from Kissam's John Street office at New York's old city hall on Wall Street, where Federal Hall now stands. There the Stamp Act Congress convened in October 1765, only the second time that representatives of the American colonies had ever met together and the first time they themselves, rather than royal authorities, had convened such a conclave—a measure that shocked the Lords of Trade in London.[11] More important, it was the first time that the colonies unitedly drafted a Declaration of Rights, in which they claimed "the Freedom of a People, and the Undoubted Right of Englishmen, that no Taxes be imposed on them, but with their own Consent."[12] Such big doings down the street—especially since one of New York's five delegates to the Congress was a Bayard cousin of Jay's, and another was Judge Robert R. Livingston, father of Jay's best friend—made so strong an impression on the nineteen-year-old that eleven years later, at the First Continental Congress, he effortlessly recalled in debate the rules that the Stamp Act Congress had followed.[13]

Historians speak of the 1765 Congress, with its fulsome pledges of loyalty to the king, as conservative. It was a funny kind of conservatism, though; for when Judge Livingston, probable author of the group's *Address to the King*, wrote New York's London agent that no one should view the meeting as factious, since it aimed to divert Parliament from a course that sooner or later "will naturally render the colonies independent,"[14] he was veiling a threat under an assurance. The *New-York Gazette* had already made that threat explicit four months earlier, writing that with Britain and her colonies at such cross-purposes, "the Connection between them ought to cease—and sooner or later it must inevitably cease."[15]

Unambiguously unconservative was the response of a New York mob a week after the Congress broke up. At dusk on November 1, the day the Stamp Act was to take effect, a mob of sailors, youths, farmers, and blacks, along with some more properous folk, began to form, armed with clubs and torches, and threatening to bury Royal Artillery major Thomas James, who reportedly had vowed to cram the stamps down New Yorkers' throats with the point of his sword. Outside Fort George at Manhattan's southern tip, where the first shipment of stamps lay under Lieutenant Governor Cadwallader Colden's protection, the crowd hanged effigies of Colden and ex–Prime Minister Lord Bute, before burning them in a bonfire, along with the outraged Colden's cherished carriage of state. Then the rioters surged to Major James's newly furnished house and wrecked it, frenziedly smashing rich furniture, mirrors, paintings, and even windows and doors, slitting and shredding the mattresses and silk curtains, stealing the silver, trampling the garden, guzzling the wine, and smearing butter over what remained. At four in the morning they straggled off.[16] Peter Jay witnessed part of the riot and rushed his family "to our more peaceable habitation in the country."[17] Rumors of mobs coming to plunder the town swirled for the next week, and British commander in chief Thomas Gage warned Colden that if such a mob materialized and his redcoats opened fire on it, the result would be insurrection and civil war.[18]

In this turbulent atmosphere—and rioting went on sporadically in the city of 18,000 for the next decade—John Jay came of age and worked out his view of the world and of himself.[19] A week after the Stamp Act passed (but before the news reached America), he was still an adolescent, writing one of his few letters of this period, a passionate, unguarded avowal of friendship to Judge Livingston's son, also named Robert R. Livingston, with an eager pleasure in young Robert's having "opened wide those Doors of Friendship, into which I had long desired to enter" and looking forward to "our voyage to Eternity."[20] But after New York's November riots, the city's thirty or so lawyers suspended business because they refused to use the hated stamps required for legal documents (with unerring stupidity, young George III and his ministers had passed a radicalizing measure that fell hardest on America's opinion-forming lawyers and journalists). Hence law clerk Jay had ample time to meditate upon the ferment seething around him. By the last year of his legal apprenticeship, 1768, everyone at the lawyer-dominated Debating Society that Jay belonged to knew what one of the debaters meant (in a match that Jay's side won) when he spoke feelingly of "the Blessings of order and Tranquility and of the pernicious Consequences of Faction and Riot."[21]

Looking back on this period a decade later in a letter to young Livingston—who had been his law partner from 1768 to 1770 and would go on to become chancellor of New York, secretary for foreign affairs, one of the negotiators of the Louisiana Purchase, and the backer of Robert Fulton's steamboat enterprise—Jay mused on the changes he saw in himself. Back in 1765, he wrote, "Bashfulness and Pride, rendered me . . . sensible of Indignities . . . [and] prone to sudden Resentment."[22] How right he was about the stiff-necked pride, a mixture of ambition, stubborn principle, and hair-trigger defensiveness against an ever-present sense of threat. A few weeks before his college graduation, he got briefly suspended for refusing to snitch on a classmate and brandishing the college bylaws to show that no rule required him to do so. As a novice lawyer he had all but challenged the colonial attorney general to a duel for conduct he thought "represents me in an insignificant Point of View," and he even expressed willingness to duel with an aggrieved young man he'd turned down for membership in the fashionable dancing assembly he cochaired.[23] But though in those days he seemed more suited for life as a professor in some ivory-tower village than as "a citizen of the World," he told Livingston, he had since developed the requisite urbanity, flexibility, and self-mastery.[24]

Though he didn't mention it, he'd gained one other quality he'd confessed to having lacked in 1765—an understanding of women. For in 1774 he married his friend Robert's second cousin, Sarah Van Brugh Livingston, who shines out from her vivid letters like all of Jane Austen's winsome heroines rolled into one, with sense and sensibility to spare. Then seventeen while her husband was twenty-eight, Sally was one of the witty, spunky, and beautiful daughters of New Jersey governor William Livingston, of *Independent Reflector* fame. Of Sally, the courtly Gouverneur Morris bantered the year before her marriage, "Never was a Little Creature so admired (I speak seriously). . . . As to her Heart when in the Midst of her Admirers it singeth with Joy. . . . The rosy Fingers of Pleasure paint her Cheeks with double Crimson. . . . And so it will continue if the Whim does not take her to get in Love."[25] But the whim did take her, and as her sister Kitty wrote a few years later, "Mr. & Mrs. Jay can be unhappy no where. They love each other too well."[26]

When the couple returned from their wedding trip in late May, though, Jay, like grandfather Augustus before him, found the world turned upside down. While he was gone, news had reached New York of the first of Parliament's Intolerable Acts, closing Boston's port in retaliation for the December 1773 Boston Tea Party—of which New Yorkers had held their own version the week before the Jays' wedding, dumping overboard the first cargo of East India tea to reach town.[27] Jay, by now a leading lawyer earning £1,000 a year, found himself already named to a committee to correspond with the other colonies and decide what to do, a committee whose numbers, form, and name shifted over the next two years as the currents of New York politics—Livingstonite and De Lanceyite, merchant and mechanic—ebbed and flowed, but that ended up running New York City and the entire colony. The committee joined the call for a continental congress, to which Jay won election in July 1774.[28]

Jay's townsmen pegged this youngest of all the congressional delegates as a conservative, as did Benjamin Franklin from his perch in London; and certainly when an overwrought Patrick Henry exclaimed at the Congress's start that "Government is at an End. All distinctions are thrown out. . . . We are in a State of Nature," Jay mildly retorted, "I cant yet think all Government is at an End. The Measure of Arbitrary power is not full, and I think it must run over, before We undertake to frame a new Constitution." Delegates shouldn't get carried away and think "We came to frame an American constitution, instead of indeavouring to correct the faults in an old one."[29] A reasonable remonstrance to Britain, Jay hoped, coupled with a determined trade boycott, ought to bring the ministry to its senses. Jay's conservatism consisted chiefly in this: that he would omit no effort—consistent with the rights of man and of Englishmen—to avoid an irreparable breach.

Assigned to write Congress's *Address to the People of Great Britain*, Jay explained what those rights were. There's no reason, he declared, "why English subjects, who live three thousand miles from the royal palace, should enjoy less liberty than those who are three hundred miles distant from it." As English subjects, "no power on earth has a right to take our property from us without our consent" or our "inestimable right of trial by jury"—the last shield of ordinary citizens against arbitrary state power—as Britain has done in setting up vice-admiralty courts, in which "a single man, a creature of the crown," sits in judgment in tax-evasion cases on defendants presumed guilty until they prove their innocence. If Britons allow such injustices to befall their American cousins, they should keep two things in mind, Jay cautioned. First, "We will never submit to be hewers of wood or drawers of water for any ministry or nation in the world." Second, "take care that you do not fall into the pit that is preparing for us."[30] Still, even after the king ignored Congress's first petition, even after Concord and Lexington, Jay pressed for one last-ditch try in the Second Continental Congress, John Dickinson's fruitless July 1775 *Olive Branch Petition*, some of whose language Jay supplied. But he remained realistic: in expressing his hope for an enduring American union with Great Britain, he conceded, "God knows how the Contest will end."[31]

More realistically still, while Congress was extending its olive branch with one hand, it was gathering up arrows with the other. In May 1775, in response to rumors that Britain was readying troops to enforce its will and might land them in New York, Congress advised New Yorkers "to persevere the more vigorously in preparing for their defence, as it is very uncertain whether the . . . conciliatory Measures will be successful."[32] In June, Congress began to raise an army and named George Washington its chief, two days before the Battle of Bunker Hill showed the British they faced an unexpectedly hard war. Passing through New York when news of the fierce fighting arrived, Washington, realizing that the politically divided colony's royal governor, William Tryon, would probably start arming the Loyalists, issued his first official order—to arrest Tryon if he did.[33]

Both the rumors of invasion and Washington's instincts about the Loyalists proved correct, and John Jay rushed to counter each threat. To prepare for the invasion, he had to deal with an unintended consequence of the trade boycott he had championed and helped enforce. Not only did the ban fail to stem England's harshness, as planned, but also it kept the colonies from stockpiling war supplies they turned out to need desperately. By the time even reluctant rebels like Jay understood that "the Sword must decide the Controversy," New Yorkers were reduced to stripping the lead out from between their windowpanes to cast into bullets, and melting down their door knockers and church bells for cannon.[34] Pathetically, until better weapons turned up, Jay sent from Philadelphia a well-designed spear for New York craftsmen to copy.

After the new British commander in chief William Howe moved the strategic center of the war to New York, aiming to use its great harbor as the hub of naval operations and to take control of the Hudson River, cutting off New England from the rest of America and then conquering the colonies one by one, Jay went on a wild ride through Connecticut, rounding up cannon from the Salisbury foundry to defend the river and heavy chain to block the Royal Navy from sailing up it.[35] But supplies—everything from bullets to blankets to boots—remained scarce for the entire war, and in later years Jay never forgot Washington's account of how his barefoot soldiers left bloody tracks in the snow.[36]

As for the Loyalists, New York was notable among the colonies for the strength of its residents' attachment to the Mother Country; at least a third wholeheartedly supported the king and another third trimmed from side to side. After the brothers Howe, general and admiral, sailed into New York Harbor on June 29, 1776, turning it, over the next few weeks, into "a wood of pine trees" with the masts of eighty-two warships from the Lower Bay to the Tappan Zee, so that it seemed "all London was afloat"—once the British occupied the city in September and kept it as a stronghold for the next seven years—the whole colony became a dragon-ridden theater of threat, fear, and violence.[37] If John Jay had seen one kind of ferocious anarchy in the urban riots of 1765, when he watched men in a frenzy of murderous destructiveness of the sort that had haunted his imagination from childhood, he lived through a different kind of anarchy, no less fearsome and instructive about human nature and its brutish capacity for evil, from 1776 to 1778.

Sitting on the cool veranda of his Westchester farmhouse before moving in to dinner in his richly carpeted dining room, with its "JJ"-monogrammed Chinese-export dishes bought for his wedding, its table and twenty-four chairs of the finest and heaviest mahogany skillfully carved in the simplest, least pretentious late-eighteenth-century style, an elderly John Jay talked of these times one memorable evening to his son William's boyhood schoolmate, James Fenimore Cooper, who became the new country's first major novelist.[38] Two weeks before the British entered New York Harbor, the colony's Provincial Congress, of which Jay was a member even while he was a Continental Congressman, had assigned him to chair a committee to deal with spies and saboteurs, and he evoked for his young friend Cooper the shadowy world of what he called "plots, conspiracies, and chimeras dire" that he would occupy for some time to come.[39] He found that Governor Tryon had indeed been raising a corps of New York's British sympathizers to support the invading army when it arrived, funneling money to them through the city's mayor. More alarmingly, he found that the plotters included a soldier of George Washington's bodyguard, who, according to later rumor (never proved), plotted to kill the General. The mayor went to jail, the guardsman to the gallows.[40]

What Cooper remembered from that long evening's talk was Jay's description of how, as head of the Committee for Detecting Conspiracies, he had run a spy ring in Westchester and the Hudson Valley, once the British had occupied Manhattan, Staten Island, and all of Long Island, a tale Cooper elaborated in 1821 into the very first best-selling American novel, *The Spy*.[41] With the Royal Navy commanding Long Island Sound and part of the Hudson, and the British army driving Washington's ragged force across New Jersey, politically divided Westchester, Cooper recounts, "had many of the features of a civil war," with the British invaders stoking internal strife by arming troops of Loyalist auxiliaries.[42] In response, the Americans formed their own bands of irregulars to harass both the redcoats and their ragtag auxiliaries. Both guerrilla groups, the Patriot "Skinners" and the Loyalist "Cow-Boys," tended to degenerate into pitiless marauders, Cooper wrote, "whose sole occupation appears to have been that of relieving their fellow-citizens from any little excess of temporal prosperity they might be thought to enjoy"—as happened to John Jay's father and siblings, leaving them only their clothes and their lives. They were lucky, though, as this gang of Cow-Boys murdered some of their other victims.[43]

Oppression and injustice reigned, says Cooper; "the law was momentarily extinct in that particular district, and justice was administered subject to the bias of personal interests and the passions of the strongest." The locals lived in doubt and fear of predators—banditti of ruffians, as Tom Paine described the State of Nature's savage hordes—often too demoralized to plant crops, distrustful of their neighbors, and hiding their real sympathies, if they had them.[44] Patrick Henry was wrong in saying that America had returned to the State of Nature in 1774, but in Westchester in the late 1770s—and in war-ravaged New Jersey, where the same marauding gangs clashed and pillaged—it was Thomas Hobbes's war of all against all, a laboratory demonstration for political philosophers and a graduate education for John Jay.[45]

Though Jay never named him, he told Cooper the story of one of the spies he had run: Enoch Crosby, whose 1832 deposition requesting a federal pension recounts adventures much like those of Cooper's hero, Harvey Birch. A virtuoso of deception and double-dealing, brave, cool, resourceful, and patriotic, Crosby, surviving hair-raisingly narrow escapes, helped American troops capture some hundred recruits to the British forces, some wholehearted Loyalists, some opportunistic freebooters.[46]

Once elected chief justice of New York in May 1777, Jay remained ankle-deep in such banditti. "I am now engaged in the most disagreeable part of my duty—trying criminals," he wrote Gouverneur Morris in the spring of 1778. "The Woods afford them Shelter and the Tories Food. Punishments must of course become certain, and Mercy dormant, a harsh System repugnant to my Feelings, but nevertheless necessary."[47] He had before his court in Albany a gang of Cow-Boys, who'd looted two Columbia County farms, killing the son of one farmer, a Continental soldier home on leave. They were "tory criminals," according to the *New-York Journal*, bandits and traitors rolled into one. "Their thefts and robberies they justified, under the pretense of the goods being lawful prizes, forfeited to the King." Jay sentenced ten of them to hang.[48]

Anyone who wants to keep his hands clean and his conscience pure had better not choose politics as a vocation, Max Weber famously wrote, because politics operates through "power backed up by *violence*," and its guiding principle—the very opposite of the Christian command to "Resist not him that is evil with force"—is "'Thou *shalt* resist evil by force,' or else you are responsible for the evil's winning out." But here one enters a moral morass, for "he who lets himself in for politics, that is, for power and force as means, contracts with diabolical powers, and for his action it is not true that good can follow only from good and evil only from evil, but that often the opposite is true."[49] John Jay came to understand this ethical dilemma with all his being once he began detecting conspiracies. For if it's disagreeable enough to hang men for their heinous actions, what about jailing or banishing people from their homes on suspicion—on information from spies about their political beliefs, or on their refusal to take loyalty oaths?[50] Should people be punished not just for their action but also for their inaction? For their beliefs?

As early as November 1775, Jay answered by proposing harsh measures when Congress asked him how to handle disaffection in Queens County on Long Island, which declared itself neutral in the looming conflict and voted not to send delegates to Philadelphia. It's not acceptable, Jay declared, to be "inactive spectators," hoping, if the British win, "to purchase their favour and mercy at an easy rate," while, if America wins, "they may enjoy, without expense of blood or treasure, all the blessings resulting from that liberty which they, in the day of trial, had abandoned." Accordingly, he recommended that the declared neutrals "be put out of the protection of the United Colonies," confined to their county, excluded from the law courts, and disarmed by New Jersey and Connecticut troops.[51]

Some who claimed neutrality, Jay suspected, were liars, actively supporting the enemy by "collecting and transmitting intelligence, raising false reports, and spreading calumnies of public men and measures."[52] Or worse—as he found when Beverly Robinson, a prosperous merchant (and a distant relative), came before his committee in February 1777. "Sir we have passed the Rubicon and it is now necessary every man Take his part," Jay told Robinson. "Cast off all alliegiance to the King of Great Britain and take an oath of Alliegiance to the states of America or Go over to the enemy for we have Declared our Selves Independent." This was an age, remember, when giving your word or swearing in God's name put your honor or your soul at stake.

Replied Robinson, "Sir I cannot Take the Oath but should be exceeding Glad to Stay in the Country." Think it over, Jay advised. "You can Take a Month or Six weeks." Jay wrote Robinson's wife, urging her to persuade him to take the loyalty oath; but by then Robinson had started to raise a Loyalist regiment, and by March Jay got news that he'd guided British regulars to attack American soldiers at Peekskill, wounding two.[53]

But some of the neutrals were neither traitors, liars, nor trimmers, and Jay faced no harder case than that of his honorable King's College friend Peter Van Schaack, who "condemned the conduct of the Home government" in London, Van Schaack's son reported, but "was yet opposed to taking up arms in opposition to it" and felt conscience-bound not to take the loyalty oath against his king. Jay ordered him to appear before the Albany authorities, whose proceedings led to his ultimate banishment to London, from which he wrote Jay in 1782, as the Revolution was drawing to a close, tentatively hoping to reopen communication. Jay replied at once. "I have adhered to certain fixed Principles, . . . without regarding the Consequences of such Conduct to my Friends, my Family, or myself; all of whom, however dreadful the Thought, I have ever been ready to sacrifice, if necessary, to the public Objects in Contest. Believe me, . . . I felt very sensibly for you and for others; but as Society can regard only the political Propriety of Men's Conduct, and not the moral Propriety of their Motives to it, I could only lament your unavoidably becoming classed with many whose morality was convenience. . . . No one can serve two Masters: either Britain was right, and America wrong; or America was right, and Britain wrong. . . . Hence it became our Duty to take one Side or the other." He closed by asking how his old friend and his children are doing. "While I have a Loaf, you and they may freely partake of it. Don't let this Idea hurt you. If your Circumstances are easy, I rejoice; if not, let me take off their rougher Edges."[54]

Van Schaack wrote back with equal magnanimity. "Be assured, that were I arraigned at the bar, and you my judge, I should expect to stand or fall only by the *merits of my cause*." He had reasons for his choice, he continues. "Even in a doubtful case, I would rather be the patient sufferer, than run the risk of being the active aggressor." But now that the fighting is over, "if America is happier for the revolution, I declare solemnly that I shall rejoice that the side I was on was the unsuccessful one. . . . I have always considered you as one of the foremost enemies of this country, but since what has happened, *has* happened, there is no man to whom I more cordially wish the glory of the achievement." As for his children, his son has been accepted at Yale. "I hope the poor fellow will not be reproached with the *malignity* of his father. . . . I would not let him come to England, because I mean he should never leave America."[55] In time Van Schaack returned to his New York law practice, and the friendship bloomed again.

Loyalty oaths, wartime un-American-activities committees: William Jay asserts that, while his father "was ever ready to adopt all proper measures for preventing the tories from injuring the American cause, he abhorred the idea of *punishing* them for their opinions."[56] Not so. He believed America was in a fight for its existence against enemies who, as he wrote to his fellow New Yorkers, "plunder your houses; ravish your wives and daughters; strip your infant children; expose whole families naked, miserable and forlorn, to want, to hunger, to inclement skies, and wretched deaths," and who seek to impose a slavery such as "Egypt, Babylon, Syria, or Rome" imposed upon the Jews—or Catholics, he might have said, imposed on Huguenots.[57] The greatest sin and dishonor would be not to fight to win, whatever it took. A life-or-death struggle has no margin for error.

Along with these indelible lessons in anarchy, Jay learned five great lessons about anarchy's antidote—government—in his education as a statesman during his presidency of the Continental Congress from December 1778 through September 1779. First, he grasped that American unity was permanent. Our enemies, he wrote in his *Circular Letter from Congress to Their Constituents*, argue "that the confederation of the States remains to be perfected; that the union may be dissolved." They are wrong. "These states are now as fully, legally, and absolutely confederated as it is possible for them to be." The ongoing war is making the bond ever stronger. "A sense of common permanent interest, mutual affection (having been brethren in affliction), the ties of consanguinity daily extending, constant reciprocity of good offices, . . . all conspire in forming a strong chain of connexion, which must for ever bind us together."[58] Jay welcomed every sign of growing unity. He cheered the marriages of two fellow congressmen to ladies from states not their own: "I am pleased with these Intermarriages," he wrote John Adams; "they tend to assimilate the States, and to promote one of the first wishes of my Heart, vizt. to see the People of America become one Nation in every Respect."[59] And he objected to Massachusetts' description of itself "as being in *New England*, as well as America. Perhaps it w^d. be better if these Distinctions were permitted to die away."[60]

Second, a Federalist by instinct even before there was Federalism, he understood that union required a strong central government sovereign over the states. As early as October 1775, he wrote, "The Union depends much upon breaking down provincial Conventions." Accordingly, during his presidency, Congress for the first time—and in his handwriting—declared its supremacy over the state governments, overturning a Pennsylvania statute (and a Pennsylvania jury decision) in the allocation of the sloop *Active* as a war prize. "Congress," Jay pronounced in taking these actions, "is by these United States invested with the supreme sovereign power of war and peace."[61]

Third, assuming the presidency when the quarrel between diplomats Silas Deane and Arthur Lee had reached its climax of bitterness, with charges of malfeasance and spying flung about in Congress, Jay learned a wariness toward his own colleagues. "There is as much Intrigue in this State House as in the vatican," he commented, "but as little Secrecy as in a boarding School."[62] His distrust only deepened when General Horatio Gates, part of a cabal of senior officers seeking to displace George Washington as commander in chief, sent him an insinuating letter critical of Washington's military strategy. Rightly judging the letter mere Machiavellian self-serving on Gates's part, like so much of the unprincipled self-interest he had seen in Congress, Jay sent Washington the relevant passage as a heads-up and received in response a letter of such nobility of character and comprehensive strategic and managerial brilliance as to teach him his fourth great lesson: that Washington was a world-historical leader.[63] The two became friends and confidants; within weeks Washington moved from signing himself "Yr. obliged & obed. Ser." to "Yr. most obed. & affect. Servt.," though it took Jay six months to get up the nerve to tell the "master-builder" (as he termed the great man) that "With sincere affection & Esteem, I am your friend & Servt."[64]

The fifth lesson proved the most useful of all to the man who set the future course of U.S. foreign policy: in the world of diplomacy, nothing is what it seems, so trust no one. He entered that murky world in November 1775, well before the colonies declared independence, when Congress sent him, Franklin, and Jefferson to see a nameless Frenchman who'd requested a secret meeting in Philadelphia. As William Jay remembers his father often recounting, the elderly, lame man stated that the king of France, then officially at peace with George III, favored the colonists' defense of their rights and wished to help with arms and money. When the trio repeatedly asked by what authority he spoke, the man merely drew his hand across his throat and replied, "Gentlemen, I shall take care of my head." Shortly thereafter, Congress—impressed by this drama, Jay thought—appointed him to a secret committee to seek aid from abroad.[65]

A year later, after further foreign encouragement—especially a secret French loan that Arthur Lee negotiated through the playwright Beaumarchais—the committee sent Silas Deane to France, posing as a merchant and equipped with invisible ink for reporting home, to obtain the promised arms and supplies, which France furnished through a front company to hide its role.[66] One of Arthur Lee's accusations in the Deane-Lee catfight raging in Congress when John Jay assumed its presidency was that Deane had charged Congress for materiel that

France had given as a gift. When Tom Paine, secretary to Congress's Committee for Foreign Affairs, leaked in the press the secret information that France had most certainly given such a free gift, French ambassador Conrad Gérard, to preserve the fiction that France had not aided America while still at peace with Britain, demanded that Congress refute what he claimed was a calumny against "the Dignity and the Reputation of the King my Master"—even though by then France, convinced by the American victory at Saratoga in October 1777 that the rebels could win, had signed a formal alliance with the United States in February 1778. So John Jay, in one of his first acts as president, had to call Paine before the bar of Congress to discipline him for telling the truth. Sacrificial whistle-blower Paine resigned in outrage before Jay could fire him.[67]

During Jay's nine months as president, Ambassador Gérard "used frequently to spend an evening with me," Jay wrote, "and sometimes sat up very late," urging on Jay the wisdom of drawing Spain into the war as an ally, and outlining the inducements America might offer.[68] He made the same argument to Congress, which in late September 1779 named Jay minister plenipotentiary to Spain, with instructions to seek such an alliance.

So SUDDEN was the appointment that Jay could say good-bye to his family only by letter—as could his wife, who, as sharp an observer of the era and as sparkling a writer as Abigail Adams, had with utter unconventionality decided to go with him. "Considering the mortality of man, and my time of life," Sally's loving father wrote her, "it is probable I may never see you again. O may God Almighty keep you in his holy Protection, & if it should please him to take you out of this World, receive you into a better!"[69]

That very nearly happened. Eighteen days out of Philadelphia, their 185-foot frigate sailed into a winter gale that tore away her masts and bowsprit, and damaged her rudder. The falling spars had injured two sailors, Sally told her mother in a long and typically vivid letter. One, "poor fellow! surviv'd not many days the amputation of his arm."

By no possibility could the jury-rigged ship reach Europe, her officers concluded, though Gérard, who was on board, demanded they continue eastward. Jay, in his first diplomatic negotiation, got the ambassador to agree to head south to Martinique. Sally marveled at her husband's "firmness & serenity of mind." As she wrote her mother: "Your whole family love Mr. Jay, but you are not acquainted with half his worth, . . . for his modesty is equal to his merit. It is the property of a Diamond (I've been told) to appear most brilliant in the dark; and surely a good man never shines to greater advantage than the gloomy hour of adversity."

Now, wrote Sally, as the frigate rolled and fellow passengers played checkers at her cramped table, she is dreaming of Martinique's fruit, "&, if what I hear of crabs, fresh fish, & Oysters be true, I'll make papa's mouth water, & make him wish to forego the pleasures of pruning trees, speechifying Assemblies, & what not for the greater pleasure of messing with us." A few days later, she added, "A land bird! A land bird! Oh! the pleasure of being near land!"[70]

Ashore, she set off to explore the exotic island, which she described with characteristic verve and economy. She always noticed and praised landscapes cultivated and improved by labor. "It is really surprising to trace the effects of industry on the very summits of the hills which are covered with coffee, coconuts, and cane," she remarked, and went on to describe, with her lifelong delight in how things work, the island town's ingenious plumbing system. To her father-in-law, once the Jays had left Martinique and were "sweetly sailing before the wind" toward Europe, she wrote two observant paragraphs describing with crisp precision how a sugar mill turns cane into sugar and molasses.[71]

Jay's mission to Spain was doomed from the start. With a colonial empire in the New World, the Spanish king, who had his own imperial ambitions in North America that competed with American claims, shuddered at the idea of colonial rebellion and would never officially support one, even to harass Britain. Making matters worse, Spain and France were conspiring behind America's back. While Congress dithered about whom to send abroad, the two Bourbon powers secretly revived their decades-old Family Compact in the Treaty of Aranjuez, which bound Spain to join the war against Britain in exchange for France's pledge not to make peace until the Spanish got Gibraltar back—a deal that not only ignored America's claims but also violated France's treaty with America by its clandestine change in the peace requirements. Also unfriendly to America, France agreed to let Spain share the Grand Banks fishery, long an American fishing ground, if France could wrest Newfoundland from Britain. And there was one more thing Jay didn't know: though Spain had helped America with money and supplies early in the Revolution, now that she was herself at war, for goals having nothing to do with American independence, she had no money to spare, despite the legends about her wealth.[72]

Jay might have figured out the economic truth beneath the façade early on. The first leg of his trip from Cadiz, where he landed in January 1780, to Madrid, was pure pomp, with sixteen or twenty oarsmen rowing "a very handsome Barge . . . ornamented by a crimson damask canopy handsomly fringed," Sally wrote in one of her letters, which provide the best account of the Jays' day-to-day life in Europe. But soon the travelers transferred to something "they've the impudence to call . . . Coaches, it's true they are made of wood and have four wheels, but there the resemblance ceases." As for the inns, "the awkwardness and filth of every thing exceed description. . . . The very first evening we found that a broom was absolutely essential," for sweeping out "several loads of dirt in which were contain'd not [less] than two or 3000 fleas, lice, buggs, &c." Their mules occupied the next room. To add insult to injury, her husband wrote, the landlord charged their party of eight for the fourteen beds in their rooms, observing "that we might have used them all if we pleased."[73] Hardly signs of a rich country.

For the two and a half years of his "honorable Exile," as he called it, Jay fruitlessly trailed after the Spanish court as it accompanied the king from palace to palace. Given his paltry salary, Jay lived in furnished single rooms with one servant and could barely afford to hire mules and a chaise to follow the monarch. "So circumstanced[,] I cannot employ Couriers to carry my Dispatches to the Sea Side or to France. My Letters by the Post are all opened"—and indeed the Spanish secretary of state once handed over a top-secret letter that Congress had sent Jay, without bothering to conceal that he'd intercepted and read it. Lack of funds obliged Jay to leave Sally in Madrid, where, as the court had never officially recognized him as an ambassador, she knew almost no one. When a daughter, conceived on shipboard, was born in July 1780, Sally's "whole heart overflowed with Joy & gratitude." But the baby died three weeks later. "Excuse my tears," Sally wrote—"you too mamma have wept on similar occasions, maternal tenderness causes them to flow & reason, tho' it moderates distress, cannot intirely restrain our grief, nor do I think it should be wish'd."[74]

JAY'S FINANCIAL PROBLEMS weren't just domestic. In its desperation for funds, Congress began spending the money it hoped he could raise from Spain, drawing bills of exchange on him for £200,000 (these typical financial instruments of the time order a second person—Jay—to pay a supplier or lender a specified amount by a given date). Though at first Spain's minister of state, the Count of Floridablanca, came up with funds when pressing bills came due, and hinted further help, the flow trickled off, the count temporized, and Benjamin Franklin, America's ambassador to France, had to raise money there to pay both the bills and Jay's salary.[75]

After nearly two years in Spain, Jay diplomatically told Floridablanca to put up or shut up. Was an "intimate union" possible or not? The count told him to outline a treaty, and three days later Jay came back with an offer to let Spain have the exclusive right to navigate the lower Mississippi River in exchange for an alliance, most-favored-nation commercial status, and financial aid—an offer, Jay shrewdly stipulated, that would expire if Spain didn't sign the treaty before Britain made peace. As always, Spain shied away from accepting American independence. A disgusted Jay wrote to Gouverneur Morris in code: "This government has little money, less wisdom, no credit, nor any right to it." And he added in his draft but didn't send,

"They have Pride without Dignity, Cunning without Policy, Nobility without Honor." Seven months later—and six months after Cornwallis surrendered to Washington at Yorktown and the fighting ended—Franklin wrote Jay to come to Paris and help him negotiate the peace treaty with Britain. "Spain has taken four years to consider whether to treat with us or not," Franklin wrote. "Give her forty, and let us in the mean time mind our own business."[76]

While from the moment of the Jays' arrival in Spain, Sally wrote her usual dazzling descriptions, Jay himself, always prudent, waited until they were about to leave before he offered a portrait. No doubt, he wrote, the palace of Aranjuez, south of Madrid, was a charming place, with the king's parks, meadows, and woods. But "it is not America. A Genius of a different Character . . . reigns over these. Soldiers, with fixed Bayonets, present themselves at various Stations in these peaceful Retreats; and tho' none but inoffensive Citizens are near, yet Horsemen with drawn swords guarding one or other of the royal Family . . . , renew and impress Ideas of Subjection. Power unlimited, and Distrust misplaced, thus exacting Homage & imposing awe, occasion uneasy Reflections. . . . Were I a Spaniard, these decorated Seats would appear to me like the temporary Enchantments of some despotic Magician, who, by re-extending his wand, could at pleasure command them to vanish, and be succeeded by Presidios, Galleys and Prisons." All human relations in Spain, and indeed people's inner souls, catch a tinge of the same despotic spirit. "This is a kind of Prudence which naturally grows out of a jealous and absolute Government, under which the People have, for many Generations been habituated to that Kind of Dependence, which constrains every Class to watch and respect the opinions and Inclinations of their Superiors in Power." No European splendor can equal "the free Air, the free Conversation, the equal Liberty, . . . which God & Nature, and Laws of our making, have given and secured to our happier Country."[77]

In May 1782, Jay, Sally, and their new baby, three-month-old Maria, left for Paris, with Sally brightening up as they traveled through what struck her as "one of the favorite spots of Nature," which "the gaiety & industry of the inhabitants" had adorned everywhere with gardens and bowers.[78] Admired for her beauty and modishness—a Paris theater audience once mistook the dainty blonde for Marie Antoinette—and with friends like Franklin and the Marquise de Lafayette, Sally flourished. So did Jay, who met his toughest challenge and won his greatest triumph.

Right after he arrived on June 23, he emerged as the chief American peace negotiator, and the task first looked to him something like a game of pool, with four balls on the table—Britain, France, Spain, and the Continental Congress—except that the balls moved of their own accord, he quickly saw, and didn't obey the laws of physics when hit. But within weeks he grasped that he was playing a different game entirely, a game of poker for global stakes against the sharpest diplomatic cardsharper of them all, French foreign minister Charles Gravier, Comte de Vergennes. At sixty-three, the worldly aristocrat, with the star, sash, and haughty bearing of the ancien régime, could draw on over forty years' experience in foreign affairs, as ambassador to Trier, Sweden, and the Ottoman Empire, where he had himself painted lounging on silk cushions in a sultanic turban and fur-trimmed caftan. By the time of the Franco-American alliance, he had conceived a grand global strategy, whose finishing touches he planned to complete in the negotiations at Paris.

With the privilege of historical hindsight, let's peek over the count's shoulder and see what cards he was holding. He had predicted when the French and Indian War ended in 1763 with Britain having driven France out of North America that "England will ere long repent of having removed the only check that could keep her colonies in awe. They stand no longer in need of her protection," and they will respond "by striking off all dependence."[79] Smarting at France's defeat, he saw that he could punish and permanently weaken France's most formidable rival by patiently helping the colonists in their inevitable rebellion, amputating a rich and important limb of the British Empire.

To produce a balance of power advantageous to France, though, he also had to control the shape that a newly independent America would take. She mustn't be strong or rich enough to be a global power in her own right, and she certainly must not end up allied with Britain. A weak America, squabbling with and distracting England, hemmed in narrow geographical boundaries by foreign powers, and dependent on French protection, would be the best of all possible worlds for Versailles, and it was his task as foreign minister to bring that world into being. Here Spain, his secret ally, could serve as a useful and willing tool, blocking American control of the Mississippi River—barring her westward expansion and hampering her economic growth by cutting off a key trade route.

Vergennes had begun laying the groundwork for this strategy in 1779, when he sent Ambassador Gérard for his late-night talks urging President of Congress Jay to entice Spain into the war by offering to give up American claims to navigate the Mississippi—a deal that Jay favored until Spain joined the war for goals separate from American independence. Without missing a beat, at the very moment that Jay landed in Spain, Gérard's successor, the Chevalier de la Luzerne, pressured Congress to change Jay's instructions and order him to give up America's claim on the Mississippi, which Jay did, but with the escape clause he had added on his own initiative, voiding the offer if Spain failed to recognize America before peace came. Finally, Vergennes dealt himself an ace in the hole when he persuaded Congress in 1781 to instruct its peace commissioner to hide nothing in his negotiations from "the ministers of our generous ally the King of France; to undertake nothing in the negotiations for peace or truce without their knowledge or concurrence; . . . and ultimately govern yourself by their advice and concurrence."[80]

"Our way of thinking," Vergennes wrote Luzerne as the peace negotiations began, "must be an impenetrable secret from the Americans."[81] Certainly Jay's co-commissioner Franklin, now seventy-six and a Parisian celebrity who had found the French nothing but generous allies, understandably credited their goodwill. But Jay smelled a rat. As Spain, which he despised, would be a party to the treaty, he called first on her ambassador to France, the immensely rich Count d'Aranda, who, like Jefferson, combed the vineyards to stock his cellars with treasures, who employed a full-time silversmith to shine his magnificent plate, and who became Jay's friend.[82] The count unrolled a map of North America and asked Jay where he thought America's western border was. The Mississippi, Jay replied; where did the count think it was? Would he draw it on the map? The count replied that there was no point quarreling about a few acres and he would send Jay the map with his proposed border in a day or two. When it arrived around August 6, 1782, Jay found Aranda had lopped off all the land north of the Ohio, plus what became Alabama and Mississippi, along with part of the future Kentucky and Tennessee.[83]

Flabbergasted, Jay and Franklin rushed to tell Vergennes of Aranda's "utterly inadmissable" landgrab, Jay recounted in his official report of the negotiations. Instead of sympathetic reassurance, they met with unexpected reserve, with Vergennes' secretary, Joseph-Matthias Gérard de Rayneval, hinting that "we claimed more than we had a right to." A few weeks later, Rayneval sent Jay a pettifogging memo, backing up the Spanish by saying that, as England never owned the territory just east of the Mississippi and south of the Ohio, America could have no claim to it either—and with no territory adjoining much of the river, America also had no navigation rights to it. As for the territory north of the Ohio, America would have to sort out with Britain whether or not that should be part of Canada. When Jay protested that, when he had negotiated with Count Floridablanca in Madrid, the Spanish had taken for granted that America owned much of the east bank of the Mississippi, the French official casually replied that Floridablanca hadn't then understood the matter.

"Hence it became evident," Jay concluded, "from whom [the Spanish] had borrowed their present ideas." And it became evident to him as well that, when the final negotiations took place, France, for all its protestations of goodwill, "would oppose our extension to the Mississippi" and "our Claim to the free navigation of that River," and also would back Spain's right to divvy up the lands east of the Mississippi with Britain.[84]

Jay found France similarly a hindrance in his negotiations with the British. When Lord Shelburne became prime minister in July 1782 and fired the pro-American foreign secretary Charles James Fox, he sent a gifted young friend, Benjamin Vaughan, to Paris as an unofficial envoy to assuage American anxiety. Vaughan showed Jay and Franklin a document stating that George III, "to give a striking proof of his royal magnanimity and disinterested wish for the restoration of peace," had commanded the new foreign secretary to acknowledge America's independence unconditionally, in advance of a general treaty. Perfect, said Jay; but when he exchanged credentials with the official British negotiator, Richard Oswald, a well-connected seventy-seven-year-old merchant and former slave trader who'd lived in America for six years, he found with disappointment and "disapprobation" that Oswald's commission authorized him to treat with representatives of the American "colonies." If the king really meant what Vaughan's documents stated, why didn't he commission Oswald to negotiate with the independent United States of America? Vergennes told Jay he was being silly, that he "was expecting the effect before the cause," and Franklin agreed that Oswald's commission "would do."[85]

From mid-August, while he was still trying to negotiate with Aranda, to mid-September, Jay patiently explained to Oswald what Vergennes was up to. The French, as Jay summed up his analysis in his official report, "are interested in separating us from Great Britain" and planting "Seeds of Jealousy, Discontent, and Discord" that will prevent "Cordiality and mutual Confidence" between the two English-speaking nations. Vergennes wants a treaty that will "render Britain formidible in our Neighbourhood" and will "leave us as few resources of wealth and power as possible," so that we must "perpetually keep our Eyes fixed on France for Security." The longer the French keep the war going, the more chance they will have to accomplish their goals, while a forthright British acknowledgment of

American independence will end the war promptly and stymie them. Vergennes strengthened Jay's argument about French deviousness by having a top-secret document purloined from Oswald's locked writing desk.[86] The now-experienced Jay told Oswald not to worry: the paper would be back in place when Vergennes had finished reading it—as it was.[87]

Jay's larger argument was that it would benefit Britain to treat America as magnanimously as George III had promised. Treaties are just words, he told Oswald, and he "would not give a farthing for any Parchment security whatever. They had never signified any thing since the World began, when any Prince or State of either Side, found it convenient to break through them." What Jay proposed was "that the Peace should be lasting," framed so that "it should not be the *Interest* of either party to break it." At first, the worry-prone Oswald blanched at Jay's expression, a *lasting* peace. Did it have some dark connotation of forceful imposition? Did Jay have some deep-laid scheme to make the United States the arbiter of the European balance of power? Franklin set his anxious mind at ease with an anecdote from Roman history: a peace whose terms and conditions are fair, he patiently explained, will be lasting. A relieved Oswald said in that case he thought he had the authority to recognize America's independence and would just check with Lord Shelburne to make sure.[88]

And now a race to London took place between envoys from Jay and Vergennes. On September 7, Vergennes dispatched Rayneval across the Channel, which Jay learned on the tenth—the same day he got an intercepted letter to Vergennes from France's American envoy, boasting that Congress would leave the French king "Master of the Terms of the Treaty of Peace" and plotting to split the Newfoundland fishery between France and Britain.[89] Rayneval's mission, Jay guessed, must be to tell Shelburne that France endorsed neither America's demand for quick recognition of its independence nor its claim to navigate the Mississippi, and to see if England would divide the fishery with France and the land east of the Mississippi with Spain.[90] Clearly, Jay guessed right. When Shelburne told Rayneval he'd decided to grant America immediate independence, the Frenchman's whole tone to him changed: "the point of independence once settled," the prime minister wrote George III, Rayneval "appears rather Jealous than partial to America upon other points, as well as that of the Fishery."[91]

To counter Vergennes, Jay asked young Vaughan to rush to London that day and lay out a rosy vision for postwar Anglo-American relations. Since America had plainly won the war, and "as every Idea of Conquest had become absurd, nothing remained for Britain to do, but to make friends of those whom she could not subdue, . . . by leaving us nothing to complain of," Jay asked Vaughan to tell Shelburne. After all, Britain had much more to gain by a treaty with America than "a mere suspension of hostilities." It could gain "Cordiality, Confidence and Commerce"—along with the "extensive and lucrative Commerce" that a commercial power naturally wants. If America ended up with the lands east of the Mississippi and the navigation of the river, said Jay, its population would explode westward, and the two English-speaking nations could share an inland waterway carrying "from the Gulph of St. Lawrence to that of Mexico . . . an immense and growing Trade" that on the European side "would be in a manner, monopolized by Great Britain." If, by contrast, Britain excluded America from the Mississippi and the fishery, and seized the land north of the Ohio, she would end up with "vast tracts of wilderness" that she wouldn't be able to settle or supply, and she would "sow the Seeds of future War in the very treaty of Peace." With such great advantages in prospect, the British would do well to win America's confidence—and America holds the acknowledgment of her independence "as the touchstone of British Sincerity."[92] Without it, as Jay had told Vaughan a couple of weeks earlier, "he would rather the war should go on to his grandsons."[93]

Shelburne agreed, and on September 27 Oswald's new commission arrived, authorizing him to treat with the United States of America. During the first week of October, Oswald and Jay hammered out a preliminary treaty, giving Jay most of what he wanted—a much bigger country than otherwise would have emerged, with everything it needed to become powerful, rich, and independent. When a scandalized Vergennes, whom Jay had kept out of the loop during these negotiations, saw the draft, he was shocked by the extent of territory America had won and by the defeat of his plans for a dependent client state in the New World. Aranda, tapping Jay on the shoulder, murmured, "*Eh bien, mon ami, vous avez très bien fait*"—well done, my friend.[94]

ALSO SCANDALIZED was American secretary for foreign affairs Robert Livingston, Jay's old friend and law partner. Along with his many pro-French colleagues in Congress, he condemned Jay's "separate and secret manner" toward Vergennes, which flagrantly disobeyed Congress's instructions to consult and defer to the count.[95] Jay stoutly rebuffed his former friend's "doubts respecting the propriety of our conduct." As Vergennes opposed America on all key points, Jay argued, he "ceased to be entitled to . . . confidence"; as he wanted a very different treaty than would most benefit America, it would have been imprudent to let him shape it. As to Jay's not following Congress's instructions: "The object of that instruction was the supposed interest of America, and not of France." They are not the same. "So far and in such matters as this Court may think it in their Interest to support us, they certainly will; but no farther," Jay wrote from Paris. Moreover, he had to seize the moment (a point he emphasized later in *Federalist* 64). Because Shelburne needed to make peace quickly, before a war-weary Britain pushed him out of office, he and Oswald "became less tenacious on certain points, than they would otherwise have been," and Jay got a great treaty by acting fast and pressing hard—and not because Britain had "either Wisdom, Virtue or Magnanimity enough to adopt a perfect and liberal System of Conciliation. If they again thought they could conquer us they would again attempt it."[96]

Nevertheless, between the two great European powers, Jay had already made his choice and committed his country, though it was the opposite of Congress's choice. America had fought a war with a French ally against a British enemy, but in the peace negotiations and for the rest of his public career, Jay, often on his own initiative and against much resistance from his colleagues and countrymen, led the way in building the foundation of future U.S. foreign policy, the special relationship between the two English-speaking peoples. And why? "Not being of British Descent," Jay explained years later, "I cannot be influenced by . . . that Partiality . . . , which might otherwise be supposed not to be unnatural." But in Europe he came to loathe "arbitrary Governments," which "debase and corrupt their Subjects," even subjects as talented and accomplished as the French (as his Huguenot ancestors had found, he well knew). Very different is Britain's political culture and therefore its national character. "It certainly is chiefly owing to Institutions Laws and Principles of Policy & Government, originally derived to us as British colonists, that with the favor of Heaven the People of this Country are what they are." Hence his "sentiments of esteem" for the British nation.[97]

On September 3, 1783, Jay and Franklin signed the final Treaty of Paris, along with their co-commissioner John Adams, who joined the tail end of the negotiations. Oswald's successor, David Hartley (son and namesake of the philosopher), signed for Britain. "The peace, which exceeds in the goodness of its terms the expectations of the most sanguine, does the highest honour to those who made it," Hamilton wrote Jay, who at this moment in American history had been *the* indispensable man. "The New-England people talk of making you an annual *fish-offering*, as an acknowledgment of your exertions for the participation of the fisheries."[98] Jefferson echoed the sentiment: "The terms obtained for us," he wrote, "are indeed great."[99]

Later that month, the Montgolfier brothers made the first manned balloon flight over Paris, which Sally Jay watched from her terrace, and which fired the whole world's imagination with ideas, Jay wrote, that "Travellers may hereafter litterally pass from Country to Country on the Wings of the wind."[100] "Don't you begin to think of taking yr. passage next spring in a Ballon?" Sally asked him.[101] But instead they set out for New York on an ordinary sailing ship on June 1, 1784, and arrived home—without incident this time—on July 24.

It is one thing to sign a treaty but quite another to get it carried out, as Jay discovered on his return, when he learned he'd been named secretary for foreign affairs while still at sea. He knew before he left for Europe that America needed a strong central government sovereign over the states; now, finding himself the key official of a government too weak to carry out promises he himself had made, he felt that need acutely. According to the treaty, America would void state laws that barred British creditors from suing U.S. citizens for prewar debts, and British troops would leave U.S. territory. When America's London envoy, John Adams, remonstrated with the British for keeping their frontier forts, they replied that they intended to honor the treaty—as soon as America held up its end of the deal. Secretary Jay, echoing his opinion in the 1775 sloop *Active* case, pronounced that the Articles of Confederation gave Congress alone the right to make a treaty, which "immediately becomes binding on the whole nation," so Congress told the states to repeal the offending laws—but had no power to make them do so.[102] And they temporized, protecting powerful citizens who owed big sums, and the British soldiers stayed put. "The federal government," Jay fumed, "is rather paternal and persuasive than coercive and efficient."[103]

Less than a year into his job, Jay started pushing to make the United States "one Great Nation, . . . divided into different States merely for more convenient Government, . . . just as our several States are divided into Counties and Townships for the like purposes."[104] Moreover, since the faction-ridden Congress, which held both legislative and executive power, couldn't make timely decisions, Jay also sought to "divide Sovereignty into its proper Departments. Let Congress legislate—let others execute—let others judge"—for efficiency rather than for checks and balances.[105] He was quick to support a convention to correct the "errors in our national Government," but when the Constitutional Convention met, his duties as secretary kept him from attending.[106] Once the conclave produced its great document, though, he eagerly joined Madison and Hamilton in writing *The Federalist* to defend it—until a rock thrown in yet another New York riot sidelined him for a long convalescence.[107]

Of the five *Federalist* papers he wrote, four are what you'd expect from a minister without the power to execute his decisions and a diplomat who'd learned from experience that "to be constantly prepared for War is the only Way to have Peace."[108] *Federalist* Numbers 2 through 5 argue that Americans, forged by the Revolution into a "band of bretheren," need to form a single, powerful union that can make good on its treaties, ensure security against foreign threats, and avoid the constant skirmishing inevitable if the states, as some anti-Federalists suggested, broke into several separate confederations.

BUT HIS FIFTH *Federalist* paper, Number 64—which supports the Constitution's plan of having the president elected not directly but by "select assemblies . . . of the most enlightened and respectable citizens," and the senators appointed by the state legislatures, to ensure leaders of "abilities and virtue"—raises a large issue that Jay's letters and speeches fully developed and that remains as pertinent as ever. Jay liked to quote Gouverneur Morris's maxim, "What is, is," and he often told his friends and children that "To see things as they are—to estimate them aright—and to act accordingly, is to be wise."[109] No wishful thinking for this realist: "To look at Objects through our Passions is like seeing through *colored* Glass, which always paints what we view, in its own, and not in the *true* Color," he cautioned.[110] Instead, "we must take men and Things as they are."[111] And since his whole experience had taught him, above all, that "the mass of men are neither wise nor good," he was bound to ask how government by the people can yield leaders of distinction.[112]

"The Rulers in democratic Republics are generally men of more Talents than morals," history shows; "there can be but little connection between Cunning and Virtue, and therefore . . . our affairs will commonly be managed by political Intrigues," and "a succession of Demagogues must be expected."[113] In democracies, after all—and especially in one that prizes opportunity and social mobility as America's does—men on the make will see politics as a bonanza: these "political Mountebankes" will be "less solicitous about the Health of the credulous Crowd, than abt. making the most of their Nostrums and Prescriptions."[114]

Since their fortunes depend on public opinion, they will mold and manipulate it. Because the "Knaves and Fools of this World are forever in Alliance," Jay wrote Jefferson, "they who either officially or from Choice fabricate opinions for other Peoples use, will always find many to receive and be influenced by them. Thus Errors proceeding from the Invention of designing Men, are very frequently adopted and cherished by others who mistake them for Truths."[115] Worse, "actuated by Envy ambition or avarice," these politicians and pundits "will always be hostile to merit, because merit will always stand in their way."[116]

Democracy is a magnificent idea: "Without a portion of it there can be no free Government," Jay was certain.[117] But "*pure* Democracy, like *pure* Rum, easily produces Intoxication, and with it a thousand mad Pranks and Fooleries,"[118] he thought, so he wanted to mix it with other elements, with an eye to the British constitution's system of checks and balances, poising the magnates against the commons. That's why he favored the existing property qualifications for electors and officials: "they who own the Country," he thought, "are the most fit Persons to participate in the Goverm$^{t.}$ of it."[119] Such men, he expected, would share his horror of redistributive taxation, which his favorite author, Cicero, identified as the demagogue's vote-getting "kind of liberality which involves robbing one man to give to another," rather than taxing everyone proportionally to his wealth or income only for common purposes, like defense.[120] But above all, he took it for granted that the propertied would include those "enlightened and respectable citizens" whom he thought best capable of choosing leaders with abilities and virtue.

Such leaders, despite all human nature's failings, were there for the finding. Men such as George Washington, "who ascended to the Temple of Honor through the Temple of Virtue," had absorbed the "maxims and precepts of sound Policy, which enable Legislators and Rulers to manage and govern public affairs wisely and justly," Jay noted.[121] By studying the accumulated thought and experience of the wisest of mankind about human nature and the social order, coupled with reflection on his own experience, a leader can learn wisdom. But to have virtue, Jay believed, he also needs religion. The most devout of the Founders, he once told an atheist "that if there was no God, there could be no moral obligations, and I did not see how Society could subsist without them." When his acquaintance replied that "society would find a Substitute for them in enlightened self Interest," Jay impatiently changed the subject.[122]

His own life movingly exemplified the link between religion and virtue. "I have done nothing but serve my Country for these six Years past and that most faithfully," he wrote in 1780. "But I confess that I did it . . . because I thought & think it my Duty, without doing which I know I cannot please my Maker & go to Heaven—provided he is satisfied with my Conduct, the mistaken Opinions of others cannot deprive me of Happiness."[123] In this spirit he calmly met George Clinton's squalid theft of the 1792 New York gubernatorial election from him: "A few years more will put us all in the dust," he wrote Sally; "and it will then be of more importance to me to have governed *myself* than to have governed the *State*."[124] And early in the war, when he wrote Sally from "a hot little Room" full of "Bugs & Fleas" in "Poghkeepsy," where Congress had fled before the British onslaught, he told her that he kept up his spirits with the "Pre-Sentiment that we shall yet enjoy many good Days together." But if this fantasy "be a Delusion" that will "like a Bubble vanish into Air," he wrote, "a firm Persuasion of after Bliss give[s] me Consolation. Then my dear Wife shall we fear no Tyrants Power, neither shall we know Anxiety any more, and if ,

I cant fill up the blank, we shall again join Hands and Hearts & continue our virtuous Connection forever."[125]

America was a brand-new democracy, and experience, Jay foresaw, would increasingly teach its citizens and legislators to pursue the public interest in addition to their self-interest. "It takes time to make Sovereigns of Subjects," he wrote, and like Jefferson he favored cheap and widespread schooling, and even state subsidies to universities, to mold a civic culture of self-government alongside "the Spirit of Enterprize and adventure" that already prevailed.[126] He thought churches equally essential to improve the national culture, and he helped fund both the new building that replaced the Trinity Church where he'd been baptized, which had burned in the great Manhattan fire of 1776, and the exquisite little brick St. Matthew's Church near his farm, where he worshipped with his dog, Bob.[127]

But these institutions could accomplish only so much, he knew. Especially after two years in Enlightenment Paris, he had no patience with the *philosophe* notion of human perfectibility, an idea he jeered at more sarcastically the older he got. You just have to read the newspapers, he wrote, to know "the Vanity of expecting, that from the Perfectability of human Nature and the lights of Philosophy, the Multitude will become virtuous and wise, or their Demagogues candid and honest."[128] Advances will be real but finite: "Human knowledge and experience will doubtless continue to do good, in proportion to their extent and influence," he wrote; "but that they will ever be able to reduce the passions and prejudices of mankind to such a state of subordination to right reason as modern philosophers would persuade us, I do not believe one word of."[129] Furthermore, this human reality means that teachers, pastors, and leaders of abilities and virtue will never make permanent gains: "political like other fields, require constant attention—when neglected, they soon become unproductive; and fresh Weeds Briars and Thorns will gradually spring up."[130] Even after all our labors, Jay concluded, "I do not expect that mankind will before the Millennium be what they ought to be."[131]

With the Constitution ratified—Jay helped persuade New York's convention to sign on with a soothing *Address to the People of the State of New York* and a bare-knuckled threat that Federalist New York City would otherwise secede from the anti-Federalist state—George Washington took the oath as the nation's first president on April 30, 1789, on the balcony of New York's city hall, where the Stamp Act Congress had met almost a quarter century earlier. Renamed Federal Hall, the 1699 building, home to the U.S. Congress since December 1784, sported a new façade designed by Pierre L'Enfant and finished only days before the inauguration.[132] Around the corner at 133 Broadway, in one of the capital city's grandest houses, lived John Jay, now the father of four (with one more to come), rich (thanks to inheritance and his own New York real-estate investments), the accomplished host of glittering dinner parties "*à la Française*," according to John Adams's daughter, and, from September 26, 1789, the first chief justice of the United States.[133]

It turned out to be a less glamorous job than he expected, however. Much less. With the Constitution brand-new, few issues required Supreme Court rulings: the Court's first session, with only four of the six justices present and no cases, broke up after a week in February 1790. And then the really unglamorous part of the job began, since the justices also presided over the federal courts in the states. Twice a year, they "rode circuit," so in 1791, after the nation's capital moved to Philadelphia, Jay had to travel there for his Supreme Court sessions, then return to New York for the circuit court, and press on to courts in New Haven; Boston; Portsmouth, New Hampshire; Newport, Rhode Island; and finally Bennington, Vermont—"carrying justice as it were to every man's door."[134] He rode on horseback, often on "Roads rendered bad by Snow and Ice," he wrote Sally. "I have had so much to do with cold and wet, that I really do wish for a Respite." Thinking it improper for a judge to accept the many invitations to stay with friends on his circuit, he slept at inns that ranged from "clean" and "obliging" to "*bad*."[135] He and Sally hated the separation: "Oh! my dr. Mr. Jay," Sally wrote, when all the kids had fevers, "shd. you too be unwell & absent from me, & I deprived of the satisfaction & consolation of attending you how wretched I shd. be!"[136]

He had told Washington he wanted the job chiefly because he thought the Court could complete his great work, the Treaty of Paris, by solving the British debt problem, which was now not merely keeping the redcoats stubbornly in their American forts but also stoking up red-hot anger that Jay and Washington feared could ignite a new war.[137] So piece by piece, he chipped away at the issue on his circuit-court rounds. In Connecticut in 1791, his court overturned—as a violation of the treaty, which was now the law of the land—a state law preventing British subjects from collecting interest due on prewar debts from Connecticut citizens, probably the first time a federal court overruled a state law on constitutional grounds. In Rhode Island the next year, he threw out a state law granting a three-year delay to debtors whom a British merchant was suing for repayment, ruling that the law violated the Constitution's contract clause. In 1793, he rode the circuit that included Virginia, a state that accounted for almost half the debts to British creditors, more than a hundred of whom were suing Virginians. The defendants' lawyers, Patrick Henry and John Marshall, put on "one of the most brilliant exhibitions ever witnessed at the Bar of Virginia," one observer exclaimed. But they lost. The court ruled that the Declaration of Independence didn't cancel debts to Britons and that a Virginia law shielding debtors was an unconstitutional violation of the Treaty of Paris.[138]

But just when John Jay, Patrick Henry, and John Marshall were performing their drama in a Richmond courtroom, "the astonishing Tragedy which the French Revolution has introduced on the Theatre of the World," as Jay termed it, had raised the curtain on its darkest act, with the beheading of Louis XVI in January 1793 and France's declaration of war against England the next month.[139] For all Jay's efforts to resolve the debt issue, the revolution stirred up the smoldering anger between Britain and America to explosive rage.

The British believed that America planned to join its old ally, France, in the war against them—with good reason, given the antics of Paris's fiery envoy, Edmond Genêt, who arrived in April charged with making that alliance happen. When he at once began commissioning American privateers to attack British shipping from U.S. ports, Jay, outraged by such a gross provocation of British retaliation against America, publicly condemned him, declaring that "the subjects of belligerent powers are bound while in this country to respect the neutrality of it, and are punishable . . . for violations of it." But the British government paid more attention to the fervid avowals of America's Democratic Societies that anyone "who is an enemy to the French revolution cannot be a firm republican."[140]

London responded in June by decreeing that it would seize the cargoes of all ships carrying grain or flour to French or French West Indian ports—a direct blow to American trade—and in November it announced it would seize the ships too. British naval captains also began impressing American sailors into the Royal Navy, claiming they were British nationals. Along the northern U.S. border, the eight forts the British still held turned from an irritation into a mortal threat. In February 1794, the governor of Canada made a speech denying American sovereignty over land Jay had won in the Treaty of Paris and telling the Indians along the border, who had been fighting the intermittent Northwest Indian War against the Americans for a decade, to prepare to join him in war against the United States. He ordered the lieutenant governor of Upper Canada, John Graves Simcoe, the founder of Toronto, to arm British vessels on the Great Lakes to keep U.S. ships off them, and in April he sent Simcoe, who nursed dreams of reconquering America from the north, to build Fort Miamis at Maumee, Ohio, to supply the Indians.[141]

That month, an angry and alarmed George Washington asked Jay to go to London on a last-ditch peace mission, to try to clear up the forts and debt issues once and for all, to get compensation for seized U.S. ships and cargoes, and to reach a commercial agreement allowing

U.S. ships to trade in the Caribbean. "Nothing can be more distant from every wish on my own account," Jay wrote Sally from Philadelphia about the president's request. "I regard it as a measure not to be desired, but to be submitted to. . . . If it should please God to make me instrumental to the continuance of peace, and in preventing the effusion of blood, . . . we shall both have reason to rejoice."[142]

"How my dr. Mr. Jay is it possible!" Sally replied. "The Utmost exertion I can make is to be silent. Excuse me if I have not philosophy or patriotism to do more." When the Senate confirmed his appointment as envoy extraordinary on April 19, Jay wrote her: "Your own Feelings will best suggest an Idea of mine. God's will be done; to Him I resign; in him I confide. Do the like. Any other philosophy applicable to this occasion is delusive."[143]

On May 12, Jay left for London. "Farewell my best beloved!" Sally wrote in parting. "Your wife 'till Death & after that a ministring spirit."[144]

When Jay landed a month later, he found the situation dire. The British government, he wrote Washington, clearly had "looked upon a War with us as inevitable," both because of "the indiscreet reception" America had given Genêt and because the ministry assumed that American troops fighting the Northwest Indian War would storm the British forts. That's why London had begun to seize U.S. shipping and to stir up Simcoe in Canada.[145] By August, when Jay felt he'd made enough headway to write that George III had remarked, "Well Sir: I imagine you begin to see that your mission will probably be successful," things suddenly turned sharply worse.[146] On August 20, when U.S. general "Mad" Anthony Wayne won the last battle of the Northwest Indian War under the walls of Fort Miamis, his soldiers discovered—and hanged—several Englishmen in war paint among the captives. A furious Washington wrote Jay on the thirtieth that not only was Simcoe supplying the Indians with arms and supplies to carry on "their hostilities, the murders of helpless women and innocent children along our frontiers," he was providing "men also, in disguise" (though the men turned out to be British traders whom the Indians had conscripted, not British soldiers). If the British want peace, they'd better surrender the forts, Washington thundered; if not, "war will be inevitably."[147]

That eventful August, Washington also declared martial law to put down the Whiskey Rebellion in western Pennsylvania—a revolt he was sure the pro-French Republican Societies had precipitated.[148] Unfortunately, the British government shared his belief and feared the rebels would depose the president (whom they trusted), take over the government, and send American troops to fight as allies of France—a belief only strengthened on August 15, when Republican James Monroe, neutral America's new envoy to France, presented an address expressing fraternity and union to the French National Convention, to which the convention's president replied with a kiss.[149] When printed in London, where the French Reign of Terror had sparked a "dread of Jacobin Politics and Jacobin Scenes," the speech, Jay wrote Washington, "made a strong and disagreeable impression."[150]

With tempers so inflamed, Jay strove "to acquire the confidence and esteem of this government, not by improper compliances, but by that sincerity, candour, truth, and prudence which . . . will always prove to be more wise and effectual than finesse and chicane," he wrote Secretary of State Edmund Randolph from London.[151] Long experience had taught him diplomatic patience and tact: he liked to quote a Spanish proverb that says, "We cannot catch Flies with Vinegar."[152]

British pride, he knew, could never stand the indignity of admitting that the capture of U.S. ships had broken international law, though he sought compensation for those seizures. So he proposed to veil the ugly truth with a polite disguise: a joint commission of Britons and Americans would award payment for vessels taken "under colour" of royal authority—a formulation that neither admitted nor denied the legality of that authority and that ultimately produced \$10.3 million in compensation. He proposed a similar commission to compensate British creditors for their unpaid American debts, and in return Lord Grenville agreed to get all redcoats off U.S. soil by June

1796.[153] A fervent believer in free trade, through which "the Bounties of Nature and conveniences of art pass from Nation to Nation without being impeded by the selfish Monopolies and Restrictions, with which narrow Policy opposes the Extension of Divine Benevolence," Jay strove to get American ships admitted to both the British West and East Indies.[154] He succeeded only within strict limits as to the size and destination of U.S. ships allowed in the British West Indies trade. He and Grenville sorted out the northern U.S. boundary, very favorably to America, but only partly solved the impressment issue, which ultimately ignited the War of 1812.

Jay and Grenville signed what came to be called the Jay Treaty on November 19, 1794. "I have no reason to believe, or conjecture, that one more favourable to us is attainable," Jay wrote of the treaty, and "we have reason to be satisfied." Moreover, it was hard work getting what we got, though it may not seem so, he remarked: "They who have levelled uneven ground, know how little of the work afterward appears."[155]

Outrage greeted the treaty in America, however. Pro-French Republicans, still resentful not only of England but also of the Federalists' Constitution and Hamilton's financial system, would naturally be opposed, an unsurprised Jay wrote, as would southern debtors, who hoped for a war that would finally cancel what they owed to British creditors.[156] Moreover, he didn't even try to get compensation for slaves the British had freed and carried off. When he arrived home in May 1795, Jay joked that he could travel across the country by the light of burning effigies of himself, and he met such newspaper squibs as:

May it please your highness, I John Jay
Have traveled all this mighty way,
To inquire if you, good Lord will please
To suffer me while on my knees,
To show all others I surpass,
In love, by kissing of your ____.[157]

Don't worry about it, Washington wrote: "I have little doubt of a perfect amelioration of sentiment, after the present fermentation . . . has evaporated a little more. —The dregs however will always remain, and the slightest motion will stir them up."[158] By 1796, as peaceful trade began to feed a boom, Republican Benjamin Rush grumbled that the treaty, "once reprobated by nineteen twentieths of our citizens, is now approved of, or peaceably acquiesced in, by the same proportion of the people."[159]

ONCE AGAIN Jay returned from abroad to find himself unexpectedly in a new job: without campaigning, he'd been elected governor of fast-growing New York State, prospering wildly as settlers moved to its hinterland now that the British forts were gone, and as Eli Whitney's new cotton gin sparked a boom in U.S. cotton production that New York merchants very profitably shipped to British mills.[160] Jay's two terms as governor of a state whose constitution he had written almost twenty years earlier left two great legacies. The first was penal reform. After hanging scores of miscreants beginning in his spymaster days, he had come to think that, while murderers deserved the death penalty, there must be a better way to punish twelve other classes of felons, who until then went to the gallows, and also a better way than whipping to punish lesser infractions. He proposed building "establishments for confining, employing and reforming criminals" by hard labor, and in November 1797 the state's first prison opened on four acres in Greenwich Village.[161]

Second, as far back as 1780, Jay had written from Spain that until America abolished slavery, "her Prayers to Heaven for Liberty will be impious," and if he were a legislator, he'd introduce a bill to abolish it and "never cease moving it till it became a Law."[162] The president of the New York Manumission Society from its founding in 1785 until he became chief justice (even though he himself still owned slaves), he carried out that vow when he became governor. Four times he had a bill introduced into the state legislature for gradual abolition, until it finally passed and he signed it into law in 1799.[163]

When Jefferson won the 1800 presidential election, Hamilton urged Jay in a slightly hysterical letter to use political legerdemain (to put it nicely) to overturn New York's vote for "an *Atheist* in Religion and a *Fanatic* in politics" and bring about Adams's reelection—a letter Jay filed with the notation: "Proposing a Measure . . . it wd. not become me to adopt."[164] From the same anti-Jefferson motive, Adams re-nominated Jay as chief justice, writing him that "the firmest security we can have against the effects of visionary schemes or fluctuating theories, will be in a solid judiciary."[165] But Jay had made up his mind to retire—and certainly the attractions of getting back on his horse to ride the judicial circuit again couldn't change it, so John Marshall became chief justice. When Jay's second three-year term as governor ended in June 1801, he headed for Westchester.

There he owned nearly 600 acres in Bedford that his father and his aunt had willed him out of the 5,200 acres Grandfather Van Cortlandt had bought as an investment around 1700 from Chief Katonah. (The hamlet within Bedford where Jay's farm stands now bears the Lenape chief's name.) Between 1799 and 1801 Jay enlarged for himself the small house he'd built there for his farm manager in the late 1780s. He emphatically did not want "a seat," his son William says; he wanted a plain, republican farmhouse, just like his neighbors' and like hundreds of others built by carpenters rather than architects all over the Northeast in the Federal period—two stories tall, five windows across, with a full-length front porch for looking down the hill at the lovely rural view to the south. After the stately pomp of his house at 133 Broadway, he now wanted no "useless display, which serves only to please other people's eyes, while it too often excites their envy."[166]

The only differences about his house were that it was bigger than most, with twelve spacious but cozy rooms (excluding hallways, cellar storerooms, and servants' garrets); it had two little wings, for his study and a kitchen, with their own doors to the porch (or piazza, as the Jays called it); and it was built like a battleship. Along with simplicity, Jay wanted quality and spared no expense for the best materials. A religious friend who visited while he was enlarging the house remarked that "all his conduct seemed to have reference to perpetuity in this world and eternity in the next," William recalls.[167] In this spirit, while riding the circuit in 1792, Jay had sent his son Peter Augustus some mulberry seeds to plant. "My father planted many trees," he wrote in the accompanying letter, "and I never walk in their shade without deriving additional pleasure from that circumstance; the time will come when you will probably experience similar emotions."[168]

All his furniture, still in the house, breathes the same republican gentleman's solid simplicity: his unadorned, indestructible traveling barrister's mahogany and glass-doored bookcases that unstack for transport, his mahogany Sheraton chest of drawers with its sober, subtle oval inlays, his rock-solid Sheraton four-poster, and especially those fine mahogany dining-room chairs James Fenimore Cooper sat in, with their slender vertical-slat backs fanned out just enough to be elegantly if severely stylish, their edges carved with just enough plain molding to show that a cabinetmaker, not a carpenter, made them—and so skillfully that, even though Jay's descendants used them well past the middle of the twentieth century, not a joint is loose.

Mementoes of his career are everywhere. In the hall hang engravings his former secretary John Trumbull gave him of two of his Revolutionary War paintings; in his study stand the cylinder-top desk he used as chief justice and three of the armchairs made for the original Senate chamber of New York's Federal Hall and given to Jay as a souvenir when he retired.

Not just a Founding Father but a family patriarch as well, he surrounded himself with portraits of his ancestors, his children, and his friends. The works and brass dial of his father's grandfather clock, its case broken in a move, now tick in a replacement case Jay had made—plain and mahogany. He kept (and neatly labeled) the certificate, signed in 1686 by James II's colonial governor of New York, Lord Limerick, that allowed his immigrant grandfather Augustus to live and work there. The four generations of descendants who lived in the house after Jay were equally reverent, carefully preserving their eminent forebear's relics, and enlarging the building (with modern plumbing too) toward the back without erasing the original structure.

Jay and his middle daughter, Ann, seventeen, moved into the house in the summer of 1801 to supervise the remodeling's finishing touches. Sally, ailing after a slight stroke in December 1800, had been taking the waters at Lebanon Springs and Ballston Spa, New York, and staying with relatives to avoid the construction noise and dust. "Oh my dear Mr. Jay! The distance that separates us is too, too great," she wrote from her sister Kitty's house up the Hudson—as she had so often written before. When she traveled south to Jay's childhood house at Rye, where his brother Peter lived, she wrote, "I have been rendered very happy by the company of our dear children but could we have been *All together* it would have heightened the satisfaction."[169] By December 2, 1801, she was in the new house, writing her newly married daughter Maria that, with the unusually mild weather, "Ann is at this moment in the garden planting peach-stones."[170] In May 1802 she wrote assuring Maria "that my health & appetite increases daily & that I really & truly feel very well indeed."[171]

That was the last letter Maria had from her mother: she died suddenly on May 28, aged forty-five, with her husband at her side. Jay led his children into the next room and read them from Corinthians: "Behold, I show you a mystery; We shall not all sleep, but we shall all be changed, in a moment, in the twinkling of an eye, at the last trump: for the trumpet shall sound, and the dead shall be raised incorruptible, and we shall be changed."

Jay wrote no letters for a long time. In January 1803, he wrote Rufus King, then U.S. envoy in London, of Sally's "long and painful Illness, and (when she appeared to be fast recovering) her unexpected Death." But he had a house and farm to finish and improve, an ill son, Peter Augustus, to care for and worry about (he recovered and became a successful New York lawyer), and Ann to look after (and look after him)—though Maria brought up her youngest sister, Sarah Louisa, and William went off to Yale. "My Expectations from Retirement have not been disappointed, and had Mrs. Jay continued with me,

I should deem this the most agreeable part of my Life," he told King. "Many Blessings yet remain and I enjoy them."[172]

He was up at dawn, in the saddle before breakfast on a horse whose grandam his father had given him in 1765 and whose mother he had then ridden. Outdoors most of the day, he supervised improvements, crops, and cider-, grist-, and saw-mills. He presided over morning and evening worship with his family and servants, and carefully annotated his prayer book with the appropriate prayers for specific days. He expanded his landholdings to about 750 acres and corresponded with British agricultural innovators on the latest advances in scientific farming. He rarely commented on politics or visited New York City, once letting eight years pass without a trip to town. "A stranger might have resided with him for months together, without discovering from his conversation that he had ever been employed in the service of his country," writes William, who came to live with him in 1809, raised six children in the house at Bedford, and helped his father turn the farm into a profitable dairy operation, while also founding the American Bible Society and becoming a prominent abolitionist.[173]

"The burden of time I have not experienced," Jay wrote, adding that he enjoyed "frequent conversations with the 'mighty dead,' who, in a certain sense, live in their works."[174] Christian stoic that he was, he most often turned to the Bible and to Cicero, that beguiling conversationalist who loved virtue, revered private property, hated tyranny and taxation, and brought Greek stoic philosophy to Rome and to posterity. Like his fellow lawyer-statesman Jay, he understood that in a world of adversity, injustice, and suffering, where one must often "choose the least among evils," one must live according to "the moral law which nature itself has ordained" and which philosophers have painstakingly (if inconsistently) elucidated, in order to better the human community and to feel whole and decent in one's "own soul, which is the most godlike thing that God has given to man."[175] Along with that bracing doctrine, Jay also had his belief in the afterlife. Two years after Sally's death, that Christian stoicism illuminates his condolence letter on the death of his friend Alexander Hamilton to Hamilton's father-in-law, Jay's old and dear friend, Philip Schuyler: "The philosophic topics of consolation are familiar to you," he wrote, "and we all know from experience how little relief is to be derived from them. May the Author and only Giver of consolation be and remain with you."[176]

As his twenty-eight years of temperate and contented retirement neared their halfway mark, his worldview had grown, if anything, more wry. His health was better than a year ago, he wrote a friend, "so that at present, there is some Prospect of my living to see further Proofs of the Perfectibility of human nature by modern Philosophers, and of the increased Illumination of this Age of Reason."[177] On May 17, 1829, at the age of eighty-three, he died, as perfect in virtue as human imperfection allows.

7

Alexander Hamilton and the American Dream

In stark contrast to Washington, Jefferson, or the Lees, descendants of seventeenth-century Virginians—or to Harvard-educated John Adams, whose forebears settled in Massachusetts Bay in 1638—Alexander Hamilton resembled those tempest-tost millions who sailed beneath the Statue of Liberty's welcoming beacon in the three decades before World War I, fulfilling George Washington's prediction that "the poor, the needy, & oppressed of the Earth" would find America "the second Land of promise."[1] A poor immigrant from the West Indies, Hamilton, like them, had come to New York seeking his fortune.

Nor was he just poor. "My birth," as he delicately put it, "is the subject of the most humiliating criticism"—for he was, in Adams's acidulous taunt, "the bastard brat of a Scotch pedlar."[2] But rich in the ambition and enterprise that could thrive in the American opportunity society he so passionately championed, he rose to be one of the country's most powerful and celebrated men, and he multiplied and strengthened the means for countless others to follow his footsteps up the ladder of success.

It's hard to exaggerate the squalor and dysfunction surrounding the future Treasury secretary's Caribbean childhood. When his mother, "a handsome young woman having a *snug* fortune," was only sixteen, Hamilton wrote, a Danish "fortune-hunter . . . bedizzened with gold," dazzled her widowed mother by his "glitter" and persuaded her to let him marry the unwilling teenager.[3] After five unhappy years on the Danish island of Saint Croix, the young wife abandoned her husband and their baby boy. The outraged Dane had her jailed, as Saint Croix law allowed, for "whoring with everyone," he charged. But though he expected her to return to him chastened and meek, she fled upon her release, settling on her native Nevis with James Hamilton, a seedy but still dashing younger son of a Scottish laird. On that tiny British island—where her father, a Huguenot doctor had found refuge from religious persecution in the late seventeeth century—she and James Hamilton lived as man and wife, and she bore two more sons, James Jr., and, on January 11, 1755, Alexander. Though her Danish husband finally got a divorce from her in 1759, its terms forbade her remarriage.[4]

The black sheep of a well-off family, James Hamilton had come to the sugar isles in search of riches like so many threadbare adventurers, but he had "too much pride and too large a portion of indolence," Hamilton recalled much later, so his "affairs at a very early day went to wreck" and he sank into the crowd of failures and lowlifes who overran the West Indies.[5] When Hamilton was ten, James decamped, drifting until he washed up, old and dying, near the southern Caribbean speck where Defoe shipwrecked Robinson Crusoe.[6]

Hamilton's intelligent and enterprising mother went back to Saint Croix and opened a general store. But when Hamilton was twelve, one of the tropical fevers that ravaged European fortune seekers in the islands felled her, and a sea of troubles engulfed the two Hamilton boys. The cousin who took them in killed himself two years later, leaving the boys destitute; their mother's little estate—nine slaves, chiefly—had gone to her one legitimate son, who had swooped down to snatch it away from her two "obscene children." All Hamilton had left were her thirty-four books, including the Plutarch and Pope that had been his beloved childhood companions, which his cousin had kindly bought for him in the auction of her household effects.[7]

Then, like Mr. Brownlow rescuing Oliver Twist, fairy-tale magic struck. A rich Saint Croix merchant, Thomas Stevens, took Hamilton into his orderly, sheltering household, where he became lifelong friends with Stevens's son Ned, a year older and remarkably similar in tastes and talents. And why did Stevens take in Alexander but leave his brother James Jr. to become a carpenter's apprentice? Years later, when Secretary of State Timothy Pickering first met Ned Stevens, he was flabbergasted by his "extraordinary similitude" to Hamilton. "I thought they must be *brothers*," Pickering wrote—an observation that one of Ned's relatives later told him "had been made a thousand times." So was Hamilton doubly illegitimate? Pickering thought so; perhaps someday the DNA sleuths will say for sure.[8]

Some months before the Stevenses took him in, Hamilton, without realizing it, had already attached himself to the great world beyond his little island. Though remote, Saint Croix was integral to the eighteenth-century British Empire's economic dynamo, the triangle trade, which (to oversimplify) brought slaves from Africa to work the sugar estates of Britain's and Europe's West Indian colonies, carried the sugar and molasses to colonial New England to make into rum, and returned to Africa to trade rum for more slaves, generally with a stop in England to sell sugar and rum for manufactures. At thirteen, Hamilton had begun clerking for the island outpost of Beekman and Cruger, a New York trading firm owned by two of the city's great Dutch mercantile families, key players in that business for generations.[9] As he took his modest place in world commerce, he also launched himself onto a tributary that flowed into the heart of New York's mainstream.

His stint at Beekman and Cruger, he later told his son John, was "the most useful part of his education," teaching him the facts of global economic life, from commodity prices, cash flow, and exchange rates to bill collecting and smuggling.[10] When his boss, Nicholas Cruger, fell ill and went home to New York (where his uncle was mayor), he left his luminously gifted sixteen-year-old clerk in charge. The adolescent took to management with gusto: his vivid letter to young Cruger about how he fattened up a cargo of starving mules from the firm's sloop *Thunderbolt* is a marvel of self-confident energy.[11]

On his countinghouse stool, Hamilton dreamt big. At fourteen, he wrote to Ned Stevens, in his earliest surviving letter, "my Ambition is prevalent that I contemn the grov'ling and condition of a Clerk or the like, to which my Fortune &c. condemns me and would willingly risk my life tho' not my Character to exalt my Station. . . . I mean to prepare the way for futurity. . . . [I] may be jusly said to Build Castles in the Air . . . , yet Neddy we have seen such Schemes successful when the Projector is Constant I shall Conclude saying I wish there was a War."[12]

But the upheaval that first exalted Hamilton's station wasn't a war; it was a hurricane that ripped through Saint Croix in August 1772. When Hamilton's muscular account of the storm's ferocity, its aftermath of death and desolation, and his own fears and religious hopes appeared in the local newspaper, its brio amazed readers, some of whom, led by Hamilton's employers and a kindly clergyman, raised funds to send the teenaged prodigy off to college in North America.[13] When Princeton declined to let him plow through its BA requirements as fast as he could rather than take the usual three years, the young-man-in-a-hurry enrolled instead at King's College (later Columbia) in late 1773 or early 1774 and became a Manhattanite.[14]

American culture embraces a host of microcultures—local traditions and ways of seeing the world that spring from some particular history and make different groups express their common Americanism in their own distinctive accents. The egalitarian Quaker culture of Philadelphia, to take sociologist Digby Baltzell's example, nurtured many fewer strivers who made it into the *Dictionary of American Biography* than Boston's more individualist Puritanism. Similarly, historian David Hackett Fischer has shown how the "folkways" of colonists from four different British regions, with their own variants of Protestantism, subtly molded the cultures of the sections of America they settled, so that their inhabitants ended up with differently inflected understandings even of so basic an idea as liberty.[15]

The New York that welcomed Alexander Hamilton had its own distinctive culture, too, whose uniqueness went far deeper than John Adams's description of a town where "they talk very fast, very loud, and all together."[16] Its Dutch past, from Peter Minuit's 1626 purchase of Manhattan to Peter Stuyvesant's forced handover of the flourishing New Netherland colony to the British in 1664, left an indelible legacy. After decades of brutal religious war, the Dutch Republic had embraced tolerance with fervor and transplanted to its trading post on the Hudson its constitutional promise that "each person shall remain free, especially in his religion, and no one shall be persecuted or investigated because of his religion." So, for example, when Governor-General Stuyvesant wanted to limit the rights of twenty-three Jews who sought asylum in New Amsterdam in 1654, they petitioned the Dutch authorities, who commanded Stuyvesant to treat them with Dutch tolerance, reminding him also that Jews were big investors in the West India Company. And then—as if Jews weren't bad enough—Quakers appeared in the Long Island village of Vlissingen, whose mostly English residents called it Flushing. When Stuyvesant forbade the villagers from taking in the Quakers, they disobeyed, citing in their 1657 *Flushing Remonstrance*, one of the foundation documents of American religious liberty, the Dutch principle that "love peace and libertie" must extend even to "Jewes Turkes and Egiptians" and reminding the governor-general of their charter, which granted the right "to have and Enjoy the Liberty of Conscience, according to the Custome and manner of Holland."[17]

And so New Amsterdam became a melting pot like no other place in North America, with settlers arriving from all over the globe and not only living side by side but also marrying each other. A quarter of the couples married in the town's Dutch Reformed Church were of different ancestries, with Germans marrying Danes, Italians Dutchmen, a man from "Calis in Vranckryck" wedding a girl from "Batavia in the East Indies."[18]

The tolerance, which also welcomed sectarian refugees from Massachusetts' intolerant Puritanism, was a matter of policy as well as principle: the business of New Amsterdam was business, and the authorities wanted to recruit traders of any stripe. The town was quick to make newcomers full citizens. Whereas only 20 percent of that era's New Englanders were freemen, New Amsterdam, in addition to the "great burgher" status it conferred on substantial taxpayers like the first Beekmans, also gave out "small burgher" status to almost anyone who asked. In the benign glow of such equal-opportunity inclusiveness, commerce boomed: Manhattan became a key shipping center even for Virginia tobacco.[19]

With its "frank acceptance of differences and a belief that individual achievement matters more than birthright," concludes Russell Shorto in *The Island at the Center of the World*, his dazzling history of Dutch New York, "this island city would become the first multiethnic, upwardly mobile society on America's shores, a prototype of the kind of society that would be duplicated throughout the country." It produced prototypical New Yorkers, too, says Shorto, "worldly, brash, confident, hustling." When the British took over, they promised to preserve the regime of tolerance and free trade (and did so for a century). "The Dutch here shall enjoy the liberty of their consciences," they proclaimed. "Dutch vessels may freely come hither."[20] Why meddle with success?

Into the theater of opportunity that had developed from such beginnings—the town where, in Gouverneur Morris's words, "to be born in America seems to be a matter of indifference"—stepped the upwardly mobile young immigrant of dubious parentage and prodigious talent, just at the moment of the Boston Tea Party.[21] Within months of entering King's College, overlooking the Hudson and adjoining the port city's busy red-light district, the nineteen-year-old threw himself into revolutionary politics. At a mass rally against England's punitive Coercive Acts, he made himself famous with an impassioned impromptu speech, calling for a boycott of British goods in defense of American liberties, that electrified the crowd. He followed up with two pamphlets prophetic in their assumption that war would come, that the colonists (with the aid of France and Spain) would win with a guerrilla insurgency, and that they would outstrip Britain in population and wealth.[22] Again and again in his career, Hamilton showed such premonitory insight: he saw complex things at a glance, saw them whole, and saw their consequences. And he had no patience with those who couldn't keep up with his brilliance.[23]

The moment that news of Concord and Lexington reached New York, Hamilton, with his own brand of student activism, joined the militia and then, early in 1776, the Continental Army. In the dismal retreat from New York—which the British occupied for the next seven years—and in the famous victories at Trenton and Princeton, the twenty-one-year-old artillery captain earned the nickname "the little lion" for his cool determination and unflappable courage under fire. An excellent commander and superb organizer, he won the admiration of a quartet of generals, including Washington, who invited him to join his staff as an aide-de-camp and lieutenant colonel in March 1777, aged twenty-two.[24] So the war he had wished for back in Saint Croix had come and had indeed exalted his station. As he said much later, revolutions, for all their horrors, "serve to bring to light, talents and virtues, which might otherwise have languished in obscurity, or only shot forth a few scattered and wandering rays."[25]

His connection with Washington turned out to be the greatest opportunity in Hamilton's life. Almost everything he achieved, he achieved as the commander in chief's right-hand man. As Hamilton said at his patron's death, "I have been much indebted to the kindness of the General; and he was an Aegis very essential to me."[26] They were each other's completing counterparts; neither would have achieved such greatness alone. "As a team, they were unbeatable and far more than the sum of their parts," says Hamilton's splendid biographer Ron Chernow.[27]

In the war, Hamilton quickly became, wrote Washington to Adams, his "principal and most confidential aide, . . . enterprising, quick in his perceptions," with "judgment intuitively great" and ambition "of that laudable kind which prompts a man to excel in whatever he takes in hand."[28] The aide worked out strategy with his commander, dealt with his subordinate generals, wrote letters exactly expressing Washington's intention from only the vaguest hint. "During the whole time that he was one of the General's aides-de-camp," recalled Secretary of State Timothy Pickering, "Hamilton had to *think* as well as *write* for him in all his most important correspondence."[29]

It was more than a professional relationship. Following conventional eighteenth-century usage, Washington called his staff of aides his "family," and, convention aside, that word catches the emotional tone. Certainly the general's closest aides-de-camp—Hamilton, the Marquis de Lafayette, and John Laurens—became a band of brothers, reminiscent, Hamilton's son said, of the Three Musketeers.[30] "All the family send their love," Hamilton wrote to Laurens in April 1779. "In this join the General & Mrs. Washington & what is best, tis not in the stile of ceremony but sincerity."[31] Increasingly secure in Washington's affection, he closed a letter to Laurens ten months later, "All the Lads embrace you. The General sends his love."[32] The orphaned and abandoned Hamilton acquired the greatest father figure of them all; and of no less emotional importance, the childless Father of his Country gained a surrogate son, whom he often called "my boy." And indeed the rumor later went round, sparked by Hamilton's enemies, that the slight, fine-boned West Indian with the gently pensive face was the strapping general's illegitimate offspring.[33]

Wherever there's a father figure and a son, the Viennese doctor would say, there's tension. In this case at least, there came to be. After four years with Washington, Hamilton had risen far above his "grov'ling" condition, but he remained a sort of "Clerk" and began to feel stifled in a job "having in it a kind of personal dependance," as he put it. He nursed dreams of further, personal, glory and chafed when Washington vetoed his requests for his own command. He came to feel his patron's affection a burden—a demand not just for affection in return but also for self-suppression. For his part, Washington surely felt stung not only by Hamilton's eagerness to move on but also by his brilliant protégé's return of increasingly stiff reserve to his own warmth, the aide's correct "Your Excellency" to the General's "my boy." "The pride of my temper would not suffer me to profess what I did not feel," wrote Hamilton at the time. "Indeed when advances of this kind have been made to me on his part, they were received in a manner that showed at least I had no inclination to court them, and that I wished to stand rather on a footing of military confidence than of private attachment."[34]

The inevitable explosion came, as usually happens, over a trifle. The two passed each other on the stairs, Washington told Hamilton he wanted to speak to him, and Hamilton said he'd be right back and went to finish his errand, returning, "I sincerely believe," in less than two minutes. He found Washington in a rage. "Col Hamilton (said he), you have kept me waiting at the head of the stairs these ten minutes. I must tell you Sir you treat me with disrespect." How much suppressed heartache that last sentence contains! "I am not conscious of it Sir," replied Hamilton, "but since you have thought it necessary to tell me so we part." "Very well Sir (said he) if it be your choice." And though the General almost immediately tried to "heal a difference which could not have happened but in a moment of passion," Hamilton, his pent-up, proud resentment unappeasable, quit the staff.[35]

In July 1781, Washington finally gave him the command he craved, and it brought him all the glory he wished. When American and French armies had bottled up British general Lord Cornwallis on the Yorktown peninsula, with a French fleet blocking him offshore, Washington and the French general, Comte de Rochambeau, needed to sweep away two British redoubts to squeeze their siege tighter. Washington ordered Hamilton's New York light infantry to clear one and a French brigade the other. Hamilton did it with panache, jumping gallantly onto the redoubt's parapet at the head of his troops, who bayoneted the enemy into quick submission; his French counterpart did it with less grace and more blood. But the two victories checkmated Cornwallis, who surrendered five days later, on October 19, 1781, ending the last great battle of the long war—though it was two more years before the British finally left New York City.

WHILE SOLDIERS starved and froze throughout the war, Hamilton, at Washington's right hand, bitterly watched how Congress's shortcomings worsened their sufferings with fecklessness and corruption that turned scarcity into famine. He mused over how to fix what was broken, and read widely, filling the blank pages of his old artillery-company paybook with facts and quotations from Bacon, Cicero, Hobbes, Hume, Montaigne, and Plutarch, along with Postlethwayt's *Trade and Commerce*.[36] By 1780, still Washington's aide-de-camp, he had concluded, earlier than most, that the United States needed a constitutional convention to form an entirely new governmental structure. That year, in a prophetic letter to Congressman James Duane, with his characteristically brilliant grasp of a complex whole in all its details, he sketched out that new government: energetic, strongly centralized, with power to raise an army and build a navy, assess taxes and contract foreign loans to support these forces, declare war and peace, regulate trade, coin money, and establish banks.[37]

Having played his heroic part in the battle that won the war, he returned to civilian life aiming to help create that new order. Late in 1780, he had married Elizabeth Schuyler, the levelheaded, endlessly kind daughter of General (later Senator) Philip Schuyler, head of a great patroon family, owner of tens of thousands of upstate acres, and a proud friend and powerful ally of his son-in-law ever after. The young couple moved into the Schuyler mansion in Albany, the gabled town founded by Stuyvesant, where Eliza listened to sermons in Dutch, still spoken in the Hudson Valley until well into the nineteenth century.[38] There Hamilton taught himself law by ravening through his friend Duane's legal library, learning in six months what usually took three years and writing a study guide for himself that, passed around in manuscript copies, served other law students as a textbook for the next decade. In October 1782, three months after passing the bar, he also became the equivalent of a British barrister.[39]

When the British finally left New York City, leaving behind a half-burnt-out town stinking of sewage, Hamilton moved back with Eliza and brand-new baby Philip to a rented house at 57 Wall Street and became one of the city fathers who rebuilt Gotham. He joined the board of the now renamed Columbia College, helped create the New York Board of Regents, and founded the Bank of New York—all within the first year or so of his return. He also became one of the greatest lawyers of them all—up there with Daniel Webster, one judge later averred.[40]

All the while, the project of recasting the national government ripened in his mind. While still cramming for the bar in 1782, he won election to Congress, headed two of its key committees six months later, and grew even more fervent for reform from his firsthand congressional experience. In 1786, he sought a New York legislature seat, which he planned to use, he told a friend, "as a stepping stone to a general convention to form a general constitution." His maneuvering in the months after he won it made him, says Catherine Drinker Bowen, arguably "the most potent single influence toward calling the Convention of '87."[41]

At the Convention, besides ensuring that immigrants like himself had full, New York–style opportunity to serve in Congress, he made only one other contribution: a six-hour speech outlining his ideal government, very "dissimilar," he conceded "with the greatest diffidence," from the two plans already under consideration. He proposed a highly democratic Assembly elected directly by the people every three years, counterbalanced by a president and senate to serve for life (unless impeached for misbehavior), chosen by electors picked by men of property.[42] No believer in what we now call federalism, he foresaw that the "general power" of this new central government "must swallow up the State powers. Otherwise it will be swallowed up by them."[43]

His purpose was threefold. He wanted to combine, as he'd suggested in his letter to Duane, the advantages of a monarchy's energetic executive with republican liberty—to unite, as he thought the British constitution did so well, "public strength with individual security." In the second place, he aimed to ensure real checks and balances between the rich and powerful and the rest. "Give all power to the many, they will oppress the few," he explained, according to Madison's Convention notes. "Give all power to the few, they will oppress the many."[44] His was a scheme that would ensure true equilibrium among monarchy, aristocracy, and democracy, like the British constitution's system of king, lords, and commons checking and balancing one another's power to prevent a slide into tyranny, oligarchy, or anarchy. Flying in the face of this long-standing British constitutional theory—which fellow Founders John Adams, John Dickinson, and Richard Henry Lee also held—the other schemes proposed at the Convention, he argued, envisioned merely having "democracy, checked by democracy, or *pork still, with a little change of the sauce*," as New York delegate Robert Yates recorded in his notes.[45]

His third purpose—and this was the goal of the equilibrium he sought—was "to go as far in order to achieve stability and permanency, as republican principles will admit." While "the demagogue or middling politician, who, for the sake of a small stipend and the hopes of advancement, will offer himself as a candidate" for the Assembly, and will sway with every wayward puff of "the amazing violence & turbulence of the democratic spirit," he wanted senators to be more like British lords, who have "nothing to hope for by a change, and . . . form a permanent barrier agst. every pernicious innovation." His president-for-life idea had the same object of keeping officials "faithful to the national interest," a view Patrick Henry shared: without the need to run for re-election, Hamilton argued, such an executive "is placed above temptation. He can have no distinct interests from the public welfare."[46] Of course, he foresaw, "It will be objected probably that such an Executive will be an *elective Monarch*." Not so, he countered: "by making the executive subject to impeachment, the term monarchy cannot apply."[47]

Behind these ideas lay his deepest worry: that direct democracy could decline into mindless mob rule. He had seen that happen after

Concord and Lexington, when a Patriot mob had stormed King's College president Myles Cooper's house, aiming to tar and feather him for his rigid Toryism. The twenty-year-old Hamilton boldly harangued the drunken, anarchic crowd about how they were about to "disgrace and injure the glorious cause of liberty"—just long enough to let their target flee out the back door and take ship for England. So, too, in November did Hamilton try, unsuccessfully, to defend Tory newspaper publisher James Rivington when Patriots destroyed his print shop.[48]

"The same state of the passions which fits the multitude, who have not a sufficient stock of reason and knowlege to guide them, for opposition to tyranny and oppression, very naturally leads them to a contempt and disregard of all authority," Hamilton wrote John Jay after the Rivington incident. "When the minds of these are loosened from their attachment to ancient establishments and courses, they seem to grow giddy and are apt more or less to run into anarchy. . . . In such tempestuous times, it requires the greatest skill in the political pilots to keep men steady and within proper bounds, on which account I am always more or less alarmed at every thing which is done of mere will and pleasure, without any proper authority."[49]

But it's not just the multitude who have a small stock of reason. At the heart of Hamilton's political vision lay the belief that men in general are reasoning rather than reasonable animals. "Has it not . . . invariably been found, that momentary passions and immediate interests have a more active and imperious controul over human conduct than general or remote considerations of policy, utility or justice?" he asked—a vision as different from Jefferson's Enlightenment rationalism as Edmund Burke's was.[50] "Why has government been instituted at all?" he asked. "Because the passions of men will not conform to the dictates of reason and justice, without constraint."[51]

So while the Constitution that finally emerged from the Convention couldn't bring about "the deceitful dream of a golden age," which no earthly government can accomplish, Hamilton noted, it was unquestionably a practical framework for ensuring liberty while keeping men steady and within proper bounds.[52] Drawing from all the advances of "the science of politics," it provided for the "regular distribution of power into distinct departments—the introduction of legislative balances and checks—the institution of courts composed of judges, holding their offices during good behaviour—the representation of the people in the legislature by deputies of their own election. . . . These are . . . powerful means by which the excellencies of republican government may be retained and its imperfections lessened or avoided"—exactly what he was seeking in his marathon Convention speech.[53]

THIS WAS A CONSTITUTION that Hamilton thought worth fighting for, offering everything he had called for in his 1780 letter to Duane. With his then-friend James Madison and John Jay (whom injury soon sidelined), he began history's noblest propaganda campaign ever in favor of the Constitution's ratification—the *Federalist Papers*, eighty-five newspaper columns, some fifty of which Hamilton wrote, sometimes two, occasionally five or even six, a week. The first, which Hamilton penned on board a passenger sloop from New York to Albany, appeared on October 27, 1787, and stressed how high the stakes in the debate were: "whether societies of men are really capable or not, of establishing good government from reflection and choice, or whether they are forever destined to depend for their political constitutions, on accident and force."[54]

Americans learned from their "unequivocal experience . . . in the course of the revolution" that their existing governmental structure didn't work, Hamilton argued. They knew even then that they had to make some basic change. Now the trade disputes raging between different states showed yet another defect in the old structure: it might prove too weak to hold the union together in the future.[55] America could end up, like the European countries, divided into several warring confederacies, each too weak to defend itself against the depredations of the European powers.[56] By now all citizens should all have learned "that the vigour of government is essential to the security of liberty."[57]

The new Constitution, he argued as *The Federalist* progressed, fixes these defects by creating "a vigorous national government" with sufficient powers to protect citizens "as well against internal convulsions as external attacks,"[58] to regulate international and interstate commerce, and to carry on foreign affairs. It provides for vital "energy in the executive." It allows the federal government to raise armies and build a navy, as it must "if we mean to be a commercial people."[59] And it permits the government to tax, since "money is . . . the vital principle of the body politic," government's "essential engine."[60] But government should levy taxes with wisdom and restraint, Hamilton cautioned: "If duties are too high they lessen the consumption . . . ; and the product to the treasury is not so great as when they are confined within proper and moderate bounds."[61] And of course, "if we are in earnest about giving the Union energy and duration, we must abandon the vain project of legislating upon the States in their collective capacities: We must extend the laws of the Fœderal Government to the individual citizens of America," making the national government supreme at the expense of the state governments.[62]

Standing guard over the whole machinery, to keep the legislators "within the limits assigned to their authority," will be "the rights of the courts to pronounce legislative acts void, because . . . [n]o legislative act . . . contrary to the Constitution, can be valid." After all, this fundamental law, which embodies "the intention of the people," must always be of "superior obligation and validity . . . to the intention of their agents" in the legislature. And since the "interpretation of the laws is the proper and peculiar province of the courts," it "therefore belongs to them to ascertain [the Constitution's] meaning."[63] This was fifteen years before Chief Justice John Marshall wrote *Marbury v. Madison.*

In June 1788, the Constitution took effect when the ninth state ratified it. In July, New York State decided to sign on, too, thanks primarily to a month of Hamilton's heroic speechifying at the Poughkeepsie ratifying convention. Wildly pro-Constitution Gothamites celebrated their townsman's magnificent achievement as author and orator with a rollicking parade, featuring a flag that depicted Hamilton beneath trumpet-blowing Fame, and climaxed by a twenty-seven-foot-long, frigate-shaped float pulled by ten horses and christened the Federal ship *Hamilton*. Marching down Broadway with the celebrants was Hamilton's old Saint Croix boss, Nicholas Cruger.[64]

ONCE GEORGE WASHINGTON took office under the new Constitution on April 30, 1789, that "energy in the executive" that *The Federalist* had extolled turned out largely to be Hamilton himself, at least in the first term. Appointed Treasury secretary in September—the startled Washington had only recently learned that his ex-aide was a financial whiz—Hamilton, now thirty-four, turned to the financial crisis undermining the nation.[65] He did more than solve it. He used it as an occasion to spread the contagion of liberty, accelerating the transformation of what historian Forrest McDonald calls a "hierarchical and deferential social order"—in which freely elected justices of the peace always turned out to be generation after generation of the same family, and Harvard listed students in its records in order of family prominence—into a free-market, opportunity society in the New York tradition.[66]

"The fabled birth of Minerva from the brain of Jove," Daniel Webster exclaimed, "was hardly more sudden or more perfect than the financial system of the United States, as it burst forth from the conception of Alexander Hamilton."[67] Certainly all the complex pieces came into being almost simultaneously and meshed together with Swiss-watch precision. But the exquisite mechanism had a moral as well as an economic purpose, which Hamilton explained in his 1791 *Report on Manufactures*, and it's worth understanding the *why* before quickly considering the *how*.

If Americans were going to pursue happiness, Hamilton aimed to give them powerful means to do it. Now that they had gained unprecedented "personal independence" and "perfect equality of religious privileges" from the "more equal government" that the Revolution and new Constitution had established, he wrote, Americans next needed a vibrant, diversified economy that would include manufacturing, to further both their material and their spiritual well-being. The object of such an economy would not be just the production of more goods and services but also the human fulfillment, the realization of human potential, that comes from thinking them up and creating them.

In this sense, Hamilton saw, economics is soulcraft. So while "a more ample and various field of enterprize" will certainly increase the wealth of the nation, he said, it will also allow all "the diversity of talents and dispositions which discriminate men from each other" to develop to their fullest excellence. In a society with limited opportunity, "minds of the strongest and most active powers for their proper objects . . . labour without effect, if confined to uncongenial pursuits." But "when all the different kinds of industry obtain in a community, each individual can find his proper element, and can call into activity the whole vigour of his nature. . . . To cherish and stimulate the activity of the human mind, by multiplying the objects of enterprise, is not among the least considerable of the expedients, by which the wealth of a nation may be promoted."[68] In Hamilton's hands, the dismal science became a humane and optimistic one.

Who knows how far the flow of opportunity and progress can spread? Machines that "facilitate and abridge labour" proliferate; the man who conceives and designs them is an "Artist."[69] As invention and enterprise flourish, the increase of supply creates its own demand, in turn sparking further enterprise. "Every new scene, which is opened to the busy nature of man to rouse and exert itself, is the addition of a new energy to the general stock of effort. . . . The bowels as well as the surface of the earth are ransacked for articles which were before neglected. Animals, Plants and Minerals acquire an utility and value, which were before unexplored."[70] Talent, ingenuity, and innovation blossom, prosperity increases, and dependence on (and vulnerability to) foreign powers shrinks.[71]

BUT TO REACH that point takes a money economy, and that's what Hamilton created out of the $76 million that the nation and various states owed to soldiers, army suppliers, and foreign lenders. That debt, said Hamilton in his January 1790 *Report on Public Credit*, "was the price of our liberty," and it would be shameful to repudiate it, as some politicians urged. It would be impolitic too: for if the federal government could convert all the various bonds and promissory notes representing those debts into federal government securities that people believed would actually be paid in full, those securities could serve as money. They could serve as a medium of exchange that would "give greater means for enterprize," extending trade, manufacturing, and agriculture.[72] But they could do so, to repeat, only if people believed they were really worth what they said they were worth, and government creates such belief by keeping its promises, not repudiating them.

Of course the nation had insufficient gold and silver to pay these debts in full, so Hamilton proposed instead to renegotiate and restructure them into several kinds of interest-bearing annuities. He would pay the interest by levying import duties and excise taxes sequestered in a special "sinking fund" that he'd also use to buy up bonds in the market whenever they fell below their face value, thus pushing the price back up to "par" (as he did spectacularly to calm the markets like a seasoned central banker when the bursting of a speculative bubble gave way to the panic of 1792). Thus stabilized in value, the securities could serve as money.[73]

But in the process, Hamilton had to untangle a jumble. Some original holders had sold their promissory notes at big discounts (as Washington had predicted they would have to); and in converting these to federal bonds, some legislators asked, shouldn't the government in fairness discriminate among holders, paying a speculator who had bought an IOU from a hard-up ex-soldier only what the spectator had paid for it, plus interest, and giving the rest of the face value to the veteran whose wounds had earned it? Hamilton managed to talk Congress out of such discrimination, arguing that it would be an administrative nightmare of dubious justice, and that it would subvert the whole enterprise, because unless people believed that government securities were worth their face value, they wouldn't be negotiable and so wouldn't serve as money.[74]

And what of the state debts? Hamilton thought that the federal government—meaning everybody—should assume responsibility for paying them, since they had been incurred in the national cause.[75] But Virginians, who had already settled most of their debt for pennies on the dollar, and who had lots of House votes, disagreed. And so Hamilton made his famous deal with Jefferson and Madison over dinner on June 20, 1790. They would provide the votes for the federal assumption of state debts if Hamilton delivered the votes for moving the national capital from New York to Philadelphia for ten years and then to a permanent site on the Potomac, where the Virginia statesmen incidentally had bought up lots of land. By the end of July, the necessary legislation had passed. And by December, paper worth $15 million when Hamilton first went to work in his Broadway office just below Wall Street had tripled in value.[76]

THAT MONTH, now in the new capital of Philadelphia, Hamilton sent Congress his *Report on a National Bank*, laying out the last parts of his plan—a bank to issue currency and lend it, a mint to print and coin it, and a customs service to collect duties and catch smugglers. Paper money, Hamilton understood, has an almost magical aspect. Like a bond, a banknote is just a promise, resting on the credit of the issuer, and credit is mere belief. He had already noted in his *Report on Public Credit* that "in nothing are appearances of greater moment, than in whatever regards credit. Opinion is the soul of it, and this is affected by appearances, as well as realities."[77] Now he intended to use the prestidigitation of credit to levitate the nation into economic modernity.

"Gold and silver, when they are employed merely as the instruments of exchange and [transfer of ownership], have been not improperly denominated dead Stock," he explained in the *Report on a National Bank*; "but when deposited in Banks, to become the basis of a paper circulation, which takes their character and place, as the signs or representatives of value, they then acquire life, or, in other words, an active and productive quality."[78] That's because, first, the bank can issue paper currency way beyond the value of the precious metal in its vault, since individuals have so much faith that they can redeem their dollar bill for a dollar's worth of gold or silver that they never do the experiment—at least not all at once.[79] How far beyond the value of the gold and silver can the paper currency grow? In a breathtaking leap of daring, Hamilton arranged that, of the bank's $10 million capitalization, only $2 million would be actual precious metal; the rest would be . . . federal government bonds—mere promises—so that the national debt would support an even larger superstructure of credit. The bank's stockholders would pay for their shares in four installments over two years, one-fourth in specie and the rest in bonds.[80] For the first six months, therefore, Hamilton balanced a $10 million elephant of currency on a $500,000 ball of specie.

So why was this not a pyramid scheme?

Hamilton made one of those leaps of faith that, once made, prove true. He believed that the country had a vast latent productive capacity—an "unequalled spirit of enterprise, which . . . is in itself an inexhaustible mine of national wealth"—and raw developable land that just needed to be unlocked with capital to start gushing riches.[81] As things stood, he had written as far back as 1780, "the money in circulation is not a sufficient representative of the productions of the country."[82] The bank's ability to put its capital to work, incessantly circulating it in notes or in loans at interest, so that it never lies idle, is to "all the purposes of trade and industry an absolute increase of capital," he observed. "And thus by contributing to enlarge the mass of industrious and commercial enterprise, banks become nurseries of national wealth." By giving loans to the creditworthy, banks "enable honest and industrious men, of small or perhaps no capital to undertake and prosecute business, with advantage to themselves and to the community," he wrote, as one self-made man hoping to give others the same opportunity; and indeed he took care to issue currency in small denominations, so that even the humblest could reap the benefits of the new economy.[83] "He smote the rock of the national resources," Daniel Webster marveled, "and abundant streams of revenue gushed forth."[84]

Hamilton insisted that the bank be run privately, not by government (which held a 20 percent stake, to give it some oversight power). A private bank would take care not to print more money than its capital could support or than the economy could productively employ, since otherwise people would try to cash in superfluous banknotes for specie, depleting the bank's reserves. Underlying the magical belief, he repeatedly insisted, had to be a foundation of hard reality: some specie is really there; loans go to people whose character and business plans the bank finds, after careful inspection, solid enough to pay back the money. Politicians are less prudent. "The stamping of paper is an operation so much easier than the laying of taxes," Hamilton noted, that in an emergency, government would too readily roll the presses, producing inflation and ruining the bank's credit. Stupid, yes: "But what government ever uniformly consulted its true interest," he asked, "in opposition to the temptations of momentary exigencies?"[85] In this case, at least, government did the right thing, and Washington signed the bank bill in February 1791.

As Hamilton rolled out his new revolution, opponents rose up in outrage. Not only agriculturalists like Jefferson believed that the Hamiltonian system would turn the country over to corrupt "stock jobbers"; even Harvard-trained Adams lacked the economic acumen to know that bankers could be anything more than "swindlers and thieves," who levy "an enormous tax on the people for the profit of individuals."[86] Jefferson, Madison, and their followers also believed that Hamilton's energetic expansion of federal power threatened constitutional liberty. They pooh-poohed his contention that Congress's power to make any law "necessary and proper" for carrying out its enumerated powers armed government with what Hamilton called "*implied*" powers, including the authority to charter a bank. They rejected his argument that a sovereign government has the "right to employ all the *means* requisite and fairly *applicable* to the attainment of the *ends*" for which it was established, an argument that is a *Federalist* leitmotif, even in the numbers written by a younger and wiser Madison. If government goes down the Hamiltonian road, Jefferson warned, it takes "possession of a boundless field of power, no longer susceptible of any definition"—exactly the arbitrary, monarchical power that Americans fought a revolution to overthrow.[87]

Patrick Henry had given just this warning about the doctrine of implied powers in the Virginia ratifying convention, and, like Jefferson and Madison's fear that northern bankers would lord it over southern planters, his warning expressed a sectional as well as a constitutional fear. "Implication is dangerous because it is unbounded," Henry argued; "if it be admitted at all, and no limits be prescribed, it admits of the utmost extension."[88] What would such power do? It would bring about, he said, what "I have ever dreaded—subserviency of southern to n[orther]n interests."[89] By which he meant, as he reportedly had phrased it in the ratifying convention, "*They'll free your niggers!*"[90]

The Framers hoped they'd found a way of finessing the slavery issue: southerners agreed to end the importation of slaves after 1808 in exchange for being awarded seats in Congress proportional to their white populations plus three-fifths of their slaves, giving them extra political power.[91] But northern abolitionists never heeded the Constitutional Convention's promise to stop belaboring the issue, and the tension remained, becoming the mainspring of American history from the 1820 Missouri Compromise to the Civil War. Hamilton himself, who hated slavery from growing up amidst its barbarities in the West Indies, had become a founding member of the New York Manumission Society in 1785, and after the Revolution he had declared the idea of making Britain return or pay for slaves it had freed "odious and immoral."[92] It took decades, but Patrick Henry's prediction proved correct.

Hamilton's rivals depicted his "federalist" program not as a completion of the Revolution but as a counterrevolution against liberty and limited government, and their opposition was bitter. For his own part, aside from his wry awareness that, in Doctor Johnson's phrase, "we hear the loudest yelps for liberty among the drivers of negroes," Hamilton abhorred the version of liberty that the "anti-federalists" increasingly embraced—the *liberté* of the French Revolution, which began two months after Washington took office and filled Hamilton with a "foreboding of ill."[93] In *The Federalist*, he had rejected, in favor of practical real-world experience and the lessons of history, all "Utopian speculations," all "those idle theories which have amused us with promises of an exemption from the imperfections, the weaknesses, and the evils incident to society in every shape."[94] Now, he wrote Lafayette, "I dread the reveries of your Philosophic politicians . . . who being mere speculists may aim at more refinement than suits . . . with human nature."[95] They mistakenly saw men as reasonable rather than merely reasoning creatures, able to re-create society logically from first principles rather than modestly building on "ancient establishments and courses," in the light of "that best oracle of wisdom, experience." Human nature being the imperfectible thing it is, he thought that the French would more than likely fail "to keep within Proper bounds" and "run to anarchy."[96]

As they did. And when pro–French Revolution Republicans (as the anti-Federalists renamed themselves) started calling each other "citizen," and French atrocities worsened, Hamilton began to fear that the homegrown "spirit of Jacobinism" could lead in America to "calamities of which the dreadful incidents of the French revolution afford a very faint image."

The ferocity of this clash of views, which marked the birth of our two-party system, startles us today. Did Republicans and Federalists really mean it when they cursed each other as "monarchists" and "anarchists"? Yes—for their experiment in government, still brand-new, seemed fragile to them: Benjamin Franklin's famous answer to Elizabeth Powel's question of what kind of government the Constitutional Convention had produced was, "A republic—if you can keep it."[97] As Hamilton put it in 1800, in terms that echoed Burke and

Washington: "A new government, constructed on free principles, is always weak, and must stand in need of the props of a firm and good administration; till time shall have rendered its authority venerable, and fortified it by habits of obedience."[98] Along with the sectional conflict, the Hamiltonians and Jeffersonians each saw the other as perverters of Franklin's trust.

And they said so pseudonymously in their party newspapers, the Republicans with sour scurrility. Hamilton, wrote New York governor George Clinton or one of his henchmen, was "Tom S***," a "mustee" (the origin of the false belief that Hamilton had African blood).[99] Hamilton's "antirepublican" followers, wrote Madison in Philip Freneau's no-holds-barred *National Gazette*, are "more partial to the opulent than to the other classes of society; and having debauched themselves into a persuasion that mankind are incapable of governing themselves," they believe "that government can be carried on only by the pagentry of rank, the influence of money, . . . and the terror of military force." They wish that "the government itself may by degrees be narrowed into fewer hands, and approximated to an hereditary form."[100] Hamilton, writing in John Fenno's *Gazette of the United States*, mildly asked if readers thought it right for Jefferson to use government funds to employ Freneau to attack a government in which he himself was secretary of state—and if they really agreed with Jefferson's denunciations of Hamiltonian policies. "If to National Union, national respectability[,] Public Order[,] and public Credit they are willing to substitute National disunion, National insignificance, Public disorder and discredit—then let them unite their acclamations and plaudits in favour of Mr. Jefferson."[101]

Jefferson recalled that he and Hamilton were "daily pitted in the cabinet like two cocks," and in a now-familiar tactic, the Republicans tried to wear down Hamilton with two congressional inquests, requiring written reports and days of testimony on his personal as well as official financial dealings.[102] In truth, the two cabinet members wore each other down. Jefferson left as secretary of state at the end of 1793, Hamilton resigned as Treasury secretary just over a year later, and Washington decided that two terms were enough and returned to Mount Vernon in 1797.

One of the silliest things ever said about a land settled by immigrants seeking a new start across the sea is that there are no second acts in American lives. America, especially Hamiltonian opportunity America, is all about second chances—and third and fourth ones. But Hamilton himself had done almost everything he could to make his own political comeback very difficult.

Surely any Treasury secretary ought to know that, were a pretty twenty-three-year-old to turn up at his door saying that her husband had left her and asking for money, he should not offer to bring her some cash at her house later that evening, and he should not start an affair within moments of his arrival.[103] But Hamilton was a sucker for pretty young women in distress (perhaps hoping to rescue someone like his mother). He'd been at West Point when Benedict Arnold's treachery came to light, for example, and he completely fell for artful coconspirator Peggy Arnold's charade of innocence as she tearfully received him, Washington, and Lafayette, in bed, all heaving bosom out of a cheap romance. "Her sufferings were so eloquent," Hamilton wrote his fiancée, "that I wished myself her brother, to have a right to become her defender."[104] And at the height of his power, as he was guiding his bank bill through Congress in the summer of 1791, he fell just as easily for Maria Reynolds, who with her husband seems to have made a career of shaking down prominent men.

At first, the husband, who soon claimed to have reconciled with Maria, just "happened" to ask Hamilton for a Treasury job, without success. A wary Hamilton thought he'd better break off the affair, but Maria's "appearances of violent attachment, and of agonizing distress at the idea of relinquishment" played on his "sensibility, perhaps my vanity," so he planned "a gradual discontinuance . . . as least calculated to give pain, in case a real partiality existed"—meaning he couldn't keep away from her.[105] "Do something to Ease My heart Or Els I no not what I shall do for so I cannot live," she wrote, in one of a series of such letters. "The variety of shapes which this woman could assume was endless," Hamilton exclaimed with a half-admiring exasperation.[106]

Just before Christmas, the husband pretended to "discover" the goings-on and extorted $1,000 in blackmail "as the plaister of his wounded honor," as Hamilton put it. A month later, Reynolds wrote Hamilton, "*inviting me to renew my visits to his wife*," which Hamilton did, allowing Reynolds systematically to "levy contributions upon my passions on the one hand, and upon my apprehensions of discovery on the other." With studied professionalism, Reynolds made sure that a witness, another lowlife named Clingman (who later himself lived with Maria), saw Hamilton several times as he came to his house to visit Maria—as he did, all told, for nearly a year.[107] Having risen so high, Hamilton was back among the grifters he thought he'd left behind.

Of course no amount of money would stop such blackmailers from using the power they had over him, and they passed it on to his enemies. When Reynolds and Clingman landed in jail as swindlers (on a different matter), Clingman, appealing to his ex-boss, Congressman Frederick Muhlenberg, for help, claimed he could "hang" Hamilton for conspiring in financial hanky-panky at the Treasury with Reynolds, showing notes from Hamilton to Maria as evidence. Duty bound to investigate, Muhlenberg, together with another congressman and Senator James Monroe, called upon Hamilton in December 1792 to ask. Yes, said Hamilton, he had had dealings with Reynolds—but not "for purposes of improper pecuniary speculations," but rather because of Reynolds's "design to extort money from me" for "an amorous connection with his wife." Hamilton showed the three embarrassed legislators a sheaf of documents that amply persuaded them, and they declared themselves satisfied and sorry to have troubled him.[108]

But the matter didn't end there. In the summer of 1797, a Republican journalistic hit man named James Callender revived the corruption charges against Hamilton and revealed the sex scandal, which he'd learned from Monroe.[109] (In Jefferson's pay like Freneau, Callender later turned on the sage of Monticello and revealed the then-president's long affair with his slave Sally Hemings.) The official-misconduct charge ignited Hamilton's fury. Scrupulously incorruptible and indifferent to riches, he had retired as Treasury secretary poor: the notoriously corruptible and rich French diplomat, the Prince de Talleyrand, who had become Hamilton's friend when he took shelter in America from the Terror, reported with amazement, after glimpsing Hamilton through the candlelit window of his New York law office, "I have seen a man who made the fortunes of a nation laboring all night to support his family."[110]

With remarkably poor judgment—Washington seems to have supplied *all* of the political prudence in their long partnership—Hamilton churned out a luridly explicit pamphlet, which I have been quoting, denying financial corruption and explaining his dealings with Reynolds by baring his affair with Maria. Had he kept silent, the gutter-press rumormongering would have died away. But now his enemies roasted him. Hamilton's "whole proof in this pamphlet rests upon an illusion," cackled Callender. "'I am a rake and for that reason I cannot be a swindler. I have not broken the *eighth* commandment. . . . It is only the *seventh* which I have violated.'" Hamilton's friends kept an embarrassed silence.[111]

But there was a worse pamphlet to come. Late in the 1800 presidential campaign three years later, he wrote the *Letter from Alexander Hamilton, Concerning the Public Conduct and Character of John Adams, Esq. President of the United States*, which Adams believed cost him reelection. He already believed that Hamilton's support of a rival Federalist had pared his 1796 presidential victory to a razor-thin margin, and he resentfully spurned his advice once in office. Hamilton nevertheless gave sub-rosa counsel to cabinet members, and Adams, suspecting "a mischievous plot against his independence," summarily fired two of them. The two clashed repeatedly over policy, and Adams believed that Hamilton was working against his reelection, when the reverse was true.[112]

All this dirty linen Hamilton aired in his pamphlet, going on to argue that Adams had "great and intrinsic defects in his character, which unfit him for the office of Chief Magistrate," including "a vanity without bounds, and a jealousy capable of discoloring every object." His "ungovernable temper" makes him "liable to paroxisms of anger, which deprive him of self-command" (to the point, Jefferson recalled, of his "dashing and trampling his wig on the floor"). Nevertheless, he's a Federalist, Hamilton concluded, and "I have finally resolved not to advise the withholding from him of a single vote."[113] Adams went down in defeat, the Federalist Party split in two and slowly died, Hamilton entered the political wilderness, and the southern Republicans he so despised—Jefferson, Madison, and Monroe—reigned for the next quarter century.[114]

Some think that Hamilton went into his duel with Aaron Burr five years later out of suicidal despair over the wreck of his political career. That wasn't the case. He had built a beautiful yellow villa at the very top of Manhattan's Harlem Heights in 1802—the only house he ever owned—and was happy to work on his highly successful law practice in his little book-lined study there, to take his gun around his thirty-five acres of woods looking for game birds, to tend the garden laid out by his friend Dr. David Hosack (whose own famous medicinal garden grew where Rockefeller Center now stands), to read to his seven children, and to gaze out his floor-to-ceiling bow windows at the magnificent rural views, eastward to Long Island Sound from his long dining room, and westward across the Hudson from the adjoining drawing room. "A disappointed politician is very apt to take refuge in a garden," he explained.[115]

But he wasn't even done with politics. Late in 1801, he and nine partners founded the *New-York Evening Post*—still operating today as the morning *New York Post*—and its editor recalled often visiting Hamilton late in the evening to get help judging some important political development. "As soon as I see him, he begins in a deliberate manner to dictate and I to note down in shorthand," William Coleman recounted. "When he stops, my article is completed."[116] And when Vice President Aaron Burr, knowing that Jefferson would drop him from the ticket in the 1804 election, decided to run for governor of New York instead, Hamilton roused all his political skill and passion to stop him. Hamilton had met the handsome, dapper, well-born roué when Burr momentarily served on Washington's wartime staff; their legal careers had intertwined ever since they both joined the bar.[117] Hamilton thought Burr a cynical opportunist with "no principle, public or private," who had never produced "a single measure of public utility" in political life, and who should not be governor of his home state. "If we have an embryo-Caesar in the United States," he thought, " 'tis Burr."[118]

WHAT ACTUALLY led him to the duel was a tragic choice he had made just after the *Post* was born. He was a man torn between two irreconcilable ideals. Having come into the world with a congenital disgrace, he was self-made even in the matter of honor, thinking his own so precarious that he was quick to take offense at any slight, large or small. He castigated Adams, for example, for not asserting "the national dignity" after "the mortifying humiliations we had endured" from revolutionary France's undeclared war on U.S. shipping in 1797 and 1798.[119] Like most soldiers, he believed in asserting honor through dueling, and he had nearly challenged Monroe over the Virginian's leaking the supposedly confidential facts of the Reynolds affair. On a practical level, he believed that the disgrace of evading a duel would ruin anybody's political future. But as he got older, his early religious belief returned, with its condemnation of dueling.

So when he learned in November 1801 that his beloved nineteen-year-old "highest and eldest hope," Philip—whom he had often taken with him on long official trips—was to fight a duel the next day, he was torn over what advice to give, especially since Philip had gotten into the duel by calling his opponent a "rascal" for a speech insulting Hamilton himself. Hamilton advised a course he thought would reconcile honor and morality. Philip should shoot in the air, honorable behavior in the dueling code. His opponent might do the same or might miss; only one duel in five was fatal. But this one was. Taken to his uncle's house with a bullet in his gut, Philip died after hours of agony, his weeping parents lying on either side, clinging to him.[120]

And that drove Hamilton's seventeen-year-old daughter mad. She lived to be seventy-three in a kind of permanent, fearful girlhood, talking of Philip as if he were still alive and singing the songs she used to sing with her father. Poor Angelica, said her younger sister when they were both old. "Lost to herself for half a century."[121] Material enough for novels by all the Brontës.

HAMILTON COULD easily, and honorably, have avoided his duel with Burr. Enraged by his loss in the gubernatorial race, blaming Hamilton for working against him and wrongly thinking him the author of slashing campaign attacks, Burr wanted revenge.[122] He found the occasion in a letter printed in a newspaper, commenting on its report that Hamilton had called Burr "a dangerous man and one who ought not to be trusted with the reins of government." Actually, said the letter writer—a guest at the dinner party where Hamilton had made the remark—"I could detail to you a still more despicable opinion which General HAMILTON has expressed of Mr. BURR."[123]

That did it for Burr, who sent his second to demand that Hamilton explain what "despicable opinion" he held.[124] The second diplomatically advised Hamilton to say he had no idea what the dinner guest was talking about, which would have ended the matter right there. Hamilton replied instead that Burr had no business asking him such questions.[125] When Burr then demanded that Hamilton take back anything he'd ever said "derogatory to my honor," the duel was on.[126]

Hamilton told his friends he would "throw away" his shot: just what he'd advised his son to do.[127] Hamilton's friends told him not to do that, for Burr, a crack marksman, had been doing target practice and meant to kill him.[128] But Hamilton was thinking more about Philip than about Burr. Whether he lived or died, what he was seeking was atonement.

Rowing across the Hudson to Weehawken on July 11, 1804, he famously looked back at the New York he had done so much to shape "and spoke of the future greatness of the city."[129] Arriving at the secluded ledge on the Jersey bank, he took his position, put on his glasses, and fired above Burr's head, shooting some twigs off a cedar tree.[130] Burr shot him through the liver and shattered his spine. "This is a mortal wound," Hamilton said; and surrounded by his family and a dozen weeping friends, in the middle of the next afternoon, aged forty-nine, he died.[131]

He left a statement apologizing to his creditors if he didn't leave enough to pay off the debt from building his little villa, explaining that he had looked forward to a "comfortable retirement" there after having "been so much harassed in the busy world," and that he expected the house, "by the progressive rise in property on this Island, and the felicity of its situation to become more and more valuable."[132] Indeed it did, as the engine of prosperity he had set in motion enriched his city and nation.

As a result, his villa—the "sweet project" he enjoyed planning and building—got moved not once but twice.[133] In 1889, as his country landscape became urban, a developer bought part of his thirty-five acres to build row houses, and offered Hamilton Grange, as the house was called, to anyone who would move it. An Episcopal church rolled it two blocks from its original site at 143rd Street and Convent Avenue down to 141st Street, to use as a rectory, wedging the house in sideways to fit the space, moving the front door to the side, and shearing off the verandas. Hemmed in between the brownstone Romanesque church and a tall apartment building, the Grange, growing ever more shabby, looked like a ninety-five-pound old lady meekly squeezed on a subway seat between two hulking football players.

In 2008, the National Park Service, which had owned the Grange for nearly half a century and had long hoped to move it to a better site, finally acted. Since the church, built just after the house's first move and partially blocking its access to the street, wouldn't let the Park Service disassemble the arcade around its apse and then rebuild to let the

The Grange, Kingsbridge Road. The Residence of Alexander Hamilton.

Picture Collection, The New York Public Library, Astor, Lenox and Tilden Foundations

house be moved in the normal way, the Park Service slowly jacked up the Grange about ten feet over several days, gently slid it across a temporary bridge of steel girders over the church onto Convent Avenue, gradually jacked it down again, and rolled it in what seemed the blink of an eye down to its new site around the corner—an amazing spectacle, which I watched for hours on two beautiful summer days, as the nineteenth-century-garbed children of the square-bearded Old German Baptists who were doing the move (doubtless descendants of a pietist sect that settled near Germantown, Pennsylvania, in the early eighteenth century) played on the Convent Avenue sidewalk. The new site is still on Hamilton's land, and the Grange looks out as it originally did over a wooded hillside, right next to City College, where another generation of ambitious immigrants prepares itself to plunge into Hamilton's opportunity America.

The Park Service has beautifully restored the house, rebuilding the portico and airy piazzas, putting back the front door, and moving the stairs to their original position, discovering in the process that what seemed a Victorian replacement staircase is the original mahogany-railed one, its 1802 carvings preserved by being turned backward against a wall for a century. You can now see what an ambitious architectural marvel the house is for its modest size, with two twenty-two-foot-long, octagonal main rooms, placed end to end, opening into each other to form one axis of an intricate, perfectly balanced, and rational cruciform plan, the work of John McComb, Jr., architect of New York's city hall and Gracie Mansion. You can see why Hamilton chose the layout: it's a perfect embodiment of his elegant, logical, complicated Enlightenment mind, and, for all its rationality, it opens surprising and interesting vistas as you move through its spaces.

Park Service architectural preservation chief Stephen Spaulding's crew scraped away dozens of layers of paint to discover the original pale yellow of the drawing-room and dining-room walls, and they discovered, by taking down plaster, that early descriptions of the dining room, with three mirrored doors echoing the ten-foot-tall bow window at the room's other end and reflecting its view, are correct. They even found the doors, which had been glued together to form one thick door. A young architect, realizing no 1802 door was that heavy, pried apart the pieces, to reveal the marks of the glazing bars that had held the original mirrored panels in place. Now restored, with new mirrors made from early-nineteenth-century glass backed with silver, they gleam ethereally. Though made of wood, the house is more strongly built than it appears, with a layer of brick just inside the outer walls, and a layer of plaster between the first-story ceiling and the second-story floor, to keep out vermin. Shielded for a hundred years by the two neighboring buildings, most of the original, handblown windowpanes are intact. The second floor, still containing what looks like Hamilton's washstand, is largely unrestored: to install an elevator would ruin the architecture, and the Americans with Disabilities Act decrees that if everyone can't access someplace in certain buildings, no one can.[134]

Park Service curators have found the delicate London-made Clementi square piano that Angelica Hamilton used to play, five of the original French-style drawing-room chairs, Hamilton's pair of demilune card tables, and the long, mirrored plateau that stood at the center

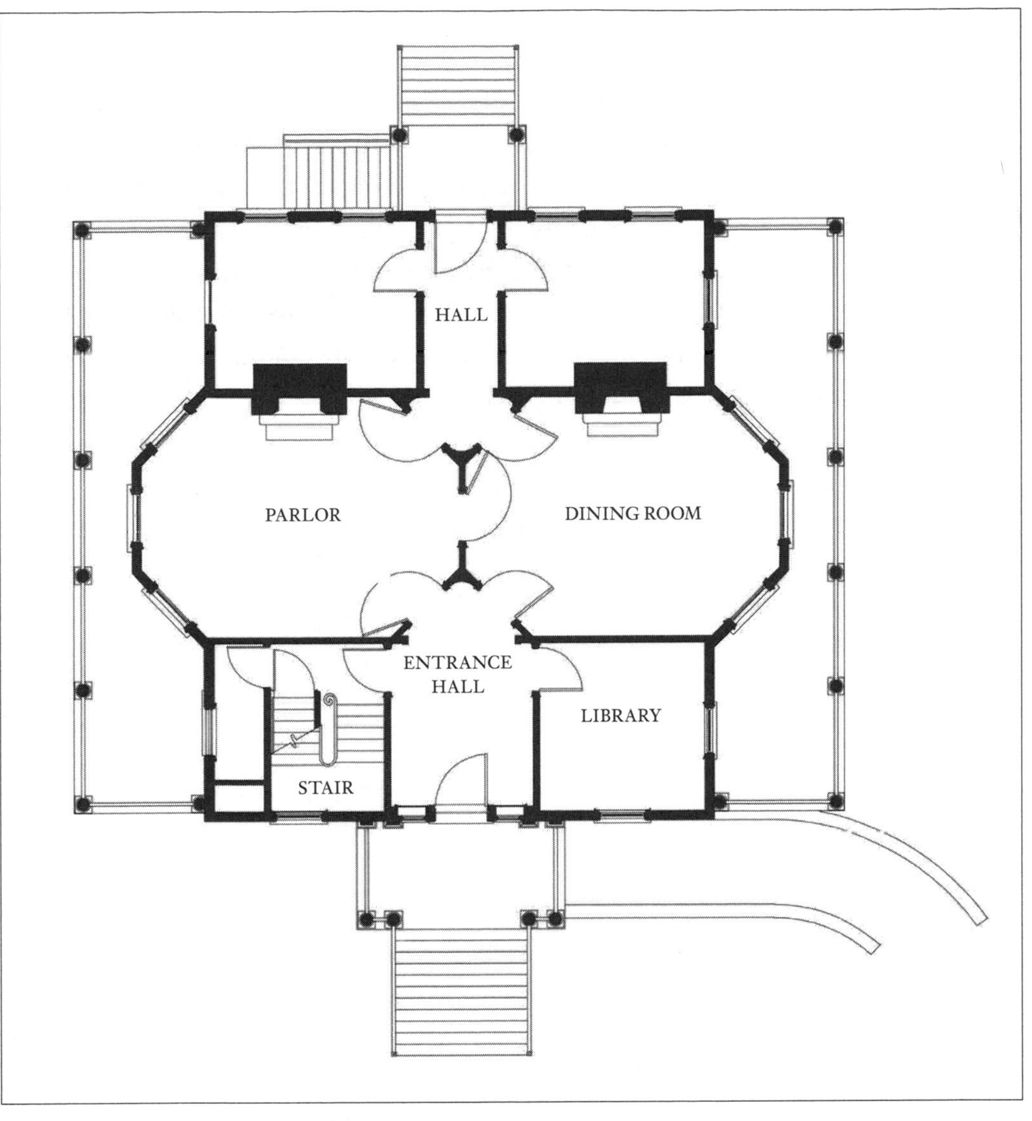

Hamilton Grange Main Floor
Drawing courtesy of John G. Waite Associates, Architects PLLC

of the dining-room table reflecting the candlelight up to the cheerful guests' faces. They've made beautifully crafted reproductions of Hamilton's rolltop desk and of his silver-plated ice bucket, the original of which a Hamilton descendant recently sold out of New York to an Arkansas collector. To me it seems the Holy Grail of American history, an artifact laden with consecrated meaning: for it arrived at Hamilton's door when the scandal over the Maria Reynolds affair was at its height and he badly needed some support. In the box, he found this note: "Not for any intrinsic value the thing possesses, but as a token of my sincere regard and friendship for you and as a rememberancer of me; I pray you to accept a Wine cooler for four bottles. . . . It is one of four I imported in the early part of my late Administration of the Government; two only of which were ever used. I pray you to present my best wishes, in which Mrs. Washington joins me, to Mrs. Hamilton & the family; and that you would be persuaded, that with every sentiment of the highest regard, I remain your sincere friend and Affectionate Hble. Servant Go: Washington."[135]

He understood better than anyone the man's incomparable worth.

PART III

The Republicans

8

Thomas Jefferson: Monticello's Shadows

In the summer of 1786, still mourning his beloved wife's death four years earlier and soon to begin sleeping with her fifteen-year-old half sister, his slave Sally Hemings, Thomas Jefferson fell in love with a beautiful English painter named Maria Cosway. Head over heels in love: for the forty-three-year-old minister to France tried to impress the twenty-something Maria by jumping a fence, and the resulting dislocated wrist troubled him the rest of his life.[1] With his good hand, he wrote Maria a 4,500-word love letter, a half-mock philosophical "dialogue" in which his "Head" contends that he should have stuck to "intellectual pleasures" that "ride serene & sublime above the concerns of this mortal world," while his "Heart" replies, in highly charged terms, that the happiness of love is worth the pain of loss, and that "the solid pleasure of one generous spasm of the heart" outweighs all the philosopher's "frigid speculations."[2] The letter, whose stated conflict stands for an unspoken conflict over Jefferson's love for a married woman, goes on to spin a fantasy that one day Maria will come and stay with him at Monticello, the mountaintop architectural masterpiece near Charlottesville, Virginia, that is the outward embodiment of this Enlightenment magus's brilliant mind. And like the letter to Maria, it too reveals the deep conflicts

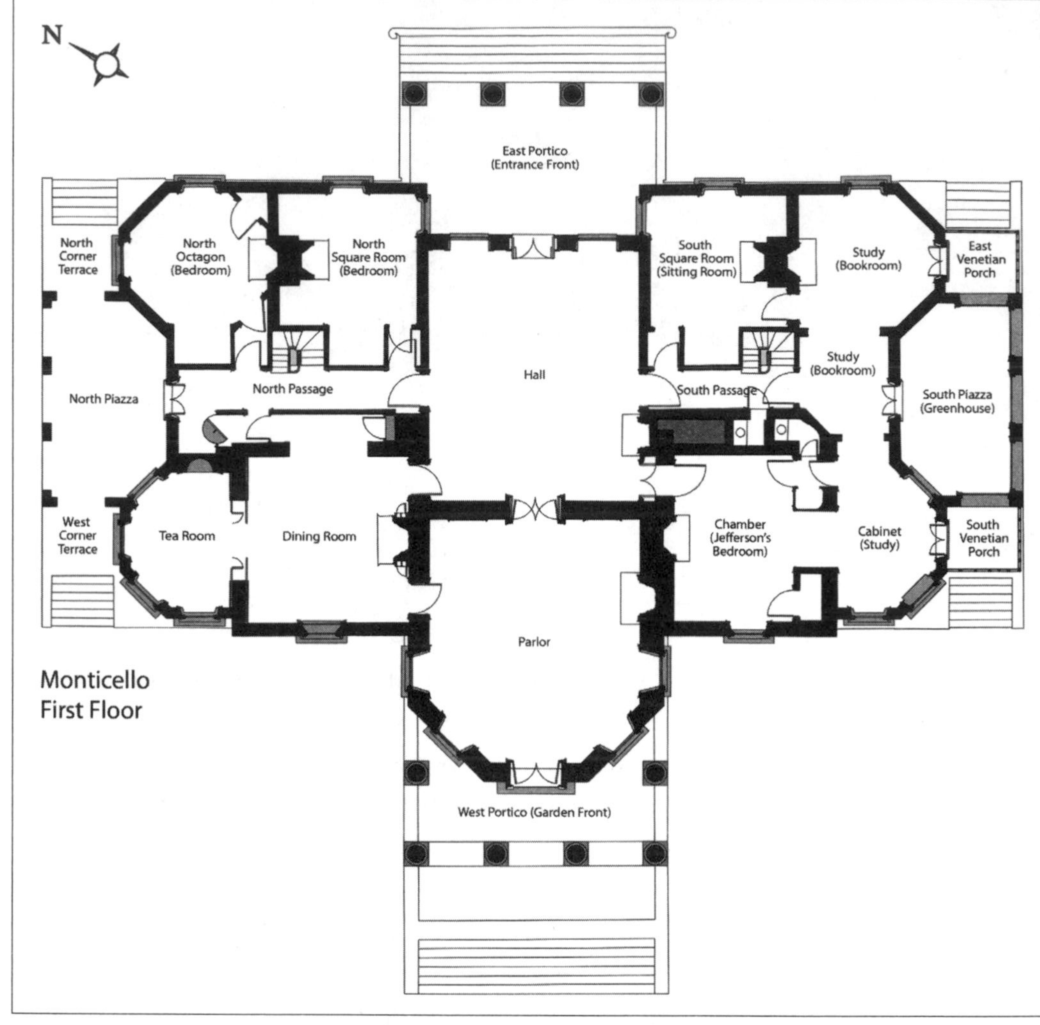

Thomas Jefferson Foundation, Inc., at Monticello

between its author's intellectual Head and the confused, darker realities that his philosophy can't resolve.

To walk through the house is to feel oneself in a microcosm of Jefferson's conception of the universe, a complex order whose parts mesh precisely, as one sees once one grasps the plan. With blueprint in hand I wandered from room to room, figuring out how the octagons fit together with the squares and rectangles to compose the balanced recessions and projections of the brick exterior, glowing deep red in the hot summer sunshine, beneath the sparkling white pediments and dome. You can't feel closer to the Great Watchmaker of the eighteenth-century philosophers than in the demi-octagon of Jefferson's study, or "cabinet," with its beautifully crafted brass models of the universe—an armillary sphere whose rings show how the stars revolve over the earth, and an orrery, a clockwork model of the solar system in which tiny planets revolve around a little brass sun. Next to them stand a brass-mounted telescope and microscope to peer into the workings of that universe, along with compasses and other instruments to map out its structure.

Jefferson built his house on a mountaintop so that he could "look down into the workhouse of nature, to see her clouds, hail, snow, rain, thunder, all fabricated at our feet! and the glorious sun, when rising as if out of a distant water, just gilding the tops of the mountains, & giving life to all nature!"[3] Such a late-eighteenth-century taste for the sublime didn't come cheap: Jefferson had to level the mountaintop to construct his house, and water, building materials, and supplies were costly and slow to get to the summit.[4] But sitting in Monticello's always cool and breezy garden pavilion and looking out over the rolling clouds and Blue Ridge mountains below, as Jefferson liked to do, you can see why he took the trouble.

In the parlor, a different set of precision instruments, a superb London-made harpsichord and a little American piano, speak of the many evenings when Jefferson, a keen violinist, together with his musical daughters, filled the house with the eighteenth-century compositions whose complex architecture weaves an order and harmony that intimates another, transcendent, order and harmony. Certainly Jefferson intuited that higher order. "[W]hen we take a view of the Universe," he wrote, "it is impossible for the human mind not to perceive and feel a conviction of design, consummate skill, and indefinite power in every atom of it's composition. The movements of the heavenly bodies, so exactly held in their course by the balance of centrifugal and centripetal forces; . . . insects mere atoms of life, yet as perfectly organised as man or mammoth . . . it is impossible, I say, for the human mind not to believe that there is, in all this, design, cause and effect, up to an ultimate cause, a fabricator of all things . . . , their preserver and regulator."[5]

THIS IS A rational universe, and human reason can grasp its laws. Jefferson set out to know them as fully as possible. Just beyond his cabinet, his cozy book room formed as complete a repository of what philosophers and naturalists had discovered of those laws as America could then boast. Jefferson owned not just the works of his intellectual heroes—Locke, Newton, and Bacon, pioneers of scientific rationalism—but also their portraits, hung high on Monticello's parlor walls. Assembled over fifty years from booksellers across Europe, the library became the nucleus of the Library of Congress when the debt-ridden ex-president had to sell its 6,487 volumes to the nation for $23,950 in 1814.[6]

He was especially proud of his book room's works on America—dealing with "whatever belongs to the American statesman," he boasted—and he turned Monticello's airy two-story hall into a museum of Americana.[7] Big maps of the country adorned the walls, including the first accurate one of Virginia as surveyed by his father. Prominently on display were the thighbone, jawbone, and tusk of a mastodon dug up in Kentucky—which clearly refuted, in Jefferson's view, famed French naturalist Georges-Louis Leclerc, Comte de Buffon's derogatory theory that the productions of nature had degenerated in the New World, so that plants, animals, and men were smaller, weaker, less various, less sexually ardent, and shorter-lived in the Americas than in Europe.[8] Could Europe produce an animal so . . . mammoth? And how about the elk and moose, whose antlers bristled challengingly above the maps?

Most striking was Jefferson's display of Indian objects—pipes and headdresses, spears and buffalo robes—many brought back by Lewis and Clark, whose epochal expedition to the Pacific he sent out in 1804 to plumb the vast lands gained in the Louisiana Purchase, his presidency's greatest (if not wholly constitutional) achievement.[9] Jefferson admired the Indians' daring and eloquence, yet further refutation of

Buffon's degeneration theory, and he liked being "the Great Father."[10] He understood the Indians in terms of the Enlightenment theory of human "perfectibility," the idea that man, having developed through barbarism to civilization, can achieve yet higher development of intellect and refinement.

In fact, he wrote toward the end of his life, a trip across the American continent is a "survey, in time, of the progress of man from the infancy of creation to the present day." If a "philosophic observer" were to start with "the savages of the Rocky Mountains" and travel eastward, he would begin by seeing man "in the earliest stage of association living under no law but that of nature," hunting animals for food and wearing their skins. He would next come upon men "in the pastoral state, raising domestic animals to supply the defects of hunting. Then succeed our own semi-barbarous citizens, the pioneers of the advance of civilization, and so in his progress he would meet the gradual shades of improving man until he would reach his, as yet, most improved state in our seaport towns. . . . I have observed this march of civilization advancing from the seacoast, passing over us like a cloud of light, increasing our knowledge and improving our condition. . . . And where this progress will stop no one can say."[11] As for the Indians, the sooner they join the march of progress the better. They need to give up their hunting and communal agriculture and settle down to a life of private property and individual farms, with arithmetic and writing to keep accounts.[12] And to speed the process, as president he sent out Christian missionaries to teach them to be less Indian and more American—to the continuing consternation of today's multiculturalists and strict separationists.[13]

It's true that Jefferson had his moments of wanting to withdraw into "intellectual pleasures" that "ride serene & sublime above the concerns of this mortal world," as he told Maria Cosway. His taste for unworldly abstraction is nowhere clearer than inside Monticello's empty dome, a stupendous and costly exercise in pure geometry, breathtakingly beautiful with its giant, Michelangelesque baseboard and the light pouring in from its round windows and central oculus—but virtually unusable, because its echoes make conversation impossible, it is unheated, and its access is steep and narrow. Even the sumptuous mahogany double doors built for symmetry opposite the dome's entrance open only onto a jumble of rafters and attics.

But usually Jefferson's intellectual pleasures fully engage the world: for him, the increase of knowledge is meant to improve man's condition. When Buffon "affected to consider chemistry but as cookery," for instance, and to equate the laboratory with the kitchen, Jefferson took sharp issue; chemistry, he lectured the count, is "big with future discoveries for the utility and safety of the human race."[14] Did not people justly esteem "Dr. Franklin's science because he always endeavored to direct it to something useful in private life"?[15] Were not phosphorous matches, for example, a boon to mankind, and would not interchangeable musket parts, which he saw in France long before the Colt factory mass-produced them in America, change history?[16]

Jefferson was himself an amateur inventor who designed—purely by mathematical reasoning rather than by digging in the earth—a plow blade that needed less than half the pulling power of ordinary plows.[17] In addition, he constantly sought seeds and plants from abroad, looking for better fruits and grains for Americans to grow, from rice that didn't need disease-breeding paddies to olive trees and continental wine grapes that would flourish in the New World. Presiding over the senate as John Adams's vice president and feeling the lack of a guide to parliamentary procedure, this compulsive improver wrote one that the House of Representatives still uses today.[18]

But it was his special intellectual achievement—and that of the American Revolution, in his view—to use reason to bring the march of civilization to government. "We can surely boast of having set the world a beautiful example of a government reformed by reason alone, without bloodshed," he wrote.[19] "We had no occasion to search into musty records, to hunt up royal parchments, or to investigate the laws and institutions of a semi-barbarous ancestry. We appealed to those of nature, and found them engraved on our hearts."[20]

What they found, of course, when they directed their power of reason to political matters, were the "self-evident" Lockean truths that no one could ever express with the exquisite economy and crystalline precision of Jefferson's Declaration of Independence: "that all men are created equal; that they are endowed by their creator with certain inalienable rights; that among these are life, liberty, & the pursuit of happiness: that to secure these rights, governments are instituted among men, deriving their just powers from the consent of the governed; that whenever any form of government becomes destructive of those ends, it is the right of the people to alter or abolish it, & to institute new government."[21] People's rights are not "the gift of their chief magistrate," he wrote in his 1774 *Summary View of the Rights of British America* (over which that magistrate, George III, was still fuming twelve years later, when Jefferson met him), but are "derived from the laws of nature." Moreover, "kings are the servants, not the proprietors of the people."[22]

These truths were always true, but they were not always self-evident, since kings, aristocrats, and priests had obfuscated them. Intellectually, men had long slumbered in "the sleep of despotism," their minds "shackled by habit and prejudice," as Jefferson wrote of the French before their revolution.[23] Not just external coercion but also a state of mind keeps people unfree: in the 1760s, for instance, the American colonists' "minds were circumscribed within narrow limits by a habitual belief that it was our duty to be subordinate to the mother country," and to this day the Indians have remained in "barbarism" because of their "bigotry" in favor of "the practices of [their] forefathers."[24] So a revolution involves reforming not just political and social institutions but also the minds of the citizenry. It was in this spirit that Jefferson famously declared: "I have sworn upon the altar of god, eternal hostility to every form of tyranny over the mind of man."[25] And in the last public letter he wrote, he was happy to say that "The general spread of the light of science has already laid open to every view the palpable truth, that the mass of mankind has not been born with saddles on their backs, nor a favored few booted and spurred, ready to ride them legitimately, by the grace of God."[26]

Shortly after writing the Declaration of Independence, Jefferson left the Continental Congress to join the Virginia legislature, aiming to carry out, as a model for the rest of the states, a program of liberation "by which every fibre would be eradicated of ancient or future aristocracy and a foundation laid for a government truly republican." He outlawed the inheritance practices of entail and primogeniture, which, by keeping land in the family and passing it undivided to the eldest son, served to perpetuate a landed aristocracy. He disestablished the Episcopal Church—though only from year to year until he succeeded permanently in 1779—on the ground that people had a natural freedom of opinion and should not be taxed to support a sect (and "the religion of the rich," at that) they didn't believe in.[27] On the same ground, he later tried, unsuccessfully, to repeal the laws against heresy, since "the opinions of men are not the object of civil government, nor under its jurisdiction."[28]

To wake up Virginians from the intellectual sleep of despotism, he envisioned an educational system that would make every child literate and numerate in three years and then send the ablest kids to tough regional grammar schools. The best of those who made it through six grueling years there would go on to college at William and Mary. Since all this schooling would be at public expense, the talented poor could rise to the top—"the best geniuses will be raked from the rubbish," as Jefferson put it—and the "aristocracy of wealth" would have to make room for "the aristocracy of virtue and talent, which nature has wisely provided for the direction of the interests of society, & scattered with an equal hand through all it's conditions."[29] More crucially, the ordinary Virginian would be well enough educated to understand that he was a free man with equal rights, a citizen not a subject. That's why a republic should fund education: "the tax which will be paid for this purpose," argued Jefferson, a small-government libertarian in most other matters, "is not more than the thousandth part of what will be paid to kings, priests, and nobles who will rise up among us if we leave the people in ignorance."[30] But his fellow legislators voted down his plan.

However decisive a step, the American Revolution did not achieve all the perfectibility of which man is capable—as how could it, since no one can foresee what heights mankind might reach? To progress further, men's minds must be left free to experiment and invent. "Reason and free inquiry," Jefferson pronounced, "are the only effectual agents against error," and, by implication, the wilderness of prejudice and superstition will shrink as the empire of reason grows.[31] Accordingly, he didn't believe that Americans should hold even their own Constitution "too sacred to be touched." No "society can make a perpetual constitution, or even a perpetual law," for "laws and institutions must go hand in hand with the progress of the human mind. As that becomes more developed, more enlightened, as new discoveries are made, new truths disclosed, and manners and opinions change with the change of circumstances, institutions must advance also, and keep pace with the times." In his most extreme mood, he believed that *all* the laws should expire after each generation, to be made anew every nineteen years. "We might as well require a man to wear still the coat which fitted him when a boy, as civilized society to remain ever under the regimen of their barbarous ancestors"—even ancestors such as the Founders, to whom we now ascribe "a wisdom more than human, and suppose what they did to be beyond amendment. I knew that age well; I belonged to it, and labored with it," he wrote in old age. "It was very like the present, but without the experience of the present; and forty years of experience in government is worth a century of book-reading." So, since "the earth belongs to the living and not to the dead," once one generation has passed into history, the next "may change their laws and institutions to suit themselves. Nothing then is unchangeable but the inherent and unalienable rights of man."[32]

That implacable spirit of Enlightenment inquiry pervades Monticello in a way that dawns on you only gradually as you walk through the rooms. The house seems to be saying, as Goethe cried on his deathbed, More light! It's not just that there are few dark corners in a house made up of so many demi-octagons, but that Jefferson has designed it so that light pours in from everywhere—through oversized, triple-hung windows and lots of them, through glass doors, through multiple skylights made up of glass louvers that let in the sunshine but keep out the rain, all reflected and bounced back across the lofty rooms by mirrors everywhere, from huge ones in the parlor to mirrored panes in the two round windows flanking the door into the dome, where the building itself would have obscured clear glass ones. Nowhere is the flood of light more intense than in Monticello's exaggeratedly high dressing room, its ceiling mostly glass louvers. One can imagine the lanky Jefferson getting out of his bed between his cabinet and dressing room as soon as he could see the clock that hung at the bottom of his sleeping alcove, rinsing his feet as he did every morning in the basin of cold water that has stained the dressing-room floor, and bathing in light.

When he left the presidency in 1809 and returned to his native state, which he never again left, Jefferson threw himself into a new scheme for enlightening his fellow citizens—the University of Virginia, of which he was not just the founder and rector but also served as its campus architect, construction supervisor, curriculum designer, faculty recruiter, and chief lobbyist with the state legislature.[33] This "hobby of my old age," Jefferson said, "will be based on the illimitable freedom of the human mind to explore and to expose every subject susceptible of its contemplation."[34] As architecture, it is breathtaking, a work of genius; beside its purity and delicacy even McKim, Mead & White's later buildings, at a respectful distance, seem ponderous and flabby. Jefferson aimed to make the connected pavilions of his "academical village," each based on a different Roman model as built or drawn by Palladio, "models of taste and good architecture, . . . no two alike, so as to serve as specimens for the architectural lectures."[35] And indeed vast numbers of American houses for the next half century seem to spring straight out of his designs.

John Jay Homestead Historic Site, New York State Office of Parks, Recreation and Historic Preservation

Sarah Jay and Her Youngest Children, William and Sarah Louisa
by James Sharples (1798)

Overleaf: John Jay
by Gilbert Stuart (the head, 1783)
and John Trumbull (the rest, 1804–8)
National Portrait Gallery, Smithsonian Institute / Art Resource, NY

Courtesy of New York State Office of Parks, Recreation and Historic Preservation

Above: John Jay Homestead dining room;
below: John Jay Homestead

Courtesy of New York State Office of Parks,
Recreation and Historic Preservation

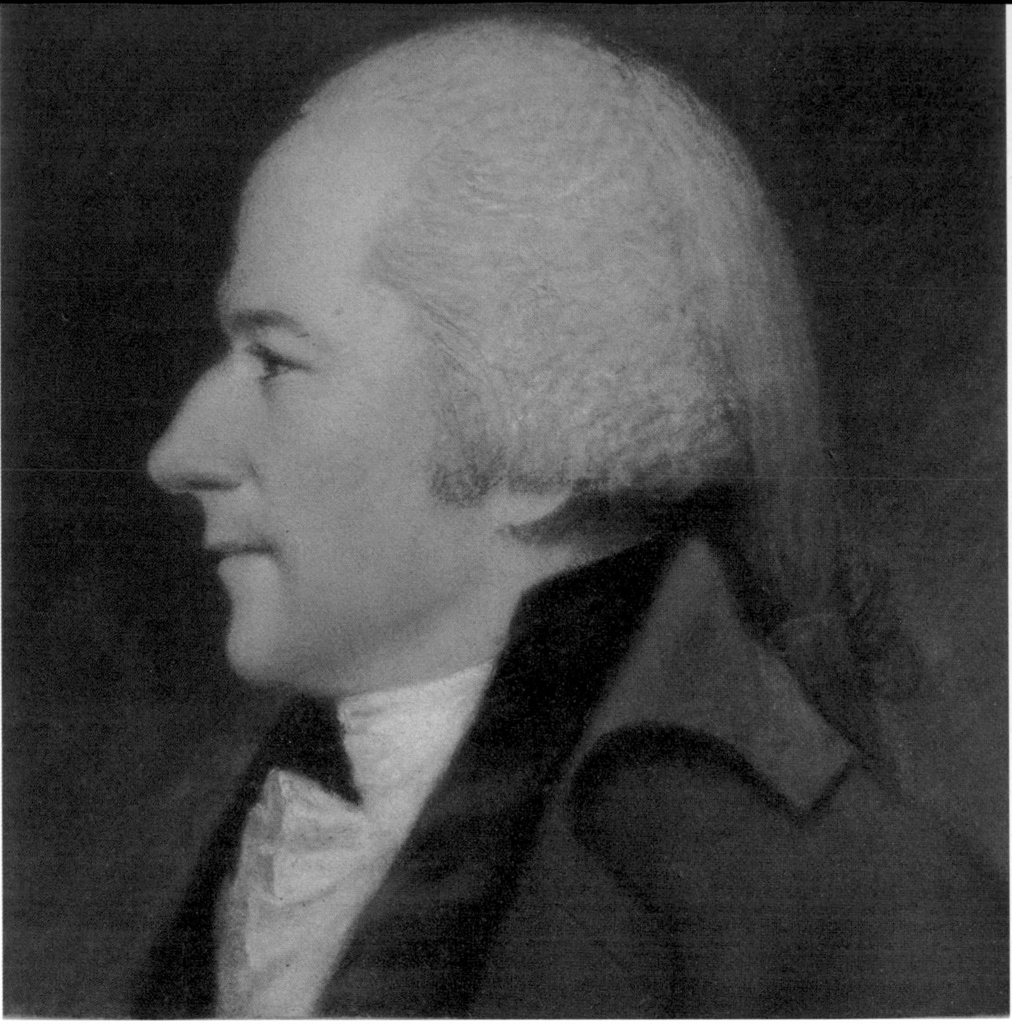

Above: *Alexander Hamilton* at age forty-one by James Sharples (1796);
below left: *Alexander Hamilton* at age twenty-five by Charles Willson Peale (1780)
below right: *Alexander Hamilton* by Charles Shirreff (undated)

The Granger Collection, New York

© R. W. Norton Art Foundation

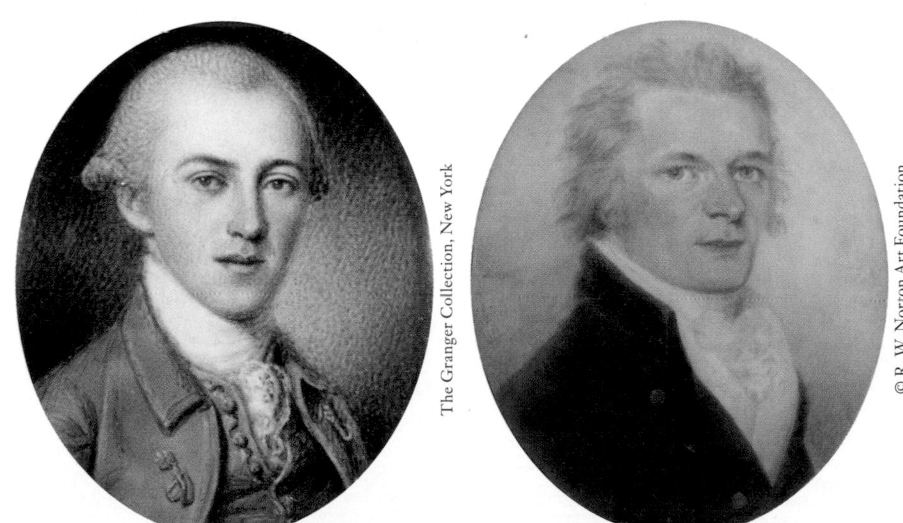

Private Collection / Photo © Christie's Images / The Bridgeman Art Library

National Park Service photographer Kevin Daley

Above: The wine cooler George Washington gave Alexander Hamilton at a time of need in 1797; *right*: Hamilton Grange entrance hall; *below*: Hamilton Grange parlor

National Park Service photographer Kevin Daley

Hamilton Grange, restored

National Park Service photographer Kevin Daley

The moving of Hamilton Grange from Convent Avenue, far left, around the corner to St. Nicholas Park, far right, in 2008

National Park Service, Kevin Daley and Mindi Rambo

Above: Hamilton Grange dining room

National Park Service photographer Kevin Daley

Private Collection / Peter Newark Pictures / The Bridgeman Art Library

Above: *Thomas Jefferson*, minister to France, by Mather Brown (1786);

below: Thomas Jefferson, secretary of state, by Charles Willson Peale (1791)

Independence National Historic Park

Above: Monticello west front

©Thomas Jefferson Foundation at Monticello, photograph by Robert Lautman

Right: Monticello dome room

© Thomas Jefferson Foundation at Monticello, photograph by Leah H. Stearns

© Thomas Jefferson Foundation at Monticello, photograph by Robert Lautman

Monticello entrance hall

© Thomas Jefferson Foundation at Monticello, photograph by Charles Shoffner

© Thomas Jefferson Foundation at Monticello, photograph by Robert Lautman

Monticello parlor

© Thomas Jefferson Foundation at Monticello, photograph by Carol Highsmith

Above: Monticello cabinet;
below left: Monticello tea room; *below right*: Monticello underground passage

The Granger Collection, New York

Above: *James Madison* at age thirty-two by Charles Willson Peale (1783);
below: *Dolley Payne Todd Madison* by Gilbert Stuart (1804)

The Granger Collection, New York

Montpelier

Courtesy of the Montpelier Foundation

Courtesy of the Montpelier Foundation

Photograph by Alfredo Mail.
Courtesy of the Montpelier Foundation,
James Madison's Montpelier

Above: Montpelier's Old Library, where Madison crammed for constitution making in 1786; *left*: Montpelier as enlarged by the du Ponts; *below*: the *tempietto* over Montpelier's ice house

Courtesy of the Montpelier Foundation

James Madison at age eighty-two by Asher Brown Durand (1833)

Courtesy of the Century Association

But as an intellectual enterprise the university proved less satisfactory to its creator when it opened the year before he died. The students turned out to be not so much an aristocracy of virtue and talent as a gang of rowdy youths with a taste for drink, gambling, breaking windows, firing guns into the air, and thrashing professors who tried to stop them. The horrified Jefferson came down from his mountain to Charlottesville to reprimand them. Flanked by his dear friends and fellow trustees James Madison and James Monroe, the frail eighty-two-year-old patriarch drew himself up to his full six foot two, began to speak—and burst into tears.[36]

At Monticello, too, that temple of Enlightenment, there were dark spots. In Palladian fashion, two pavilions flank the main house, connected by L-shaped wings, which from the front appear to be low terraces, made for promenades. From the back, because of the mountain's slope, you can see that the wings are in fact covered passages that lead out of the cellar of the house and contain the semi-subterranean kitchen, dairy, and other rooms for those who waited on Jefferson. Since those latter were slaves, it's hard not to walk through these passages without thinking of H. G. Wells's *The Time Machine*, with its airy, playful creatures of light enjoying the surface of the earth, while the dark Morlocks toil hidden beneath the surface, not to be spoken of.

Everyone knows about Monticello's gadgets—the cannonball-weighted clock visible both inside and outside the house; the double doors that open at one touch, thanks to a figure-of-eight pulley joining them beneath the floorboards; the space-saving clothes closet built in above the alcove bed. But two of this inspired tinkerer's most famous contrivances—the little dumbwaiters hidden on either side of the dining-room fireplace to bring bottles of wine up from the cellar, and the lazy Susan pantry door on whose shelves platters of food could be laid and then rotated into the dining room—seem designed to keep the slaves out of sight and out of mind, hiding even from its master the grim reality on which Monticello rested.[37]

From the start of his public life, slavery was the circle Jefferson couldn't square. His wealth depended on it—without slaves, southern land was much less valuable—but he knew the institution was evil. True, he believed blacks to be an inferior race, genetically low in intelligence and without the capacity to assimilate that he ascribed to Indians.[38] (When, to refute Jefferson's assertions of black inferiority, an ex-slave and self-taught mathematician sent him a complex almanac of his own devising, Jefferson concluded that the man must have had help.)[39] Even so, with unflinching logic, Jefferson insisted that selling men into slavery was a "cruel war against human nature itself, violating it's most sacred rights of life and liberty," as he said in a passage condemning George III for not ending the slave trade that his fellow congressmen edited out of the Declaration of Independence.[40] "Whatever be their degree of talent it is no measure of their rights," he wrote of slaves. "Because Sir Isaac Newton was superior to others in understanding, he was not therefore lord of the person or property of others."[41] Slaves are men; all men are created equal; QED.

Slavery didn't just contravene America's fundamental principle of liberty but subverted it, Jefferson believed. "Can the liberties of a nation be thought secure when we have removed their only firm basis, a conviction in the minds of the people that these liberties are of the gift of God?" he wrote. "That they are not to be violated but with His wrath?"[42] If our liberty rests on self-evident propositions rather than musty parchments, what happens to freedom when the propositions no longer seem so self-evident—when beliefs, which are as powerful as institutions, begin to waver?

JEFFERSON WRESTLED with this problem beginning with his first House of Burgesses term, when the twenty-six-year-old newly fledged lawyer tried (and failed) to make it legal for Virginians to free their slaves. In 1778 he persuaded the state legislature to ban further importation of slaves. He believed that the institution could be limited and then gradually eradicated, after which the slaves would be expatriated—largely because their owners would have much to fear from their resentment.

And justly: "The whole commerce between master and slave is a perpetual exercise of the most boisterous passions, the most unremitting despotism on the one part, and degrading submissions on the other," he wrote.[43] The American slave owner who fought for independence inflicts "on his fellow men a bondage, one hour of which is fraught with more misery than ages of that which he rose in rebellion to oppose. . . . When the measure of their tears shall be full, when their groans shall have involved heaven itself in darkness," Jefferson wrote in words that prefigure Lincoln's prophetic Second Inaugural, "doubtless a god of justice will awaken to their distress, and by diffusing light & liberality among their oppressors, or at length by his exterminating thunder, manifest his attention to the things of this world, and that they are not to be left to the guidance of a blind fatality."[44]

As a member of Congress under the Articles of Confederation, Jefferson strove to ban slavery in any new states carved out of the western territory won from Britain in the Revolution, but a sick delegate didn't show up to cast the vote needed for victory.[45] Four decades later, when Congress did exactly the opposite and passed the 1820 Missouri Compromise, permitting slavery in Missouri and in any new states formed in the southern part of his Louisiana Territory, he was aghast, hearing it as "a fire bell in the night" that "filled me with terror," for "I considered it at once as the knell of the Union." He correctly predicted that the antagonism of slavery and antislavery factions would spark a nationwide conflagration. Though he held fast to his original solution, he no longer thought it would come to pass. The slave-owning states, he ruefully concluded, "have the wolf by the ears, and we can neither hold him, nor safely let him go. Justice is in one scale, and self-preservation in the other."[46]

So what to make of Jefferson's relationship with Sally Hemings, which has come to symbolize the conflict, tragic to some and merely hypocritical to others, between America's highest ideals and its slaveholding Founding Fathers—a conflict that Jefferson fully recognized and that Irish poet Tom Moore satirized as early as 1806, when he jeered at President Jefferson as "the patriot" who liked to "dream of freedom in his bondsmaid's arms"?[47] The Hemings family, whom Jefferson had inherited when his father-in-law's death left him one of Virginia's biggest slave owners, made up almost all of Monticello's household staff, probably because they were so light-skinned that visitors mistook them for white.[48] The Hemings matriarch, Betty, was said to be half white, the daughter of an English sea captain, and many of her children had white fathers, including Sally, the daughter of Jefferson's own father-in-law, John Wayles.[49] Such was the state of race relations on the eighteenth-century Virginia plantation.

DNA tests showing that Sally's youngest son had a Jefferson father, cross-checked with records showing which Jefferson men were at Monticello nine months before each child's birth, suggest that Sally's son Madison Hemings was most likely correct in alleging in a lengthy 1873 newspaper interview that his mother had been Jefferson's "concubine," and that he and his siblings were Jefferson's children.[50] The story he told is this. Jefferson had sent for his eight-year-old daughter, Polly, to join him in France in 1787, and her thirteen- or fourteen-year-old nursemaid, Sally, brought her across the ocean, one little girl in charge of another. When Jefferson was to return to America shortly after the fall of the Bastille, the pregnant Sally refused to come, since French law made her free. Jefferson promised her special privileges if she would return, and vowed to free her unborn child and any others she might have at twenty-one, a promise he kept with the four children who reached adulthood. And all Sally's children bore Jefferson-connected names, unlike Monticello's other slaves.[51]

No one can know the nature of their relationship, which some eminent historians and social scientists still believe was not sexual.[52] But, in addition to the DNA data, Jefferson was sufficiently hot-blooded in a propriety-breaking way to have tried vigorously but unsuccessfully to seduce a neighbor's wife, nearly sparking a duel, and, except for his infatuation with Maria Cosway, we hear nothing of any other woman in his life after Martha's death but Sally.[53] She lived in one of Monticello's semi-underground rooms and looked after Jefferson's apartments and wardrobe, very light work. The only two extant eyewitness accounts describe her as "decidedly good looking" and "mighty near white"—three-quarters white, in fact—with "long straight hair down her back."[54] Some historians opine, on no evidence, that she must have looked like her half sister, Jefferson's beloved wife Martha, whose deathbed she and her mother (who had helped raise Martha) never left, while the faint and grief-stricken Jefferson, then thirty-nine, had to be carried to his room.[55] Perhaps the widower loved Sally in Martha's place, they theorize. Perhaps she welcomed the attentions of her powerful and fascinating master.[56]

One hopes so; but it's all speculation. One can't forget Jefferson's own description of the master-slave relationship, with despotism on one side and submissions on the other—written to be sure before Sally arrived in Paris. Nor can one forget that Jefferson's greatest anxiety—panic, almost—about having Polly cross the ocean was that she might be captured by the Barbary pirates, then holding twenty-two Americans in slavery. "My mind revolts at the possibility of a capture," he wrote, as well it might, since he knew what slavery meant.[57]

When you compare the houses of Virginia's other Founding Fathers to Monticello, what strikes you is how they've grown up organically, the products of historical development. You can see George Washington's increasing importance written all over Mount Vernon, for example, as his father's story-and-a-half house grew inexorably bigger and more presidential. Similarly, you can read James Madison's history in Montpelier, as he built a private four-room extension for himself and his new bride onto his parents' house, like a duplex town house in a modern condo development, and then added a ceremonial portal when he became president.

Monticello, by contrast, looks like the product of a single, unified conception, springing from Jefferson's brain like Athena from the head of Zeus. It didn't, of course. It was over fifty years in the making: Jefferson and his wife began their ten years of marriage in one of the little pavilions, basically a studio apartment with a basement kitchen, all that then existed of Monticello.[58] Jefferson kept changing his mind about what he wanted, especially after he returned from his four years in Paris, filled with visions of French neoclassicism and smitten with the Roman *Maison Carrée* at Nîmes, which he gazed at "whole hours," he said, "like a lover at his mistress."[59] He tore down walls, designed historically accurate details in all the classical orders, extended porticoes, moved stone columns, enlarging and perfecting. "Putting up and pulling down [is] one of my favorite amusements," he commented, with the result that for years he found himself "living in a brick-kiln," with unplastered walls.[60] But he produced something transcendent, like Palladio's villas or Lord Burlington's Chiswick House.

The years of turmoil to reach this result make one reconsider skeptically his description of the American Founding as "a beautiful example of a government reformed by reason alone, without bloodshed." What about the years when Washington's men froze and starved trying to outlast British armies that chased them for six hundred miles? As Jefferson's experience building Monticello should have taught him, nothing springs forth like a fully formed Platonic ideal. Yes, there is a self-evident right to liberty, but it took six years of bloodshed to establish that right in the New World. And many of those fighting believed they were safeguarding not an abstract idea of liberty but the historical liberty that they had enjoyed during five or more generations of self-rule in America and that belonged to them as free-born Englishmen, protected by such "musty records" as *Magna Carta.*

There is a certain otherworldliness to Jefferson's political philosophy (compared with his bursts of hardheaded pragmatism as president). But one remembers that he did not fight in the Revolution, since he was serving as Virginia's governor. An unintentionally funny story he tells about having dinner with Alexander Hamilton and John Adams in New York in 1791 perfectly encapsulates this quality. Hamilton gestured toward Jefferson's beloved portraits of Bacon, Newton, and Locke, and asked who they were. "[My] trinity of the three greatest men the world had ever produced," Jefferson replied, naming them. Hamilton paused a moment. "'The greatest man,' said he, 'that ever lived was Julius Caesar.'"[61] The aghast Jefferson took this crack as yet one more proof of the antirepublicanism and monarchism he ascribed to Hamilton. But most likely Hamilton was having fun pricking Jefferson's piety, reminding him that statecraft isn't a matter of reason alone.

Jefferson's casualness about how the ideal actually gets made into reality, his willingness to put up and tear down and put up again, and live oblivious to the rubble meanwhile, rather than to extend and update what already exists, led him to another political obliviousness, this one bloody rather than bloodless: his ardent support of the French Revolution, which broke out several weeks before he returned home to become secretary of state. He even helped Lafayette draft the *Declaration of the Rights of Man and the Citizen.*

As the revolution lurched leftward and the Terror sent some of the uprising's early, moderate supporters—Jefferson's close friends—to the guillotine, his support did not waver. He deplored his friends' deaths, but the "liberty of the whole earth was depending on the issue of the contest," he averred. They were like battlefield casualties, who "would never have hesitated to give up their lives" for the goal that was at stake—though it was their supposed friends who had killed them, not their enemies. "My own affections have been deeply wounded by some of the martyrs to this cause," Jefferson wrote, "but rather than it should have failed, I would have seen half the earth desolated. Were there but an Adam and an Eve left in every country, and left free, it would be better than as it is now."[62] As Burke said of the French revolutionaries and their effort to rebuild the world from scratch according to their idea of reason alone, without regard for history, prudence, or human life, "In the groves of *their* academy, at the end of every visto, you see nothing but the gallows."[63]

One other remark Jefferson made about Hamilton sums up his curious tinge of otherworldliness. The Treasury secretary "avowed the opinion," Jefferson complained, "that man could be governed by one of two motives only, force or interest." Government by force was "out of the question" in America, Hamilton added, and that left interest.[64] Here one remembers that Jefferson also didn't take part in the Constitutional Convention, since he was in Paris. Far from envisioning a republic of philosophers, where carefully educated citizens reason their way to self-evident truths about liberty and republican government, the writers of the Constitution created, through politically realistic compromise, a republic of ordinary men, moved by ordinary interests that, checking and balancing one another like the centrifugal and centripetal forces that keep the planets in their orbits, would add up to liberty. Hamilton was merely expressing the fundamental American principle of government. At more than a few moments, Jefferson's rationalism clouded his realism.

Yet his rationalism proved invaluable to the republic not just at its Founding but at its moment of greatest crisis, when it had to break with its historical past and square the circle he himself couldn't square. At Gettysburg, in the midst of the Civil War, Lincoln invoked the words of the Declaration of Independence to explain what the war was about: that the nation "conceived in Liberty, and dedicated to the proposition that all men are created equal," needed "a new birth of freedom" to include all men in that proposition. The abstraction, not the history, was at that moment our true national identity. And in the ever-growing consciousness of man's freedom that is the true meaning of history, as Jefferson might have said, so it became.

"Mine, after all, may be a Utopian dream," Jefferson said in old age in another context, "but being innocent, I thought I might indulge in it till I go to the land of dreams, and sleep there with the dreamers of all past and future times."[65] He is among the greatest of those dreamers.

9

James Madison: Theory

In the roster of famous last words—from Nathan Hale's "I regret I have but one life to give for my country" and Lord Nelson's victorious "God be praised, I have done my duty" to François Rabelais' "Drop the curtain; the farce is over" and John Maynard Keynes's debonair "I should have drunk more champagne"—surely the final utterance of James Madison deserves an honored place. Bedridden with rheumatism at eighty-five, the fourth president had spent nineteen years in retirement in Montpelier, the columned brick Virginia plantation house where he had grown up since age nine or ten, where as a young legislator he had pored over history and political philosophy to help frame his plan for the U.S. Constitution, and where, as a forty-six-year-old ex-congressman, he had brought his wife of three years to live with his parents on their 5,000 rich Piedmont acres. That final morning in 1836, Sukey, his wife's longtime maid, had brought him his breakfast, as usual; another slave, his valet Paul Jennings, got ready to shave him, as he had done every second day for sixteen years; his favorite niece sat by him to keep him company, as the June sun filtered through the twin poplars in the backyard and warmed the book-filled sickroom. The old man, his intellect as sharp as his body was worn, tried to eat but could not swallow.

"What is the matter, Uncle James?" his niece asked.

"Nothing more than a change of *mind*, my dear," the president replied. And then, writes Jennings in a memoir of Madison published just after the Civil War, "his head instantly dropped, and he ceased breathing as quietly as the snuff of a candle goes out."[1]

A change of *mind*! How utterly fitting a farewell for the most cerebral of the Founders, the nation's great political theorist, whose biography is, more than any other president's, the record of his thought. How fitting, too, for a man whose intellectual journey has sparked debate for two centuries. Was the Father of the Constitution consistent? Did he shift his views—and if so, why?

And thereby hangs a most interesting, and most human, tale.

True Enlightenment intellectual that Madison was, the liberty he most hotly defended as the Revolution loomed was freedom of thought, man's God-given birthright and the engine of human progress. At Princeton, he had wholly embraced the Scottish Enlightenment ethic of President John Witherspoon, an Edinburgh-educated Presbyterian iconoclast (like Madison's beloved schoolmaster Donald Robertson), who strove to "cherish a spirit of liberty, and free enquiry" in his scholars, "and not only to permit, but even to encourage their right of private judgment."[2] With teenaged bravado, Madison upped the free-enquiry stakes: he persuaded Witherspoon to let him try to do two years of work in one, "an indiscreet experiment of the minimum of sleep and the maximum of application, which the constitution would bear," an older and wiser Madison ruefully judged. Though he graduated in two years rather than the usual three, he stayed on for another because the effort had left him too ill to travel home. Finally back at Montpelier in 1772, he wrote his college friend William Bradford that he couldn't settle down to choose a career. His illness, recurring with epilepsy-like seizures at times of stress, "intimated to me not to expect a long or healthy life," he said, so it seemed silly to learn skills "difficult in acquiring and useless in possessing after one has exchanged Time for Eternity."[3]

But his lassitude had vanished when he wrote Bradford with flaming indignation in early 1774, shortly after the Boston Tea Party. A handful of Baptist preachers languished in jail in the next county "for publishing their religious Sentiments which in the main are very orthodox," he wrote his Philadelphia friend. Locked up for their *opinions*! "I have squabbled and scolded[,] abused and ridiculed so long about it, to so little purpose that I am without common patience. So I leave you to pity me and pray for Liberty of Conscience to revive among us." After all, he asked, echoing Doctor Witherspoon's thunderous denunciations of "lordly domination and sacredotal tyranny," what can you expect when you have an established church that tells everyone to believe and pray alike? Had the Church of England been established in the northern as well as the southern colonies, "slavery and Subjection might and would have been gradually insinuated" throughout British America, since, without a clash of opinions, "Union of Religious Sentiments begets a surprizing confidence" that breeds "mischievous Projects."[4]

Two months later, with the dissenting ministers still locked up, he was still fuming, and he expanded his criticism in another letter to Bradford, later George Washington's attorney general. His fellow Virginians were harming themselves as well as the ministers. They should imitate Bradford's fellow Pennsylvanians, who have "long felt the good effects of their religious as well as Civil Liberty. Foreigners have been encouraged to settle amg. you. Industry and Virtue have been promoted by mutual emulation and mutual Inspection, Commerce and the Arts have flourished and I can not help attributing those continual exertions of Genius which appear among you to the inspiration of Liberty and that love of Fame and Knowledge which always accompany it." Freedom of thought and belief, of unbounded speculation, of invention and innovation, make up an indivisible whole. "Religious bondage shackles and debilitates the mind and unfits it for every noble enterprize[,] every expanded prospect."[5] There is no progress without intellectual freedom.

THAT YEAR, Madison found his vocation when he joined the Orange County Committee of Safety, which enforced the colonies' ban on British trade: he became a professional politician. Two years later, elected to the Virginia Convention that pushed Congress to declare American independence, the twenty-five-year-old revolutionary made his first public splash on the question, not surprisingly, of religious freedom, since in his view any government attempt to dictate religious belief was an attack on his cherished freedom of thought, which necessarily includes the freedom to hold unorthodox ideas about anything, including church doctrine. When the Virginia Convention, which turned into the state's official legislative Assembly, drew up a Declaration of Rights, Madison objected to the article declaring that "all men shou'd enjoy the fullest Toleration in the Exercise of Religion, according to the Dictates of Conscience." Toleration, he pointed out, implied that government had the authority to withhold or to grant freedom of conscience. But it doesn't. Freedom of thought is "a natural and absolute right" not subject to any government control whatever. His suggested amendment, which would have disestablished the Anglican Church completely, proved too radical for the Convention, but its members accepted his second draft, which declared that religious belief and practice "can be directed only by reason and conviction, not by force or violence; and therefore, that all men are equally entitled to enjoy the free exercise of religion, according to the dictates of conscience, unpunished and unrestrained by the magistrate."[6]

Almost a decade later, in June 1785—when, because of the Articles of Confederation's term limits, he had left the Continental Congress after four years of toil and had rejoined the Virginia Assembly—Madison made clear that his musings on freedom of conscience had matured into a fully formed political theory that took the ideas William Livingston had voiced thirty years earlier into new, self-governing territory. Patrick Henry and other legislators had proposed a tax to support teachers of the Christian religion; Madison responded with a ringing defense of intellectual freedom, *Memorial and Remonstrance*

Against Religious Assessments, that swept the state—and swept Henry's bill into oblivion.

"All men are by nature equally free and independent," he wrote, quoting the Virginia Declaration of Rights, which in turn paraphrased Locke. They voluntarily give up their liberty of aggression upon entering society, to ensure mutual safety and to secure from invasion the rights and freedoms they have retained. These rights and freedoms—which belong to us not because society or government bestows them but because they are the "gift of nature"—are "unalienable," none more so than freedom of thought, "because the opinions of men, depending only on the evidence contemplated by their own minds cannot follow the dictates of other men." Since on entering society, no man surrenders more rights than any other man, we who glory in our freedom "to profess and to observe the Religion which we believe to be of divine origin . . . cannot deny an equal freedom to those whose minds have not yet yielded to the evidence which has convinced us"—even, Madison implies, if they believe in no religion.

Even under the free, popularly elected government that the Revolution brought into being, man's God-given rights remain off-limits to state interference. Yes, the "will of the majority" ultimately rules, "but it is also true that the majority may trespass on the rights of the minority," and such a trespass on fundamental rights is as illegitimate as the arbitrary will of an absolute monarch. Any rulers who "overleap the great Barrier which defends the rights of the people"—even popularly elected rulers carrying out the will of the majority—"exceed the commission from which they derive their authority, and are Tyrants," differing from the Inquisition "only in degree." A democratic tyranny may seem a contradiction in terms, but when a democratically elected government tramples rights bestowed by nature, that tyranny becomes all too real. How to prevent that oppression became the focus of Madison's intellectual and political life.

Lovers of freedom, he knew, must snuff out such despotism before it has "strengthened itself by exercise, and entangled the question in precedents." So the Assembly's bill allowing the state to meddle in matters of conscience and to tax all citizens to pay state-approved teachers of a Christianity some citizens may not profess puts the most basic choice before us. "Either then, we must say that the Will of the Legislature is the only measure of their authority; and . . . they may sweep away all our fundamental rights; or that they are bound to leave this particular right untouched and sacred." If citizens let the legislature overturn a single natural, fundamental right—as if individuals exist for the state rather than the state for individuals and the protection of their rights—then all their rights are at risk, and they have what Richard Henry Lee called an "elective despotism." In that event, popularly elected rulers "may controul the freedom of the press, may abolish Trial by Jury, may swallow up the Executive and Judiciary powers of the State," and may even "despoil us of our right of suffrage, and erect themselves into an independent and hereditary Assembly." Virginia's growing numbers of Baptists, Methodists, and other Dissenters, who painfully remembered having to support the established Anglican clergy before its tacit disestablishment in 1776 and wanted no further government interference in religion, devoured Madison's *Remonstrance*, flooded the Assembly with passionate petitions, and killed the bill.[7]

As a practical matter, Madison's view that government should never dream of "making laws for the human mind," because there are areas of human freedom where government may not tread, made him a firmer believer in the separation of church and state even than Jefferson—as firm a believer as Livingston, whose liberty-of-thought creed he had absorbed through his college reading of the *Independent Reflector*. He rejected as "an old error, that without some sort of alliance or coalition between Govt. and Religion neither can be duly supported." On the contrary, "a due distinction . . . between what is due to Caesar and what is due to God best promotes the discharge of *both* obligations," he wrote. "A mutual independence is found most friendly to practical religion, to social harmony, and to political prosperity." When church and state collude, history shows, the result is "pride and indolence in the Clergy" and "superstition, bigotry, and persecution" in the society.[8]

He came to think it wrong for Congress and the military to appoint tax-funded chaplains; it smacked too much of a religious establishment, and it discriminated against Catholics and Quakers, who, he thought, would never be appointed to such chaplaincies. Congressmen so inclined could hire their own clergymen out of their own pockets. As president, though he had planned to follow Jefferson in never proclaiming days of thanksgiving or fasting, when Congress pushed him to change course, "I was always careful to make the Proclamations absolutely indiscriminate, and merely recommendatory," he recalled, simply designating "a day on which all who thought proper might unite in consecrating it to religious purposes, according to their own faith and forms."[9]

Beyond showing him that democratic majority rule could turn tyrannical, his early political career proved an education in popular government's dangers and shortcomings at all levels: individual, state, and national. In his bid for reelection to the Assembly in 1777, he wouldn't lay out the usual free drinks that voters expected, thinking the custom "inconsistent with the purity of moral and republican principles" that he was "anxious to promote by his example," he later wrote. The voters, short on the requisite republican purity, viewed his behavior "as the effect of pride or parsimony," and voted him down as a prig.[10] Both as a professional politician and as the framer of a government, he never again made the mistake of expecting ordinary people to be prodigies of virtue.

As consolation for his loss, then-governor Patrick Henry got him named to his eight-man Council of Advisors, where, on his first workday in January 1778, he helped deal with a letter from George Washington that sounded what became a keynote of his next decade in politics. Freezing and hungry that dire winter in Valley Forge, with no supplies coming in, "this Army must inevitably . . . Starve, dissolve, or disperse," the General wrote two days before Christmas. "Sir this is not an exaggerated picture."[11] The governor and council managed to send meat and salt, "good rum," and sugar northward, and Madison had his first taste of the desperate, hand-to-mouth difficulty of getting self-governing citizens to pay taxes, and states to cooperate with the national government, even with survival at stake.[12]

Elected to the Continental Congress two years later, he vividly wrote a week after taking his seat in Philadelphia in March 1780 of the "alarm and distress" prevailing there to Jefferson, his close friend ever since his Piedmont neighbor had succeeded Henry as governor and had begun working hand in glove with Madison on the Council of Advisors. With the victory at Yorktown still nineteen months in the future, problem piled upon problem: "Our army threatened with an immediate alternative of disbanding or living on free quarter; the public treasury empty; public credit exhausted; . . . Congress complaining of the extortion of the people; the people of the improvidence of Congress, and the army of both; our affairs requiring the most mature & systematic measures, and the urgency of occasions admitting only of temporizing expedients, and those expedients generating new difficulties"—and that was just for starters. His colleagues were lightweights, often wrong, but even when right they were unable to get the separate states to back their plans without constant second-guessing that bred universal distrust.[13]

With inflation exploding, Congress took exactly the wrong course. Thinking that inflation sprang only from too much paper money chasing too few goods, Congress called in its paper currency, devalued it forty to one, and vowed to print no more. But as Madison saw, the real problem was that no one believed Congress could ever make the paper it emitted worth anything, so inflation barreled on: Madison's expenses for his first six months in Philadelphia came to $21,000 for room and board for himself and $6,034 more for his three horses, $2,459 for liquor and mixers, $1,776 for laundry, and $1,020 for barbering. The twenty-nine-year-old congressman, still getting an allowance from his rich planter father, was also "a pensioner on the favor of Haym Salomon, a Jew Broker," who patriotically refused to charge interest on loans to the "necessitous Delegate." By May 1781, one thousand Continental dollars equaled one gold dollar.[14]

Perhaps worse, "the situation of Congress has undergone a total change," Madison wrote Jefferson after the currency reform. "Whilst they exercised the indefinite power of emitting money on the credit of their constituents, they had the whole wealth and resources of the continent within their command, and could go on with their affairs independently and as they pleased." With the money presses stopped, "they are now as dependent on the States as the King of England is on Parliament. They can neither enlist, pay nor feed a single soldier, nor execute any other purpose," unless the state legislatures vote them money the states themselves have printed. Otherwise, "every thing must . . . come to a total stop."[15]

To SOLVE the economic meltdown and the military-supply problem it exacerbated, Madison saw, America had to inspire confidence by showing it could win its Revolution—which for most of 1780 seemed uncertain—and it needed to borrow hard currency from abroad. Since France was both its chief foreign lender and its main military ally, Madison saw the French alliance as a strategic sine qua non. Moreover, he liked the French, whose diplomats began wooing him soon after his arrival in Philadelphia with glittering dinners at their lavish legation, which "Mr. Mutterson," as a French nobleman called him, attended weekly. Unlike some of his fellow Founders, Madison had never traveled abroad (and never did), had never before lived in a big city, and found these hyper-refined blossoms of the ancien régime fascinating—too fascinating, as it turned out.[16]

The French diplomats, for their part, quickly saw his value. Madison joined Congress when the feud between two of America's secret commissioners to France raged most fiercely, with Arthur Lee accurately accusing Silas Deane of harboring British spies and colluding with French agents to profiteer, while Deane falsely accused Lee of double-crossing America's French ally by seeking a separate peace with Britain. The feud split Congress for the first time into two factions, one pro-French, the other anti. By late 1780, Madison had emerged as deputy leader of the pro-French party; and the French minister in Philadelphia, the Chevalier de la Luzerne, and his secretary, François Barbé-Marbois, lobbied him with indefatigable suavity.[17]

They had their own national interest to advance, and they used Madison to further Foreign Minister Comte de Vergennes' geostrategic vision. France aimed to humiliate, weaken, and impoverish Britain, its longtime adversary, through a costly war that would end by splitting off a precious chunk of its empire; but it wanted the independent United States that emerged to be weak, hemmed in by irritating and predatory foreign powers, and dependent on Versailles for protection and trade.[18] John Adams, who had arrived in France in 1780 as an American peace commissioner, sniffed out these intentions and wrote Congress that France meant to "Keep us weak. Make us feel our obligations. Impress our minds with a sense of gratitude." By July 1780, the wily Vergennes fathomed the undiplomatic Adams's increasingly anti-French views, declared he would deal with him no further, and got Congress to recall him.[19]

To counter the John Adams–Arthur Lee Francophobes, Ambassador Luzerne, mainly by playing Madison like a violin, inveigled Congress to instruct the American peace commissioners in June 1781 to keep no secrets from "the ministers of our generous ally the King of France; to undertake nothing in the negotiations for peace or truce without their knowledge or concurrence; . . . and ultimately govern yourself by their advice and concurrence." The next June, Madison and Barbé-Marbois took this message to the American public, collaborating on a letter to the *Pennsylvania Packet*, signed "a gentleman in office" in Philadelphia. They extolled "the happy alliance which unites us to France," from which "we have every year received new benefits, . . . without being able to make any other return than barren acknowledgments," and they suggested that America should at least repay that debt "with an unlimited confidence and constant communication of every thing which relates to our mutual interests."[20]

But once George Washington, with crucial French military backing, ended the fighting on American soil with his victory at Yorktown in October 1781, America's need of France ebbed. Moreover, the new chief U.S. peace commissioner, John Jay, had reached exactly John Adams's conclusions about French duplicity and sent proof of it to Congress in an intercepted letter from Barbé-Marbois to Vergennes, which showed that in the peace negotiations France planned to oppose key U.S. aims (as Chapter Six recounts). Ignoring Congress's instructions to defer to the French, Jay, unknown to Vergennes, hammered out a peace treaty with Britain infinitely more beneficial to the newly independent United States than the aghast French foreign minister ever dreamed.[21]

Madison was scarcely less aghast. He had incredulously insisted that the Barbé-Marbois letter was a forgery, and he feared, as Jay negotiated, that America was "more in danger of being seduced by Britain than sacrificed by France." When he saw the treaty's text, he couldn't help applauding the "extremely liberal" terms Jay had brilliantly won from Britain, but he was scandalized not only that Jay had acted without consulting Vergennes but also that he had settled a key border issue with Britain in complete secrecy. Unless Congress revealed that secret treaty provision, Madison exploded, "all confidence with France is at an end which in the event of a renewal of the war, must be dreadful as in that of peace it may be dishonorable." And squirming under Luzerne and Barbé-Marbois' dark mutterings that even though Vergennes diplomatically didn't complain of Jay's conduct, he "*felt* and *remembered*," Madison urged not just disclosure but abject apology.[22]

He was dead wrong but utterly sincere, and he remained sincere and wrong about France for the rest of his political career, with unhappy consequences for his nation. But his original premise—the indispensability of French economic and military support in the dark days of the Revolution—was sound, and the affection he formed for America's French allies ran deep. One of his most vivid memories was the 1784 visit he made with Barbé-Marbois and the Marquis de Lafayette to the Oneida Indians near present-day Rome, New York, a six-day wilderness ride west from Albany and the farthest Madison ever ventured from home in his life. Barbé-Marbois volunteered as chef and whipped up "delicious" soups over the campfire, especially welcome in the freezing, wet autumn; Lafayette was "as amiable a man as his vanity will admit"; the servants enjoyed the Indians' custom of temporarily marrying their girls to visitors for the duration of their stay. Nevertheless, Barbé-Marbois sniffed, "These children of nature are not at all what the writers of Europe say, who have never seen them."[23]

But the French alliance solved only part of the economic and military-supply problems that Madison faced daily in Philadelphia. The larger solution, he saw, had to address a deeper political problem. Under British oppression, American colonists had focused on the free, self-determination part of "free self-government." Having declared independence, and fighting a war that demanded concerted national effort, Americans now had to stress the *government* part of that formula—a formula Madison knew was almost an oxymoron, with irresolvable tension at its heart, since, as he later quipped, "an *advisory* Govt is a contradiction in terms."[24] The politics of the 1780s taught him "that liberty may be endangered by the abuses of liberty, as well as by the abuses of power." As he rhetorically phrased the issue, "Can any government be established, that will answer any purpose whatever, unless force be provided for executing its laws?"[25]

To win the war, therefore, Americans would have "to give greater authority and vigor to our public councils."[26] Just days after the ratification of the 1777 Articles of Confederation in March 1781, Madison proposed an amendment giving Congress "a general and *implied* power" to force the states "to abide by [Congress's] determinations." As he explained to Jefferson, "The necessity of arming Congress with coercive powers arises from the shameful deficiency of some of the States which are most capable of yielding their apportioned supplies." All it would take to jolt the needed food, materiel, and cash out of them is "a small detachment" of soldiers or "two or three vessels of force employed against their trade." But he changed his mind about the amendment: as he explained to Jefferson, he believed that Congress already *had* "an implied right of coercion," which if push came to shove "will probably be acquiesced in." Therefore, it made no sense to give balky states the chance to deny preemptively that such government power legitimately existed.[27]

Congress also needed the power to tax, Madison saw. After the fighting ended at Yorktown, he, Alexander Hamilton, and other congressmen worked out a financial plan that not only would provide for federal levies but also, at his instigation, would have had the federal government assume responsibility for the states' war debts and would not discriminate among the various classes of public creditors—positions he repudiated when his and Hamilton's close alliance later turned to enmity. Congress approved a watered-down tax but not Madison's two war-debt proposals a few months before the Treaty of Paris, signed in September 1783, brought the Revolution formally to a close.[28]

Back in the Virginia Assembly in 1784 after his congressional term ended, he relearned firsthand just how little the state legislatures cared about the national interest, strengthening his wish for "greater authority and vigor" in the federal government. He tried and failed to get the Assembly to let British creditors sue Virginia debtors in the state's courts as the peace treaty required, so that Britain would ship all its troops home, as it had agreed. Moreover, he grumbled, other states wouldn't pay contributions due to the central government or join in an embargo to counter new British trade restrictions.[29] And the central government itself seemed ready to pit one region against another; John Jay, now foreign secretary, was negotiating with Spain to swap America's right to navigate the lower Mississippi for twenty-five years in exchange for commercial agreements that would most benefit northeasterners—a scheme that enraged southwestern pioneers. Jay reasonably but impoliticly thought that, because U.S. population growth over twenty-five years would inevitably swallow up the lower Mississippi without the need for a war the nation couldn't presently win, it made sense, for now, to "forbear to use, what we know it is not in our power to use," in exchange "for a valuable consideration"—but not, he finally realized, if that deal would be "disagreeable to one half of the nation."[30] As Madison realized much sooner—since he and Jefferson had first discussed the river's crucial importance in 1779—Jay's negotiations, soon broken off, could only make southerners and westerners feel "sold by their Atlantic brethren" and "absolved from every federal tie."[31]

Madison also saw how willing the popularly elected legislatures were to harm a minority to please the majority, above all in their "general rage for paper money." Backed by little or nothing in most states, "this fictitious money" inevitably depreciated, and the resulting price inflation aided debtors by decreasing the real value of the sum they owed, while "Creditors paid the expence of the farce." Since debtors are many and creditors few, the "clamor for [paper money] is now universal," Madison wrote Jefferson in 1786, and state legislators opposed to printing it—and in effect transferring wealth from creditors to debtors by government fiat—were likely to get turned out of office or, if not, "will require all their firmness to withstand the popular torrent," as he himself found when he successfully kept Virginia from joining the paper stampede.[32]

In the same letter, Madison told Jefferson that all these problems made him support a meeting of deputies from the various states scheduled for September 1786 in Annapolis. He and others hoped that meeting would lead to "a Plenipotentiary Convention for amending the Confederation," he wrote, "yet I despair so much of its accomplishment at the present crisis."[33] As it happened, only five states sent delegates to the Annapolis Convention; but two of them were Madison and Hamilton, and out of their determination came the next year's Constitutional Convention.

Despite his profession of despair, all through the spring and summer of 1786 leading up to the Annapolis meeting, Madison crammed for constitution making by ravening through a "literary cargo" of books that Jefferson, then U.S. minister in Paris, had sent him by the hundreds from Europe—histories of confederations from ancient Greece to modern Switzerland in French and Latin as well as English, works of political theory from the Enlightenment and earlier, Diderot's great *Encyclopédie*—all in the faith that "the past should enlighten us on the future: knowledge of history is no more than anticipated experience," Madison wrote. "When we see the same faults followed regularly by the same misfortunes, we may reasonably think that if we could have known the first we might have avoided the others."[34]

Most men have a hard enough time learning from their own experience; the theoretical Madison, to his great credit, paid close attention to realities and consequences, and repeatedly adjusted his theories to the lessons of experience, both personal and historical. In his second-floor library looking west to Montpelier's spectacular panorama of the Blue Ridge mountains twenty miles away, the zealous student absorbed over 2,000 years of experience of why past confederations failed. All this he summarized in a handwritten booklet—the library's floor still bears his ink splatters—which he consulted in debates at the Constitutional Convention and mined freely for three of his twenty-nine *Federalist* papers. His reading reinforced what his congressional experience had already suggested: confederacies fail when they lack a strong central authority. So he undertook the "political experiment" of the Constitutional Convention with the aim of "combining the requisite stability and energy in government with the inviolable attention due to liberty, and to the republican form."[35]

Before the Convention opened on May 25, 1787, in the Pennsylvania statehouse, where eleven years earlier eight of the fifty-five delegates had signed the Declaration of Independence, Madison prepared zealously. In December 1786, he persuaded George Washington that his "name could not be spared from the Deputation to the Meeting" as "a proof of the light in which he regards" its importance; as for the rest of the Assembly, Madison wrote Jefferson, "the names of the members will satisfy you that the states have been serious in this business."[36] The list of governors, judges, congressmen, and war heroes, Jefferson wrote John Adams, read like "an assembly of demi-gods."[37]

In April 1787, Madison drew up a brilliantly lucid analysis of the *Vices of the Political System of the United States*, in which he worked out fully the constitutional theory that guided him in the months ahead. On May 3, he arrived in Philadelphia, and a week or so later, when the other six Virginia delegates had settled in, he led them in adopting an outline of an entirely new government, which Governor Edmund Randolph, young, tall, handsome, and eloquent, presented to the Convention on May 29, four days after it began. The Virginia Plan, which Madison almost certainly wrote, served the delegates as a blueprint during the nearly four months of debate that followed—debate that Madison, seated in the front row opposite presiding officer George Washington's thronelike chair, tirelessly transcribed "with a labor and exactness beyond comprehension," as Jefferson judged, never missing a day and scarcely even an hour. In his "researches into the History of the most distinguished Confederacies," Madison explained, he had yearned to know "the principles, the reasons, & the anticipations, which prevailed in the formation of them," and now he wanted to make sure that posterity would have the "materials for the History of a Constitution on which would be staked the happiness of a people great even in its infancy, and possibly the cause of Liberty throughout the world."[38]

The drama that followed is part of American legend: everyone knows how the delegates locked themselves into their forty-foot-square room with its twenty-foot ceiling and swore themselves to secrecy, so they could debate freely and air even their most unformed ideas without public censure; how they kept the windows locked all through the sweltering Philadelphia summer, so that eavesdroppers couldn't overhear their deliberations; how, in Benjamin Franklin's calming phrase, they came "to *consult*, not to *contend*, with each other" in a spirit, said Madison, of "mutual deference and concession," compromising even up to the Great Compromise of July; how the aged Franklin, who wafted in every day in his Paris-made sedan chair, unique in Philadelphia, pronounced at the end that he had wondered if the sunburst painted on the back of Washington's chair represented dawn or dusk: "But now I have the happiness to know it is a rising and not a setting sun."[39] Summed up Madison, "There never was an assembly of men, charged with a great & arduous trust, who were more pure in their motives, or more exclusively or anxiously devoted to the object committed to them, than were the members of the Federal Convention of 1787." And given "the natural diversity of human opinions on all new and complicated subjects," he wrote, "it is impossible to consider the degree of concord which ultimately prevailed as less than a miracle."[40]

After persuading the Annapolis Convention to call for the Constitutional Convention (with Hamilton) and conjuring up the Virginia Plan that became the assembly's road map, Madison further earned his title of "Father of the Constitution" by taking a leading role in the debates, writing twenty-nine of the eighty-five *Federalist* papers urging the Constitution's ratification (and those twenty-nine the most profound in the collection and classics of political thought), and pushing a balky and fractious Virginia Ratifying Convention, with Patrick Henry and George Mason forcefully leading the opposition, to approve the new government by a cliffhanging 89 to 79 vote in June 1788.

And out of all these writings and speeches, what theory of government emerges—and how much of that political theory grew out of Madison's experience of the Convention itself?

The Virginia Plan—which outlined a federal government with an executive, a judiciary, and a bicameral legislature, and sketched procedures for ratifying and amending the Constitution as well as admitting new states to the union—proposed that the legislature assume all of the old Congress's lawmaking powers, plus the authority "to legislate in all cases to which the separate States are incompetent, . . . to negativc all laws passed by the several States, contravening . . . the articles of Union, and to call forth the force of the Union agst. any member of the Union failing to fulfill its duty under the articles thereof."[41] Strong stuff, this using force against the states and the citizens. It was one of Madison's key ideas, and it rested, as all political theories must, on a psychological theory—a view of human nature—that he luminously set forth in *Federalist* 51.

"What is government itself but the greatest of all reflections on human nature?" he asked. "If men were angels, no government would be necessary." But they are not. In spite of the Lockean social contract they have made, men, under the power of their passions and their interests, sometimes break their pledge not to invade one another's rights and property (and note that from the American Revolution's first slogan, "Liberty, property and no stamps!" to the Continental Congress's 1774 declaration of the colonists' rights to "Life, liberty and property," the Founders took the Lockean view that the protection of property is a key governmental charge). "What is the meaning of government?" Madison asked. "An institution to make people do their duty. A government leaving it to a man to do his duty, or not, as he pleases, would be a new species of government, or rather no government at all."[42]

Yet once a free people gives government the power to use force as the Framers were doing through the Constitution, a further problem arises. Men must administer that government, men with the same human nature as everyone else, often with its worst defects in abundance. What motives, after all, drive men to seek elective office? "1. ambition 2. personal interest. 3. public good. Unhappily the two first are proved by experience to be most prevalent." Such men often have "interested views, contrary to the interest, and views, of their Constituents," whom they too often hoodwink by masking their "base and selfish measures . . . by pretexts of public good and apparent expediency." Since "power is of an encroaching nature,"Madison warned, "all men having power ought to be distrusted to a certain degree." One can argue that honesty is the best policy or that considerations of reputation and religion ought to make officials behave virtuously, but experience shows that they don't—and they especially don't in large groups like legislatures, where "passion never fails to wrest the sceptre from reason. Had every Athenian citizen been a Socrates, every Athenian assembly would still have been a mob."[43]

"In framing a government of men over men, the great difficulty lies in this: You must first enable the government to control the governed; and in the next place, oblige it to control itself." And here political theorist Baron de Montesquieu's version of checks and balances does its work, with power divided not among king, lords, and commons, but among executive, legislative, and judiciary, with each branch of the federal government limiting and policing the power of all the others—very different from the old, unicameral Congress, which wielded executive as well as legislative authority. "Each department should have a will of its own," Madison wrote, its officers as independent as possible from the other branches for their appointment and their salaries. To Montesquieu's well-known theory, which *Federalist* 47 had brilliantly parsed, Madison added a psychological wrinkle. Yes, politicians are ambitious, so the new Constitution will take advantage of what eighteenth-century psychology saw as the most fundamental of the passions. "Ambition must be made to counteract ambition," he wrote: an individual officer must feel his own power, importance, and self-interest bound up with the constitutional rights of his office, which he will jealously protect. By splitting the legislature into two independent branches elected differently, by assuring that judges are independent because they have lifetime tenure, and by arming the executive with a veto, the Constitution's "constant aim is to divide and arrange the power of the several offices in such a manner that each may be a check on the other; that the private interest of every individual, may be a centinel over the public rights,"[44] for every elected official will be dependent for his continued employment not on other officials but on the citizens who elected him.

THOSE CITIZENS have interests and passions of their own, however; and despite the supreme value Madison placed on free, popular government, he knew from all his political experience that when a majority succumbs to such impulses, even free, democratic governments can wield power tyrannically. "As air is to fire," freedom nourishes the interests and passions that can overwhelm reason and justice. That's true even of the intellectual freedom so precious to Madison. "As long as the reason of man continues fallible, and he is at liberty to exercise it, different opinions will be formed," which in turn—because man's "opinions and his passions will have a reciprocal influence on each other"—will nurture a multiplicity of passions: a "zeal for different opinions concerning religion, concerning government," for example, or "an attachment to different leaders ambitiously contending for pre-eminence and power."[45] As for the interests, a "distinction of property results from the very protection which a free Government gives to unequal faculties of acquiring it. There will be rich and poor; creditors and debtors; a landed interest, a monied interest, a mercantile interest."[46] Such differences, "sown in the nature of man," inevitably will give rise to factions, which Madison defined as "a number of citizens . . . united and actuated by some common impulse of passion, or of interest, adverse to the rights of other citizens, or to the permanent and aggregate interests of the community."[47]

Once a faction amounts to a majority, tyranny threatens, as Madison explained in his greatest *Federalist* essay, Number 10. "The most common and durable source of factions, has been the various and unequal division of property," he argued. "Those who hold, and those who are without property, have ever formed distinct interests in society."[48] How does such factionalism breed oppression? "The apportionment of taxes on the various descriptions of property, is an act which seems to require the most exact impartiality, yet there is perhaps no legislative act in which greater opportunity and temptation are given to a predominant party, to trample on the rules of justice. Every shilling with which they overburden the inferior number, is a shilling saved to their own pockets."[49] In other words, taxation *with* representation can be tyranny, if the unpropertied majority levies disproportionate taxes on the richer minority, unjustly transgressing the natural right to property that society exists to protect.

The poorer majority can cook up sundry other "improper or wicked project[s]" to invade the property of the rich through state power, including a "rage for paper money" (which, by debasing the currency, expropriates by inflation), "for an abolition of debts" (as Virginia tried to do by barring British creditors from suing debtors in its courts and as Shays's Rebellion tried to accomplish by stopping mortgage foreclosures in Massachusetts just before the Constitutional Convention began), and even "for an equal division of property."[50]

The great challenge of constitution making for a free people, Madison argued, is to "secure the public good, and private rights against the danger of such a faction," while preserving "the spirit and the form of popular government."[51] His safeguard against the tyranny of a democratically elected majority—which generally, he thought, would take the form of unjust taxation—entirely contravenes conventional wisdom as Montesquieu had formulated it. The French philosopher had declared that democracies had to be small in area, so that all citizens could gather for face-to-face deliberation—a view that caused some thoughtful Founders to oppose the Constitution on the grounds that a strong popular government over America was bound to decline into tyranny because the country's vastness precluded such face-to-face lawmaking.

On the contrary, Madison argued: history shows that small "democracies have ever been spectacles of turbulence and contention; . . . incompatible with personal security, or the rights of property; and have in general been as short in their lives, as they have been violent in their deaths."[52] That's because the smaller the society, the fewer the interests it contains, and the easier for one of them to form a majority. The smallest democracies are the worst of all: only consider "the notorious factions and oppressions which take place in corporate towns limited as the opportunities are"—a reality that anyone will acknowledge who considers how today's city councilors are generally more corrupt than congressmen, congressmen more corrupt than senators, and senators (probably) more corrupt than presidents. And, Madison would say, just look at the antics of state legislators.[53]

The Constitution, by contrast, provides Americans with a form of government that has "no model on the face of the globe"—an extended republic.[54] Its rationale is Madison's great contribution to political theory and practice.[55] Unlike a pure democracy, where all the citizens meet and vote on every law, a republic delegates power to "a small number of citizens elected by the rest," and the selection process aims to produce representatives "whose wisdom may best discern the true interest of their country, and whose patriotism and love of justice, will be least likely to sacrifice it to temporary or partial considerations." Since it's easy for a handful of representatives to gather from great distances for lawmaking sessions, such a government can embrace a very large territory, which yields a further advantage. "Extend the sphere," Madison argued, "and you take in a greater variety of parties and interests; you make it less probable that a majority of the whole will have a common motive to invade the rights of other citizens." A multiplicity of competing interests—like the multiplicity of sects that kept Virginia from imposing a religious tax early in Madison's political career—prevents a single interest from predominating. "We behold," Madison triumphantly concluded, "a republican remedy for the diseases most incident to republican government."[56]

For all Madison's worry that it was in man's nature for passion and interest to overwhelm his reason and virtue—that man was a creature more given to rationalizing than to rationality—he nevertheless believed that, while "there is a degree of depravity in mankind which requires . . . circumspection and distrust: So there are other qualities in human nature, which justify . . . esteem and confidence. Republican government presupposes the existence of these qualities in a higher degree than any other form." If "there is not sufficient virtue among men for self-government," he wrote in *Federalist* 55, then only "the chains of despotism can restrain them from destroying and devouring each other."[57]

That's why he set such store by the Senate, which he idealistically envisioned as "the great anchor of the Government"—a "temperate and respectable body" of "enlightened citizens," who would "watch & check" the representatives, lest they err "from fickleness or passion" or even "betray their trust." Such a body (which John Adams had first envisioned as part of a bicameral legislature in his 1776 *Thoughts on Government*) would defend "the people against their own temporary errors and delusions" and against "the artful misrepresentations of interested men," demagogues seducing citizens to "measures which they themselves will afterwards be the most ready to lament and condemn," Madison wrote in *Federalist* 63. "What bitter anguish would not the people of Athens have often escaped, if their government had contained so provident a safeguard against the tyranny of their own passions. Popular liberty might then have escaped the indelible reproach of decreeing to the same citizens, the hemlock on one day, and statues on the next," as the Athenians honored Socrates after condemning him to death by poison.[58]

Madison recommended a Senate "so small, that a sensible degree of the praise or blame of public measures may be the portion of each individual," and he thought senatorial terms should be long—nine years, he first suggested, before settling on six—so that each member's "pride and consequence . . . may be sensibly incorporated with the reputation and prosperity of the community," again mobilizing personal ambition in the public service. Long terms would also give senators "an oppy. of acquiring a competent knowledge of the public interests" and the chance to plan and carry out "a succession of well chosen and well connected measures, which have a gradual and perhaps unobserved operation," whereas congressmen's two-year terms allow them to see only "one or two links in a chain of measures, on which the general welfare may essentially depend." Without such a "stable institution" as this ideal Senate, there will be "mutability in the public councils" that will unsettle both commerce and foreign affairs. "What prudent merchant will hazard his fortunes in any new branch of commerce, when he knows not but that his plans may be rendered unlawful before they can be executed?" Madison asked in *Federalist* 62.[59]

In addition, Madison saw the Senate, like the House of Lords in British constitutional theory, as the principal guardian of "the rights of property," which should "be respected as well as personal rights in the choice of Rulers," because property "chiefly bears the burden of government & is so much an object of Legislation."[60] Since propertyless Americans will in time outnumber the Americans with land, capital, slaves, factories, ships, warehouses, and so on, the propertyless, he feared, "will either combine under the influence of their common situation: in which case, the rights of property and public liberty, will not be secure in their hands," or else they will become the bought and paid-for "tools of opulence & ambition." A safeguard, he thought, would be to make the right to vote for congressmen as wide as possible, while narrowing the right to vote for senators to the propertied.[61] "Give all power to property, and the indigent will be oppressed. Give it to the latter and the effect may be transposed. Give a defensive share to each and each will be secure," he concluded.[62]

Shortly before the Convention opened, Madison wrote Washington outlining his plans for a new government, which included his precious federal veto "*in all cases whatsoever* on the legislative acts of the States," to ensure federal supremacy. But in the same letter, it's clear he had begun formulating a different way of achieving the same goal. He told the General that he had been meditating "some middle ground" between complete "independence of the States" and "a consolidation of the whole into a simple republic"—a middle ground that would rest on "an equality of suffrage," so that every citizen's vote "in the national Councils" would be of equal weight. No longer, as under the Articles of Confederation's system of voting by states, would a citizen of little Delaware have more weight than a Pennsylvanian.[63] As the Convention debates unfolded, the notion of a "middle ground" grew upon him, and he withdrew the Virginia Plan's call for a national veto over state laws, and federal force to make states comply with national measures, which, he conceded, "would look more like a declaration of war."[64] He came to see that the Constitution's supremacy clause—declaring the Constitution and the federal laws the supreme law of the land, which every judge in the nation would have to enforce—would serve just as well as a federal veto over state laws to establish the federal government's preeminence. The national government, he explained to Jefferson, "instead of operating on the States, should operate without their intervention on the individuals composing them" with "every power requisite for general purposes" (as enumerated in Article I, Section 8 of the Constitution), leaving to the states "every power which might be most beneficially administered by them."[65]

His three key points—the extended republic as a shield against liberty-destroying faction, the Senate as the concentrated distillate of the nation's wisdom and virtue, and the federal government as supreme—required, in Madison's view, an equal principle of representation, whether by population or tax contribution. By definition, representatives in an extended republic—senators as well as congressmen—ought "to bear a proportion to the votes which their constituents, if convened, would respectively have."[66] Proportional representation was equally necessary to allow the senate to draw on the whole pool of the country's talent for disinterested guardians of the national interest.

Little wonder, then, that Madison vehemently opposed the Constitutional Convention's Great Compromise, put forth on June 11 by Connecticut delegate Roger Sherman, "an old Puritan, honest as an angel," in John Adams's phrase, a cobbler's son who in Thomas Jefferson's estimation "never said a foolish thing in his life."[67] The small states, continuing an argument that had simmered since the very first discussions about the Articles of Confederation in 1776, had declared that they wouldn't accept proportional representation and give up the equal representation of one vote for each state's delegation that they had already exercised for a decade under the Articles of Confederation. They'd sooner erase all state boundaries, said Delaware's George Read derisively, or redraw them, according to David Brearley of New Jersey, so "that a new partition of the whole be made in thirteen equal parts."[68] To Sherman's suggestion that the large states meet them halfway by adopting proportional representation in the House and representation by states in Madison's precious Senate, which would now be a creature of state interests rather than his ideal conclave of philosopher-kings, Madison objected strenuously in speech after speech.

Such a Senate, he correctly argued, had no theoretical justification whatsoever. The new government was not designed to act on the states, as Congress under the Articles of Confederation does, he pointed out. There is not "a single instance in which the Genl. Govt. was not to operate on the people individually," in both its lawmaking and tax-collecting capacities.[69] On what principle of legitimacy, then, could representation by state rest? Would not a constitution that contained that principle, even in part, fail to cure the Articles of Confederation's chief defect: that it created something that is more like a league or "a treaty of amity of commerce and of alliance" than a nation?[70] Wouldn't it create once again "a sovereignty over sovereigns, a government over governments, a legislation for communities, as contradistinguished from individuals"—which every political philosopher has argued is a theoretical absurdity? Worse, "in practice, it is subversive of the order and ends of civil polity," because its lack of adequate power dooms it to failure, as all historical experience—which is "the oracle of truth"—unequivocally proclaims.[71]

Madison lost that argument. The Great Compromise passed on July 16, after a month's increasingly testy deadlock, while the heat baked the delegates and the flies bit them. Madison accepted that at times principle has to yield to politics, that the Convention was "compelled to sacrifice theoretical propriety to the force of extraneous considerations." In fact, he concluded with gracious patriotism after battling so heatedly, "the real wonder is, that so many difficulties should have been surmounted; and surmounted with a unanimity almost as unprecedented as it must have been unexpected."[72] The delegates "formed the design of a great confederacy, which it is incumbent on their successors to improve and perpetuate. If their works betray imperfections, we wonder at the fewness of them."[73] As to whether Americans should ratify the document, it was now or never. "The multiplied inducements at this moment to the local sacrifices necessary to keep the States together, can never be expected to coincide again."[74] Concluded Madison, "The only option . . . lies between the proposed government and a government still more objectionable. Under this alternative, the advice of prudence must be, to embrace the lesser evil."[75]

Still, he had misgivings. The small states could now gang up in the Senate to block essential legislation until congressmen from the big states made concessions to them in the House, meaning that "the minority could negative the will of the majority." But his deepest anxiety was that now the critical division in the nation would not be the gap between the propertied and the propertyless but rather between the North and the South, with slavery the crucial "line of discrimination," he said with unintended resonance.[76] And while he claimed in Virginia's Ratifying Convention to be amazed by Patrick Henry's fear—entirely unwarranted, he said—that the Constitution could lead to the end of slavery, he himself worried about the arithmetic of "5 States on the South, 8 on the Northn. Side of this line," a disproportion in the Senate likely only to worsen as new states joined the Union.[77]

The Constitution, after all, outlined a government that would safeguard persons and property. And what were slaves? In explaining in *Federalist* 54 the Convention's compromise counting slaves as three-fifths of a person in reckoning the southern states' population for apportionment of representatives and taxation, slave owner Madison set forth the southern view that slaves "partake of both these qualities; being considered by our laws, in some respects as persons, and in other respects as property." In being deprived of his liberty and forced to work for a master who can sell and beat him, "the slave may appear to be degraded from the human rank, and classed with those irrational animals, which fall under the legal denomination of property." But insofar as the law protects him from the violence of all others, and punishes him for violence he commits, he is "a member of the society" and "a moral person." Reasonable enough then, writes Madison (in words it's hard to transcribe), to adopt "the compromising expedient of the constitution . . . , which regards them as inhabitants, but as debased by servitude below the equal level of free inhabitants, which regards the *slave* as divested of two fifths of the *man*."[78] None of the brooding over slavery's evil that Washington and Jefferson committed to paper appears in Madison's surviving writings.

Having gone into the Convention seeking a strong central government supreme over fractious states—and assuring the delegates that there was "less danger of encroachment from the Genl. Govt. than from the State Govts."—Madison, as a slave owner and representative of slave owners with particularly sordid interests as well as a lawmaker of wisdom and virtue, began to have second thoughts about federal power.[79] With non-slave-owning northern states predominant in the Senate, he fretted, a government designed to protect property might someday threaten the South's peculiar and crucially valuable property in slaves—property on which his own wealth rested. During the Convention, Madison had come to see that giving the central government supreme but strictly limited and enumerated powers over all citizens would serve the national purpose just as well as giving it a veto over state laws.[80] Now he grasped more fully that such a plan would not only give the federal government its needed energy but would also protect the states from illegitimate encroachments—especially emancipation of the slaves, which in his view would be so illegitimate as to be almost unthinkable. As he began his slow shift from being a federalist in his era's meaning of the term—a proponent of a strong federal government—to the states'-rights position that our era understands by federalism, he embraced the limited and enumerated powers idea all the more firmly.

The federal government's powers, he explained in *Federalist* 45, "are few and defined," largely confined to "war, peace, negociation, and foreign commerce," while state powers will concern most issues that have to do with "the lives, liberties and properties of the people; and the internal order, improvement and prosperity of the state."[81] In the same speech in the Virginia Ratifying Convention in which he assured Patrick Henry that the federal government had no power to emancipate the slaves, he also assured the state's foremost law professor, George Wythe, that "the powers granted by the proposed constitution, are the gift of the people," and "every power not granted thereby, remains with the people, and at their will."[82] The tension between the states and the federal government would form yet another mechanism of checks and balances, another safeguard of rights and property. As Delaware's John Dickinson explained it to the Constitutional Convention: "Let our government be like that of the solar system. Let the general government be like the sun and the states the planets, repelled yet attracted, and the whole moving regularly and harmoniously in their several orbits."[83]

Like so many delegates, Madison loved this image from the Newtonian "planetary system" and echoed it, describing the federal government as "the great pervading principle that must controul the centrifugal tendency of the States; which without it, will continually fly out of their proper orbits and destroy the order & harmony of the political System."[84] That image had sunk deep into the eighteenth-century imagination, which often thought in terms of opposed forces, centrifugal against centripetal, creating a dynamic harmony, a music of the spheres, which, as Madison's favorite author, Joseph Addison of *Spectator* fame, put it in 1712, has "no real voice nor sound," as medieval men believed, but vibrates only in "reason's ear."[85] As early as the 1730s, Alexander Pope, whom every educated eighteenth-century English speaker read, had anticipated Madison in describing how "jarring int'rests of themselves create / Th'acording music of a well-mix'd State."[86]

As Madison explained, "This policy of supplying by opposite and rival interests, the defect of better motives, might be traced through the whole system of human affairs, private as well as public."[87] Modern readers will think of Adam Smith, whose analysis of how each individual's pursuit of his private, selfish interest adds up to the public interest Madison had read by the time of the Constitutional Convention; other Founders might have thought of Bernard Mandeville's famous 1714

Fable of the Bees, which similarly showed how "Private Vices" can add up to "Publick Benefits," as people send money coursing through the economy to gratify such passions as vanity or pride, gluttony or lust, just as Madison, wearing his psychologist's hat, set ambition to counteract ambition in *Federalist* 51, making the baser, sometimes immoral, human energies of passions and interests, rather than wisdom, virtue, or reason, power the machinery of government and society.

The only problem in such a dynamic equilibrium, a balance of opposed forces, is that, under the extreme tension that binds it, things can slip out of whack. Pope described the consequences thus:

And if each system in gradation roll,
Alike essential to th' amazing whole;
The least confusion but in one, not all
That system only, but the whole must fall.
Let Earth unbalanc'd from her orbit fly,
Planets and Suns run lawless thro' the sky,
Let ruling Angels from their spheres be hurl'd,
Being on being wreck'd, and world on world.[88]

Madison certainly shared the anxiety that things could "fly out of their proper orbits and destroy the order & harmony of the political System." And in his view, that happened soon enough.

10

James Madison: Practice

THE NEW GOVERNMENT that James Madison had done so much to design hummed into motion smoothly—though with a bump for Madison himself. Patrick Henry, doubting his fellow Virginian's ratifying-convention assurances on slavery and loath to cede state power to the central government, made sure that the thirty-seven-year-old federalist didn't become one of the state's senators, declaring his election would produce "rivulets of blood throughout the land." He tried to keep Madison from being elected congressman, too, by gerrymandering his district to make him run against his friend James Monroe on Monroe's home turf. Despite his distaste for politicking, Madison campaigned gamely, debating Monroe for hours in the snow and getting a frostbitten nose on the frigid ride home.[1] He won, 1,308 to 972—and bore his frostbite battle scar for life.[2]

Heading to New York for the start of the first Congress under the Constitution, Madison stopped for a week at Mount Vernon, where he drafted president-elect Washington's Inaugural Address—to which, as Congress's de facto leader for its first two years, he wrote the legislature's ceremonial reply.[3] He helped the new president choose cabinet secretaries and other officials, remained his closest advisor until those appointees took over, and fired up the new government machinery on April 8, 1789, by proposing import duties to fuel its operations—an independent revenue source that the Confederation Congress had never possessed. On April 30, he marched with the president to his inauguration as one of five congressional escorts.[4]

Madison's chief goal in the new government's first year was shepherding the Bill of Rights through Congress. He had at first strongly opposed such amendments, arguing that the Constitution, by its precise enumeration of the federal government's strictly limited powers, makes clear that any power not on that short list remains off-limits. A bill of rights would reverse the emphasis, he feared, opening the way to an enlargement of federal prerogative and a shrinking of the powers reserved to the states and the people. "If an enumeration be made of our rights," he at first argued in the June 1788 Virginia Ratifying Convention, "will it not be implied, that every thing omitted, is given to the general government?"[5]

But the ratifying convention changed his mind. Under the new Constitution, he knew, Americans didn't have rulers; they had public servants. Yet since many of his republican compatriots remained stuck in the pre-Revolutionary view of rights as something to be wrested from rulers, he saw he couldn't muster a majority in favor of the Constitution without vowing that he and his fellow federalists would promptly pursue a bill of rights.[6] "As an honest man, *I feel* my self bound by this consideration," he wrote.[7]

A few months later, he had persuaded himself that this pragmatic position was principled. "My own opinion has always been in favor of a bill of rights," he disingenuously wrote Jefferson—as long as no one could mistakenly believe that these are the *only* rights the central government can't infringe, thus emboldening federal authorities to usurp powers that the Constitution doesn't explicitly confer. Not of course that such "parchment barriers" as a bill of rights would prevent "overbearing majorities" from violating individual rights: "Wherever there is an interest and power to do wrong, wrong will generally be done," Madison dryly observed. But a bill of rights could beneficially shape the nation's political culture. "The political truths declared in that solemn manner acquire by degrees the character of fundamental maxims of free Government, and as they become incorporated with the national sentiment, counteract the impulses of interest and passion."[8]

What's more, warily attentive to his constituents ever since his 1777 electoral defeat, he had made promises about a bill of rights in his January 1789 congressional campaign that he felt duty bound to honor. "Antifederal partizans" had warned Baptists in his district that he "had ceased to be a friend to the rights of Conscience." However incredible, the rumor gained traction, so he responded with public letters pledging support for a bill of rights, "particularly the rights of Conscience in its fullest latitude."[9] By the time he proposed the Bill of Rights on June 8, 1789, he told his fellow congressmen that he wished they had made it "the first business we entered upon; it would stifle the voice of complaint, and make friends of many who doubted [the Constitution's] merits."[10]

Only one disappointment tempered his pleasure in the result. He wanted the Bill of Rights to include an amendment protecting citizens against *state* violations of "the equal rights of conscience, or the freedom of the press, or the trial by jury in criminal cases," which in his view would be the "most valuable amendment on the whole list"; but his fellow congressmen wouldn't cede so much of the states' powers in the name of individual rights.[11] He graciously acquiesced, "as a friend to what is attainable."[12] It would not be until after the Civil War that the Fourteenth Amendment extended the Bill of Rights to ban infringements of constitutional rights by the states—though the Supreme Court's *Slaughter-House Cases* decision narrowed that protection in 1873.[13]

Congress submitted the Bill of Rights to the states on September 25, 1789, and long before the states had finished ratifying the ten amendments during 1791 and '92, Treasury secretary Alexander Hamilton had seized the initiative of the new government from Madison with his sweeping plan for repairing the nation's ruined finances at the start of 1790, igniting a smoldering feud with the Virginia congressman that ended in an explosive battle over what the Constitution meant. In his January *Report on Public Credit* to Congress, Hamilton had proposed restructuring the nation's $76 million of war debts by calling them in and replacing them with interest-bearing long-term notes backed by specially designated tax revenues, so that investors would be certain they would be repaid and would receive their interest like clockwork, making them willing to lend to the U.S. government once again.

But they would have confidence in the full faith and credit of the government, Hamilton grasped, only if they saw that the existing federal and state promissory notes were worth their face value. So in exchanging the old jumble of debt for new securities, the federal Treasury would have to treat all bondholders alike—whether they were soldiers who had received the government notes as their pay or investors who had bought them up at discounts from cash-strapped veterans or suppliers. And to be sure the state debts would get paid, the Treasury would have to shoulder them itself. Seven years earlier, Madison, in consultation with Hamilton, had proposed to Congress a financial plan that included exactly such a federal assumption of state debts, and, just as Hamilton was now urging, he had also pleaded with the states not to discriminate among different classes of creditors.[14]

But now Madison turned against these ideas and against his *Federalist Papers* collaborator, and in his much later fragment of autobiography, he took pains to claim that he hadn't understood back in the 1780s "the magnitude of the evil" of leaving soldiers who had sacrificed so much with only pennies on the dollar, while the "stockjobbers" who had bought their government promissory notes at predatory discounts raked in the lion's share of the money originally owed the battle-scarred veterans.[15] As for federal assumption of state debts, Virginia and some other states had already paid their debts, so in helping to pay the debts of the remaining states with their taxes, Virginians would in effect be paying for the war twice—though their state in fact had discharged its own debt also for pennies on the dollar. Accordingly, Madison blocked Hamilton's plan in Congress all through the winter and spring of 1790.

Still, as one of the few Founders who had never been a lawyer, a soldier, or a foreign envoy, Madison was a practical, professional politician—indeed from this moment even a political party leader—and he was willing to make a deal. Over a famous Madeira-fueled dinner at Jefferson's rented house on Maiden Lane in late June, Madison agreed to get two of his Virginia allies to vote for the funding plan, in exchange for Hamilton's pledge to persuade some Pennsylvania congressmen to vote for building the nation's permanent capital on the Potomac. By August, Congress had passed both measures.[16]

Nevertheless, Madison's resistance to Hamilton's plan ran deeper than such horse trading could reach. Uneasy about northern power now that the Great Compromise had dashed his dreams of a best-and-brightest senatorial faculty club and assured northern dominance of that body, he had no wish to boost northern economic might further, as Hamilton's plan would do, since northern states had the most debts for the federal government to pay off, and speculators in depreciated government paper were mostly northerners.[17] Some of those speculators, he learned to his disgust, were "members of Congress, who did not shrink from the practice of purchasing thro' Brokers the certificates at little price," knowing they would then vote "to transmute them into the value of the precious metals."[18] Such sharp practice differed little from the notorious corruption of those legislators whom John Trenchard and Thomas Gordon had famously lashed in *Cato's Letters* for shielding the perpetrators of the South Sea Bubble while speculating in the company's stock.

Nor did Madison like Hamilton's idea of a funded debt, perpetually rolled over, never extinguished, and requiring taxation to service it. Such a market in government paper called into being a class of financiers and investors, dependent on the Treasury and prone to the corruption that Trenchard and Gordon and their American followers believed was an inherent tendency of a government-bond market.

Madison shared that suspicion: "the stockjobbers will become the praetorian band of the Government," he wrote Jefferson, "at once its tool and its tyrant."[19] For all his belief in the efficacy of constitutional checks and balances, he still deeply valued republican virtue—the polar opposite, he thought, of the stockjobbers' worldview. And he also feared that the Treasury faction would gain enough political might to carry all before it.

After Jefferson returned from his four years in France in late 1789 and the two Piedmont neighbors began working together during Washington's presidency, the friendship between Secretary of State Jefferson and Congressman Madison deepened, with Jefferson's radical republicanism fanning Madison's own republican flame. Madison remained an independent thinker, of course, and had no trouble pooh-poohing Jefferson's wilder notions, including his airy dismissal of Madison's hope that the Constitution would last: "No society can make a perpetual constitution, or even a perpetual law," Jefferson scoffed.[20] But John Randolph of Roanoke—the outrageous House Ways and Means chairman who thought himself the purest and indeed the *only* republican, and who slanderously accused his cousin Nancy of working as a Richmond whore before she married Gouverneur Morris and of killing a baby he alleged that she had had with a slave—nevertheless hit a truth in saying, "Madison was always some great man's mistress—first Hamilton's,—then Jefferson's."[21]

Without doubt, Madison craved Jefferson's approval, and that passion deeply if subliminally tinged his worldview and shaped his career thereafter. As John Quincy Adams judged, "The mutual influence of these two mighty minds upon each other is a phenomenon, like the invisible and mysterious movements of the magnet in the physical world, and in which the sagacity of the future historian may discover the solution of much of our national history not otherwise easily accountable."[22]

Not long after he left Princeton, Madison had warned his friend William Bradford against "the impertinent fops" who "breed in Towns and populous places, as naturally as flies do in the Shambles, because there they get food enough for their Vanity," but this conventional trope, which the young man knew from literature not experience, began congealing into Jeffersonian rural sentimentality by the 1790s.[23] "The life of the husbandman," Madison declared in a 1792 article on republicanism, is the best life for "*health, virtue, intelligence,* and *competency* in the *greatest number* of citizens," not to mention "*liberty* and *safety*" for all. The life of workers in the various "branches of manufacturing, and mechanical industry," to the extent it differs from the yeoman's life, is proportionally less "truly independent and happy."[24]

How bad can it get? he asked in a subsequent article. Take the buckle makers of Britain, 20,000 of whom have lost their jobs and are "almost destitute of bread," because the trendsetting Prince of Wales, a "wanton youth" acting on "a mere whim of the imagination," has chosen to tie his shoes rather than buckle them. You don't find such "servile dependence of one class of citizens on another class" among "American citizens, who live on their own soil," exempt from "the *mutability of fashion.*"[25]

The bad faith in this pose jars. In 1792, Madison's younger brothers managed the Montpelier plantation, along with their father, nearing seventy; the congressman had surely never set hand to plow. Jefferson, who as minister to France had had himself painted in 1786 in a daintily curled wig, striped silk waistcoat, and dandified ruffled shirt, with a matching expression of supercilious foppery worthy of any ancien régime aristocrat, did run his own plantation, using the most modern methods, some of his own invention.[26] But sturdy yeomen? These hereditary landed grandees had their farming done for them by slaves. Their dependence on another class, though tyrannical rather than servile, was just as absolute as that of the buckle makers of Britain. They wanted the fiction of being republican husbandmen, "who provide at once their own food and their own raiment," as Madison rhapsodized, in order to oppose their pretense of virtuous rootedness-in-the-soil to urban life's foppery and fashion, phantom paper wealth, speculative bubbles, useless and precarious occupational diversity, debt, debauchery, and disease. No finance capitalism for them, no large-scale industry, no northern cosmopolitanism—in short, no Hamiltonianism.

THE LAST STRAW for Madison was Hamilton's December 1790 proposal for a federally chartered bank, empowered to print money, sell stock, and make loans to the government and private entrepreneurs. The capstone of Hamilton's financial edifice, the bank would leverage $2 million of precious metal into $10 million in currency, enough to galvanize the nation's economy into full productive vigor. Madison, writing in his old Princeton friend Philip Freneau's snarling *National Gazette*, thundered that such a measure would only "pamper . . . speculation," "promote unnecessary . . . debt," and "encrease . . . corruption"—all "in opposition to the republican spirit of the people."[27] Understandably scarred by the inflation of Revolutionary War paper currency, Madison, now the hardest of hard-money fundamentalists, didn't understand how paper money—firmly anchored in specie and backed by reliable credit—could safely increase both the quantity and velocity of money, greatly enlarging the money supply. All the bank would accomplish, he mistakenly told Congress in February 1791, would be to banish precious metals to foreign lands and substitute another medium of exchange for them, without increasing the overall quantity.[28]

As this speech gathered steam, Madison moved beyond such backward-looking mercantilism and magnificently set forth his main point: that the Constitution did not give Congress the power to establish an incorporated bank. Hamilton, he said, was urging the legislators to charter the bank based on the power that Article I, Section 8 of the Constitution gives them "to make all laws which shall be necessary and proper for carrying into Execution the foregoing Powers"—specific, limited powers that the section had just enumerated. But notice what "ductile" language Hamilton must use "to cover the stretch of power contained in the bill." As the bill puts it, the bank "might be conceived to be conducive to the successful conducting of the finances; or might be *conceived* to *tend* to give *facility* to the obtaining of loans," Madison quoted, adding emphasis oozing with incredulous contempt. So to begin with, the bank wasn't even "necessary," as the "necessary and proper" clause required; "at most it could be but convenient."

Worse, Madison suggested, Hamilton's reliance on a doctrine of implied powers instead of explicit ones courts disaster. "The doctrine of implication is always a tender one," he warned. "Mark the reasoning" behind the bill: "To borrow money is made the *end* and the accumulation of capitals, *implied* as the *means*. The accumulation of capitals is then the *end*, and a bank *implied* as the *means*." Such a chain of implication can lead to "a charter of incorporation, a monopoly, capital punishments, &c.," until finally it takes in "every object of legislation, every object within the whole compass of political economy"—even down to incorporating, should Congress wish it, a fraud-ridden, government-corrupting "South-Sea company." In that case, Madison cautioned, the "essential characteristic of the government, as composed of limited and enumerated powers, would be destroyed," and Congress would bear "the guilt of usurpation."[29] We should not, he later wrote, "by arbitrary interpretations and insidious precedents . . . pervert the limited government of the Union, into a government of unlimited discretion, contrary to the will and subversive of the authority of the people."[30]

Here we stand at one of the fateful crossroads of American history. One great man proposes a brilliant innovation that another great man says the Constitution whose design team he led does not permit. What should have happened?

Madison himself provides an ideal model. In the Constitutional Convention, he and Pennsylvanian James Wilson, his chief ally, had moved to give Congress power to build canals, but their colleagues rejected the plan as costly and unnecessary.[31] Three decades later, on his last day as president—March 3, 1817—Madison vetoed a bill providing federal funds for canals and roads. "I am not unaware of the great importance of roads and canals," his veto message remarked, with some understatement; nor did he doubt that spending federal money on them would yield "signal advantage to the general prosperity." But the power to do so is not among the powers "specified and enumerated" in Article I, Section 8, and any reading of the "necessary and proper" clause, or the commerce clause, or the clause "to provide for the common defense and general welfare" that would justify Congress's exercise of such power "would be contrary to the established and consistent rules of interpretation"—which, Madison explained at different epochs in his life, should stick to what those who had framed and ratified the text meant by it.[32] "Such a view of the Constitution," the veto message concluded, "would have the effect of giving to Congress a general power of legislation instead of the defined and limited one hitherto understood to belong to them." If legislators want to build roads and canals, let them frame a constitutional amendment asking the people for the requisite power.[33] Couldn't be clearer.

But even Madison didn't always find the question so simple.

At other times, he willingly embraced the doctrine of implied powers himself. As early as 1781, remember, he had asserted Congress's "implied right of coercion" of the states, by gunboats if need be, to make them provide their share of Revolutionary War supplies. And in his defense of the "necessary and proper" clause in *Federalist* 44 against those who thought it too elastic, he pointed out that the Constitution purposely didn't follow the Articles of Confederation in prohibiting Congress from exercising "any power not *expressly* delegated" to it, because no legislative body can carry out its duties "without recurring more or less to the doctrine of *construction* or *implication*." It would otherwise face "the alternative of betraying the public interest by doing nothing; or of violating the constitution by exercising powers indispensably necessary and proper; but at the same time, not *expressly* granted." In words Hamilton later flung back at him, Madison concluded, "No axiom is more clearly established in law, or in reason, than that wherever the end is required the means are authorised; wherever a general power to do a thing is given, every particular power necessary for doing it, is included."[34] And even as recently as the debates over the Bill of Rights, Madison had dissuaded his colleagues from wording the Tenth Amendment so that it would reserve to the states and to the people powers not *expressly* delegated to the United States. Not even the Constitution, he argued, could foresee every eventuality, so some latitude was in order.[35]

He found he needed that flexibility when, as secretary of state, he opposed President Jefferson's strict constructionism and embraced Hamilton's broad-construction constitutional approach to justify the Louisiana Purchase. With the army Napoleon had sent to quell the slave revolt in Haiti destroyed, and the fleet he had readied to reinforce its planned occupation of New Orleans icebound in Holland, the French dictator concluded that he now had no geostrategic use for the Louisiana Territory and would be better off at least getting some money for it by selling it to the Americans. The flabbergasted American envoys in Paris, James Monroe and Robert Livingston, realized that Napoleon wasn't joking about offering to sell only when Madison's old friend François Barbé-Marbois solemnly assured them that the offer was serious—but that time was short.

Jefferson objected that the Constitution gave neither the president nor Congress power to pay $15 million to double the size of the United States, but Madison argued that the deal was too good to lose and that Congress's treaty-making power implied a power to buy land, so Jefferson decided to shelve the constitutional amendment he had already drafted and "acquiesce with satisfaction" in Madison's view. Madison confessed to Senator John Quincy Adams that the Constitution didn't entirely authorize the transaction, but he expected that the "magnitude of the object" would excuse the stretch.[36]

In the case of Hamilton's bank, what actually happened was this. After the House and Senate approved it by big majorities, President Washington, troubled by Madison's opposition, asked him to prepare a veto message, just in case, and he asked Jefferson and Attorney General Edmund Randolph for their written opinions about the bank's constitutionality.[37] They echoed Madison's objections, and Washington sent their memos to Hamilton for rebuttal.

In his extensive, forceful brief—which urged interpreting the

Constitution "on principles of liberal construction" (liberal not in a partisan sense but in the sense of free, open-minded, unprejudiced, expansive rather than crabbed)—Hamilton argued that the "criterion of what is constitutional . . . is the *end* to which the measure relates as a *mean*. If the end be clearly comprehended within any of the specified powers, & if the measure have an obvious relation to that end, and is not forbidden by any particular provision of the constitution—it may safely be deemed to come within the compass of the national authority." Moreover, Hamilton advised the practical-minded president, "All the provisions and operations of government must be presumed to contemplate things as they *really* are."[38] Washington received Hamilton's brief on February 23, 1791, and signed the bill into law the next day, providing all the "energy in government" that Madison had once sought—and more—and supercharging American prosperity.

In the summer of 1798, when President John Adams signed the Alien and Sedition Acts—for which Vice President Jefferson justly dubbed his administration "the reign of witches"—Madison had to ponder a starker constitutional question: What is the right response to federal measures so grossly unconstitutional that they trample liberty? As the Napoleonic Wars raged across the globe and the United States found itself locked in an undeclared but costly naval "Quasi-War" with France, U.S. diplomats sought peaceful relations, only to meet with demands for a £50,000 bribe from their French counterparts, code-named X, Y, and Z in their dispatch. When news of the XYZ Affair reached America in March 1798, with reports (slightly embellished) that the American envoys had indignantly replied, "Millions for defense, but not one cent for tribute," sour national politics reached its climax of bitterness.

Adams's and Hamilton's Federalists tarred Madison's and Jefferson's Republicans as dupes or fifth columnists for clinging to their affection for France all through the Reign of Terror and the rise of Napoleon—and indeed X, Y, and Z's dark hints of aid from "friends of France" in America, as the published diplomatic dispatches reported, fanned the spies-and-saboteurs hysteria that hatched the Alien and Sedition Acts.[39] Republicans dismissed the Federalists as Francophobe "anglomen," pageantry-loving "monocrats," and plutocratic stock-jobbers, who were using French misbehavior as an excuse to forge a British alliance and move toward a British-style monarchy or hereditary aristocracy, British-style political corruption, and a British-style standing army that would underpin a British-style "fiscal-military" state—all the liberty-killing "known instruments for bringing the many under the domination of the few," Madison concluded.[40]

As the partisan press battle blazed with swollen-veined passion, Adams never employed the power the Alien Act gave the president to deport any noncitizen he deemed a national security threat, even though he believed that the country "swarmed" with "Spies in its own Bosom."[41] But the government did bring prosecutions under the Sedition Act, which criminalized "false, scandalous, and malicious writing" intended to bring the president or Congress "into contempt or disrepute, or to excite against them . . . the hatred of the good people of the United States." Madison proposed a mordant July 4 toast: "The freedom of speech; May it strike its enemies dumb." But joking aside, since the act forbade conspiring "with intent to oppose . . . measures of the government," Madison and Jefferson, fearful that Federalist spies were opening their mail, worried about prosecution as they conspired in figuring out what to do.[42] Indeed, an uncharacteristic six-month break in the correspondence between the author of the Declaration of Independence and the Father of the Constitution testifies to their anxiety; their friend and neighbor James Monroe even cautioned them against being seen together on the Piedmont lanes.[43]

Meanwhile, the government indicted bare-knuckled Republican journalist Benjamin Franklin Bache, Benjamin Franklin's grandson, for seditious libel, though he died before trial, while Republican hack James Callender got a nine-month sentence, and Vermont Republican congressman Matthew Lyons got four months and a $1,000 fine, for volunteering, with some truth, that Adams had "an unbounded thirst for ridiculous pomp, foolish adulation, and selfish avarice." He won reelection from jail.[44]

The Piedmont conspirators responded by writing resolutions that two state legislatures passed. Jefferson drafted one for Kentucky, declaring that, because the Constitution was a pact among the states to delegate certain limited and enumerated powers to the federal government, the states might justly complain if the federal government exceeded those powers, as it did in the Alien and Sedition Acts, and might declare its action "void and of no force." In fact, read Jefferson's draft of the Kentucky Resolutions, "where powers have been assumed which have not been delegated, a nullification of the act is the rightful remedy."[45] The Kentucky legislature, however, dropped the word "nullification" from the resolution it finally passed, sticking to the slightly less incendiary "void and of no force" language.[46]

Madison too shied away from the extremism of nullification in his Virginia Resolutions, and though Jefferson slipped the phrase "utterly null, void, and of no force or effect" into one draft of them, the words never appeared in the final copy.[47] The resolutions Madison wrote declared that the "unconstitutional" Alien Act "subverts the general principles of free government," overturning the separation of powers by making the president both judge and jury in deciding whom to deport.

Worse by far, the Sedition Act violates the Virginia Ratifying Convention's solemn statement "that, among other essential rights, the liberty of conscience and of the press cannot be cancelled, abridged, restrained or modified by any authority of the United States." The act usurps a power that the Constitution not only doesn't confer but indeed positively prohibits in the Bill of Rights—and the usurpation "ought to produce universal alarm, because it is levelled against the right of freely examining public characters and public measures, and of free communication among the people thereon, which has ever been justly deemed, the only effectual guardian of every other right."[48] And remember, Madison wrote in a later report on the Virginia Resolutions, "that to the press alone, chequered as it is with abuses, the world is indebted for all the triumphs which have been gained by reason and humanity, over error and oppression." Without freedom of the press, the United States might still "possibly be miserable colonies, groaning under a foreign yoke."[49] As for journalistic abuses: out of the clash of assertions and opinions, however false and biased, would emerge truth, he believed, with a radical faith in freedom of thought and expression, and a belief in the power of information, that uncannily prefigure John Stuart Mill's *On Liberty*.

As to what to do, the Virginia Resolutions are less clear, merely advising that the states "are in duty bound, to interpose for arresting the progress of the evil" that threatens their citizens' "rights and liberties."[50] When in September 1799, Madison, Monroe, and Jefferson gathered at Monticello to discuss how best to proceed, Madison was aghast to hear Jefferson say that Virginia and Kentucky should declare themselves ready "to sever ourselves from that union we so much value, rather than give up the rights of self government . . . in which we alone see liberty, safety and happiness." Spluttered Madison, "We should never think of separation except for repeated and enormous violations."[51] He trusted in the wisdom of the electorate and the diffusion of republican culture through the newspapers to right this wrong, and soon enough Jefferson became president and let the Alien and Sedition Acts lapse.

Imagine Madison's horror, then, when in the late 1820s South Carolinians opposed to a protective tariff began to speak of their state's right to nullify it, citing the authority of Madison and Jefferson's Virginia and Kentucky Resolutions. As Vice President (and, later, Senator) John C. Calhoun fanned the flames into the 1830s, the elderly Madison wrote one earnest letter after another, recalling that the Constitution was not a pact among the state legislatures but among "the people in each of the states, acting in their highest sovereign authority," so no state legislature had the authority to nullify an act of Congress, which was the supreme law of the land. If states seized such authority, they would "speedily put an end to the Union itself."[52] And to gain what?

"The idea that a Constitution which has been so fruitful of blessings, and a Union admitted to be the only guardian of the peace, liberty and happiness of the people of the States comprizing it should be broken up and scattered to the winds without greater than existing causes is more painful than words can express."[53]

By 1833, Madison noted, northerners began voicing "unconstitutional designs on the subject of . . . slaves" (as Patrick Henry had predicted they would forty-five years earlier), and talk in the South turned from nullification to secession. If a state or bloc of states were actually to secede, Madison wrote, what the other states might do raises questions too painful to consider. "God grant," he concluded, that we are spared "the more painful task of deciding them!"[54] The next year, he wrote a note of *Advice to My Country*, to be read after his death: "The advice nearest to my heart and deepest in my convictions is that the Union of the States be cherished and perpetuated. Let the open enemy to it be regarded as a Pandora with her box opened; and the disguised one, as the Serpent creeping with his deadly wiles into Paradise."[55] However inadvertently, and much to his sorrow, he was complicit in opening the lid of that box, if only a tiny crack, and letting the evils loose. And when his *Advice* first appeared in print in 1850, inflamed states'-rights partisans dismissed it as a forgery.[56]

James Madison was a remarkable mind. But what of his heart—his passions as well as his reason, as he would say? That too is an extraordinary story, with a sadly unpromising start ending in one of the legendarily successful political marriages in American history.

Madison was not the stuff of which fairy-tale lovers are made. Not for nothing did his detractors dismiss him as "Little Jemmy." Five foot six at the highest estimate, though some guess five four (and we do shrink with age), slight and delicate in build, he was, one contemporary said, "no bigger than half a piece of soap."[57] When he first arrived in Congress at twenty-nine, one delegate mistook him as being "just from the College."[58] By his midthirties, suffering periodic attacks of "bilious indisposition" and chronic hypochondria, he was balding and wore his powdered hair in a comb-over that ended in a little point on his forehead.[59] In his customary suits of solemn black, with knee breeches and black silk stockings, he looked, thought Jacques-Pierre Brissot de Warville (later a leading Girondin), like "a stern censor, . . . conscious of his talents and duties."

As a public speaker, swaying back and forth, and consulting notes in his hat, he had, according to an unsympathetic congressional colleague, "no fire, no enthusiasm, no animation; but he has infinite prudence and industry."[60] An admiring Bushrod Washington, by contrast, saw the intellectual brilliance behind the low-voiced, undramatic presentation and told his uncle, the General, that Madison spoke "with such force of reasoning, and a display of such irresistible truths, that opposition seemed to have quitted the field."[61] The *Virginia Journal* blossomed into verse to praise his Constitutional Convention oratory:

Maddison, above the rest
Pouring, from his narrow chest
More than Greek or Roman sense
Boundless tides of eloquence.[62]

Many observers noted the contrast between his awkward reserve with crowds and strangers, and his genial fluency with intimates. Perhaps Edward Coles, Madison's secretary and his wife's cousin, caught it best: "his form, features, and manner were not commanding, but his conversation exceedingly so and few men possessed so rich a flow of language, or so great a fund of amusing anecdotes, which were made the more interesting for their being well-timed and well-told. His ordinary manner was simple, modest, bland, and unostentatious, retiring from the throng and cautiously refraining from doing or saying anything to make himself conspicuous."[63] But in private, ever since Princeton, he even liked a dirty joke.

Most delegates to the Continental Congress lived in boardinghouses, and at Mrs. Mary House's harmonious and agreeable one a block from Independence Hall, Madison's Philadelphia lodging from

1780 to 1793, the Virginia congressman met his New York colleague and fellow boarder, William Floyd, who brought his family to stay in late 1782. Madison, thirty-one, fell in love with the youngest Floyd daughter—harpsichord-playing Catherine, then fifteen—and by April 1783, just when Kitty was about to turn sixteen, Madison wrote Jefferson that he "had sufficiently ascertained her sentiments" and that "the affair has been pursued" so successfully that the "preliminary arrangements" were "definitive"—a roundabout way of saying that they were engaged.[64] They exchanged miniature portraits by Charles Willson Peale, and when the congressional session ended, the thirty-two-year-old swain accompanied his betrothed and her family on their trip home and stayed for a brief visit.

But in July, in a letter brattily sealed with a blob of rye dough, Kitty wrote Madison to break it off, doubtless because she preferred the young medical student she had also met at Mrs. House's and whom she married in 1785. It's a problem for biographers that Madison asked his correspondents to return his letters and destroyed or defaced most of the personal ones, directing his wife to burn the remaining nonpolitical ones after his death. Though his August 11, 1783, letter to Jefferson survives, he crossed out its account of the Kitty Floyd affair; but the heartache still bleeds out from under the inkblots: "one of those incidents to which such affairs are liable . . . profession of indifference . . . more propitious turn of fate." Jefferson replied with the usual bromides, enlivened by his golden pen: "the world still presents the same and many other resources of happiness, and you possess many within yourself." He had thought the match a done deal, he wrote, "[b]ut of all machines ours is the most complicated and inexplicable."[65]

As Madison shepherded the Constitution, the new government, and the Bill of Rights into existence, he himself entered into middle age as a confirmed bachelor. But instead of being just a short, slight, balding, diffident middle-aged bachelor, he was a famous and powerful one—so when he asked his friend Senator Aaron Burr in May 1794 to introduce him to Philadelphia's most eligible young widow, Dolley Payne Todd, she readily, if nervously, agreed to meet the man she called "the great little Madison."[66] All the young and youngish men of Philadelphia were "in the Pouts" for the famously buxom twenty-five-year-old and would "station themselves where they could see her pass," one friend recalled.[67] She was "the first & fairest representative of Virginia, in the female society of Philada," her old friend Anthony Morris wrote, "and she soon raised the mercury there in the thermometers of the Heart to fever heat."[68] It wasn't just her external charms that fascinated everyone; she had an inner radiance, visible to all, which she herself summed up better than anyone. "Everybody loves Mrs. Madison," Senator Henry Clay once said to her, much later. "That's because," she replied without missing a beat, "Mrs. Madison loves everybody."[69]

For all her sunniness, Dolley was acquainted with grief, which perhaps explains her habitual caginess about her past. Her father was a high-principled failure, who therefore inflicted upon his family some of the cost of those principles. He and Dolley's mother had moved from Virginia to join a Quaker settlement in North Carolina, where Dolley was born three years later, in May 1768. But the Paynes didn't make a go of Carolina farming, and, a year after Dolley's birth, they sold their farm at a big loss and returned to farm in Virginia, with their slaves. When Virginia legalized manumission in 1782, the state's Quakers faced a stern choice: free their slaves, since the Quakers increasingly found slavery morally intolerable, or leave the sect. John Payne chose emancipation, moved to Philadelphia and became a laundry-starch merchant, failed, got thrown out of the Pine Street Meeting for insolvency, shut himself in his room, and died in 1792.[70]

By then, his temperature-raising Dolley had been married for two years to Quaker lawyer John Todd and had borne her first child, John Payne Todd. In the summer of 1793, she gave birth to her second son, just as a horrific yellow-fever plague was about to scourge Philadelphia. It killed perhaps one in every ten inhabitants and devastated Dolley's family. After sending her and the babies to supposed safety in the countryside, John Todd stayed in town to look after his parents, who refused to leave and soon succumbed. By the time he fled, it was too late. He died on October 14, 1793, as did his infant son, leaving Dolley a twenty-five-year-old widow with a toddler to raise.[71]

Seven months later, within days of Dolley's twenty-sixth birthday in May 1794, Burr introduced her to Madison. In June, one of Dolley's young relatives wrote her that forty-three-year-old "Mad—" told her to say that "he thinks so much of you in the day that he has Lost his Tongue, at Night he Dreames of you & Starts in his Sleep a Calling on you to relieve the Flame for he Burns to such an excess that he will be shortly consumed."[72] In August, Dolley accepted Madison's proposal. "I can not express, but hope you will conceive the joy it gave me," he wrote her.[73] In September, they were married at Harewood in West Virginia, home of Dolley's younger sister, Lucy, wife of George Steptoe Washington, the General's ward and nephew (so interconnected were the Virginia oligarchs).

That day, Dolley wrote to her oldest friend, Eliza Collins Lee, wife of Light-Horse Harry Lee's brother, Congressman Richard Bland Lee: "I have stolen from the family to commune with you—to tell you in short, that in the cource of this day I give my Hand to the Man who of all other's I most admire," and she signed herself "Dolley Payne Todd." Later, after Madison had slipped on her tiny finger a ring with a circle of modest diamonds lovingly preserved at Montpelier, she penned this addendum: "Evening: Dolley Madison! Alass!" The paper being torn off at this point, who knows what was in her heart on her wedding night?[74] The Society of Friends, however, knew what it thought of her marrying a non-Quaker eleven months after her first husband's death: it expelled her.

BEGINNING IN January 1793, when the French revolutionaries murdered Louis XVI, the Republican embrace of France caused a steady erosion of the party's influence, which Republican adulation of French ambassador Edmond Genêt speeded up. But the envoy's presumptuous disregard of President Washington's neutrality proclamation soon began to "surprize and disgust" Republican leaders, wrote Madison; they grasped that the young man's "folly" would "do mischief which no wisdom can repair."[75] When Washington himself publicly blamed the "self-created" Democratic-Republican Societies, with their glorification of the increasingly radical and violent French Revolution, for sparking the antitax Whiskey Rebellion in western Pennsylvania in the summer of 1794, Madison lost heart.

Federalist journalists had already been calling the societies "Madisonian" and terming their "Jaco-Demo-Crat" members "the Mads"—a dig that stuck.[76] "The game," said Madison, "was to connect the democratic Societies with the odium of insurrection—to connect the Republicans in Congress with those Societies—to put the President ostensibly at the head of another party, in opposition to both" the Republicans and the societies.[77] By the end of the 1796–97 congressional session, a dispirited Madison, having failed to stop the Jay Treaty with Britain from going into effect and no longer leader of what had been called "Mr. Madison's Party" or the "French Party," chose to retire from Congress and take Dolley home to Virginia.

His parents needed him there. As his father, James Madison, Sr., had grown old and frail, Madison's brother Ambrose had taken over the management of Montpelier. But Ambrose died suddenly in 1793, and when Madison returned home, he grasped the reins of the plantation and became, for the first time, a Virginia farmer.

He moved his wife, her young son, and her beloved youngest sister Anna—whom Dolley called her sister-daughter—into his parents' nine-room brick house, Orange County's biggest when his father had built it in the mid-1760s. To this conventional five-bay, two-story Georgian house—in other words, it had four windows and a central doorway on the first floor, and five windows on the second—he immediately began adding a four-room extension to the north, with its own internal staircase. By ingeniously adding three more bays—another door and two more windows on the first floor, with three windows above—he produced a still-symmetrical eighty-six-foot-long building,

The Evolution of Montpelier

Courtesy of The Montpelier Foundation and Partsense, Inc.

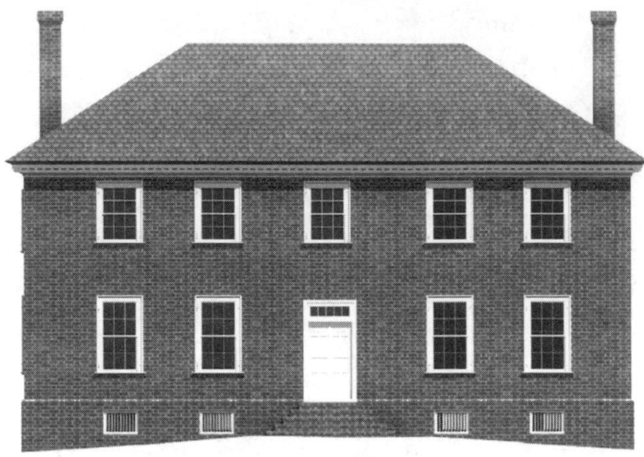

The house Madison's father built in the mid-1760s

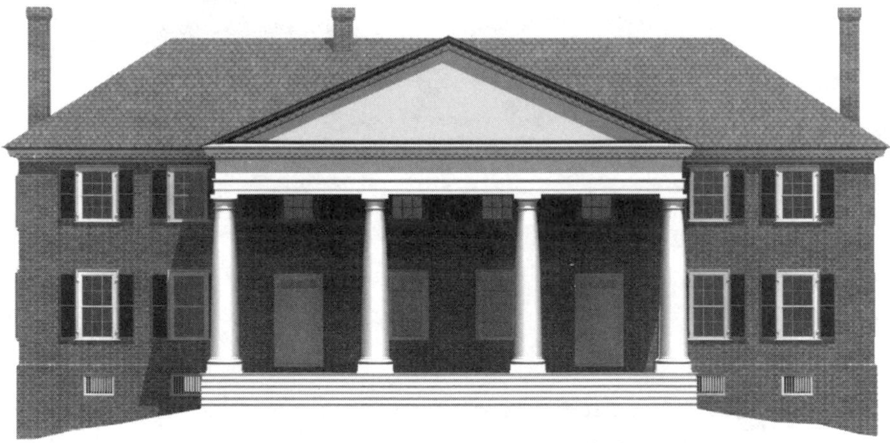

The house with the extension Madison added after his return to Montpelier with his new bride in 1797, with its entrance between the two left-hand columns of the new portico

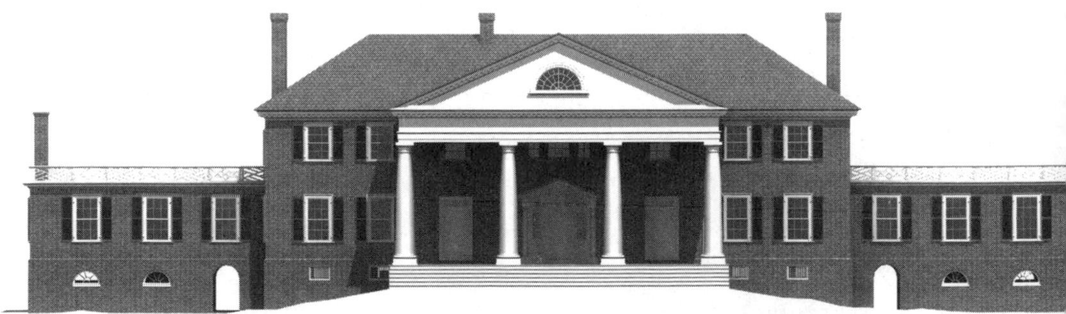

Montpelier as enlarged during President Madison's first term

with three pairs of windows on the first floor, separated by doorways on each side of the central pair. To emphasize the symmetry and unify the façade further, he built a two-story columned portico as a central focal point, embracing the two doorways. The second floor of the enlarged building was a connected whole, but to get from the new first floor to the old meant going out one front door and walking across the porch to the other, so that Madison's young family had some sense of privacy from his elderly parents.

When Madison became president in 1809, he began preparing for his second retirement by enlarging Montpelier further, adding two one-story wings with roof terraces on each side, one of them housing a grand library, and the other a comfortable residence for his mother—still living there when Madison retired for good, visited daily by her son and daughter-in-law, until her death at ninety-seven in 1829, when Madison was seventy-eight and more wrinkled than she.[78] With advice (and workmen) from his friends Jefferson, Capitol architect William Thornton, and White House interior designer Benjamin Henry Latrobe, he reunified the first floor and added a stylish, pedimented central entrance door with a fanlight above, and he knocked down more walls to make a large, stately, presidential drawing room, hung with a mini-museum of second-rate old-master paintings, at the heart of the house. He also built a lovely domed *tempietto*—a whimsical, classical covering for an icehouse dug into the ground below—just to the northwest of what was now a serene, self-confident, late-Georgian mansion, tripartite, harmoniously proportioned, unostentatiously grand, and looking out to the heart-melting Piedmont view over Madison's 5,000 lush patrimonial acres.

These details, so easy to relate, cost restorers and archeologists immense labor to discover, not simply because Montpelier grew up through three successive stages of Madison family development but more especially because the presidential mansion underwent continual "modernization" and enlargement almost from the moment the widowed Dolley Madison had to sell it in 1844. The family who bought it in 1848, for example, stuccoed over the rose-colored handmade bricks and replaced the wooden-shingle roof with a metal one, to make the house look more fashionably Greek Revival. But William du Pont, Sr., an heir to the great chemical and gunpowder fortune, made the biggest change after he took over Montpelier in 1901. A mere presidential mansion seems not to have been grand enough for him: he more than doubled the size of the house, from twenty-two rooms when he started to a Brobdingnagian fifty-five. His daughter Marion, married for a time to cowboy-movie idol Randolph Scott, inherited the house in 1928, making the grounds into a famous thoroughbred center and turning part of Mother Madison's wing into an art deco fantasy of chrome and lacquer, with a Steuben crystal mantelpiece, that more evokes a streamlined diner than the metropolitan suavity of an art deco icon like Rockefeller Center—and that the restorers have moved to a separate building.

I first saw Montpelier when the restoration team had torn down most of the du Pont additions and scraped all the stucco off Madison's bricks. As they demolished, they had found intact pieces of Madison's original house—a door frame, paneling, floorboards, a mantelpiece, a hearthstone—and they were placing them back in their original positions by matching up nail holes and chisel marks. They had removed all the modern, waterlogged plaster, leaving behind lathes dating from the 1760s to 1812, so that I could peer through the spaces between the hand-cut slats into room after room after room, as if in a ghost house. The lanky, electrically intense restoration chief, John Jeanes, for whom Montpelier is a calling not a job, showed me how he had been able to re-create missing chair rails by tracing faint profiles of the originals he had found on the sides of the window frames under several layers of paint.

When I returned almost three years later, he showed me how his crew had laid 30,000 new, handmade cypress shingles on the roof (copied from original ones that had fallen into the attic); replastered the walls with the original lime, horsehair, and sand formula; re-created the Chinese Chippendale railings crowning the roof-terraces on the wings; and repaired a structural beam that some previous remodeler had insouciantly sawn through to make a doorway. Of the original furnishings, little remained, having been sold off piece by piece by Dolley's spendthrift son, and I talked to other restorers about wallpapers and curtains, based on scraps that had turned up, along with a piece of one of Madison's letters, in a two-century-old mouse's nest uncovered in a wall. And I couldn't help thinking of the whole project as a metaphor for the restoration that Madison's Constitution needs—a clearing away of some of the more vainglorious excrescences added on by twentieth-century modernizers, defacing the simple, classical restraint and balance of the original, which every stage of Madison's alterations had preserved.

The Revolution of 1800—as Jefferson dubbed the electoral sweep that gave the Republicans the presidency and control of both houses of Congress—took Madison away from Montpelier for a sixteen-year stretch in Washington, first as President Jefferson's secretary of state and closest confidant until 1809 and then as his two-term successor.[79] Those opening years of the nineteenth century transformed American politics, society, and foreign relations in ways that Madison only marginally controlled; most often, he seemed like a swimmer stroking bewilderedly on time's ever-rolling stream toward a destination he neither chose nor relished. The magisterial command he showed as a lawgiver deserted him as an executive. Partly because of his deeply ingrained deference to Jefferson, partly because ideology and politics rather than experience and history increasingly became his guides, and partly because he had almost never run anything, he proved no leader at a time when the country badly needed one.

In May 1801, he arrived in the new capital he had won in his bargain with Hamilton—two months after Jefferson's inauguration, because his father had died in February and he had to wind up the old squire's affairs before leaving Montpelier to take the oath as secretary of state. The city of Washington, despite architect Pierre L'Enfant's grandiose plan for its streets and squares, seemed still to be emerging from the primeval ooze. A sad flock of shanties, falling into ruin even as they were built, punctuated the swampy wastes between the capital's 109 habitable brick houses and 263 wooden ones and promised to doom their "wretched tenants to perpetual fevers," Treasury secretary Albert Gallatin predicted. "Washington would be a beautiful city if it were built," an English traveler scoffed, "but as it is not, I cannot say much about it."[80] For the first few weeks, the Madisons moved in with Jefferson at the unfinished President's House, still as scantily furnished as when Abigail Adams had used what's now the East Room to hang out her washing.[81]

Even with Goose Creek off the Potomac ambitiously renamed the Tiber, Washington was still frontier, like so much of the country.[82] The population west of the Alleghenies, 150,000 in 1795, exploded to more than a million of the nation's more than 7 million inhabitants by 1810; that year 70 percent of the country's white population was twenty-five or younger. Young settlers were filling even the frontier parts of settled states: "Axes were resounding and the trees literally were falling about us as we passed," reported a traveler through the upstate New York woods in 1805.[83] And the 1803 Louisiana Purchase, the Jefferson administration's greatest accomplishment (or stroke of luck), expanded by 900,000 square miles the frontier yet to settle. As part of the Revolution of 1800, Congress made it ever easier for settlers to buy western land in smaller and smaller parcels, at cheap prices and on easy credit terms.[84]

WHAT KIND OF CULTURE would this young, mobile society invent for itself? Above all, Madison and Jefferson vowed, it would be republican. Even at the start of George Washington's administration, Madison had urged the new president to resist anything that smacked of aristocratic or monarchist pretension. As he saw it, "the more simple, the more Republican we are in our manners, the more rational dignity we shall acquire."[85]

By manners he meant more than using the correct fork. He meant, as Hobbes had defined it long before, "those qualities of man-kind, that concern their living together in Peace, and Unity"—the customs and ceremonies, allied to virtue, by which men humanize their interactions: we wait our turn, we dine, we thank, we marry, we mourn.[86] For Madison and Jefferson, republican manners would ban all show of deference or superiority. "The principle of society with us, as well as of our political constitution, is the equal rights of all," Jefferson explained; "and if there be an occasion where this equality ought to prevail preeminently, it is in social circles collected for conviviality."[87] With proud simplicity, Jefferson set the tone by walking from his boardinghouse to his inauguration. That day, he declared, "buried levees, birthdays, royal parades, and the arrogation of precedence in society by certain self-stiled friends of order, but truly stiled friends of privileged orders." Away with George Washington's controlled, majestic bearing and his yellow coach with six white horses. The slouching Jefferson, when he rode at all, rode in a one-horse cart.[88]

Soon enough, these republican manners created an international incident. As a national capital, raw little Washington, with around 3,000 whites and 750 blacks when the Madisons arrived, acquired its share of more or less exotic foreign diplomats: General Louis-Marie Turreau, the French ambassador, who often beat his wife, Dolley Madison's close friend, at home and in public, and who reportedly danced quadrilles in his embassy with naked ladies, for example, and the turbaned Sidi Suleiman Melli Melli, the Bey of Tunis's envoy, who earnestly discussed women and God with several Creek and Cherokee chiefs at a President's House reception, and for whom Secretary of State Madison procured one "Georgia a Greek," whose fee he expensed on the State Department ledger as "appropriations to foreign intercourse."[89] But the real scandal concerned Anthony Merry, Britain's envoy extraordinary and minister plenipotentiary—and it was a scandal Jefferson and Madison precipitated.

As DIPLOMATIC PROTOCOL required, the newly arrived Merry, escorted by Madison and "all bespeckled," the envoy's secretary wrote, "with the spangles of our gaudiest court dress," came to the President's House in late 1803 to present his credentials.[90] Jefferson, having by now recoiled against that aristocratic finery and hauteur he had sported in his portrait as ambassador to France, received Merry in sloppy dress and bedroom slippers, lounged in his chair in his characteristic slouch, legs crossed and one hip cocked higher than the other, and dangled a slipper off one toe. Merry took this demeanor as an "actually studied" insult.[91]

His next President's House visit a few days later, for a dinner in his and his wife's honor, confirmed this interpretation. Instead of ushering Elizabeth Merry into the dining room and seating her to his right, as custom dictated, Jefferson offered his arm to a startled Dolley Madison, who whispered, "Take Mrs. Merry." The secretary of state took charge of Mrs. Merry, however, leaving His Britannic Majesty's envoy to fend for himself. As Merry pulled out a chair to sit beside the Spanish ambassador's wife, a young congressman elbowed him aside, and Merry stumbled down the table until he found an empty place.

Making things even worse, the French envoy was there too, a gross breach of the commonsense diplomatic rule of never inviting representatives of two warring countries to the same event, and Merry later heard with disgust that Jefferson had specially asked the Frenchman to come back from out of town for the dinner. A few days later, the Merrys went to dinner at the Madisons' and got the some treatment, though this time Mrs. Merry stared down Treasury secretary Gallatin's wife and displaced her from the seat at Madison's right hand.[92]

Jefferson was an ex-ambassador to the French court, and he and Madison, as Virginia grandees, knew better than this, as indeed Madison later admitted, when he said that he would have escorted Mrs. Merry to his own dinner table but felt obliged to toe the presidential line. "Mr. Jefferson and Mr. Madison were too much of the gentlemen not to feel ashamed of what they were doing," the British legation secretary reported, "and consequently did it awkwardly, as people must do who affect bad manners for a particular object."[93] Their object of course was to express resentment at Britain, and Merry got the message all too clearly—as did the Spanish ambassador's wife, who exclaimed, as Jefferson snubbed Mrs. Merry, "This will be the cause of war!"[94]

Knowing they had gone too far, Jefferson and Madison tried to backpedal; they printed up and presented to Merry a pamphlet misspelled *Cannons of Etiquette*, stating that American diplomatic occasions, large or small, would follow the rule of *pêle-mêle*, meaning that guests would crowd in and take whatever place they could, though ladies would go first. Merry huffed that they should have told him this before and that he'd seek instructions on how to proceed; meanwhile he continued to turn down President's House dinner invitations. "I shall be highly honored," Jefferson acidly remarked, "when the King of England is good enough to let Mr. Merry come and eat my soup."[95]

But he never did. Convinced by this charade of America's implacable hostility to Britain and partiality for France, Merry consistently advised his government never to make concessions to the United States or to believe American overtures of friendship. So the "Merry Affair" helped sow the seeds of the War of 1812.[96]

THE MERRY AFFAIR, said Madison, was about "the right of the *government here to fix its rules of intercourse* and the sentiments and *manners of* the country."[97] But the kind of manners he and Jefferson were "fixing" at once reflected and legitimated a trend that was already running strong in the country: a powerful streak of resentment in the assertion of independence and equality.

In the 1790s, the pro-French Democratic-Republican Societies thronged with farmers and tradesmen who seethed with class anger against "aristocrats" who devalued them, they believed, for having "not snored through four years at Princeton." And who were these aristocrats? "Judges, Lawyers, Generals, Colonels," and "all men of talents," sneered one Republican, whom his party strove "to prevent . . . from being elected" to office.[98] Another northern Republican in the late 1790s railed against "the merchant, phisition, lawyer & divine, the philosopher and school master, the Juditial & Executive Officers" who "asotiate together and look down with two much contempt on those that labour." Such men "that git a Living without Bodily Labour" use their "art & skeems" to control the banks, the newspapers, and the government, which they employ to keep themselves rich and the poor poor.[99] By 1800, the country's eighty-five Republican newspapers were constantly vibrating with resentment against the Federalist "prigarchy"—the "great men," such as "merchants, speculators, priests, lawyers," and government officials, who, enriched "by their *art* and *cunning*," supposedly looked down "upon the honest laborer as a distinct animal of an inferior species."[100]

Madison and Jefferson recognized the political force of such passions and played them for all they were worth. Having shed his former yearning to leaven government with the wise and virtuous, Madison wasn't content merely to flay the Hamiltonians as monocrats itching to reinstate an aristocracy, but went on to tar them as "Tories"—not just opponents but enemies with blood on their hands, supporters of the actual hierarchical oppressors whom Americans had only recently stopped with bullets. These Federalists, whom Madison renamed "anti-republicans" while rebranding the anti-Federalists as the Republicans, believe the "people are stupid, suspicious, licentious," and "should think of nothing but obedience, leaving the care of their liberties to their wiser rulers," Madison wrote.[101]

Jefferson, the philosopher and polymath who boasted on his tombstone that he was "Father of the University of Virginia," declared: "State a moral case to a ploughman and a professor; the former will decide it as well, and often better than the latter, because he has not been led astray by artificial rules."[102] This was long before the politicization of academe, of which William F. Buckley, Jr., could jibe he'd rather be governed by the first 200 names in the Boston phone book than by the highly partisan Harvard faculty; and if Jefferson meant to uplift the ploughman rather than denigrate the professor, his was a generously commendable sentiment. But in fact he was pandering to know-nothingism. Montpelier and Monticello are pure embodiments of the Enlightenment spirit, in their classical balance, harmony, restraint, order, urbanity, and deep historical learning, and their builders were sons of the Age of Reason. But the Revolution of 1800 marks the end of the Enlightenment in America.

The society that republican manners fostered was a society of inflamed egos, of I'm-just-as-good-as-you self-assertion and readiness to take offense. By 1800, foreign visitors spoke of Americans as slobs who pushed and shoved in public and trampled ordinary civilities. The incivility increased as one traveled west, where there were "no private or publick associations for the common good," and "every man is for himself alone and has no regard for any other person farther than he can make him subservient to his own views," one acute observer noted. "Natural freedom," a foreign traveler remarked, "is what pleases them." Out in the West, a Kentuckian told Madison, "society is yet unborn," there is "no distinction assumed on account of rank or property," and a "certain loss of civility is inevitable."[103]

That was an understatement. Out west, "savage" fights were common, complete with "choking, gouging out each other's eyes, and biting off each other's noses," recalled another Kentuckian. "But what is worst of all," according to an English visitor, "these wretches in their combat endeavor to their utmost to tear out each other's testicles."[104] In the rest of the world, a New Englander mused, "progress has been from ignorance to knowledge, from the rudeness of savage life to the refinements of polished society." But in America, "the case is reversed. The tendency is from civilization to barbarism." Maybe the naturalist Buffon was right: that in the unhealthful climate of the New World, species degenerated.[105]

Out on the frontier that was Washington—where some backwoods congressmen had never before seen a piano or a Frenchman,[106] where Republican congressman Matthew Lyons notoriously spat in Connecticut Federalist Roger Griswold's face in the legislative chamber and later beaned him with the House of Representatives' fire tongs after Griswold caned him, and where Dolley Madison's brother-in-law, Congressman John G. Jackson, got badly hurt in a duel over policy differences, while her cousin (President Madison's secretary) horsewhipped yet another congressman in the Capitol for the same reason—Dolley resolved to do some civilizing.[107]

She made her first try while her husband was still secretary of state. As de facto first lady—President Jefferson and Vice President Aaron Burr were widowers—she presided with her sunny good nature over the presidential table at dinners that ladies attended. But these were few. Believing that women had no place in politics, Jefferson mostly held weekday dinners for eight or a dozen congressmen at a time, all Republicans or all Federalists, where he wooed them to his views with his good wine, high cuisine, and fascinating talk, even though they could sometimes see their breath in his cold dining room.[108]

So Dolley took it upon herself to bring the sexes and the political parties together, at her famously convivial New Year's Day celebrations at her F Street house, to which all Washington trooped with relief after the stiff, obligatory President's House reception, and at her weekly dinners for up to seventy guests, which Elizabeth Merry sniffed were "more like a harvest-home supper than the entertainment of a Secretary of State." Dolley had her own ideas of hospitality, however. She told her friend and first biographer, Margaret Bayard Smith, that "she thought abundance was preferable to elegance; that circumstances formed customs, and customs formed taste; and as the profusion, so repugnant to foreign customs, arose from the happy circumstance of the superabundance and prosperity of our country, she did not hesitate to sacrifice the delicacy of European taste, for the less elegant, but more liberal fashion of Virginia."[109] The sentiment is Dolley's, the prose Mrs. Smith's: Dolley served ham and called visitors "Honey," and after supper she liked a pinch or two of snuff from her monogrammed silver snuffbox and a few hands of loo, for money.

Madison's inauguration as president on March 4, 1809, marked Dolley's launch as "the Presidentess," as the *National Intelligencer* dubbed her, and she went to work in earnest.[110] Congress had voted $20,000 to complete and furnish the White House, as it now came to be called, and Madison put Dolley in charge of architect Benjamin Henry Latrobe's redesign. With clear-sighted self-assurance, she aimed to create a theater where she would dramatize her own vision of American civility, hospitality, and republican manners. Stiff, courtly, European-style "etiquette she delighted to throw aside at all times," a niece recalled; "she liked no form which separated her from her friends."[111] At her celebrated weekly receptions, "Mrs. Madison's Wednesday nights," she set the model of how the political parties, sexes, and classes could mingle with democratic equality but also with style, sociability, and decorum. She united, said Margaret Bayard Smith, "all the elegance and polish of fashion" with "unadulterated simplicity, frankness, warmth, and friendliness."[112]

At her first Wednesday night in May 1809, visitors oohed and aahed at her parlor's "very latest Sheraton style" furniture, upholstered in the same sunflower-yellow silk as the curtains, which shimmered in the glow of the Argand lamps and superfine wax candles. Her pièce de résistance, the oval drawing room, ready for her New Year's reception in 1810, sported red silk-velvet curtains framing the French windows that overlooked the newly landscaped grounds, all reflected in the sparkling mirrors opposite.

Like every other important visitor to the capital, Washington Irving went to one of the White House's "genteel squeezes," and pronounced the "blazing splendor" so dazzling that he thought he was in "fairy land."[113] Dolley aimed all the splendor at glorifying not herself but the nation and the people: everything that could be American made was, especially the furniture, some of which had such patriotic motifs as the U.S. seal carved or painted on it. And everywhere were evocations of republican Rome and democratic Greece. The furniture was Greek Revival because classical "Greece was free," Latrobe explained; "in Greece every citizen felt himself a part of the republic."[114]

Certainly the citizens who attended Dolley's festivities—300 or so at a time, including often "a perfect rabble in beards and boots" rather than gentlemanly shoes—felt enlarged not diminished by being there, and the force of Dolley's personality wove the spell. "She spared no pains to please all who might visit her, and all were pleased from the most exalted to the most humble," wrote playwright George Watterston. "There was nothing about her that looked like condescension, or bordered on haughtiness: everything she did had the appearance of real kindness, and seemed to spring from a sincere desire to oblige and to gratify those who came to see her." She never forgot a name, and like the deftest politicians, she often knew who people were before they'd been introduced.[115] "You like yourself more when you are with her," her niece explained.[116]

Dolley's challenge was not just to bring Federalists and Republicans together, which she did with aplomb, but also to reconcile the various Republican factions, nastily sniping at each other now that the party held so overwhelming a majority. "By her deportment in her own house you cannot discover who [are] her husband's friends or foes," a congressman marveled. "Her guests have no right to complain of her partiality."[117] He was among many who noted what Anthony Morris called "the peculiar power she always possessd, of making & preserving friends, and of disarming Enemies."[118]

If only her husband had the same knack. While she, in her resplendent gowns, plumed turbans, and republican pearls rather than diamonds highlighting the famous bosom, sat at the head of the dinner table, "as easy as if she had been born & educated at Versailles," said Vice President Elbridge Gerry's son, the president found a quieter place down in the middle, where he didn't have to, well . . . preside.[119] "The little Man looks sometimes, as if the cares of the nation and the toll of seeing so much company had almost exhausted him," said one guest, echoing a common sentiment.[120] Madison struck many visitors as "a schoolmaster dressed for a funeral," and, "being so low in stature," one remarked, "he was in danger of being confounded with the plebeian crowds and was pushed and jostled about like a common citizen." To make sure everyone knew who he was, Dolley had the band play "Hail to the Chief" when he came into the room.[121]

Even those who agree that that government is best which governs least might think that the Revolution of 1800 took a good idea way too far. As "real a revolution in the principles of our government as that of 1776 was in its form," Jefferson boasted, his was arguably a counterrevolution, a rejection of the Madisonian Constitution's energetic federal government and a return to something closer to the weaker Articles of Confederation regime.[122] "When we consider that this government is charged with the external and mutual relations only of these states; that the states themselves have the principal care of our persons, our property, our reputation, constituting the great field of human concerns," Jefferson told Congress in 1801, "we may well doubt whether our organization is not too complicated, too expensive; whether offices and officers have not been multiplied unnecessarily."[123] He set out to fix all that.

But even in its own terms, Jefferson's revolution didn't make sense. Yes, he cut and cut. He dumped all internal excise taxes and fired the tax collectors, slashing the Treasury's head count by 40 percent. By 1810, even with the $15 million spent for the Louisiana Purchase, he and Madison had cut the federal debt to half the $80 million it totaled when they began.[124] But they cut muscle, not just fat. They reduced foreign embassies to just three, in Britain, France, and Spain. Jefferson halved military spending, letting the army dwindle to 3,000 men and the navy to the handful of frigates George Washington had built to fight the Barbary pirates, which Jefferson proposed to supplement with a swarm of light, undergunned patrol boats for coastal defense.[125] The federal government claimed responsibility for external relations, but it had trashed foreign policy's essential diplomatic and military instruments.

That might be less reckless in a time of profound peace, but from 1792 until 1815—before Jefferson became president, in other words, and until midway through Madison's second term in the White House—more or less continuous war between France and England and their allies and vassals convulsed the globe, with battles raging on land and sea not just across Europe but from the West Indies to Egypt to Moscow. True, an ocean appeared to protect America from Europe's troubles; but French shippers—as well as those from Spain, which declared war against Britain in 1796—dared not run the British naval gauntlet by carrying goods between their West Indian islands and Europe, so American seafarers filled the vacuum. United States ship tonnage trebled from 1793 to 1807; American shippers—mostly New Englanders—became the world's largest neutral carriers, and their profits skyrocketed. So the nation had something to protect, even though Jefferson considered the carrying trade mere unproductive "gambling," unlike honest agriculture.[126]

A LEGAL FICTION made this golden age for U.S. seamen possible. American officials invoked the time-honored international-law precept that "free ships make free goods," meaning that in wartime neutral ships had the right to carry any non–war-materiel cargo to belligerents. But Britain countered by dusting off a trade regulation from the Seven Years' War—the Rule of 1756—and reinterpreting it to mean that U.S. ships couldn't carry cargoes from French and Spanish West Indian ports to Europe.[127] So U.S. shippers seized the fig leaf of the "broken voyage." They carried cargo from the French or Spanish West Indies to the United States, unloaded it and paid the duty, reloaded it and got a tax rebate, and carried it on to Europe as American goods.

Britain tolerated this charade, both for eastward and westward trade, until the spring of 1805, when the war intensified. Then, without warning, the Royal Navy started seizing cargoes from American ships whose captains couldn't prove that their loads really were bound for or coming from the United States. When Admiral Lord Nelson's crushing victory over the French and Spanish navies at Trafalgar in the fall of 1805 gave Britain total mastery of the seas, American shipping faced even higher risk. Before 1805 ended, British confiscations had cost American carriers millions of dollars, their insurance premiums had quadrupled, and President Jefferson and Secretary Madison had a major crisis on their hands.[128]

Napoleon made their troubles worse. His million-man conscript army's triumph at Austerlitz in December 1805 won him control of the

European continent, which he used the next year to choke the British economy through decrees barring ships that traded with England from entering any European harbor. If a ship had landed anywhere in the British Empire, European port troops would seize it; if its cargo was British made or Empire grown, they would confiscate it. In this life-or-death world war, which ultimately cost Britain over £1 billion and 300,000 dead, London understandably retaliated with its own 1807 Orders in Council, which made any ship trading between Continental ports subject to British seizure and required any ship trading with a single Continental port to stop in England for a license. Napoleon countered by ordering the capture of any ship that complied with the Orders in Council.[129] American captains, caught between two implacable world powers, had nowhere to turn.

Nor was that all. In its desperate need for sailors, the Royal Navy not only "impressed" men—that is, drafted them—by kidnapping them off British streets and merchant ships, but it also stopped American ships and impressed seamen it claimed were British subjects, especially galling to America in that Britain didn't recognize the right of Britons to become U.S. citizens. In June 1807, a few miles off Virginia's Hampton Roads, the British warship *Leopard* ordered the American frigate *Chesapeake* to let a boarding party search for deserters and, being refused, raked the U.S. vessel with broadside after broadside, killing three and wounding eighteen Americans. Then a press gang from the *Leopard* kidnapped four sailors, claiming they were British deserters, though only one was. An outraged Madison directed U.S. ambassador James Monroe to demand release of the seamen, punishment of the *Leopard*'s officers, and a British promise of "an entire abolition of impressments" of Americans. Jefferson ordered all British ships out of U.S. harbors.[130]

And what retaliation did Madison propose to this multitude of provocations? With no military force to speak of, the only arrow he had in his quiver was a trade embargo, a weapon of the 1770s that he persisted in believing would work in the new century. But contrary to what he thought, Britain and France were much less dependent on U.S.

trade than America was on European, especially British, trade; British foreign secretary George Canning rightly dismissed the embargo that Congress passed in December 1807, barring all U.S. vessels from foreign trade, as "an innocent municipal Regulation, which effects none but the United States themselves."[131] How right he was: during 1808, U.S. exports fell 80 percent and imports 60 percent.[132]

Soon enough, too, the bitterly unpopular embargo—along with the Jefferson administration's viciously oppressive Enforcement Act of 1809, which responded to widespread smuggling and evasion by arming the government with search and seizure powers as unconstitutional as the Alien and Sedition Acts—came to feel more like a war against Americans than against Europeans. Echoing the Virginia and Kentucky Resolutions of 1798, Connecticut's governor invoked the state's duty "to *interpose*" to protect "the right and liberty of the people" against "the general government."[133] Before Congress voted to repeal the embargo, effective on Madison's inauguration day in March 1809, New Englanders were even darkly muttering about secession.[134]

When Madison stood in the Capitol, pale and trembling in his embargo-chic suit of black Connecticut-made cloth, to deliver his First Inaugural Address on March 4, he inadvertently sounded what was to be his administration's keynote when he mentioned, with conventional modesty, his "inadequacy to [the] high duties" he was assuming. He spoke more truly than he knew, sadly: for he proved an inadequate leader, with feckless subordinates who failed to meet the stern challenges his administration faced. And thanks to his and Jefferson's ideology, he had inadequate tools to deal with those challenges, and he lacked the leadership skills to get Congress to strengthen or even to preserve those he had.[135] Only the genius and daring of General Andrew Jackson and of some naval captains off Madison's radar screen saved his presidency from failure and fortuitously gilded it with honor.

As the embargo expired, Congress renewed sanctions against Britain and France but opened trade with the rest of the world, so captains simply lied about their destinations and traded promiscuously. Bowing to reality, Congress reopened French and British trade but declared that if either combatant would drop its anti-U.S. rules, America would forbid trade with the other. A slapstick charade ensued, with both England and France promising to lift their bans but shying away once Madison had made policy changes that left him looking clueless. Whether commercial sanctions can ever substitute for force remains debatable; but one Republican congressman rightly complained that his party's embargo policy "puts out one eye of your enemy, it is true, but it puts out both your own. It exhausts the purse, it exhausts the spirit, and paralyses the sword of the nation."[136]

The Twelfth Congress, which convened in November 1811, was as solidly Republican as its five predecessors, but its many freshmen included a new breed of western Republican, young War Hawks who thought that Madison's temporizing appeasement sullied "the honor of a nation," as one congressman said. To "step one step further without showing that spirit of resentment becoming freemen," another declared in trademark Republican terms, "would but acknowledge ourselves unworthy of self-government."[137] Choosing tough-minded newcomer Henry Clay as Speaker—who took such firm control that he stopped Old Republican John Randolph from bringing his dog into the House, a practice no one dared challenge before—the Congress broke with Old Republican orthodoxy, raising taxes and beefing up the army.

"The business is become more than ever puzzling," a troubled Madison wrote Jefferson on May 25, 1812. "To go to war with Engd and not with France arms the federalists with new matter, and divides the Republicans. . . . To go to war agst both, presents a thousand difficulties." On June 1, citing impressment, the *Chesapeake*, and the Orders in Council, Madison asked the Senate to declare war on Britain, which it did on June 18—though unknown to the president, Britain had already lifted the offending Orders.[138] Federalists voted unanimously against what they called "Mr. Madison's War," which one Federalist pamphleteer, exaggerating Madison's real enough Anglophobia, charged was "undertaken for *French* interests and in conformity with repeated *French* orders."[139]

To ADMINISTER the war and command the troops, Madison assembled a group of incompetents rarely matched in U.S. history. As part of the Revolution of 1800, Jefferson had raised party loyalty above merit in government appointments; Madison, with no control of his own party despite all his political experience, used appointments to appease Republican factions or barons, choosing each official with "an eye . . . to his political principles and connections," he ruefully sighed, "and the quarter of the Union to which he belongs."[140] Even so, one party faction blocked his promotion of his first-rate, trusted Treasury secretary, Albert Gallatin, to secretary of state, so Madison elevated indolent navy secretary Robert Smith instead, to ingratiate Smith's powerful senator brother. That breathtaking failure to lead—and "to resist encroachments" of the legislative on the executive department and so to maintain the crisp and clear separation of powers that *Federalist* 51 had urged—meant in effect the president would have to keep running the State Department himself. An inoffensive southerner replaced Smith as naval chief, and, for balance, a northern ex-congressman whose father-in-law was also a congressman took over the War Department, though beyond a medical degree he had no special wartime skills.[141] Both secretaries, one senator grumbled, were "incapable of discharging the duties of their office."[142]

Incompetence aside, John Randolph warned, the cabinet "presents a novel spectacle in the world, divided against itself, and the most deadly animosity raging between its principal members—what can come of it but confusion, mischief, and ruin?"[143] War Hawk John C. Calhoun wrote more charitably but with no less foreboding, "our president tho a man of amiable manners and great talents, has not I fear those commanding talents which are necessary to controul those about him."[144]

What instruments did Madison have to fight and finance the war? For his top generals, he named men cut from the same cloth as his cabinet, chosen by the same principles from the aging "survivors of the Revolutionary band." Sneered John Adams, "Chaff, Froth, and Ignorance have been promoted," and even twenty-six-year-old Colonel Winfield Scott worried that the old officers had "sunk into either sloth, ignorance, or habits of intemperate drinking."[145] And though the War Hawk Congress approved a larger army, it clung to Republican prejudice against an oceangoing navy, believing that once the war ended, "a permanent Naval Establishment" would "become a powerful engine in the hands of an ambitious Executive," as one overwrought congressman grimly prophesied, and that it would require permanently higher taxes that would "bankrupt" the nation and "end in a revolution."[146] The previous, orthodoxly Republican Congress had refused to renew the charter of Hamilton's bank when it expired in 1811, so Madison lost his best tool for borrowing money to pay for the war. By March 1813, Treasury secretary Gallatin warned Madison that the country had scarcely a month's worth of funds. By November 1814, with no one willing to buy its bonds, the United States defaulted on its national debt.[147]

Madison's military strategy was to launch lightning attacks on Canada and seize prime swaths of territory before an unready Britain could harden its positions there—an enterprise, Jefferson wrote him, sure to be "a mere matter of marching."[148] A demoralized London would have to back off as it lost a precious chunk of its empire, which Madison hoped to annex, just as he had condoned a recent freelance American seizure of Spanish West Florida.[149] Though Madison bustled round the "departments of war and the navy, stimulating everything in a manner worthy of a little commander in chief, with his little round hat and huge cockade," one official reported, the three-pronged Canadian invasion had a less jaunty result.[150]

To the west, stroke-impaired General William Hull, fifty-nine, set out to invade Canada from Fort Detroit, but his detachment of Ohio militiamen refused to follow, saying that they couldn't leave U.S. territory. Hull returned to Fort Detroit and misguidedly sent orders to evacuate Fort Dearborn in Chicago, surrounded by hostile Indians. On August 15, 1812, the fort's sixty-five soldiers marched out: the Indians massacred them, beheading one officer and eating his dripping heart. British general Isaac Brock besieged Hull's own Fort Detroit and plied him with disinformation about the murderous intentions of the redcoats' supposedly huge detachment of Indian allies. "My God!" the petrified Hull cried. "What shall I do with these women and children"—including his own family? With no warning to any subordinate, he surrendered the fort without a shot on August 16. "Even the women were indignant at so shameful a degradation of the American character," one observer recorded, and an equally indignant court-martial sentenced him to death for cowardice and dereliction of duty, though Madison spared his life. Brock claimed the Michigan territory for the British Crown.[151]

Commanding the middle prong, at Niagara, was "the last of the patroons," General Stephen Van Rensselaer, who at forty-nine had not a shred of battlefield experience. His first effort to cross the river into Canada miscarried, as a traitor stole all his oars. Two days later, he managed to send 600 men across, who, under the command of Winfield Scott, killed the fast-moving General Brock but got pinned down. When Van Rensselaer ordered his New York militia to Scott's aid, they too refused to leave U.S. soil. Scott had to surrender with his army.[152]

Jefferson's ex–secretary of war, General Henry Dearborn—fat, sixty-one, and nicknamed "Granny"—commanded the eastern prong, charged with taking Montreal. He wouldn't move. When the War Department peremptorily ordered action, he lumbered from Albany to Plattsburgh and sent troops into Canada, where, after skirmishing with the enemy, they then shot at one another in the dark. As usual, the militia wouldn't follow the regulars onto foreign soil, and Granny retreated with his 7,000 or so men. The whole Canadian fiasco, even a Republican paper judged, added up to nothing but "disaster, defeat, disgrace, and ruin and death."[153]

Against that black backdrop, the navy's brilliant successes shone the more luminously, especially given the cloud of Republican disdain that had hung over that service. In August 1812, the frigate *Constitution*, with craven General Hull's brave nephew Isaac Hull in command, forced HMS *Guerrière* to strike her colors after a heart-stopping mid-Atlantic chase and heaven-resounding battle that crippled and dismasted the British vessel and caused one American sailor to cry of his own ship, "Her sides are made of iron," when cannonballs bounced off her, instantly winning her the nickname "Old Ironsides." An aghast London *Times* spluttered that "never before in the history of the world did an English frigate strike to an American." Madison, discarding ideology for the lessons of experience he had formerly valued so highly, sent out his little navy to patrol the high seas in late 1812, where it won renown in victory after victory against a Britannia that had hitherto ruled the waves.

Stephen Decatur, for instance, who at twenty-five had become the youngest captain in U.S. naval history during Jefferson's 1804 campaign against the Barbary pirates, when he had daringly sneaked into Tripoli Harbor and burned a U.S. frigate grounded there to keep her out of piratical hands, now won further fame when his *United States* astonishingly brought the defeated frigate HMS *Macedonian* into Newport Harbor as a prize after another mid-ocean duel. More important, since control of the Great Lakes was the strategic key to the Canadian front, was twenty-seven-year-old Oliver Hazard Perry's destruction of the British fleet on Lake Erie in late 1813, in a battle so ferocious he had to switch to a new ship when the British shot his first one out from under him. Another group of American seamen, the sailors who manned the 500 U.S. privateers, proved equally lethal, capturing 1,300 British merchantmen before the war ended.[154]

In a further bow to experience, Madison fired his war and navy secretaries at the start of 1813, and Congress, also educable, voted new ships, more soldiers with better pay, and higher taxes to pay the bills—effective the next year, when it turned out to be too late. But Britain learned faster and by the end of 1813 had clamped a blockade on

America's entire East Coast, bottling up the U.S. Navy and choking off trade.

When Napoleon's abdication in April 1814 freed seasoned British troops to turn their full force on America, the outlook darkened ominously. Though a brilliant U.S. naval victory on Lake Champlain stymied the British invasion of New York in September, British troops and ships sailed into Chesapeake Bay and looted, burned, and raped their way toward Washington. Madison ordered his new war secretary, John Armstrong, to strengthen the capital's defenses, but the pigheaded Armstrong—no improvement on his predecessor, as Madison by then knew from a long train of insubordination and duplicity that a competent leader would have punished with dismissal—disobeyed, convinced that the enemy had targeted Baltimore, even though on August 19 British admiral Sir George Cockburn had sent a message declaring that he'd dine in Washington in two days, take Dolley Madison captive, and display her in triumph in the streets of London.[155]

On August 24, 1814, the British attacked U.S. troops at Bladensburg, Maryland, the overland approach to Washington, fifteen miles away. Pluckily, Madison, in his little round hat, had spent most of six days in the saddle despite his sixty-three years, stimulating his officers there with all his heart. To no avail: the troops fled in such ignominious disarray that the "battle" became known as the Bladensburg Races. As plucky as her husband, Dolley Madison told her cousin that she did not "tremble" but felt "*affronted*" when Admiral Cockburn entered the Chesapeake and "sen[t] me notis that he would make his bow at my Drawing room *soon*." After all, she said, "I have allways been an advocate for fighting when *assailed*, tho *a Quaker*," and she had her "old Tunesian Sabre within my reach."[156]

In a famous letter to her sister Lucy, written the night of August 23, added to twice the next day, and clearly edited and copied after the fact, since it is mostly free of Dolley's endearingly haphazard spelling, Dolley tells of staying in the White House until the last possible moment, "with no fear but for [Madison] and the success of our army," packing up cabinet papers and valuables, and "ready at a moment's warning to enter my carriage and leave the city." The 200 men guarding the White House had melted away; panicked Washingtonians were angry with Madison for bringing war to their doorsteps; her French butler, hired from the Merrys on their departure, remained unconvinced that it would be bad form to booby-trap the White House with gunpowder to blow up the British if they entered.

Dawn of the twenty-fourth found her "turning my spyglass in every direction, . . . hoping to discern the approach of my dear husband." By three o'clock she could hear the cannon from Bladensburg. A friend who had come to help her escape waited impatiently as she tried to get the huge, full-length portrait of Washington unscrewed from the wall. It was taking too long. "I have ordered the frame to be broken, and the canvass taken out it is done, and the precious portrait placed in the hands of two gentlemen from New York for safe keeping"—one of the few relics of the original White House on view there today. "And now, dear sister, I must leave this house" or be trapped in Washington. "Where I shall be tomorrow, I cannot tell!!"[157]

A couple of days late but true to his word, Admiral Cockburn marched into the city a few hours after Dolley left her house for the last time. At the Capitol, British troops piled up all the furniture and set it alight, melting the building's glass and incinerating the Library of Congress. At the White House, finding the table set for a dinner party of forty that Dolley had planned, with the meat still warm, Cockburn and his officers sat down to eat the "elegant and substantial repast," toasting "Jemmy's health" in his own good wine, and carrying away Dolley's cushion, so Cockburn could "warmly recall Mrs. Madison's seat," along with one of Madison's hats and his wife's portrait, to "keep Dolley safe and exhibit her in London," the admiral joked. Then fifty men with buckets of burning coals set the building afire from end to end; the "city was light and the heavens redden'd with the blaze," a witness reported.

The redcoats fired the nearby Treasury, at the same moment that the commander of the navy yard ordered his ships and stores torched

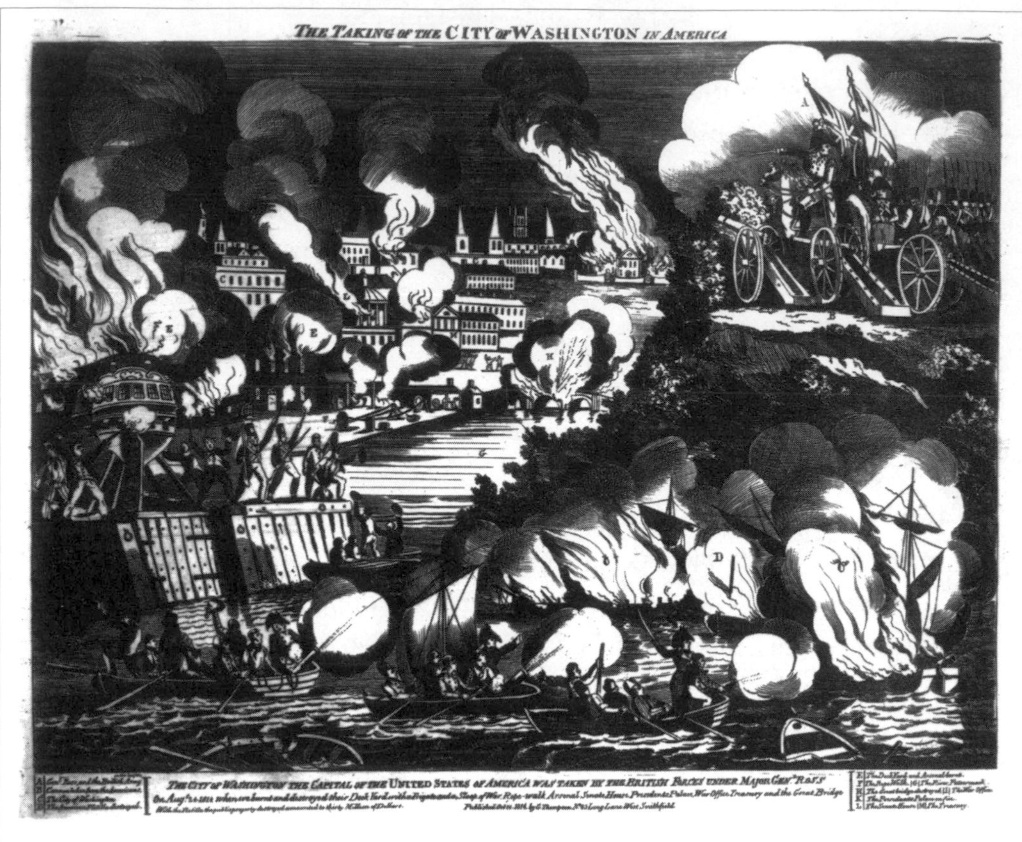

The Burning of Washington *pub. by G. Thompson, 1814*
Private Collection / The Bridgeman Art Library

to keep them out of enemy hands. Dolley could see the blaze from her refuge ten miles away. The next day, when the British accidentally exploded 130 barrels of gunpowder at an American arsenal, the whole city would have burned to the ground but for a providential thunderstorm with freak, hurricane-force winds that turned the sky black as night and extinguished the flames.[158]

In August 1814, peace talks began in Ghent. Britain demanded control of the Great Lakes, an Indian buffer zone shielding Canada, a chunk of Maine, and access to the Mississippi. The no-nonsense American commission, led by Henry Clay and John Quincy Adams, refused. But when British troops moved on from Washington and failed to take Fort McHenry in Baltimore, an American success that Francis

Scott Key immortalized in "The Star-Spangled Banner," and when the Duke of Wellington opined that the conquest of America would be difficult—and impossible without control of the Great Lakes—London's negotiators softened their harsh terms and agreed to a peace that restored the status quo antebellum. After all, while Americans viewed the War of 1812 as an urgent matter of national honor, reasserting that they were no longer colonial vassals of the British Empire, for Britain it was merely an annoyance, and half the British public didn't even know their country was at war with the United States.[159]

The commissioners signed the treaty on Christmas Eve 1814. News of the peace had not reached Wellington's brother-in-law, General Edward Pakenham, however, who had marshaled a 10,000-man army in Jamaica and sailed it to the Louisiana coast to storm New Orleans and pour into the Mississippi Valley. Nor had U.S. general Andrew Jackson heard of the treaty. After wresting Alabama from the Creek Indians, he now methodically prepared to wreak equal violence upon the British invaders of New Orleans. With pirate chief Jean Lafitte as his unorthodox aide-de-camp, Jackson built defensive earthworks stretching from the Mississippi at the western end to an impassable swamp at the eastern, and he prepared his 4,700 soldiers and artillerymen to meet 5,300 boxed-in British head-on. The unrelenting, close-range cannon, rifle, and musket fire on January 8, 1815, was "the most murderous I ever beheld," a battle-tested British veteran marveled. The numbers bear him out: 700 Britons killed (including Pakenham), 1,400 wounded, and 500 captured—compared with 7 dead and 6 wounded Americans.[160]

The burning of Washington had at last solidified U.S. public opinion in favor of the war; when the news of Jackson's victory reached Washington on February 4, topping even the U.S. Navy's dazzling feats, the celebratory crowds in the torch-lit streets felt the war effort was worth its heavy cost. To crown all, when the peace terms reached Madison on February 13, their mildness amazed him. With their honor vindicated, and the question of impressment made moot by the ending of the European war, Americans believed they had won a famous victory, even though Britain had conceded nothing. They felt all the more victorious when the next month the U.S. Navy crushed the Barbary pirates for good, freeing all their captives.[161] Madison was the man of the hour, and what one journalist dubbed the "era of good feelings" dawned.

In truth, however, America had had a close call, and Madison digested its lessons. In April 1816, he approved a new bank, a small standing army and permanent navy, and taxes and tariffs to maintain them.[162] He had learned, as all his reading of history should already have taught him, that because men are not angels, a nation needs a military establishment to defend against the passions and interests that drive other countries to trample its rights. He had learned, too, that the bank was *necessary*, not merely convenient.

And that lesson made his understanding of constitutional interpretation more nuanced. "There is certainly a reasonable medium between expounding the Constitution with the strictness of a penal law, or other ordinary statute, and expounding it with a laxity which may vary its essential character," he wrote in 1819, two years after he retired. One should neither "squeeze it to death" nor "stretch it to death," he pronounced late in life. Reasonable men will have legitimate disagreements about the means necessary to wield the government's limited and enumerated powers. All that is beyond dispute is that the means may not outstrip the ends, "which is in effect to convert a limited into an unlimited Govt."[163]

Historians like to play the game of "counterfactual history": What would have happened had Lincoln let the South secede or if Lee had won at Gettysburg? What if Britain had stayed out of World War I, if Hitler had invaded Britain, or if Russia had had no Gorbachev? So it's hard to resist the question: What if Madison and Jefferson had acknowledged the value of America's shipping trade, had recognized the skill of U.S. seamen, had built up a navy equal to U.S. maritime genius, and had sent it to protect seaborne commerce? What if they had valued finance and central banking? Would America have had to fight the War of 1812? And suppose Madison had decided that America's commercial interest lay with Britain, long its main trading partner, not France, for which he and Jefferson had, Hamilton once charged, a "womanish weakness": Would he have helped defeat Napoleon and joined Britain in the commercial mastery of the world?[164] The point of such questions is only to show that nothing is foreordained. Events unfold because people make choices, show courage (or not), have talents, have luck, have certain beliefs, not because of impersonal, ineluctable forces. The leader makes the time as much as the time makes the leader. Thinking about how things might have turned out better, Madison would say, is how we learn from the experience of history.

When the Madisons left Washington for retirement at Montpelier on April 6, 1817, the ex-president seemed like "a School Boy on a long vacation," a fellow passenger on their steamboat recalled: "as playful as a child, talking and jesting with everybody on board." He was happy with his "release from incessant labors, corroding anxieties, active enemies, and interested friends," as Jefferson described how he must feel.[165] Healthy and fit at sixty-six, he threw himself enthusiastically into managing his plantation. He and Dolley, surrounded by relatives, entertained crowds of visitors in the warm months, with ninety to dinner one Fourth of July. They walked up and down their portico when it rained, arranged and edited Madison's papers for publication, and "looked," one visitor said, "like Adam and Eve in their Bower."[166]

Madison fell at once into his comfortable role as Jefferson's second in command on the board of the University of Virginia, of which Jefferson, as founder and rector, was, said Madison, "the great projector and mainspring."[167] When the third president told the fourth how pleased he was to think that Madison would also succeed him as rector, it was something more than modesty that made Madison say that doing so—as he faithfully did—"would be the pretension of a mere worshipper [replacing] the Tutelary Genius of the Sanctuary."[168] Aside from a three-month sojourn in Richmond for the 1829 Virginia Constitutional Convention, the Madisons, increasingly dependent on each other, never left Montpelier beyond short trips to Charlottesville for Board of Visitors business and twice-yearly weeklong visits to Monticello—where one can't help wondering which of the old couple slept against the wall in the cozy but inconvenient alcove bed in what was always called "Mr. Madison's room."

When the Madisons returned to Virginia from Washington, war-inflated grain prices were falling. Like so many of his neighbors, Madison tried to diversify, raising sheep and growing corn and even tobacco again, difficult on the worn-out Piedmont clay. Bad weather throughout the 1820s shrank harvests; Virginians sold depreciating land cheap, sold slaves, and moved to greener pastures as their way of life died out. "They whose fathers rode in coaches and drank the choicest wines now ride on saddlebags, and drink grog, when they can get it," mourned John Randolph.[169]

The agricultural depression hit Jefferson especially hard, not only because high living had already swamped him with debt but also because, as the Virginia gentlemanly code demanded, he had co-signed loans for a friend who defaulted, leaving him liable for more than he could pay. In his last letter to Madison, he confided that he was trying to get permission for a lottery to sell off his lands, keeping just the Monticello house and a modest farm. Otherwise, he would lose the estate and perhaps "have not even a log hut to put my head into" or even "ground for burial." And, with a premonition of death, he said farewell: "The friendship which has subsisted between us, now half a century, and the harmony of our political principles and pursuits, have been constant sources of happiness to me," he told Madison. "To myself you have been a pillar of support through life. Take care of me when dead, and be assured that I shall leave with you my last affections."[170]

Madison replied, "You cannot look back to the long period of our private friendship & political harmony, with more affecting recollections than I do. If they are a source of pleasure to you, what ought they not to be to me?" Perhaps gently telling Jefferson that he wished he could help him financially but couldn't, he remarked that for more than a decade, "such have been the unkind seasons, & the ravages of insects, that I have made but one tolerable crop of Tobacco, and but one of Wheat; the proceeds of both of which were greatly curtailed by mishaps in the sale of them. And having no resources but in the earth I cultivate, I have been living very much throughout on borrowed means."[171]

Jefferson escaped losing Monticello, for he died soon after this correspondence, on the fiftieth anniversary of the Declaration of Independence that he wrote—July 4, 1826, the same day John Adams died. But Madison was telling the unvarnished truth about his own financial plight. He too had problems that went beyond bad crops and low prices. For if the Madisons seemed like Adam and Eve to one visitor, Montpelier had its requisite "serpent in the Garden of Eden," as Madison's secretary put it.[172] That was Dolley's surviving son, John Payne Todd, whom Madison, another childless Founding Father, treated as his own. A prototypical dissolute Southern Gothic wastrel, Todd never married, couldn't hold a job, drank, and gambled his way into perpetual debt and sometimes into debtors' prison. Madison kept bailing him out, to the tune of at least $40,000—equal to nearly $1 million today.[173] By the time the ex-president died at eighty-five on June 28, 1836, he had sold his thousand acres of investment land in Kentucky, his turnpike stock, and half his ancestral Piedmont acreage. Visitors had begun to remark that Montpelier was looking run-down, and its rooms needed painting.[174]

In 1844, Dolley sold the estate and moved back to Washington, to her dead sister's house on Lafayette Square, which Madison had owned. A living link to the Founders, she went out everywhere—including often to the White House, since she knew all of the first twelve presidents—and she had her own seat in the House of Representatives' gallery. She sent the first private telegraph message and laid the Washington Monument's cornerstone. But she was so poor that she kept wearing her old trademark dresses, shawls, and turbans from a vanished age, and Paul Jennings, the valet who had attended Madison on the day he died and now worked for Senator Daniel Webster to earn his freedom, often brought her baskets of provisions from

Webster and sometimes gave her money himself. When she died at eighty-one in 1849, Washington gave her the biggest funeral in its history.[175] She lay first in one temporary vault and then in another until 1858, when Montpelier's new owners at last gave permission for her to be buried beside her husband in the red Virginia clay, as the Civil War was about to sweep over it, making way for America's new birth of freedom.[176]

NOTES

INTRODUCTION: The Americanness of the American Revolution

1 John Locke, *Second Treatise*, IX, §123.

2 Bernard Bailyn, *The Ideological Origins of the American Revolution*, enlarged edition (Cambridge, MA: Harvard University Press, 1967), pp. x, 19.

3 Trevor Colbourn, *The Lamp of Experience: Whig History and the Intellectual Origins of the American Revolution* (Indianapolis: Liberty Fund, 1965), p. 73.

4 Bailyn, op. cit., p. 67.

5 William Livingston, *The Independent Reflector*, Milton M. Klein, ed. (Cambridge, MA: Belknap Press, Harvard University Press, 1965[IR]), XXXVIII, p. 323.

6 Bailyn, op. cit., pp. 255–56.

7 IR, XXII, p. 213.

8 James Madison, *Memorial and Remonstrance Against Religious Assessments*, in James Madison, *Writings*, Jack N. Rakove, ed. (Library of America, 1999 [Madison LoA]), p. 33.

9 Ron Chernow, *Washington: A Life* (New York: Penguin, 2010), p. 3; George Washington to Marquis de Lafayette, 25 July 1785, in George Washington, *Writings*, John Rhodehamel, ed. (Library of America, 1997 [Washington LoA]), p. 583; Exodus 33, v. 1–3; Matthew 11, v. 28–30.

10 Bailyn, op. cit., pp. 32–33.

11 Locke, op. cit., V, §48–49, 40.

12 James Madison to Thomas Jefferson, 24 October 1787 (Madison LoA, p. 150).

13 James Madison, *Federalist* 10 (Madison LoA, p. 167).

14 George Washington to Bryan Fairfax, 24 August 1774 (Washington LoA, p. 158).

15 IR, II, p. 62.

16 George Washington to Bryan Fairfax, 20 July 1774 (Washington LoA, pp. 155–56).
17 Bailyn, op. cit., p. 346.
18 Alexander Hamilton, *Federalist* 6, in Alexander Hamilton, *Writings*, Joanne B. Freeman, ed. (Library of America, 2001 [Hamilton LoA]), p. 176.
19 James Madison, *Federalist* 55 (Madison LoA, pp. 319–20).
20 IR, XXIX, p. 257.
21 IR, IV, p. 79; Bailyn, op. cit., pp. 135–36.
22 James Madison, *Federalist* 57 (Madison LoA, p. 328).
23 John C. Hamilton, *Life of Alexander Hamilton* (Boston: Riverside, 1879), VII:686.

CHAPTER 1: Conceived in Liberty: William Livingston and the Case for Revolution

1 John Adams, "The 'American Revolution,'" *Niles' Weekly Register*, March 7, 1818.
2 Bernard Bailyn, *The Ideological Origins of the American Revolution*, enlarged edition (Cambridge, MA: Harvard University Press, 1967), p. 1.
3 Milton M. Klein, *The American Whig: William Livingston of New York*, revised edition (New York: Garland, 1993), pp. 305–6.
4 Clare Brandt, *An American Aristocracy: The Livingstons* (Garden City, NY: Doubleday, 1986), pp. 12–21.
5 Ibid., pp. 38, 41–42, 45–48.
6 Klein, op. cit., p. 10; Brandt, op. cit., p. 59.
7 Brandt, op. cit., pp. 37, 40.
8 Ibid., pp. 59–62.
9 Klein, op. cit., pp. 15–17.
10 Ibid., pp. 32–37.
11 Ibid., pp. 37–38.
12 Ibid., pp. 39, 50, 161; Caroline Robbins, *The Eighteenth Century Commonwealthman* (New York: Atheneum, 1968), pp. 34–35, 43–44.
13 Trevor Colbourn, *The Lamp of Experience: Whig History and the Intellectual Origins of the American Revolution* (Indianapolis: Liberty Fund, 1965), p. 60.
14 Klein, op. cit., pp. 45–48.
15 Ibid., pp. 16, 70, 60–63; Catherine Drinker Bowen, *The Lion and the Throne: The Life and Times of Sir Edward Coke* (Boston: Little, Brown, 1956), p. 509.
16 Klein, op. cit., p. 64.
17 Ibid., pp. 60, 68–69; IR, XLIII, p. 360.
18 Klein, op. cit., pp. 70–72.
19 James Alexander, *A Brief Narrative of the Case and Trial of John Peter Zenger*, Stanley Nider Katz, ed., 2nd edition (Cambridge, MA: Harvard University Press), pp. 8–9; John Trenchard and Thomas Gordon, *Cato's Letters: or, Essays on Liberty, Civil and Religious, and Other Important Subjects*, Ronald Hamowy,

ed. (Indianapolis: Liberty Fund, 1995), I:29, 87, 94, 103–4, 110, 114–15, 138–39, 141–42, 176–80, 228–30, 233–37, 239–40, 255–58, 405–8, 413–18, 423, 427–29.

20 Alexander, op. cit., pp. 3–4, 133.

21 Ibid., pp. 7–8, 111, 17, 19–20, 49–50.

22 Ibid., pp. 18, 20, 21, 53, 56–57.

23 Ibid., p. 30; William Smith, Jr., *The History of the Province of New-York*, Michael Kammen, ed. (Cambridge, MA: Belknap Press, Harvard University Press, 1972), II:19–20.

24 Alexander, op. cit., pp. 22, 62.

25 Ibid., pp. 63, 69, 78. Andrew Hamilton was not related, as far as is known, to the much younger Alexander Hamilton.

26 Ibid., pp. 78, 81, 84, 87.

27 Ibid., pp. 91, 99; Colbourn, op. cit., pp. 9–10, 44–45; Bailyn, op. cit., p. 78.

28 Alexander, op. cit., pp. 89, 86, 84.

29 Ibid., pp. 75, 99, 29; William Smith, Jr., op. cit., II:20.

30 Bailyn, op. cit., pp. 30–31, 33, 53–54, 67–69.

31 Benson Lossing, ed., *Harper's Encyclopedia of United States History* (New York, 1902), s.v. Zenger.

32 Klein, op. cit., pp. 96–98, 100–101.

33 Ibid., pp. 101, 116.

34 Ibid., pp. 102–3, 106–7.

35 Ibid., p. 79.

36 Ibid., pp. 92–93, 233–34, 188.

37 Ibid., pp. 123, 104, 126, 131, 152.

38 Ibid., pp. 110–11.

39 Ibid., p. 189; William Livingston, *The Independent Reflector*, Milton M. Klein, ed. (Cambridge, MA: Belknap Press, Harvard University Press, 1965), p. 447.

40 IR, I, pp. 56–57.

41 IR, XI, pp. 128, 133; Pope, *Epilogue to the Satires*, Dialogue II, lines, 208–11.

42 IR, X, pp. 120–22.

43 IR, VI, pp. 89–91.

44 Klein, op. cit., p. 249.

45 IR, p. 5.

46 Ibid., p. 22.

47 Ibid., pp. 184, 271.

48 IR, VIII, pp. 181–82.

49 IR, XVII, p. 174; IR, XVIII, p. 180.

50 IR, XVII, pp. 174, 173.

51 IR, XVII, pp. 172, 174.

52 IR, XX, pp. 192–95; IR, XVIII, p. 180.

53 IR, XLVI, p. 391; James Madison, *Federalist* 10, in James Madison, *Writings*, Jack N. Rakove, ed. (Library of America, 1999), p. 167.

54 IR, XLVI; Klein, op. cit., p. 232.

55 IR, XXII, pp. 210–11; Robbins, op. cit., pp. 81–83; IR, XXXVIII, p. 320.
56 Klein, op. cit., pp. 319, 340, 352–53.
57 IR, p. 291.
58 IR, XXXVI, pp. 306–7; IR, XXXVIII, p. 323.
59 IR, XXXIII, pp. 287–88; IR, XXXVI, p. 306.
60 IR, XXXIII, p. 286.
61 IR, XXXVI, p. 307.
62 IR, XXXIII, p. 286; IR, XXXIX, p. 328.
63 IR, XXXIII, p. 289.
64 Thomas Jefferson, *A Summary View of the Rights of British America*, in Thomas Jefferson, *Writings*, Merrill D. Peterson, ed. (Library of America, 1984), p. 121.
65 Bailyn, op. cit., pp. 273–74, 276–77, 279–84, 289–90, 297–99.
66 IR, XXXIII, pp. 287–88, 290.
67 Klein, op. cit., pp. 287, 252, 171.
68 IR, IV, p. 77; IR, XXVIII, p. 326.
69 IR, XXXVI, p. 310; IR, XXXIII, p. 287.
70 IR, p. 335.
71 IR, II, p. 62.
72 IR, XXXVII, p. 313; IR, XXXVI, p. 308.
73 IR, XLVI, p. 391.
74 IR, XXXVII, p. 315.
75 IR, XLVII, p. 399.
76 IR, L, p. 419 (probably by William Smith, Jr.).
77 IR, XIII, p. 147.
78 IR, XLVII, p. 398; IR, XIII, p. 143.
79 IR, XL, pp. 336–37.
80 Klein, op. cit., p. 170; Colbourn, op. cit., pp. 16–18, 24.
81 Klein, op. cit., pp. 294–95.
82 Ibid., pp. 402–3; Bailyn, op. cit., p. 106.
83 Michael Kammen, *Colonial New York: A History* (Oxford and New York: Oxford University Press, 1975), p. 78; Klein, op. cit., pp. 161–64.
84 Klein, op. cit., pp. 403–5.
85 Ibid., p. 410; Bailyn, op. cit., pp. 106–7.
86 Bailyn, op. cit., p. 107.
87 Klein, op. cit., pp. 432–33.
88 Ibid., pp. 413–16.
89 Colbourn, op. cit., pp. 44–45.
90 Klein, op. cit., p. 419.
91 IR, XXXII, pp. 281, 284; Colbourn, op. cit., pp. 32–33, 43–45, 53.
92 Klein, op. cit., p. 419, 424.
93 Ibid., pp. 421–22.
94 Ibid., p. 422.
95 Ibid., pp. 448–49, 459; Bernard Bailyn, *The Ordeal of Thomas Hutchinson* (Cambridge, MA: Harvard University Press, 1974), pp. 35–36.

96 Bernard Bailyn, *The Ideological Origins of the American Revolution*, enlarged edition (Cambridge, MA: Harvard University Press, 1967), pp. 230ff.
97 Paul C. Nagel, *The Lees of Virginia: Seven Generations of an American Family* (New York: Oxford University Press, 1990), pp. 62–63.
98 "Slave Petition to the Governor, Council, and House of Representatives of the Province of Massachusetts," 25 May 1774 (Massachusetts Historical Society Collections, 5th ser., 3:432–33), in Philip B. Kurland and Ralph Lerner, *The Founders' Constitution*, Volume 1, Chapter 14, Document 9 (Chicago: University of Chicago Press, 1986).
99 Klein, op. cit., p. 353.
100 Ibid., pp. 487–88.
101 Bailyn, op. cit., p. 53.
102 Klein, op. cit., pp. 535, 544–47, 109, 155–56.
103 Ibid., pp. 546–47, 552–53.
104 Ibid., pp. 556–60.
105 Kitty Livingston to John Jay and Sarah L. Jay, 21 November 1777, in Linda M. Freeman, Louise V. North, and Janet M. Wedge, eds., *Selected Letters of John Jay and Sarah Livingston Jay* (Jefferson, NC: McFarland, 2005), p. 52.
106 Sarah L. Jay to Susanna French Livingston, 15 April 1783, in Linda M. Freeman, Louise V. North, and Janet M. Wedge, eds., op. cit., p. 132.
107 Klein, op. cit., pp. 559–65.
108 Ibid., pp. 544–45.
109 National Center for Education Statistics, *The Nation's Report Card: U.S. History 2010* (National Assessment of Educational Progress, June 2011).
110 Private communication, William Schroh, Jr., Director of Museum Operations, Liberty Hall Museum, Union, NJ.

CHAPTER 2: Conservative Revolutionaries: The Lees of Stratford Hall

1 Paul C. Nagel, *The Lees of Virginia: Seven Generations of an American Family* (New York: Oxford University Press, 1990), p. 97.
2 Charles Royster, *Light-Horse Harry Lee and the Legacy of the American Revolution* (Baton Rouge, LA: State University Press, 1994), p. 202.
3 J. Kent McGaughy, *Richard Henry Lee of Virginia* (Lanham, MD: Rowman & Littlefield, 2004), p. 4; Philip Alexander Bruce, *Social Life in Virginia in the Seventeenth Century* (Richmond, VA: Whittet & Shepperson, 1907), pp. 18, 103, 215.
4 Nagel, op. cit., p. 14; McGaughy, op. cit., p. 5.
5 McGaughy, op. cit., p. 7; Nagel, op. cit., p. 11.
6 McGaughy, op. cit., p. 9; Winthrop Jordan, *The White Man's Burden: Historical Origins of Racism in the United States* (New York: Oxford University Press, 1974), p. 40.
7 McGaughy, op. cit., pp. 8–9; Nagel, op. cit., pp. 14–16.

8 Nagel, op. cit., pp. 21–22, 17, 27.
9 Ibid., pp. 24; McGaughy, op. cit., pp. 9–10.
10 Nagel, op. cit., pp. 26–27, 29–32.
11 Ibid., pp. 33–37.
12 Ibid., pp. 38–39, 44.
13 Ibid., p. 36.
14 Ibid., pp. 44–45.
15 Ibid., pp. 13, 41–42.
16 John Summerson, *Architecture in Britain 1530–1830*, 9th edition (New Haven, CT: Yale University Press, 1993), pp. 514–15.
17 Nagel, op. cit., p. 43.
18 Richard M. Ketchum, *Divided Loyalties: How the American Revolution Came to New York* (New York: Henry Holt, 2002), pp. 21–22; Edmund Burke, "Speech for the Conciliation with the Colonies," 22 March 1775.
19 Gordon S. Wood, *The American Revolution: A History* (New York: Modern Library, 2002), pp. 6–7, 15; John E. Selby, *The Revolution in Virginia, 1775–1783*, revised edition (Charlottesville: University of Virginia Press, 2007), pp. 27, 29.
20 Selby, op. cit., pp. 13–15.
21 Benjamin Franklin, *Autobiography*, Russel B. Nye, ed. (Boston: Houghton Mifflin, 1958), pp. 73–74.
22 Selby, op. cit., p. 30.
23 Wood, op. cit., p. 13; Selby, op. cit., p. 26.
24 Edmund S. Morgan, *Virginians at Home: Family Life in the Eighteenth Century* (Williamsburg: Colonial Williamsburg Foundation, 1952), pp. 11, 18–19, 78–81, 83–84.
25 Nagel, op. cit., p. 39.
26 Ibid., pp. 46, 65.
27 McGaughy, op. cit., pp. 46–47.
28 Nagel, op. cit., pp. 67, 43.
29 Ibid., pp. 66–67.
30 Ibid., pp. 66–68, 70–71.
31 McGaughy, op. cit., pp. 24–25.
32 Ibid., pp. 31–32.
33 Ibid., pp. 48, 51–53.
34 Nagel, op. cit., pp. 77, 79–80; Selby, op. cit., p. 38.
35 Richard H. Lee, *The Life of Richard Henry Lee by His Grandson* (Philadelphia: Carey and Lea, 1825), I:7.
36 Ibid., I:17–19, 20–21.
37 McGaughy, op. cit., pp. 80–84.
38 Ketchum, op. cit., pp. 32–33, 35–36.
39 Ibid., pp. 38–40.
40 Ibid., pp. 40–45; Alfred Thayer Mahan, *The Influence of Sea Power Upon History, 1660–1783*, 12th edition (Boston: Little, Brown, 1890), p. 291.
41 Ketchum, op. cit., pp. 42, 46–47, 71–73, 77, 81.

42 Ibid., p. 86; Richard H. Lee (RHL) to [a gentleman in London], 31 May 1764, in James Curtis Ballagh, ed., *The Letters of Richard Henry Lee* (New York: Macmillan, 1911) [RHL Let.], I:5–7.
43 RHL to Lord Shelburne, 31 May 1769 (RHL Let., I:37).
44 RHL to Landon Carter, 22 June 1765 (RHL Let., I:8).
45 A Virginia Planter [RHL], "To the Good People of Virginia," Richard H. Lee, op. cit., I:37.
46 RHL to [J.R., a London Merchant], after 27 June 1768; RHL to Arthur Lee, 4 July 1765; RHL to Gouverneur Morris, 25 May 1775 (RHL Let., I:28, 10, 140).
47 McGaughy, op. cit., pp. 77, 55, 60, 63; RHL to William Lee, 12 July 1772 (RHL Let., I:75–6); Nagel, op. cit., p. 84.
48 RHL to William Lee, 12 July 1772 (RHL Let., I:70–71).
49 McGaughy, op. cit., pp. 78, 80; RHL to the editor of the *Virginia Gazette*, 25 July 1766 (RHL Let., I:16–17).
50 "Articles of Association, by the citizens of Westmoreland," 27 February 1766 (Richard H. Lee, op. cit., I:34–35; McGaughy, op. cit., p. 79.
51 McGaughy, op.cit., pp. 52, 56; Richard H. Lee, op. cit., I:107.
52 RHL to Arthur Lee, 19 May 1769 (RHL Let., I:35).
53 McGaughy, op. cit., pp. 56–57; RHL to William Lee, 17–20 December 1769 (RHL Let., I:40).
54 RHL to William Lee, 23 October 1772 (RHL Let., I:78).
55 RHL to General William Whipple, 29 November 1778 (RHL Let., I:454).
56 For example, RHL to William Lee, 7 July 1770, 15 January 1773; RHL to Arthur Lee, 26 June 1774 (RHL Let., I:50, 81, 118).
57 Morgan, op. cit., pp. 7–8; Richard H. Lee, op. cit., I:246. Thomas Jefferson practiced a more manipulative version of spare-the-rod child-rearing. See Fawn M. Brodie, *Thomas Jefferson: An Intimate History* (New York: W. W. Norton, 1974), pp. 239–40, on how he prevented his daughter Martha from becoming a nun.
58 RHL to Edmund Pendleton, 22 May 1788 (Richard H. Lee, op. cit., II:92).
59 RHL to John Dickinson, 25 July 1768 (RHL Let., I:29).
60 RHL to a Gentleman of Influence in England, 27 March 1768 (RHL Let., I:26).
61 RHL to John Dickinson, 25 July 1768 (RHL Let., I:29).
62 RHL to John Dickinson, 26 November 1768 (RHL Let., I:30–31).
63 Wood, op. cit., p. 33.
64 RHL to William Lee, 7 July 1770 (RHL Let., I:45–46).
65 RHL to Samuel Adams, 4 February 1773 (RHL Let., I:52–53).
66 RHL to Samuel Adams, 24 April 1774 (RHL Let., I:108); Arthur Lee to RHL, 18 March 1774 (Richard H. Lee, op. cit., I:94).
67 RHL to Arthur Lee, 26 June 1774 (RHL Let., I:114–16).
68 Joseph Warren, Suffolk Resolves, 9 September 1774.
69 McGaughy, op. cit., pp. 110–11; Wood, op. cit., pp. 47–49.
70 McGaughy, op. cit., p. 114.
71 Wood, op. cit., p. 54.
72 RHL to Arthur Lee, 24 February 1775 (RHL Let., I:130–31).

73 Wood, op. cit., pp. 53, 55.
74 RHL to Patrick Henry, 20 April 1776 (RHL Let., I:176–79).
75 Richard H. Lee, op. cit., I:168–69.
76 McGaughy, op. cit., pp. 121, 123–24.
77 RHL to Thomas Jefferson, 21 July 1776 (RHL Let., I:210).
78 A. R. Riggs, *The Nine Lives of Arthur Lee, Virginia Patriot* (Williamsburg: Virginia Independence Bicentennial Commission, 1976), pp. 12–14, 25.
79 Ibid., pp. 17, 21.
80 Ibid., pp. 22, 25.
81 Colbourn, op. cit., p. 230.
82 Henry, Lord Brougham, *Historical Sketches of Statesmen Who Flourished in the Time of George III* (London: Richard Griffin, 1858), I:431.
83 Caroline Robbins, *The Eighteenth Century Commonwealthman* (New York: Atheneum, 1968), p. 322; John Wilkes, *The North Briton*, Number 45, 23 April 1763; John Wilkes, *An Essay on Woman*, 1755.
84 Riggs, op. cit., pp. 34–35, 26–27, 33.
85 Colbourn, op. cit., pp. 229–30.
86 Bernard Bailyn, *The Ideological Origins of the American Revolution*, enlarged edition (Cambridge, MA: Harvard University Press, 1967), pp. 110–12, 120.
87 Riggs, op. cit., pp. 29–30, 32, 35–36, 41–42, 45–46; Ketchum, op. cit., p. 325.
88 Riggs, op. cit., pp. 36, 45, 43.
89 Ibid., pp. 48–49.
90 Nagel, op. cit., p. 105; Riggs, op. cit., p. 51.
91 Riggs, op. cit., p. 52; Nagel, op. cit., pp. 107–8.
92 Riggs, op. cit., p. 55; Nagel, op. cit., p. 107; Alan Taylor, *Writing Early American History* (Philadelphia: University of Pennsylvania Press, 2005), p. 173.
93 Barbara W. Tuchman, *The First Salute: A View of the American Revolution* (New York: Alfred A. Knopf, 1988), p. 84.
94 Riggs, op. cit., pp. 52, 54–56, 58; Nagel, op. cit., p. 105.
95 RHL to Samuel Adams, 23 November 1777 (RHL Let., I:355); Riggs, op. cit., pp. 58–60, 63; McGaughy, op. cit., pp. 132–34.
96 George III to Lord North, 3 March 1781 (Francis Wharton, ed., *The Revolutionary Diplomatic Correspondence of the United States* [Washington: Government Printing Office, 1889], I, 568); James West Davidson and Mark Lytle, *After the Fact: The Art of Historical Detection* (New York: McGraw-Hill, 1992), pp. xxvii–xxxv.
97 Riggs, op. cit., pp. 60–61, 69–70, 64.
98 Nagel, op. cit., pp. 110–11; McGaughy, op. cit., p. 115; RHL to General Washington, 22 October 1775 (RHL Let., I:152); Marine Committee to Silas Deane, 7 November 1775 (RHL Let., I:154–55); RHL to Thomas Ludwell Lee, 28 May 1776 (RHL Let., I:196); RHL to George Washington, 27 February 1777 (RHL Let., I:266); RHL to General Washington, 20 November 1777 (RHL Let., I:351–52); RHL to Arthur Lee, 20 April 1777 (RHL Let., I:279); RHL to Mrs. [Catharine] Macaulay, 29 November 1775 (RHL Let., I:161–62).

99 Committee of Secret Correspondence to Commissioners in France, 17 February 1777 (RHL Let., I:258–59; RHL to General Lee, 11 May 1776 (RHL Let., I:189–90); RHL to Samuel Adams, 1 March 1778 (RHL Let., I:391); RHL to the Governor of Virginia, 7 April 1777 (RHL Let., I:260).
100 Virginia Delegates in Congress to George Pyncheon and John Bradford, 16 October 1777 (RHL Let., I:332).
101 Nagel, op. cit., pp. 102–4.
102 RHL to Patrick Henry, 8 October 1777 (RHL Let., I:325).
103 RHL to John Adams, 8 October 1779 (RHL Let., II:155–56).
104 RHL to William Lee, 12 July 1772 (RHL Let., I:71); RHL to Arthur Lee, 20 April 1777 (RHL Let., I:280).
105 Nagel, op. cit., pp. 130–32.
106 McGaughy, op. cit., pp. 176–79; Nagel, op. cit., p. 136.
107 Nagel, op. cit., p. 132.
108 McGaughy, op. cit., p. 176; RHL to General Washington, 11 October 1787 (Richard H. Lee, op. cit., II:76).
109 Nagel., op. cit., pp. 135–36.
110 RHL to Governor Randolph, 16 October 1787 (Richard H. Lee, op. cit., II:78).
111 RHL to Samuel Adams, 5 October 1787 (Richard H. Lee, op. cit., II:74–75).
112 Nagel, op. cit., p. 137.
113 Ibid., p. 140.
114 McGaughy, op. cit., p. 231.
115 Charles Royster, *Light-Horse Harry Lee and the Legacy of the American Revolution* (Baton Rouge: Louisiana State University Press, 1994), pp. 14, 21, 25, 62; Nagel, op. cit., p. 161.
116 Royster, op. cit., pp. 13, 17–19, 21–24, 37, 54.
117 Henry Lee, *The Revolutionary War Memoirs of General Henry Lee* (reprint of *Memoirs of the War in the Southern Department of the United States*, 1869 edition), Robert E. Lee, ed. (New York: Da Capo, 1998), p. 108.
118 Royster, op. cit., pp. 40, 41, 43.
119 Ibid., pp. 48, 40–41; Nagel, op. cit., p. 162.
120 Royster, op. cit., pp. 40–41, 48–49.
121 Ibid., p. 57; Nagel, op. cit., p. 164.
122 Nagel, op. cit., pp. 164–65.
123 Ibid., pp. 151, 52–54; Royster, op. cit., p. 57.
124 Royster, op. cit., pp. 71–72, 74, 76, 173.
125 Ibid., pp. 14, 92, 106, 130, 126.
126 Ibid., pp. 72–73, 172–73.
127 Ibid., pp. 173–77.
128 Nagel, op. cit., p. 165.
129 Ibid., pp. 179, 195.
130 Ibid., pp. 174, 178, 181, 166; Royster, op. cit., pp. 177, 179.
131 Royster, op. cit., pp. 181–84.

132 Ibid., p. 231; Nagel, op. cit., p. 197.
133 Royster, op. cit., pp. 231, 227.
134 Ibid., p. 156.
135 Ibid., pp. 157–59, 161, 26–27.
136 Ibid., pp. 162–63.
137 Ibid., pp. 163–64.
138 Ibid., pp. 167, 232–34, 241–44, 3–4, 6–7; Nagel, op. cit., p. 184.
139 Nagel, op. cit., pp. 54–56.
140 Ibid., pp. 206–7.
141 Ibid., pp. 207–9, 212, 215, 229.
142 Ibid., pp. 273–74, 284, 287–300.
143 Robert E. Lee to Mary Lee, 25 December 1861 (Robert E. Lee, *Recollections and Letters of Robert E. Lee* [New York: Doubleday, Page, 1905], p. 59).

CHAPTER 3: George Washington: In Pursuit of Fame

1 Benjamin Franklin, *Autobiography*, Russel B. Nye, ed. (Boston: Houghton Mifflin, 1958), p. 1.
2 Ron Chernow, *Washington: A Life* (New York: Penguin, 2010), pp. 4–5, 7–8, 10; George Washington (GW) to David Humphreys, 25 July 1785, in George Washington, *Writings*, John Rhodehamel, ed. (Library of America, 1997 [LoA]), p. 580.
3 GW, *Comments on David Humphreys' Biography of Washington*, October 1786 (LoA, p. 610).
4 Nathaniel Hervey, *The Memory of Washington* (Boston and Cambridge: James Munroe, 1852), p. 23.
5 Washington Irving, *Life of George Washington*, in *Works of Washington Irving* (New York: P. F. Collier, 1897), XV, 142.
6 Chernow, op. cit., pp. 157–58, 396–97.
7 GW to Mary Ball Washington, 15 February 1787 (LoA, pp. 637–38).
8 Chernow, op. cit., pp. 423, 588–89.
9 Ibid., pp. 9, 15–16; LoA, p. 1055.
10 Chernow, op. cit., pp. 15–17, 422; LoA, p. 1094.
11 GW to George William Fairfax, 27 February 1785 (LoA, p. 574).
12 Chernow, op. cit., p. 13.
13 *Rules of Civility & Decent Behaviour in Company and Conversation* (LoA, pp. 3–5, 9–10, 1094).
14 GW, *Design for a Coat*, c. 1749–50 (LoA, p. 17).
15 GW to John Augustine Washington, 28 May 1755 (LoA, p. 52).
16 Chernow, op. cit., pp. 17–19.
17 GW, *A Journal of my Journey over the Mountains began Fryday the 11th, of March 1747/8* (LoA, pp. 11–14, 16).
18 Chernow, op. cit., pp. 22–23; James Thomas Flexner, *George Washington: The Forge of Experience* (Boston: Little, Brown, 1965), p. 7; LoA, p. 1056.

19 GW to Charles Lawrence, 26 April 1763 (LoA, p. 107); GW to Robert Dinwiddie, 18 May 1754 (LoA, p. 41); Chernow, op. cit., pp. 29–30.
20 Thomas Jefferson to Dr. Walter Jones, 2 January 1814, in Thomas Jefferson, *Writings*, Merrill D. Peterson, ed. (Library of America, 1984), p. 1319.
21 Chernow, op. cit., pp. 31–32; LoA, p. 1095.
22 GW, *Comments on David Humphreys' Biography of Washington*, October 1786 (LoA, p. 611).
23 GW, *Journey to the French Commandant*, 16–17 January 1764 (LoA, pp. 17–20); Flexner, op. cit., p. 60.
24 GW, *Journey to the French Commandant* (LoA, pp. 20–22); GW, *Comments on David Humphreys' Biography of Washington* (LoA, p. 611); Chernow, op. cit., p. 34.
25 GW, *Journey to the French Commandant* (LoA, pp. 22–24, 26).
26 Ibid., LoA, pp. 28–32.
27 Le Gardeur de Saint Pierre de Repentigny, Commander of the French Forces on the Ohio, to Governor Dinwiddie of Virginia, 15 December 1753 in GW, *Diary of George Washington from 1789 to 1791* (New York: C. B. Richardson, 1860), IV:247.
28 GW, *Journey to the French Commandant* (LoA, pp. 32–34); Chernow, op. cit., pp. 36, 32, 38.
29 Paul Johnson, *A History of the American People* (New York: HarperCollins, 1997), p. 124.
30 Chernow, op. cit., pp. 40–41; GW, *Comments on David Humphreys' Biography of Washington* (LoA, pp. 611–12).
31 GW to Robert Dinwiddie, 29 May 1754 (LoA, pp. 43–44), 1096; Flexner, op. cit., p. 89.
32 GW to Robert Dinwiddie, 29 May 1754 (LoA, pp. 44–47).
33 GW to John Augustine Washington, 31 May 1754 (LoA, pp. 48, 1096).
34 GW, *Comments on David Humphreys' Biography of Washington* (LoA, pp. 612–13); Chernow, op. cit., pp. 46–49.
35 Chernow, op. cit., p. 50.
36 GW to Robert Dinwiddie, 18 May 1754 (LoA, p. 39).
37 GW to Robert Dinwiddie, 29 May 1754 (LoA, pp. 40–43).
38 GW to William Fitzhugh, 15 November 1754 (LoA, p. 49).
39 GW, *Comments on David Humphreys' Biography of Washington* (LoA, p. 614).
40 Chernow, op. cit., p. 53.
41 Franklin, op. cit., pp. 130–31.
42 GW, *Comments on David Humphreys' Biography of Washington* (LoA, pp. 614–15); Chernow, op. cit., p. 57.
43 GW, *Comments on David Humphreys' Biography of Washington* (LoA, p. 615); GW to Robert Dinwiddie, 18 July 1755 (LoA, pp. 58–60).
44 Chernow, op. cit., p. 61.
45 GW, *Comments on David Humphreys' Biography of Washington* (LoA, pp. 615–17); GW to Robert Dinwiddie, 18 July 1755 (LoA, p. 59); Franklin, op. cit., p. 132; Chernow, op. cit., p. 60.

46 GW to Bushrod Washington, 9 November 1787 (LoA, p. 662).
47 GW, *Comments on David Humphreys' Biography of Washington* (LoA, p. 617).
48 Franklin, op. cit., p. 132.
49 Chernow, op. cit., pp. 63–64, 69; GW to Richard Washington, 15 April 1757 (LoA, p. 88).
50 GW to Christopher Gist, 10 October 1755 (LoA, p. 62); GW to Robert Dinwiddie, 22 April 1756 (LoA, pp. 74–75).
51 Franklin, op. cit., pp. 120–21; GW to Robert Hunter Morris, 9 April 1756 (LoA, p. 72).
52 GW to Robert Dinwiddie, 11 October 1755 (LoA, pp. 63–64).
53 GW to John Stanwix, 15 July 1757 (LoA, p. 90).
54 GW, *General Orders*, 1 January 1776 (LoA, p. 197).
55 Arthur O. Lovejoy, *Reflections on Human Nature* (Baltimore: Johns Hopkins University Press, 1961), pp. 157, 179, 218–19.
56 GW to John Stanwix, 10 April 1758 (LoA. p. 93); GW to Benjamin Harrison (LoA, p. 330).
57 GW to Sarah Bache, 15 January 1781 (LoA, p. 413).
58 GW, *General Orders*, 1 January 1776 (LoA, p. 196).
59 Ibid.
60 GW to Robert Dinwiddie, 10 March 1757 (LoA, pp. 86–87).
61 GW, *Comments on David Humphreys' Biography of Washington* (LoA, p. 619).
62 Chernow, op. cit., p. 91.
63 GW, *Farewell Address to the Virginia Regiment* (LoA, p. 99).
64 Richard Norton Smith, *Patriarch: George Washington and the New American Nation* (Boston: Houghton Mifflin, 1993), p. 173.
65 Chernow, op. cit., pp. 24–26, 52, 98, 78–79; Lease of Mount Vernon (Fairfax County Deed Book C, 17 December 1754), pp. 822–25, reprinted W. W. Abbot, ed., *The Papers of George Washington*, Colonial Series, vol. 1, 1748–August 1755 (Charlottesville: University Press of Virginia, 1983), 232–34; Allan Greenberg, *George Washington Architect* (London: Andreas Papadakis, 1999), p. 7.
66 GW, *General Orders*, 6 October 1755 (LoA, p. 61).
67 Chernow, op. cit., p. 51.
68 GW to James McHenry, 27 January 1799 (LoA, pp. 1020–21).
69 Greenberg, op. cit., pp. 62–67; Chernow, op. cit., p. 76.
70 GW to Isaac Heard, 2 May 1792 (LoA, p. 802).
71 Chernow, op. cit., pp. 76, 140, 77; GW to Robert Cary & Co., 6 June 1768 (LoA, pp. 127–28); GW to Richard Washington, 15 July 1757 (LoA, p. 89).
72 GW to Robert Stewart, 27 April 1763 (LoA, p. 109).
73 Chernow, op. cit., p. 82; GW to Elizabeth Parke Custis, 14 September 1794 (LoA, pp. 881–82).
74 Chernow, op. cit., pp. 101, 218, 295.
75 GW to Martha Washington, 18 June 1775 (LoA, p. 168).
76 Chernow, op. cit., pp. 153–54; GW to Burwell Bassett, 20 June 1773 (LoA, p. 146).

77 Chernow, op. cit., pp. 421, 463–64.
78 GW to Eleanor Parke Custis, 16 January 1795 (LoA, p. 901).
79 GW to Sarah Cary Fairfax, 12 September 1758 (LoA, pp. 96–97).
80 Chernow, op. cit., p. 170.
81 Ibid., pp. 124–25, 141–42, 778.
82 Ibid., p. 119; GW to William Pearce, 18 December 1793 (LoA, p. 862).
83 GW, *Reward for Runaway Slaves*, 11 August 1791 (LoA, pp. 102–3); GW to Josiah Thompson, 2 July 1766 (LoA, p. 118).
84 Chernow, op. cit., pp. 114–15, 641.
85 GW to John Posey, 24 June 1767 (LoA, p. 121).
86 GW to William Crawford, September 1767 (LoA, pp. 125–26).
87 GW to Charles Washington, 31 January 1770 (LoA, pp. 134–37).
88 Chernow, op. cit., pp. 148–50.
89 GW to Thomas Johnson, 20 July 1770 (LoA, pp. 137–40).
90 Greenberg, op. cit., pp. 65–71, 34, 46–47.
91 Ibid., p. 67.
92 Ibid., pp. 26–27; see also Allan Greenberg, *The Architecture of Democracy* (New York: Rizzoli, 2006).
93 Chernow, op. cit., pp. 136–37; GW to Robert Cary & Co., 10 August 1764 (LoA, pp. 110–11).
94 GW to Robert Cary & Co., 20 September 1765 (LoA, pp. 113–17).
95 GW to George Mason, 5 April 179 (LoA, pp. 130–32).
96 Chernow, op. cit., pp. 144–47; LoA, p. 1060.
97 Chernow, op. cit., p. 165.
98 GW to George William Fairfax, 10 June 1774 (LoA, p. 150).
99 GW to Bryan Fairfax, 4 July 1774 (LoA, pp. 152–53).
100 Fairfax Resolves, 1–3, 6–7.
101 GW to Bryan Fairfax, 20 July 1774 (LoA, pp. 155–56).
102 GW to Bryan Fairfax, 24 August 1774 (LoA, p. 158).
103 Chernow, op. cit., pp. 170–71.
104 GW to Robert McKenzie, 9 October 1774 (LoA, p. 160).
105 Chernow, op. cit., pp. 174–75.
106 GW to George William Fairfax, 31 May 1775 (LoA, p. 164).
107 Chernow, op. cit., pp. 183, 186–87.
108 GW to Burwell Bassett, 19 June 1775 (LoA, pp. 169–70).
109 Lionel Trilling, *Sincerity and Authenticity* (New York: Harcourt Brace Jovanovich, 1971), p. 1.
110 GW to Martha Washington, 18 June 1775 (LoA, pp. 168–69).

CHAPTER 4: General Washington

1 John Ferling, *Almost a Miracle: The American Victory in the War of Independence* (New York: Oxford University Press, 2007), pp. 53, 55, 58–59.
2 Ibid., p. 60.

3 GW to John Augustine Washington, 31 March 1776, in George Washington, *Writings*, John Rhodehamel, ed. (Library of America, 1997 [LoA]), p. 218.
4 GW to Joseph Reed, 10 February 1776 (LoA, p. 212).
5 GW to Joseph Reed, 14 January 1776 (LoA, p. 203).
6 Ron Chernow, *Washington: A Life* (New York: Penguin, 2010), pp. 211, 213.
7 GW to Joseph Reed, 1 February 1776 (LoA, p. 208).
8 GW to John Augustine Washington, 31 March 1776 (LoA, pp. 218–19).
9 GW to Thomas Gage, 11 August 1775 (LoA, p. 181).
10 Chernow, op. cit., p. 201.
11 GW to Thomas Gage, 19 August 1775 (LoA, pp. 182–83).
12 Ferling, op. cit., p. 62.
13 Chernow, op. cit., pp. 239–41; GW to John Hancock, 14 July 1776 (LoA, p. 230).
14 Ibid., LoA, p. 230.
15 David Hackett Fischer, *Washington's Crossing* (New York: Oxford University Press, 2004), pp. 153, 218; Chernow, op. cit., pp. 223–24; Ferling, op. cit., pp. 102–4, 123.
16 Ferling, op. cit., pp. 104–5; Chernow, op. cit., pp. 224–26.
17 Ferling, op. cit., p. 106; Chernow, op. cit., pp. 226–27; GW to John Augustine Washington, 31 March 1776 (LoA, pp. 220–21); GW to John Hancock, 19 March 1776 (LoA, p. 217).
18 Chernow, op. cit., pp. 228–29; GW to Josiah Quincy, 24 March 1776, in John C. Fitzpatrick, ed., *The Writings of George Washington* (Washington: U.S. Government Printing Office, 1931–1944), IV:421–22; *Cato*, IV, iv, 48; Cf. GW to Benedict Arnold, 5 December 1775 (LoA, p. 192).
19 Fischer, op. cit., pp. 147–48, 81. Lee was no known relation to the Lees of Stratford Hall.
20 Ibid., pp. 67–74; Henry Lee, *The Revolutionary War Memoirs of General Henry Lee* (reprint of *Memoirs of the War in the Southern Department of the United States*, 1869 edition), Robert E. Lee, ed. (New York: Da Capo, 1998), pp. 109–11.
21 Ferling, op. cit., p. 122.
22 Thomas Paine, *Common Sense and Other Political Writings*, Nelson F. Adkins, ed. (Indianapolis: Bobbs-Merrill, 1953), pp. 7, 18, 27.
23 GW to Joseph Reed, 31 January 1776 (LoA, p. 206); GW to Joseph Reed, 10 February 1776 (LoA, pp. 213–14); GW, *General Orders*, 9 July 1776 (LoA, p. 228).
24 Chernow, op. cit., p. 231; GW to Adam Stephen, 20 July 1776 (LoA, p. 233); Fischer, op. cit., pp. 83–84.
25 Fischer, op. cit., pp. 89–91, 94–99; Chernow, op. cit., pp. 245–48; Ferling, op. cit., pp. 122, 135; Theodore P. Savas and J. David Dameron, *A Guide to the Battles of the American Revolution* (New York: Savas Beatie, 2010), pp. 55–60.
26 Chernow, op. cit., p. 249; Fischer, op. cit., pp. 99–100.
27 Fischer, op. cit., pp. 21–22, 25–29; Chernow, op. cit., pp. 333–34.
28 Chernow, op. cit., pp. 249–51; Fischer, op. cit., p. 101.
29 GW to John Augustine Washington, 22 September 1776 (LoA, p. 246); Cher-

now, op. cit., pp. 253–55; Savas and Dameron, op. cit., pp. 65–66; Ferling, op. cit., pp. 141–42.

30 Ferling, op. cit., pp. 144–45, 128–29; Fischer, op. cit., pp. 109–10.

31 Ferling, op. cit., pp. 146–48; Fischer, op. cit., pp. 110–11; Chernow, op. cit., pp. 258–59.

32 Chernow, op. cit., pp. 202–3.

33 Ibid., pp. 261–62; Fischer, op. cit., pp. 111–14; Ferling, op. cit., pp. 151–53.

34 GW to John Hancock, 8 September 1776 (LoA, p. 241).

35 GW to John Adams, 25 September 1798 (LoA, p. 1011).

36 Ferling, op. cit., p. 345.

37 Chernow, op. cit., p. 287.

38 Fischer, op. cit., p. 276.

39 GW, *General Orders*, 17 December 1777 (LoA, pp. 280–81).

40 Fischer, op. cit., pp. 77, 75.

41 Ibid., p. 46.

42 Ibid., pp. 63–65.

43 Ibid., pp. 117–19, 125–26, 129–30; Chernow, op. cit., pp. 264–65, 269; Ferling, op. cit., p. 187.

44 Fischer, op. cit., p. 133.

45 Ibid., pp. 129, 149–50; Chernow, op. cit., p. 265.

46 GW to Lund Washington, 10 December 1776 (LoA, p. 260); Ferling, op. cit., p. 154.

47 GW to Lund Washington, 10 December 1776 (LoA, pp. 259, 261).

48 GW to Lund Washington, 30 September 1776 (LoA, pp. 249–50).

49 GW to John Augustine Washington, 6 November 1776 (LoA, p. 256); Micah 4, v. 3–4.

50 Ferling, op. cit., pp. 168–69.

51 Paine, op. cit., pp. 55, 59, 58; Jack Fruchtman, Jr., *Thomas Paine: Apostle of Freedom* (New York: Four Walls, Eight Windows, 1994), pp. 22–23, 27, 38–39.

52 Chernow, op. cit., pp. 270–71; Savas and Dameron, op. cit., p. 81.

53 Chernow, op. cit., p. 272.

54 Ibid., pp. 272–73; GW to John Hancock, 27 December 1776 (LoA, p. 262).

55 Ferling, op. cit., p. 176; Chernow, op. cit., pp. 274–76; Fischer, op. cit., pp. 203–5; GW to John Hancock, 27 December 1776 (LoA, p. 264).

56 Chernow, op. cit., pp. 276–77; Fischer, op. cit., pp. 235, 254–55.

57 Chernow, op. cit., p. 277; Fischer, op. cit., pp. 265, 267–68, 291.

58 Fischer, op. cit., pp. 270–73.

59 Ibid., p. 273.

60 GW to Lund Washington, 20 August 1775 (LoA, p. 184).

61 Fischer, op. cit., p. 6.

62 Ibid., pp. 293, 300–301, 307.

63 Ibid., p. 313.

64 Ibid., pp. 280–81, 315, 348.

65 Chernow, op. cit., pp. 280–81; Fischer, op. cit., pp. 316, 321.

66 Chernow, op. cit., pp. 281–83; Fischer, op. cit., p. 334.
67 GW to Henry Laurens, 31 January 1778 (LoA, p. 290).
68 Chernow, op. cit., pp. 301–5; Savas and Dameron, op. cit., pp. 129–33; Ferling, op. cit., p. 252.
69 David McCullough, *John Adams* (New York: Simon & Schuster, 2001), p. 173; Chernow, op. cit., pp. 307–11; Ferling, op. cit., p. 256.
70 Gordon S. Wood, *The American Revolution: A History* (New York: Modern Library, 2002), pp. 81–82; James Thomas Flexner, *Washington: The Indispensable Man* (New York: Signet, 1974), pp. 108–9.
71 Savas and Dameron, op. cit., pp. 125–29, 145–51; Ferling, op. cit., pp. 214, 223, 232, 238.
72 Fischer, op. cit., pp. 146–47; Chernow, op. cit., pp. 313–14, 317–18; GW to Horatio Gates, 4 January 1778 (LoA, p. 287).
73 GW to Richard Henry Lee, 17 October 1777 (LoA, pp. 275–76).
74 GW to Thomas Conway, 5 November 1777 (LoA, p. 280); GW to Horatio Gates, 4 January 1778 (LoA, pp. 287–88).
75 Chernow, op. cit., pp. 317–20.
76 Ibid., pp. 374–75, 322.
77 Fischer, op. cit., pp. 72–73.
78 Chernow, op. cit., pp. 324–25; Ferling, op. cit., pp. 258, 274, 276.
79 GW to George Clinton, 16 February 1778 (LoA, p. 292).
80 Ferling, op. cit., p. 277.
81 GW to John Banister, 21 April 1778 (LoA, pp. 303–4).
82 Ferling, op. cit., p. 277.
83 Ibid., p. 280.
84 GW to Henry Laurens, 23 December 1777 (LoA, pp. 283–84).
85 Ferling, op. cit., p. 280.
86 Chernow, op. cit., pp. 330–31, 334.
87 Ibid., pp. 332–33; Ferling, op. cit., pp. 286–88; Flexner, op. cit., p. 118.
88 Chernow, op. cit., pp. 355–56; Ferling, op. cit., pp. 262–63; GW, *General Orders*, 5 May 1778 (LoA, p. 308).
89 Ferling, op. cit., pp. 126–67, 417; Barbara W. Tuchman, *The First Salute: A View of the American Revolution* (New York: Alfred A. Knopf, 1988), pp. 177–78.
90 Ferling, op. cit., pp. 266, 269, 294, 299; Chernow, op. cit., p. 337.
91 Chernow, op. cit., pp. 339–44, 347–48; Savas and Dameron, op. cit., pp. 170–78.
92 GW to John Banister, 21 April 1778 (LoA, pp. 299–300).
93 GW to Gouverneur Morris, 4 October 1778 (LoA, p. 326).
94 Ferling, op. cit., p. 351.
95 GW to Lund Washington, 17 August 1779 (LoA, pp. 356–57).
96 GW to Gouverneur Morris, 4 October 1778 (LoA, p. 326); GW to Benjamin Harrison, 18 December 1778 (LoA, p. 333).
97 GW to Benjamin Harrison, 18 December 1778 (LoA, pp. 331, 333–34).
98 GW to James Warren, 31 March 1779 (LoA, p. 342).
99 GW to Benjamin Harrison, 25 October 1779 (LoA, p. 367).

100 Chernow, op. cit., p. 366; Ferling, op. cit., pp. 413, 399.
101 GW to Benjamin Harrison, 25 October 1779 (LoA, p. 367); Chernow, op. cit., p. 368.
102 GW to John Augustine Washington, 6 July 1780 (LoA, p. 380).
103 Ferling, op. cit., pp. 412–13.
104 GW to John Cochran, 16 August 1779 (LoA, p. 356); Chernow, op. cit., pp. 325–26.
105 GW to Joseph Jones, 31 May 1789 (LoA, p. 378).
106 GW to Benjamin Franklin, 20 December 1780 (LoA, p. 403); GW to Joseph Jones, 31 May 1789 (LoA, p. 378); GW, *Circular to the State Governments*, 18 October 1780 (LoA, pp. 399, 402); GW to William Fitzhugh, 22 October 1789 (LoA, p. 400); GW to John Laurens, 15 January 1781 (LoA, pp. 409–12).
107 GW to Joseph Reed, 28 May 1780 (LoA, pp. 374–76).
108 GW to William Fitzhugh, 22 October 1780 (LoA, p. 401); GW, *Circular to the State Governments*, 18 October 1780 (LoA, pp. 394, 397); GW to John Banister, 21 April 1778 (LoA, p. 303); GW to John Cadwalader, 5 October 1780 (LoA, p. 391).
109 GW to John Laurens, 15 January 1781 (LoA, pp. 410–11); Chernow, op. cit., p. 369.
110 GW to Henry Laurens, 14 November 1778 (LoA, p. 329).
111 Ferling, op. cit., p. 394.
112 Chernow, op. cit., pp. 349, 373.
113 GW to Benjamin Lincoln, 2 October 1782 (LoA, p. 472).
114 Ferling, op. cit., pp. 323–25.
115 Ibid., pp. 421, 423–25, 427.
116 Ibid., pp. 437–42.
117 Ibid., pp. 89, 452, 454–57, 462, 481–87, 498–99.
118 GW to Lund Washington, 30 April 1781 (LoA, pp. 420–21).
119 Ferling, op. cit., p. 504.
120 Ibid., pp. 499–500, 508, 517, 520.
121 Ibid., pp. 510–16, 566.
122 GW, *Journal of the Yorktown Campaign* (LoA, p. 428).
123 Ferling, op. cit., pp. 504–5.
124 GW, *Journal of the Yorktown Campaign* (LoA, pp. 442, 451).
125 Ferling, op. cit., pp. 524–25, 527; Chernow, op. cit., pp. 410, 412.
126 Ferling, op. cit., pp. 527–31.
127 Ibid., p. 532; GW, *Journal of the Yorktown Campaign* (LoA, p. 457).
128 Ferling, op. cit., p. 532.
129 Chernow, op. cit., p. 414.
130 Ferling, op. cit., pp. 532–33; Chernow, op. cit., p. 416.
131 Ferling, op. cit., pp. 533–54.
132 Chernow, op. cit., p. 415.
133 Ferling, op. cit., p. 534, Chernow, op. cit., pp. 413, 415.
134 Ferling, op. cit., pp. 534–35; Chernow, op. cit., pp. 416–17.

135 Ferling, op. cit., pp. 535–36; Tuchman, op. cit., p. 290.
136 Tuchman, pp. 537–38; Chernow, op. cit., p. 418.
137 Chernow, pp. 419–20, 429.
138 GW to James McHenry, 17 October 1782 (LoA, p. 476).
139 Ferling, op. cit., pp. 98, 238, 447–50.
140 Chernow, op. cit., pp. 389–90; GW, *Circular to New England State Governments*, 5 January 1781 (LoA, pp. 406–7).
141 Chernow, op. cit., pp. 430, 433–34; LoA, pp. 1107–9.
142 GW to Alexander Hamilton, 12 March 1783 (LoA, p. 492).
143 GW, *Speech to the Officers of the Army*, 15 March 1783 (LoA, pp. 497–99); Chernow, p. 434.
144 Chernow, op. cit., pp. 435–36.
145 GW to Joseph Jones, 18 March 1783 (LoA, pp. 501–2).
146 Ferling, op. cit., pp. 558–59; GW, *General Orders*, 18 April 1783 (LoA, p. 513).
147 GW, *General Orders*, 4 July 1775 (LoA, p. 175); GW, *Farewell Address to the Armies of the United States*, 2 November 1783 (LoA, pp. 543–46).
148 Chernow, op. cit., pp. 451–52.
149 GW, *Address to the New York Provincial Congress*, 26 June 1775 (LoA, p. 174).
150 GW, *Address to Congress on Resigning Commission*, 23 December 1783 (LoA, p. 548); Chernow, op. cit., pp. 454–57, 461.

CHAPTER 5: President Washington

1 GW to Marquis de Lafayette, 1 February 1784, in George Washington, *Writings*, John Rhodehamel, ed. (Library of America, 1997 [LoA]), pp. 553–54.
2 GW to Marquis de Lafayette, 4 April 1784 (LoA, pp. 558–59).
3 Ron Chernow, *Washington: A Life* (New York: Penguin, 2010), pp. 466–67.
4 GW to Tench Tilghman, 24 March 1784 (LoA, pp. 555–56).
5 Robert F. Dalzell, Jr., and Lee Baldwin Dalzell, *George Washington's Mount Vernon* (New York: Oxford University Press, 1998), pp. 114–55, 120–23.
6 Benson J. Lossing, *George Washington's Mount Vernon* (New York: Fairfax Press reprint, 1977), p. 153.
7 Robert F. Dalzell, Jr., and Lee Baldwin Dalzell, op. cit., pp. 113, 121; Allan Greenberg, *George Washington Architect* (London: Andreas Papadakis, 1999), pp. 72–77.
8 GW to William Fitzhugh, 15 May 1786 (LoA, p. 599).
9 GW to Arthur Young, 6 August 1786 (LoA, pp. 602–4).
10 Chernow, op. cit., pp. 465, 496.
11 GW to William Pearce, 6 October 1793 (LoA, p. 845).
12 GW to Marquis de Lafayette, 25 July 1785 (LoA, pp. 584–85); GW to William Fitzhugh, 15 May 1786 (LoA, pp. 598–99).
13 Chernow, op. cit., pp. 483–84.
14 GW to Marquis de Lafayette, 1 February 1784 (LoA, p. 553); GW to Alexander Hamilton, 4 March 1783 (LoA, pp. 489–90).

15 GW, *Circular to State Governments*, 8 June 1783 (LoA, pp. 518–20).
16 GW to William Gordon, 8 July 1783 (LoA, pp. 531–32).
17 GW to Benjamin Harrison, 18 January 1784 (LoA, p. 552).
18 GW to Marquis de Lafayette, 10 May 1786 (LoA, p. 595).
19 GW to James Warren, 7 October 1785 (LoA, p. 592); GW to Benjamin Harrison, 10 October 1784 (LoA, pp. 562, 560); LoA, p. 1068.
20 GW to James Madison, 10 November 1786 (LoA, pp. 621–22); Chernow, op. cit., pp. 479–81; Ian W. Toll, *Six Frigates: The Epic History of the Founding of the U.S. Navy* (New York: W. W. Norton, 2006), pp. 19–20.
21 James Madison to GW, 7 December 1786 (Madison LoA, p. 60).
22 Chernow, op. cit., p. 523.
23 GW to David Humphreys, 26 December 1786 (LoA, pp. 632–33); LoA, p. 1068.
24 GW to James Madison, 31 March 1787 (LoA, p. 648).
25 GW to Edmund Randolph, 28 March 1787 (LoA, pp. 644–45).
26 Chernow, op. cit., pp. 520–31.
27 Ibid., p. 537.
28 GW, *Diary Entry*, 17 September 1787 (LoA, p. 655).
29 GW to the Continental Congress, 17 September 1787 (LoA, pp. 654–55); GW to Marquis de Lafayette, 7 February 1788 (LoA, p. 668).
30 GW to Edward Newnham, 29 August 1788 (LoA, p. 695).
31 Ibid.
32 GW to Alexander Hamilton, 28 August 1788 (LoA, pp. 691–92); GW to the House of Representatives, 30 March 1796 (LoA, pp. 931–32).
33 GW to Bushrod Washington, 9 November 1787 (LoA, p. 661).
34 GW to Marquis de Lafayette, 7 February 1788 (LoA, pp. 668–69); GW, *Fragments of a Draft of the First Inaugural Address*, January 1789 (LoA, p. 710).
35 GW to Edward Newnham, 29 August 1788 (LoA, p. 695).
36 GW, *First Inaugural Address*, 30 April 1789 (LoA, pp. 732–33).
37 GW, *First Annual Message to Congress*, 8 January 1790 (LoA, p. 750).
38 GW, *First Inaugural Address*, 30 April 1789 (LoA, p. 733).
39 GW to Marquis de Lafayette, 19 June 1788 (LoA, pp. 684–85).
40 GW to Alexander Hamilton, 3 October 1788 (LoA, p. 697).
41 GW to Benjamin Harrison, 22 January 1785 (LoA, pp. 570–71).
42 GW to Edmund Randolph, 30 July 1785 (LoA, pp. 586–87).
43 GW to Alexander Hamilton, 3 October 1788 (LoA, p. 697).
44 GW to Benjamin Lincoln, 26 October 1788 (LoA, p. 700).
45 GW, *Fragments of a Draft of the First Inaugural Address*, January 1789 (LoA, pp. 704–5).
46 GW to Alexander Hamilton, 3 October 1788 (LoA, p. 697).
47 GW, *Fragments of a Draft of the First Inaugural Address*, January 1789 (LoA, p. 707).
48 GW to Catharine Macaulay Graham, 9 January 1790 (LoA, p. 752).
49 GW to Henry Knox, 1 April 1789 (LoA, p. 726); Chernow, op. cit., pp. 470–71; Trevor Colbourn, *The Lamp of Experience: Whig History and the Intellectual Origins of the American Revolution* (Indianapolis: Liberty Fund, 1965), pp. 52–53.

50 GW, *First Inaugural Address*, 30 April 1789 (LoA, pp. 730–31).
51 GW to Catharine Macaulay Graham, 9 January 1790 (LoA, p. 752).
52 GW to James Madison, 5 May 1789 (LoA, p. 734); GW to John Adams, 10 May 1789 (LoA, p. 738); GW to Catharine Macaulay Graham, 9 January 1790 (LoA, p. 754).
53 GW to John Adams, 10 May 1789 (LoA, pp. 736–77).
54 Arthur O. Lovejoy, *Reflections on Human Nature* (Baltimore: Johns Hopkins University Press, 1961), pp. 197–207.
55 Chernow, op. cit., pp. 575–76, 579, 581; GW to David Stuart, 15 June 1790 (LoA, p. 762).
56 GW to Catharine Macaulay Graham, 9 January 1790 (LoA, p. 752).
57 GW to Gouverneur Morris, 13 October 1789 (LoA, p. 747); Carol Borchert Cadou, *The George Washington Collection: Fine and Decorative Arts at Mount Vernon* (Manchester, VT: Hudson Hills, 2006), pp. 140–41, 144–45, 127, 130–31; Chernow, op. cit., p. 617.
58 GW to Richard Conway, 4 March 1789 (LoA, p. 719); Chernow, op. cit., pp. 582–84.
59 Chernow, op. cit., pp. 562–63.
60 GW to David Humphreys, 20 July 1791 (LoA, p. 777); Chernow, op. cit., pp. 584, 608–9; R. N. Smith, *Patriarch: George Washington and the New American Nation* (Boston: Houghton Mifflin, 1993), pp. 88–89.
61 Chernow, op. cit., p. 650.
62 Ibid., pp. 580–81.
63 Ibid., p. 370.
64 R. N. Smith, op. cit., p. 25.
65 Chernow, op. cit., p. 573.
66 GW to David Stuart, 15 June 1790 (LoA, p. 761).
67 GW to Alexander Hamilton, 29 July 1792 (LoA, p. 811); LoA, p. 1119; Thomas Jefferson to the President of the United States, 23 May 1792 (Jefferson LoA, p. 987); Alexander Hamilton, *Speech in the Constitutional Convention on a Plan of Government*, version recorded by Robert Yates, 18 June 1787 (Hamilton LoA, pp. 159, 165).
68 Chernow, op. cit., p. 620.
69 GW to David Humphreys, 20 July 1791 (LoA, p. 778).
70 GW to Thomas Jefferson, 15 March 1791 (LoA, p. 909).
71 GW to Lewis Nicola, 22 May 1782 (LoA, p. 469).
72 GW, *Fragments of a Draft of the First Inaugural Address*, January 1789 (LoA, p. 706).
73 R. N. Smith, op. cit., p. 79.
74 Thomas Jefferson, *The Anas*, 10 July 1792, in Thomas Jefferson, *Writings*, Merrill D. Peterson, ed. (Library of America, 1984), pp. 678–79.
75 Chernow, op. cit., pp. 677–78; GW to James Madison, 20 May 1792 (LoA, pp. 804–6).

76 LoA, p. 1119.
77 Chernow, op. cit., p. 678.
78 GW to Thomas Jefferson, 23 August 1792 (LoA, pp. 817–18); GW to Alexander Hamilton, 26 August 1792 (LoA, p. 819).
79 *The Papers of George Washington Digital Edition*, Theodore J. Crackel, ed. (Charlottesville: University of Virginia Press, 2008).
80 Chernow, op. cit., p. 687.
81 GW to Henry Lee, 21 July 1793 (LoA, p. 841).
82 GW to Gouverneur Morris, 13 October 1789 (LoA, p. 746).
83 GW to Chevalier de la Luzerne, 29 April 1790 (LoA, p. 759).
84 Chernow, op. cit., pp. 658–59; R. N. Smith, op. cit., p. 99.
85 GW to Marquis de Lafayette, 11 August 1790 (LoA, pp. 764).
86 GW to Marquis de Lafayette, 28 July 1791 (LoA, p. 780).
87 GW to Marquis de Lafayette, 10 June 1792 (LoA, p. 808).
88 John Kekes, "Why Robespierre Chose Terror," *City Journal*, Spring 2006.
89 Chernow, op. cit., pp. 687–89, 714.
90 GW, *Proclamation of Neutrality*, 22 April 1793 (LoA, p. 840).
91 Chernow, op. cit., pp. 692, 697–98.
92 Ibid., p. 693.
93 James Madison, *Helvidius* No. 1, 24 August 1793 (Madison LoA, pp. 537, 541); "The *Federalist*," *Detached Memoranda* (Madison LoA, p. 770).
94 Cabinet Opinion on "Little Sarah," in Paul L. Ford, ed., *The Works of Thomas Jefferson*, Federal Edition (New York and London: G. P. Putnam's Sons, 1904–5), vol. 7; Chernow, op. cit., pp. 694–95.
95 Chernow, op. cit., p. xix.
96 Ibid., p. 696.
97 GW to John Francis Mercer, 26 September 1792 (LoA, p. 824).
98 GW to Henry Lee, 21 July 1793 (LoA, pp. 841–42).
99 GW to Henry Knox, 20 September 1795 (LoA, p. 916).
100 Kekes, op. cit.; Thomas Carlyle, *The French Revolution*, in *Works* 4:247.
101 GW, *Proclamation Calling Forth the Militia*, 7 August 1794 (LoA, p. 872).
102 GW, *Fourth Annual Message to Congress*, 6 November 1792 (LoA, p. 829); GW, *Proclamation Calling Forth the Militia*, 7 August 1794 (LoA, p. 871).
103 Chernow, op. cit., pp. 718–19; LoA, p. 871.
104 R. N. Smith, op. cit., p. 212.
105 GW, *Proclamation Calling Forth the Militia*, 7 August 1794 (LoA, p. 871).
106 GW to Charles Mynn Thruston, 10 August 1794 (LoA, p. 874).
107 GW to Henry Lee, 26 August 1794 (LoA, p. 876).
108 Chernow, op. cit., pp. 721–24.
109 GW, *Sixth Annual Message to Congress*, 19 November 1794 (LoA, pp. 888–89); Chernow, op. cit., pp. 725–26.
110 GW to John Jay, 30 August 1794 (LoA, pp. 879–80).
111 Ibid.

112 GW, *Draft of the Farewell Address*, 15 May 1796 (LoA, p. 945).
113 GW to Gouverneur Morris, 22 December 1795 (LoA, pp. 927–28).
114 Chernow, op. cit., pp. 730, 740–42.
115 GW, *Farewell Address*, 19 September 1796 (LoA, p. 967).
116 GW to Thomas Jefferson, 6 July 1796 (LoA, pp. 951–52).
117 Chernow, op. cit., p. 780.
118 GW to Sarah Cary Fairfax, 16 May 1798 (LoA, p. 1004).
119 GW to Jonathan Trumbull, Jr., 3 March 1797 (LoA, p. 988); GW to Alexander Hamilton, 15 May 1796 (LoA, p. 938).
120 GW, *Farewell Address*, op. cit., pp. 969, 977, 970.
121 Ibid., p. 972.
122 Ibid., p. 971.
123 GW to the Hebrew Congregation in Newport, Rhode Island, 18 August 1790 (LoA, p. 767).
124 GW to David Humphreys, 25 July 1785 (LoA, pp. 579–80).
125 GW to Edmund Randolph, 26 August 1792 (LoA, p. 821).
126 GW to Marquis de Lafayette, 19 June 1788 (LoA, p. 685).
127 Chernow, op. cit., pp. 534, 611, 810.
128 J.-J. Rousseau, *The Government of Poland*, Ch. 1; GW, *Farewell Address*, op. cit., p. 968.
129 GW, *Farewell Address*, op. cit., pp. 964–65.
130 GW to Charles Mynn Thruston, 10 August 1794 (LoA, pp. 873–74); LoA, p. 1121.
131 GW, *Farewell Address*, op. cit., pp. 969, 971, 970, 968.
132 GW to the Commissioners of the District of Columbia, 28 January 1795 (LoA, p. 906).
133 GW, *Farewell Address*, op. cit., p. 968.
134 Ibid., p. 966.
135 GW to Henry Laurens, 14 November 1778 (LoA, p. 329).
136 GW, *Farewell Address*, op. cit., pp. 973, 975.
137 GW, *First Annual Message to Congress*, 8 January 1790 (LoA, p. 749); GW, *Fifth Annual Message to Congress*, 3 December 1793 (LoA, p. 848); GW, *Farewell Address*, op. cit., p. 972.
138 GW, *Eighth Annual Message to Congress*, 7 December 1796 (LoA, p. 980).
139 GW to James McHenry, 20 May 1797 (LoA, p. 996); GW to James McHenry, 3 April 1797 (LoA, p. 993); GW to David Humphreys, 26 June 1797 (LoA, p. 998); R. N. Smith, op. cit., p. 302.
140 GW to Robert Lewis, 18 August 1799 (LoA, p. 1047).
141 GW to Arthur Young, 12 December 1793 (LoA, pp. 852–53).
142 LoA, p. 1073.
143 Chernow, op. cit., pp. 463–64, 747.
144 Ibid., pp. 749, 615.
145 eMuseum.MountVernon.org, harpsichord.
146 Chernow, op. cit., p. 422.

147 GW to Tobias Lear, 6 May 1794 (LoA, p. 868).
148 Chernow, op. cit., p. 709.
149 GW to Marquis de Lafayette, 10 May 1786 (LoA, p. 597); GW to John Francis Mercer, 9 September 1786 (LoA, p. 607).
150 GW to Robert Lewis, 18 August 1799 (LoA, p. 1047).
151 GW to William Pearce, 10 May 1795 (LoA, p. 911).
152 Chernow, op. cit., pp. 751, 800.
153 GW to Lawrence Lewis, 4 August 1797 (LoA, p. 1002).
154 Chernow, op. cit., pp. 759–62.
155 Ibid., p. 761.
156 Ibid., p. 801.
157 GW, *Last Will and Testament*, 9 July 1799 (LoA, p. 1035).
158 Ibid., pp. 1023–24; LoA, p. 1126.
159 Chernow, op. cit., p. 808.
160 LoA, pp. 1126; GW, *Last Will and Testament*, op. cit., p. 1023.
161 Chernow, op. cit., p. 815.
162 GW to James McHenry, 29 May 1797 (LoA, pp. 996–97).
163 GW to Burges Ball, 22 September 1799 (LoA, p. 1050).
164 Chernow, op. cit., p. 806.
165 Chernow, op. cit., pp. 807–11; R. N. Smith, op. cit., pp. 353, 355; American Academy of Otolaryngology—Head and Neck Surgery (*www.entnet.org*), "Early History of the Tracheotomy"; White McKenzie Wallenborn, M.D., "George Washington's Terminal Illness," *http://gwpapers.virginia.edu*.
166 Chernow, op. cit., pp. 809, 811.
167 GW, *Last Will and Testament*, op. cit., pp. 1036–42, 1031, 1034–35.

CHAPTER 6: John Jay: America's Indispensable Diplomat

1 John Jay (JJ) to William Livingston, 19 February 1785, in Linda M. Freeman, Louise V. North, and Janet M. Wedge, eds., *Selected Letters of John Jay and Sarah Livingston Jay* (Jefferson, NC: McFarland, 2005 [SL]), p. 170.
2 William Jay, *The Life of John Jay* (New York: J. & J. Harper, 1833, reprint Bridgewater, VA: American Foundation Publications, 2000), I:3–8.
3 Walter Stahr, *John Jay: Founding Father* (New York: Hambledon and Continuum, 2006), p. 2.
4 William Jay, op. cit., I:7.
5 Ibid., op. cit., I:10.
6 Peter Jay to James Jay, 3 July 1752 O.S., in Richard B. Morris, ed., *John Jay: The Making of a Revolutionary, Unpublished Papers 1745–1780* (New York: Harper & Row, 1975 [UP I]), pp. 35–36.
7 JJ to Mrs. R. Livingston, 12 July 1783, in The Papers of John Jay, Columbia University John Jay Project [PJJ] *http://www.columbia.edu/cu/lweb/digital/jay/*) #90224 (William Jay, op. cit., II:120).
8 William Jay, op. cit., I:12.

9 Benjamin Kissam to JJ, 25 August 1766 (UP I:82–83).
10 Stahr, op. cit., p. 17.
11 Richard M. Ketchum, *Divided Loyalties: How the American Revolution Came to New York* (New York: Henry Holt, 2002), p. 125.
12 C. A. Weslager, *The Stamp Act Congress: With an Exact Copy of the Complete Journal* (Newark: University of Delaware Press, 1976), p. 201.
13 UP I: 136.
14 Weslager, op. cit., p. 109.
15 Ketchum, op. cit., p. 129.
16 Ibid., pp. 140–42.
17 Stahr, op. cit., p. 22.
18 Ketchum, op. cit., pp. 145, 147.
19 Ibid., p. 206.
20 JJ to Robert R. Livingston, Jr., 2 April 1765 (UP I:72).
21 UP I:89.
22 JJ to Robert R. Livingston, Jr., 1 January 1775 (UP I:139).
23 JJ to John Tabor Kempe, 27 December 1771 (UP I:107); JJ to Robert Randall, 2 February 1773 (UP I:116–17); William Jay, op. cit., I:14–15.
24 JJ to Robert R. Livingston, Jr., 1 January 1775 (UP I:139).
25 Gouverneur Morris to Kitty Livingston, 11 January 1773 (SL, p. 27).
26 Kitty Livingston to Brockholst Livingston, 3 September 1781 (SL, p. 14).
27 UP I:129–30.
28 Stahr, op. cit., pp. 30, 33–38; Ketchum, op. cit., p. 327; UP I:133–37.
29 Stahr, op. cit., p. 44; UP I:136.
30 JJ, *Address to the People of Great Britain*, 5 September 1774 (William Jay, op. cit., I:465–76).
31 JJ to John Vardill, 24 September 1774 (UP I:137).
32 UP I:148.
33 Ketchum, op. cit., p. 350.
34 UP I:196; William Jay, op. cit., I:29, 44, 48.
35 Stahr, op. cit., p. 57; JJ to the Secret Committee, 7 August 1776 (UP I:301–3).
36 JJ to the Count of Floridablanca, 25 April 1780 (William Jay, op. cit., II:453).
37 William Jay, op. cit., I:41; Ketchum, op. cit., pp. xii, 306.
38 SL, p. 293.
39 JJ to Edward Rutledge, 6 July 1776 (William Jay, op. cit., I:62).
40 JJ to Edward Rutledge, 11 October 1776 (William Jay, op. cit., II:7); UP I:277–78.
41 William Jay, op. cit., I:49.
42 J. F. Cooper, *The Spy: A Tale of the Neutral Ground*, Introduction.
43 JJ to Frederick Jay, 31 July 1781 (William Jay, op. cit., II:85–86); *Deposition of John Bennett*, 11 November 1785 (UP II:202–3).
44 Cooper, *The Spy*, Ch. 1; Thomas Paine, *The Rights of Man*, Ch. 2.
45 John C. Hamilton, *The Life of Alexander Hamilton* (New York: Appleton, 1840), I:216–17.

46 *Minutes of the Committee for Detecting Conspiracies*, 23 December 1776; *Enoch Crosby Describes His Career as a Spy*, 15 October 1832 (UP I:333–45).
47 JJ to Gouverneur Morris, 29 April 1778 (UP I:475).
48 JJ et al., *Report of the Judges of Oyer and Terminer to Governor George Clinton*, 19 May 1778 (UP I:479–81).
49 Max Weber, *Politics as a Vocation*, tr. H. H. Gerth and C. Wright Mills (Philadelphia: Fortress Press, 1968), pp. 45–46, 49.
50 William Jay, op. cit., I:50.
51 Ibid., op. cit., I:41–42.
52 JJ to the Count of Floridablanca, 25 April 1780 (William Jay, op. cit., I:445).
53 *Minutes of the Committee for Detecting Conspiracies*, 22 February 1777 (UP I:346–48); Beverly Robinson to JJ, 4 March 1777 (UP I:349–50); Robert Troup to JJ, 29 March 1777 (UP I:384).
54 UP I:331–32; JJ to Peter Van Schaack, 17 September 1782, in Richard B. Morris, ed., *John Jay: The Winning of the Peace, Unpublished Papers 1780–1784* (New York: Harper & Row, 1980 [UP II]), pp. 467–68.
55 Peter Van Schaack to JJ, 15 October 1782 (William Jay, op. cit., I:162–65).
56 Ibid., I:113.
57 JJ, *Address from the Convention to Their Constituents*, 23 December 1776 (William Jay, op. cit., I:52–54).
58 JJ, *Circular Letter from Congress to Their Constituents* (William Jay, op. cit., I:485–86).
59 JJ to John Adams, 4 May 1786 (JP #7461, William Jay, op. cit., I:249).
60 JJ to E. Gerry, 9 January 1781 (JP #8827, William Jay, op. cit., II:68).
61 UP I:195, 509–10.
62 JJ to George Washington, 26 April 1779 (JP #8414, William Jay, op. cit., II:48).
63 UP I:511; JJ to George Washington, 6 April 1779 (William Jay, op. cit., II:35); George Washington to JJ, 14 April 1779 (William Jay, op. cit., II:26–43).
64 George Washington to JJ, April 1779 (JP #7232, William Jay, op. cit., II:47); JJ to George Washington, 21 April 1778 (JP #7231, William Jay, op. cit., II:45); JJ to George Washington, 26 April 1779 (JP #8417, William Jay, op. cit., II:48); JJ to George Washington, 14 October 1779 (William Jay, op. cit., II:52).
65 William Jay, op. cit., I:39–41.
66 A. R. Riggs, *The Nine Lives of Arthur Lee, Virginia Patriot* (Williamsburg: Virginia Independence Bicentennial Commission, 1979), pp. 47–49, 51.
67 UP I:507–8, Conrad Alexandre Gérard to Congress, 6 January 1779 (UP I:521).
68 JJ, *Extracts from Mr. Jay's History of His Spanish Mission* (William Jay, op. cit., I:100).
69 William Livingston to Sarah Jay, 7 October 1779 (SL, p. 61).
70 Sarah Jay to Susanna French Livingston, 12–16 December 1779 (SL, pp. 65–68); Stahr, op. cit., p. 125.
71 Sarah Jay to Peter Jay, 9 January 1780 (SL, pp. 70–73).
72 UP I:649–50, 715, 824; JJ, *Extracts from Mr. Jay's History of His Spanish Mission* (William Jay, op. cit., I:96–101).

73 Sarah Jay to her sister Susan, 28 August 1780 (SL, pp. 87–88); Sarah Jay to William Livingston, 23 May 1780 (SL, p. 84).
74 JJ to Margaret C. Meredith, 12 May 1780 (SL, p. 77); Sarah Jay to her sister Kitty, 22 July 1781 (SL, p. 113); JJ to Robert R. Livingston, 23 May 1781 (SL, p. 81); Sarah Jay to Susanna French Livingston, 28 August 1780 (SL, pp. 90–91); William Jay, op. cit., I:120.
75 UP I:716–18; Benjamin Franklin to JJ, 2 October 1780 (William Jay, op. cit., II:63).
76 UP I:824; UP II:96–97; JJ to Gouverneur Morris, 28 September 1781 (UP II:108–9); UP II:146–47.
77 JJ to Robert Morris, 25 April 1782 (JP #12335, William Jay, op. cit., II:96–98).
78 Sarah Jay to Susanna French Livingston, 28 August 1782 (SL, p. 121).
79 Ketchum, op. cit., p. 77.
80 JJ, *Extracts from Mr. Jay's History of His Spanish Mission* (William Jay, op. cit., I:100); William Jay, op. cit., I:128.
81 UP II:5.
82 William Jay, op. cit., I:140.
83 JJ to Robert R. Livingston, 17 November 1782 (William Jay, op. cit., II:471–72).
84 Ibid., pp. 473–74; *M. de Rayneval's Memoir respecting the Right of the United States to the Navigation of the Mississippi* (in JJ to Robert R. Livingston, 17 November 1782 (William Jay, op. cit., II:476–80, JP #4230).
85 JJ to Robert R. Livingston, 17 November 1782 (William Jay, op. cit., II:458–61, 463); Richard Oswald, *Conversations with Franklin and Jay*, 7-9 August 1782 (UP II:292).
86 JJ to Robert R. Livingston, 17 November 1782 (William Jay, op. cit., II:493–95, JP #4230).
87 William Jay, op. cit., I: 156.
88 Oswald, op. cit., 7–9 August 1782 (UP II:289); Oswald, op. cit., 11–13 August 1782 (UP II:298–99).
89 François Barbé-Marbois to the Count de Vergennes, 13 March 1782 (William Jay, op. cit., I:491–92, JP #6407).
90 JJ to Robert R. Livingston, 17 November 1782 (William Jay, op. cit., II:483–84).
91 UP II:334.
92 JJ to Robert R. Livingston, 17 November 1782 (William Jay, op. cit., II:484–87, JP #4230).
93 Benjamin Vaughan to Lord Shelburne, 24 August 1782 (UP II:324).
94 UP II:437; John Adams, Benjamin Franklin, Henry Laurens, John Jay to Robert R. Livingston, 13 December 1782 (UP II:442); William Jay, op. cit., I:155.
95 UP II:519.
96 JJ to Robert R. Livingston, 19 July 1783 (William Jay, op. cit., I:175–78, JP #2748, 4230); JJ to Robert R. Livingston, 17 November 1782 (William Jay, op. cit., II:493–94).
97 JJ to Robert Gooloe Harper, 19 January 1796 (William Jay, op. cit., II:262–63, JP #90212).

98 Alexander Hamilton to JJ, 25 July 1782 (William Jay, op. cit., II:122–23).
99 Thomas Jefferson to JJ, 11 April 1783 (William Jay, op. cit., I:171, JP #10093).
100 JJ to Robert R. Livingston, 12 September 1783 (William Jay, op. cit., II:128, JP #846).
101 Sarah Jay to JJ, 27 November 1783 (SL, p. 154).
102 Stahr, op. cit., p. 203.
103 William Jay, op. cit., I:238–42.
104 JJ to Judge Lowell, 10 May 1785 (William Jay, op. cit., I:190, JP #1642).
105 JJ to George Washington, 7 January 1787 (William Jay, op. cit., I:256, JP #8424).
106 JJ to George Washington, 16 March 1786 (William Jay, op. cit., I:242, JP #8420).
107 William Jay, op. cit., I:261–62.
108 JJ to Governor Livingston, 19 July 1783 (William Jay, op. cit., II:122, JP #90225).
109 JJ to Rufus King, 20 January 1803 (SL, p. 283, JP #700); JJ to William Wilberforce, 8 November 1809 (William Jay, op. cit., II:320, JP #9281).
110 JJ to his children [extracts] (William Jay, op. cit., II:429, JP #6363).
111 JJ to Major General Henry Lee, 11 July 1795 (William Jay, op. cit., I:370, JP #12870).
112 JJ to General Washington, 27 June 1786 (William Jay, op. cit., I:246, JP #8422).
113 JJ to William P. Beers, 18 April 1807 (William Jay, op. cit., II:310, JP #12578); JJ to Judge Lowell, 29 February 1796 (William Jay, op. cit., II:265, JP #2959).
114 JJ to General Washington, 27 June 1786.
115 JJ to Thomas Jefferson, 27 October 1786 (William Jay, op. cit., II:190, JP #5280); JJ to the Marquis de Lafayette, 16 June 1786 (William Jay, op. cit., II:186–87).
116 JJ to Judge Lowell, 29 February 1796 (William Jay, op. cit., II:265, JP #12871).
117 JJ to William Wilberforce, 25 October 1810 (William Jay, op. cit., II:331, JP #9278).
118 JJ to Judge Richard Peters, 24 July 1809 (William Jay, op. cit., II:315, JP #1155).
119 JJ to William Wilberforce, 25 October 1810 (William Jay, op. cit., II:330, JP #9278).
120 Cicero, *De Officiis*, II:24, 85.
121 JJ to Judge Richard Peters, 29 March 1811 (William Jay, op. cit., II:338–39, JP #4050).
122 JJ to John Bristed, 23 April 1811 (William Jay, op. cit., II:347, JP #8709).
123 JJ to Silas Deane, 1 November 1780 (William Jay, op. cit., I:119, JP #7783).
124 JJ to Sarah Jay, 18 June 1792 (SL, p. 213).
125 JJ to Sarah Jay, 21 July 1776 (SL, p. 40).
126 JJ to Thomas Jefferson, 14 December 1786 (William Jay, op. cit., I:251, JP #5860); JJ to William Bingham, 31 May 1785 (William Jay, op. cit., II:166, JP #7480); JJ to Rev. Dr. Witherspoon, 6 April 1784 (William Jay, op. cit., II:154, JP #9450); cf. JJ to Dr. Rush, 24 March 1785 (William Jay, op. cit., II:162).
127 Stahr, op. cit., pp. 233, 4, 378.

128 JJ to Rufus King, 20 January 1803 (William Jay, op. cit., I:431, JP #700).
129 JJ to William Vaughan, 26 May 1796 (William Jay, op. cit., II:272).
130 JJ to George Hammond, 15 June 1796 (William Jay, op. cit., II:273, JP #8964).
131 JJ to Benjamin Vaughan, 31 August 1797 (SL, p. 262).
132 Stahr, op. cit., pp. 254, 265–67.
133 Abigail Adams Smith to Abigail Adams, 20 May 1788 (SL, p. 167).
134 Stahr, op. cit., pp. 273–80.
135 JJ to Sarah Jay, 12 December 1790 (SL, p. 196); JJ to George Washington, 14 April 1789 (William Jay, op. cit., I:277); Stahr, op. cit., pp. 277, 279.
136 Sarah Jay to JJ, 13 November 1791 (SL, p. 201).
137 Hamilton had foreseen just such a role for the "SUPREME TRIBUNAL" in *Federalist* 22 (Hamilton LoA, pp. 249–50).
138 Stahr, op. cit., pp. 281, 291, 297–300.
139 JJ to William Wilberforce, 14 April 1806 (William Jay, op. cit., II:308, JP #9284).
140 William Jay, op. cit., I:317–20; Stahr, op. cit., pp. 302–3.
141 William Jay, op. cit., I:305–6; Alan Taylor, *The Divided Ground: Indians, Settlers, and the Northern Borderland of the American Revolution* (New York: Vintage, 2007), pp. 283, 287.
142 JJ to Sarah Jay, 15 April 1794 (SL, pp. 220–21).
143 JJ to Sarah Jay, 20 April 1794 (SL, p. 223).
144 Sarah Jay to JJ, 22 April 1794 (SL, p. 224).
145 JJ to George Washington, 21 July 1794 (William Jay, op. cit., II:218–19, JP #8449).
146 JJ to George Washington, 5 August 1794 (William Jay, op. cit., II:221, JP #8450).
147 George Washington to JJ, 30 August 1794 (William Jay, op. cit., II:226–27, JP #7255); Taylor, op. cit., p. 287; George Washington to JJ, 30 August 1794 (GW LoA, p. 880).
148 George Washington to JJ, 1 November 1794 (William Jay, op. cit., II:233); George Washington, *Sixth Annual Message to Congress*, 19 November 1794 (GW LoA, p. 888).
149 JJ to George Washington, 25 February 1795 (William Jay, op. cit., II:243–44); George Morgan, *The Life of James Monroe* (Boston: Small, Maynard, 1921), p. 183.
150 JJ to George Washington, 6 March 1795 (William Jay, op. cit., II:246–47, JP #8456).
151 JJ to Edmund Randolph (William Jay, op. cit., I:325).
152 JJ to Peter Van Schaack, 28 July 1812 (William Jay, op. cit., I:445, JP #9440).
153 William Jay, op. cit., I:326, 328, 378.
154 JJ to Lord Lansdown, 20 April 1786 (William Jay, op. cit., II:185, JP #8171).
155 JJ to Edward Randolph (William Jay, op. cit., I:334); JJ to Oliver Ellsworth, 19 November 1794 (William Jay, op. cit., II:235).
156 JJ to James Duane, 16 September 1795 (William Jay, op. cit., I:375–76).

157 Stahr, op. cit., pp. 336–37.
158 JJ to Robert Gooloe Harper, 19 January 1796 (William Jay, op. cit., II:261, JP #7260).
159 Stahr, op. cit., p. 338.
160 Ibid., pp. 340–41.
161 Ibid., p. 345; William Jay, op. cit., I:396; O. F. Lewis, *The Development of American Prisons and Prison Customs, 1776–1845* (Albany: Prison Association of New York, 1922), pp. 43–44.
162 JJ to Egbert Benson, 18 September 1780 (JP #7513).
163 William Jay, op. cit., I:407–8.
164 Alexander Hamilton to JJ, 7 May 1800 (AH LoA, pp. 923–25, JP #5635); William Jay, op. cit., I:412–14.
165 Stahr, op. cit., pp. 362–63.
166 William Jay, op. cit., I:461.
167 Ibid., I:442–43.
168 JJ to Peter A. Jay, 25 April 1792 (SL, p. 205).
169 Sarah Jay to JJ, 13 July 1801 (SL, pp. 277–78).
170 Sarah Jay to Maria Jay Banyer, 2 December 1801 (SL, p. 278).
171 Sarah Jay to Maria Jay Banyer, 5 May 1802 (SL, p. 281).
172 JJ to Rufus King, 20 January 1803 (SL, p. 283, JP #700).
173 William Jay, op. cit., I:462.
174 Ibid., I:434.
175 Cicero, *De Officiis*, Book III: I, 2; XVI, 67; V, 26; X, 40.
176 JJ to Philip Schuyler, 25 July 1804 (William Jay, op. cit., II:300).
177 JJ to Judge Richard Peters, 9 January 1811 (William Jay, op. cit., II:336, JP #1156).

CHAPTER 7: Alexander Hamilton and the American Dream

1 GW to David Humphreys, 25 July 1785, in George Washington, *Writings*, John Rhodehamel, ed. (Library of America, 1997), pp. 579–80.
2 AH to William Jackson, 26 August 1800, in Alexander Hamilton, *Writings*, Joanne B. Freeman, ed. (Library of America, 2001 [LoA]), p. 930; John Adams to Benjamin Rush, 25 January 1806.
3 AH to William Jackson, 26 August 1800 (LoA, p. 931).
4 Ron Chernow, *Alexander Hamilton* (New York: Penguin, 2004), pp. 8, 10–11, 16–17, 20.
5 AH to William Jackson, 26 August 1800 (LoA, p. 931); AH to William Hamilton, 2 May 1797 (LoA, p. 880).
6 Chernow, op. cit., pp. 21, 580.
7 Ibid., pp. 22–26.
8 Ibid., pp. 27–28.
9 Richard Brookhiser, "Alexander Hamilton: New Yorker," *City Journal*, Autumn 1996.

10 John C. Hamilton, *The Life of Alexander Hamilton* (New York: Appleton, 1840), I:6.
11 AH to Nicholas Cruger, 27 February 1772 (LoA, pp. 4–5).
12 AH to Edward Stevens, 11 November 1769 (LoA, p. 3).
13 "Account of a Hurricane," *Royal Danish American Gazette*, 6 September 1772 (LoA, pp. 6–9).
14 Chernow, op. cit., pp. 37–78, 47–48.
15 E. Digby Baltzell, *Puritan Boston and Quaker Philadelphia* (New York: Free Press, 1979), pp. 34–38; David Hackett Fischer, *Albion's Seed: Four British Folkways in America* (New York: Oxford University Press, 1989).
16 David McCullough, *John Adams* (New York: Simon & Schuster, 2001), p. 25.
17 Russell Shorto, *The Island at the Center of the World* (New York: Vintage, 2005), pp. 96, 274–76.
18 Ibid., p. 272.
19 Ibid., pp. 268, 61, 271, 194–95.
20 Ibid., pp. 28, 3, 270, 304–5.
21 Gouverneur Morris to Robert Livingston, Jr., 20 March 1802, *The Diary and Letters of Gouverneur Morris, Minister of the United States to France; Member of the Constitutional Convention*, Anne Cary Morris, ed. (New York: Charles Scribner's Sons, 1888), II, Ch. 42 (Liberty Fund: Online Library of Liberty).
22 Chernow, op. cit., p. 55; AH, *A Full Vindication of the Measures of the Congress*, 15 December 1774 (LoA, pp. 15, 19–20, 29, 41); *The Farmer Refuted*, 23 February 1775 (Liberty Fund: Online Library of Liberty).
23 Catherine Drinker Bowen, *Miracle at Philadelphia* (Boston: Little, Brown, 1966), p. 108.
24 Chernow, op. cit., pp. 63, 72–73, 81, 92.
25 AH, *Eulogium on Major-General Greene, Presented to the Society of Cincinnati*, 4 July 1789 (Liberty Fund: Online Library of Liberty).
26 AH to Tobias Lear, 2 January 1800.
27 Chernow, op. cit., p. 88.
28 GW to John Adams, 25 September 1798 (LoA, p. 1013).
29 Chernow, op. cit., p. 90.
30 Ibid., p. 95.
31 AH to John Laurens, April 1779 (LoA, p. 61).
32 AH to John Laurens, 8 January 1780 (LoA, p. 66).
33 Chernow, op. cit., pp. 86–87.
34 AH to Philip Schuyler, 18 February 1781 (LoA, pp. 93–95).
35 Ibid.
36 Chernow, op. cit., pp. 110–11.
37 AH to James Duane, 3 September 1780 (LoA, pp. 70–87).
38 Chernow, op. cit., pp. 128–30, 147–48; Shorto, op. cit., p. 310.
39 Chernow, op. cit., pp. 168–69.
40 Ibid., pp. 184–85, 206, 109–201, 189.
41 Bowen, op. cit., pp. 5–6.

42 Ibid., p. 208; AH, "Speech in the Constitutional Convention," recorded by James Madison, 18 June 1787 (LoA, p. 151); AH, "Speech in the Constitutional Convention," recorded by Robert Yates, 18 June 1787 (LoA, pp. 159, 165); AH, "Plan of Government," 18 June 1787 (LoA, pp. 149–50).
43 AH, "Speech in the Constitutional Convention," recorded by James Madison, 18 June 1787 (LoA, p. 155).
44 Ibid., p. 156.
45 Bernard Bailyn, *The Ideological Origins of the American Revolution*, enlarged edition (Cambridge, MA: Harvard University Press, 1967), pp. 276, 283–84, 288–90; *Records of the Federal Convention*, Max Ferrand, ed. (New Haven, CT: Yale University Press, 1911), III:413.
46 AH, "Speech in the Constitutional Convention," recorded by James Madison, 18 June 1787 (LoA, pp. 156–57) and as recorded by Robert Yates (LoA, p. 164); Bailyn, op. cit., p. 346.
47 AH, "Speech in the Constitutional Convention," recorded by James Madison, 18 June 1787 (LoA, p. 158) and as recorded by Robert Yates (LoA, p. 165).
48 Chernow, op. cit., pp. 63–64, 68–69.
49 AH to John Jay, 26 November 1775 (LoA, p. 44).
50 *Federalist* 6 (LoA, pp. 178–79); Burke, *Reflections on the Revolution in France* (Garden City, NY: Doubleday Anchor Books, 1973), p. 100: "We are afraid to put men to live and trade each on his own private stock of reason; because we suspect that this stock in each man is small, and that the individuals would do better to avail themselves of the general bank and capital of nations, and of ages."
51 *Federalist* 15 (LoA, p. 223).
52 *Federalist* 6 (LoA, p. 181).
53 *Federalist* 9 (LoA, p. 197).
54 *Federalist* 1 (LoA, p. 171).
55 *Federalist* 23 (LoA, p. 256).
56 *Federalist* 8 (LoA, pp. 194–95).
57 *Federalist* 1 (LoA, p. 173).
58 *Federalist* 11 (LoA, p. 204); *Federalist* 23 (LoA, p. 253).
59 *Federalist* 24 (LoA, p. 262).
60 *Federalist* 30 (LoA, p. 290); *Federalist* 31 (LoA, p. 298).
61 *Federalist* 21 (LoA, p. 241).
62 *Federalist* 23 (LoA, pp. 254–55).
63 *Federalist* 78 (LoA, pp. 422–23).
64 Chernow, op. cit., pp. 263–64, 268–69.
65 Ibid., p. 286.
66 Forrest McDonald, *Alexander Hamilton: A Biography* (New York: W. W. Norton, 1979), pp. 120–21.
67 Daniel Webster, "A Speech Delivered at a Public Dinner in New York," 10 March 1831, in *The Works of Daniel Webster*, 20th edition (Boston: Little, Brown, 1890), I:200.

68 AH, *Report on Manufactures*, 5 December 1791 (LoA, pp. 662, 656, 659, 663–64).
69 Ibid., p. 660.
70 Ibid., p. 666.
71 Ibid., pp. 668–69.
72 AH, *Report on Public Credit*, 9 January 1790 (LoA, pp. 533, 535).
73 Ibid., pp. 569–71; Chernow, op. cit., p. 382.
74 *Report on Public Credit* (LoA, pp. 537–40).
75 Ibid., pp. 542, 544, 547.
76 Chernow, op. cit., pp. 328–30; Brookhiser, op. cit.
77 *Report on Public Credit* (LoA, p. 560).
78 AH, *Report on a National Bank*, 13 December 1790 (LoA, p. 576).
79 Ibid., pp. 577–78.
80 Ibid., p. 604.
81 AH, *Federalist* 11 (LoA, p. 205).
82 AH to James Duane, 2 September 1780 (LoA, p. 81).
83 *Report on a National Bank* (LoA, pp. 578, 585); Chernow, op. cit., p. 356.
84 Webster, op. cit., p. 200.
85 *Report on a National Bank* (LoA, pp. 582, 592, 601–3).
86 Chernow, op. cit., p. 346.
87 Jefferson, *Opinion on the Constitutionality of a National Bank*, 15 February 1791 (TJ LoA, p. 416).
88 Bailyn, op. cit., p. 345.
89 Chernow, op. cit., p. 350.
90 George Morgan, *The True Patrick Henry* (Philadelphia: Lippincott, 1907), p. 353.
91 Bowen, op. cit., pp. 200–204.
92 Chernow, op. cit., pp. 213–14.
93 Samuel Johnson, *Taxation No Tyranny: An Answer to the Resolutions and Address of the American Congress*, 1775, in *Works* (New York: Harper, 1846), II:437; AH to Lafayette, 6 October 1789 (LoA, p. 521).
94 *Federalist* 6 (LoA, pp. 176, 181).
95 AH to Lafayette, 6 October 1789 (LoA, p. 521).
96 AH to John Jay, 26 November 1775 (LoA, p. 44); *Federalist* 15 (LoA, p. 223).
97 *Records of the Federal Convention*, III:85.
98 AH, *Letter from Alexander Hamilton, Concerning the Public Conduct and Character of John Adams, Esq. President of the United States*, 24 October 1800 (LoA, p. 970).
99 Chernow, op. cit., p. 245.
100 Madison, "A Candid State of the Parties," *National Gazette*, 26 September 1792 (JM LoA, p. 531).
101 AH, *An American No. 1*, 4 August 1792 (LoA, pp. 756, 759).
102 Thomas Jefferson to Dr. Walter Jones, 5 March 1810 (Bernard Mayo, ed., *Jefferson Himself: The Personal Narrative of a Many-Sided American* [Charlottesville: University Press of Virginia, 1942], p. 186); Chernow, op. cit., p. 390; AH, *Observations on Certain Documents Contained in No. V & VI of "The History of the United States for the Year 1786," In Which the Charge of Speculation Against Alex-*

ander Hamilton, Late Secretary of the Treasury, is Fully Refuted. Written by Himself ("Reynolds Pamphlet," LoA, pp. 884–85).

103 Ibid. (LoA, pp. 894–95).

104 AH to Elizabeth Schuyler, 25 September 1780 (LoA, pp. 89–91).

105 AH, "Reynolds Pamphlet," (LoA), pp. 895–99.

106 Ibid. (LoA, p. 906).

107 Ibid. (LoA, pp. 898–99, 909).

108 Ibid. (LoA, pp. 891, 888, 901–3).

109 Ibid. (LoA, p. 904).

110 Chernow, op. cit., pp. 529–31, 549.

111 Ibid., p. 535.

112 AH, *Letter from Alexander Hamilton*, 24 October 1800 (LoA, pp. 940–43); Chernow, op. cit., pp. 510, 515, 554, 525, 612.

113 AH, *Letter from Alexander Hamilton, Concerning the Public Conduct and Character of John Adams, Esq. President of the United States*, 24 October 1800 (LoA, pp. 935, 937, 960, 970–71).

114 Chernow, op. cit., pp. 626, 628.

115 David Garrard Lowe, "The Triumph of Rockefeller Center," *City Journal*, Summer 1995; Chernow, op. cit., pp. 641–44.

116 Chernow, op. cit., p. 650.

117 Ibid., pp. 674, 169.

118 AH to an Unknown Correspondent, 26 September 1792 (LoA, p. 794).

119 AH, *Letter from Alexander Hamilton*, 24 October 1800 (LoA, pp. 951–52).

120 AH to Benjamin Rush, 29 March 1802 (LoA, p. 987); Thomas Fleming, *The Duel: Alexander Hamilton, Aaron Burr, and the Future of America* (New York: Basic Books, 1999), pp. 7–9, 21, 303.

121 Chernow, op. cit., p. 655.

122 Ibid., pp. 674–77.

123 Charles D. Cooper to Philip Schuyler, *Albany Register*, 24 April 1804 (LoA, pp. 1009–10).

124 Aaron Burr to AH, 23 April 1804 (LoA, p. 1008).

125 AH to Aaron Burr, 20 June 1804 (LoA, pp. 1011–12).

126 Aaron Burr to AH, 22 June 1804 (LoA, pp. 1014–15).

127 "Statement by Nathaniel Pendleton," 18 July 1804 (LoA, p. 1029).

128 Chernow, op. cit., pp. 691–92.

129 Ibid., p. 700.

130 "Statement by William P. Van Ness," 21 July 1804 (LoA, p. 1030); "Statement by Nathaniel Pendleton," 18 July 1804 (LoA, pp. 1029–30).

131 Chernow, op. cit., pp. 704, 708.

132 AH, "Statement Regarding Financial Situation," 1 July 1804 (LoA, pp. 1016–17).

133 AH to Elizabeth Hamilton, 19 November 1798 (LoA, p. 912).

134 Personal communication from Stephen Spaulding and Steve Laise, National Park Service.

135 George Washington to AH, 21 August 1797 (Papers of George Washington, Digital Edition, Charlottesville: University of Virginia Press, 2008).

CHAPTER 8: Thomas Jefferson: Monticello's Shadows

1 R. B. Bernstein, *Thomas Jefferson* (New York: Oxford University Press, 2003), pp. 62–64; Fawn M. Brodie, *Thomas Jefferson: An Intimate History* (New York: W. W. Norton, 1974), p. 29.

2 TJ to Maria Cosway, 12 October 1786, Thomas Jefferson, *Writings*, Merrill D. Peterson, ed. (Library of America, 1984 [LoA]), pp. 872, 874.

3 Ibid. (LoA, p. 870).

4 Jack McLaughlin, *Jefferson and Monticello: The Biography of a Builder* (New York: Henry Holt, 1998), pp. 34, 154–55.

5 TJ to John Adams, 11 April 1823 (LoA, pp. 1466–67).

6 Bernstein, op. cit., p. 178.

7 TJ to Samuel H. Smith, 21 September 1814 (LoA, pp. 1353–54).

8 TJ, *Autobiography* (LoA, p. 3); TJ, *Notes on the State of Virginia*, Query VI (LoA, pp. 169–77); Antonello Gerbi, *The Dispute of the New World: The History of a Polemic, 1750–1900*, Jeremy Moyle, trans. (Pittsburgh: University of Pittsburgh Press, 2010), pp. 3–9; Hugh Honour, *The New Golden Land: Images of America from the Discoveries to the Present Time* (New York: Pantheon, 1976), p. 51.

9 TJ, *Sixth Annual Message*, 2 December 1806 (LoA, p. 527).

10 Bernstein, op. cit., pp. 141–44; TJ, *Notes on the State of Virginia*, Query VI (LoA, pp. 184–85, 187–88).

11 TJ to William Ludlow, 6 September 1824 (LoA, pp. 1496–97).

12 TJ to James Jay, 7 April 1809 (Bernard Mayo, ed., *Jefferson Himself: The Personal Narrative of a Many-Sided American* [Charlottesville: University Press of Virginia, 1942], p. 293).

13 Bernstein, op. cit., pp. 144–45.

14 TJ to Rev. James Madison, 19 July 1788 (LoA, p. 925).

15 TJ to Robert Fulton, 17 March 1819 (Mayo, op. cit., p. 289).

16 TJ to Charles Thomson, 11 November 1784 (Mayo, op. cit., p. 124); TJ to John Jay, 30 August 1785 (Mayo, op. cit., p. 124).

17 TJ to Charles W. Peale, 13 June 1815 (Mayo, op. cit., p. 289).

18 Bernstein, op. cit., p. 118.

19 TJ to Edward Rutledge, 18 July 1788 (Mayo, op. cit., p. 146).

20 TJ to Major John Cartwright, 5 June 1824 (LoA, p. 1491).

21 TJ, *A Declaration by the Representatives of the United States of America, in General Congress Assembled* (LoA, p. 19).

22 TJ, *A Summary View of the Rights of British America* (LoA, p. 121).

23 TJ to Richard Price, 8 January 1789 (LoA, p. 936).

24 TJ, *Autobiography* (LoA, p. 5); TJ to Robert Fulton, 17 March 1810 (Mayo, op. cit., pp. 289–90).

25 TJ to Dr. Benjamin Rush, 23 September 1800 (LoA, p. 1082).

26 TJ to Roger C. Weightman, 24 June 1826 (LoA, p. 1517).

27 TJ, *Autobiography* (LoA, pp. 34–35, 44).

28 TJ, *A Bill for Establishing Religious Freedom* (LoA, p. 347).

29 TJ, *Notes on the State of Virginia*, Query XIV (LoA, p. 272); TJ, *Autobiography* (LoA, p. 32).
30 TJ to George Wythe, 13 August 1786 (LoA, pp. 859–60).
31 TJ, *Notes on the State of Virginia*, Query XVII (LoA, p. 285).
32 TJ to Samuel Kercheval, 12 July 1816 (LoA, p. 1401); TJ to Major John Cartwright, 5 June 1824 (LoA, p. 1494); TJ to James Madison, 6 September 1789 (LoA, p. 963).
33 Bernstein, op. cit., pp. 173–75.
34 TJ to A. L. C. Destutt de Tracy, 26 December 1820 (Mayo, op. cit., p. 327).
35 TJ to Dr. William Thornton, 9 May 1817 (Mayo, op. cit., p. 325).
36 Bernstein, op. cit., pp. 176–77.
37 McLaughlin, op. cit., p. 256.
38 TJ, *Notes on the State of Virginia*, Query XIV (LoA, pp. 265–67, 270).
39 Bernstein, op. cit., pp. 87–88.
40 TJ, *A Declaration by the Representatives of the United States of America, in General Congress Assembled* (LoA, p. 22).
41 TJ to Henri Gregoire, 25 February 1809 (LoA, p. 1202).
42 TJ, *Notes on the State of Virginia*, Query XVIII (LoA, p. 289).
43 Ibid. (LoA, p. 288).
44 TJ to Jean Nicolas Démeunier, 26 June 1786 (LoA, p. 592).
45 TJ to James Madison, 25 April 1784; TJ to Jean Nicolas Démeunier, 22 June 1786 (Mayo, op. cit., p. 109).
46 TJ to John Holmes, 22 April 1820 (LoA, p. 1434).
47 Thomas Moore, *To Thomas Hume, Esq., M.D. from the City of Washington*.
48 Lucia Stanton, *Free Some Day: The African-American Families at Monticello* (Monticello: Thomas Jefferson Foundation, 2000), pp. 114–15.
49 Ibid., p. 103.
50 Thomas Jefferson Foundation, *Report of the Research Committee on Thomas Jefferson and Sally Hemings* (January 2000). *http://www.monticello.org/site/plantation-and-slavery/report-research-committee-thomas-jefferson-and-sally-hemings* provides the report, the minority report, and further discussion.
51 Bernstein, op. cit., pp. 66–67, 111.
52 Robert F. Turner, ed., *The Jefferson-Hemings Controversy: Report of the Scholars Commission* (Durham, NC: Carolina Academic Press, 2011). An excellent summary of the controversy is Maura Singleton, "Anatomy of a Mystery: The Jefferson-Hemings Controversy in the Post-DNA Era," *University of Virginia Magazine*, Fall 2007.
53 Bernstein, op. cit., pp. 155–56.
54 Ibid., pp. 110–11; Thomas Jefferson Foundation, *Thomas Jefferson Encyclopedia*, s.v. Sally Hemings (*http://www.monticello.org/site/plantation-and-slavery/sally-hemings*).
55 Annette Gordon-Reed, *The Hemingses of Monticello: An American Family* (New York: W. W. Norton, 2008), p. 230; McLaughlin, op. cit., p. 200.
56 Brodie, op. cit., pp. 32, 228; Gordon-Reed, op. cit., pp. 122, 285–86.

57 TJ to Francis Eppes, 30 August 1785 (Mayo, op. cit., p. 117); TJ to Francis Eppes, 11 December 1785 (Mayo, op. cit., p. 118).
58 McLaughlin, op. cit., pp. 14, 153.
59 TJ to Madame de Tessé, 20 March 1787 (LoA, p. 891).
60 McLaughlin, op. cit., pp. 248, 289–90, 373, 258.
61 TJ to Dr. Benjamin Rush, 16 January 1811 (LoA, p. 1236).
62 TJ to William Short, 3 January 1793 (Mayo, op. cit., p. 185).
63 Edmund Burke, *Reflections on the Revolution in France* (Garden City, NY: Doubleday Anchor Books, 1973), p. 91.
64 TJ, *The Anas* (LoA, p. 666).
65 TJ to J. Correa de Serra, 25 November 1817 (Mayo, op. cit., p. 326).

CHAPTER 9: James Madison: Theory

1 Paul Jennings, *A Colored Man's Reminiscences of James Madison* (Brooklyn: George C. Beadle, 1865), pp. 18–19.
2 Ralph Ketcham, *James Madison: A Biography* (Charlottesville: University Press of Virginia, 1990), pp. 19, 31.
3 JM, *Autobiography* (MS, Library of Congress), p. 1; JM to William Bradford, 9 November 1772, James Madison, *Writings*, Jack N. Rakove, ed. (Library of America, 1999 [LoA], p. 3).
4 JM to William Bradford, 24 January 1774 (LoA, pp. 5, 7); Ketcham, op. cit., p. 38.
5 JM to William Bradford, 24 January 1774 (LoA, p. 9).
6 Ketcham, op. cit., pp. 63, 68–73; JM, *Amendments to the Virginia Declaration of Rights*, 29 May–11 June 1776 (LoA, p. 10); JM, *Autobiography*, p. 3.
7 JM, *Memorial and Remonstrance Against Religious Assessments*, 20 June 1785 (LoA, pp. 30–36); Ketcham, op. cit., pp. 161–65.
8 Ketcham, op. cit., pp. 165, 167; JM to Edward Livingston, 10 July 1822 (LoA, p. 788); JM, *Memorial and Remonstrance Against Religious Assessments*, 20 June 1785 (LoA, p. 32).
9 JM, "Monopolies, Perpetuities, Corporations, Ecclesiastical Endowments," *Detached Memoranda*, 1819 (LoA, pp. 762–66).
10 JM, *Autobiography*, p. 4.
11 George Washington to Henry Laurens, 23 December 1777 (Washington LoA, p. 282).
12 Andrew Burstein and Nancy Isenberg, *Madison and Jefferson* (New York: Random House, 2010), p. 62.
13 JM to Thomas Jefferson, 27 March 1780 (LoA, p. 11).
14 Ketcham, op. cit., pp. 85–86, 116, 141–42, 105.
15 Ibid., p. 90.
16 Ibid., pp. 104–5.
17 Ibid., pp. 93–95.
18 John Jay, *Extracts from Mr. Jay's History of his Spanish Mission*, in William Jay,

The Life of John Jay (New York: J. & J. Harper, 1833, reprint Bridgewater, VA: American Foundation Publications, 2000), I:100.

19 David McCullough, *John Adams* (New York: Simon & Schuster, 2001), pp. 238, 241.

20 Ketcham, op. cit., pp. 120–21, 128–29; Gaillard Hunt, ed., *The Writings of James Madison* (New York and London: Putnam, 1900), I:208.

21 Ketcham, op. cit., pp. 121–22.

22 Ibid, pp. 122–25.

23 Ibid., pp. 154–57.

24 JM, "Monopolies, Perpetuities, Corporations, Ecclesiastical Endowments," *Detached Memoranda*, 1819 (LoA, p. 764).

25 *Federalist* 63 (LoA, p. 350); *Speech in the Virginia Ratifying Convention on Control of the Military*, 16 June 1788 (LoA, p. 389).

26 Hunt, op. cit., I:67.

27 JM to Thomas Jefferson, 10 April 1781 (LoA, p. 13); Ketcham, op. cit., p. 113.

28 Ketcham, op. cit., pp. 117–18.

29 Ibid., pp. 171–72, 174–75.

30 Walter Stahr, *John Jay: Founding Father* (New York: Hambledon and Continuum, 2006), pp. 213–17.

31 Burstein and Isenberg, op. cit., p. 72; JM to Thomas Jefferson, 12 August 1786 (LoA, p. 56).

32 JM to Thomas Jefferson, 12 August 1786 (LoA, pp. 53–55); Ketcham, op. cit., p. 172.

33 JM to Thomas Jefferson, 12 August 1786 (LoA, p. 55).

34 Burstein and Isenberg, op. cit., p. 128; Ketcham, op. cit., p. 184.

35 JM to Thomas Jefferson, 19 March 1787 (LoA, p. 64); JM, *Federalist* 37 (LoA, p. 196).

36 JM to George Washington, 7 December 1786 (LoA, p. 59); JM to Thomas Jefferson, 6 June 1787 (LoA, p. 96).

37 Thomas Jefferson to John Adams, 30 August 1787 (Jefferson LoA, p. 909).

38 Catherine Drinker Bowen, *Miracle at Philadelphia* (Boston: Little, Brown, 1966), p. 30; JM, *A Sketch Never Finished Nor Applied*, 1830 (LoA, pp. 840–41).

39 Ketcham, op. cit., p. 203; JM, *Speech at the Virginia Ratifying Convention on Ratification and Amendments*, 24 June 1788 (LoA, p. 402); Bowen, op. cit., p. 263.

40 JM, *A Sketch Never Finished Nor Applied*, 1830 (LoA, p. 842); JM to Thomas Jefferson, 24 October 1787 (LoA, p. 144).

41 *The Virginia Plan* (LoA, pp. 89–91).

42 JM, *Federalist* 51 (LoA, p. 295); JM, *Speech in the Virginia Ratifying Convention on the Control of the Military*, 16 June 1788 (LoA, p. 389); Bowen, op. cit., pp. 70–71.

43 JM, *Vices of the Political System of the United States*, April 1787 (LoA, pp. 75–78); JM, *Federalist* 48 (LoA, p. 281); JM, *Speech in the Federal Convention on the Proposed Compromise on State Representation*, 5 July 1787 (LoA, p. 122); JM, *Federalist* 55 (LoA, p. 316).

44 JM, *Federalist* 51 (LoA, pp. 294–96).

45 JM, *Federalist* 10 (LoA, pp. 161–62).
46 JM to Thomas Jefferson, 24 October 1787 (LoA, p. 150).
47 JM, *Federalist* 10 (LoA, p. 161).
48 Ibid., p. 162.
49 Ibid., p. 163.
50 Ibid., p. 167; Burstein and Isenberg, op. cit., pp. 146–47.
51 JM, *Federalist* 10 (LoA, p. 163).
52 Ibid., p. 164.
53 JM, *Vices of the Political System of the United States*, April 1787 (LoA, p. 78).
54 JM, *Federalist* 14 (LoA, p. 173).
55 Perhaps he took the hint from Scottish Enlightenment thinker David Hume's essay, "The Idea of a Perfect Commonwealth."
56 JM to Thomas Jefferson, 24 October 1787 (LoA, p. 145); JM, *Federalist* 10 (LoA, pp. 166–67).
57 JM, *Federalist* 55 (LoA, pp. 319–20).
58 JM, *Federalist* 63 (LoA, p. 347); JM, *Speech in the Federal Convention on the Senate*, 26 June 1787 (LoA, pp. 110–11); Bernard Bailyn, *The Ideological Origins of the American Revolution*, enlarged edition (Cambridge, MA: Harvard University Press, 1967), p. 290.
59 JM, *Federalist* 63 (LoA, p. 345); JM, *Speech in the Federal Convention on the Senate*, 26 June 1787 (LoA, p. 110); JM, *Federalist* 63 (LoA, p. 346); JM, *Federalist* 62 (LoA, pp. 342–43).
60 JM to Caleb Wallace, 23 August 1785 (LoA, p. 43).
61 JM, *Speech in the Federal Convention on the Suffrage*, 7 August 1787 (LoA, pp. 132–33).
62 JM, *Observations on the "Draught of a Constitution for Virginia,"* 15 October 1788 (LoA, p. 411).
63 JM to George Washington, 16 April 1787 (LoA, pp. 80–81).
64 Ketcham, op. cit., p. 197.
65 JM to Thomas Jefferson, 24 October 1787 (LoA, pp. 143–44).
66 JM, *Speech in the Federal Convention Opposing Equal Representation in the Senate*, 14 July 1787 (LoA, p. 124).
67 Bowen, op. cit., p. 93.
68 Ibid., pp. 75, 84; Thomas Jefferson, *Autobiography* (Jefferson LoA, pp. 28–31).
69 JM, *Speech in the Federal Convention Opposing Equal Representation in the Senate*, 14 July 1787 (LoA, p. 124).
70 JM, *Vices of the Political System of the United States*, April 1787 (LoA, p. 72).
71 JM, *Federalist* 20 (LoA, pp. 190, 188).
72 JM, *Federalist* 37 (LoA, pp. 199–200).
73 JM, *Federalist* 14 (LoA, p. 173).
74 JM to Edmund Randolph, 10 January 1788 (LoA, p. 192).
75 JM, *Federalist* 62 (LoA, p. 339).
76 JM, *Speech in the Federal Convention Opposing Equal Representation in the Senate*, 14 July 1787 (LoA, p. 125).

77 JM, *Speech at the Virginia Ratifying Convention on Ratification and Amendments*, 24 June 1788 (LoA, p. 406); JM, *Speech in the Federal Convention Opposing Equal Representation in the Senate*, 14 July 1787 (LoA, p. 125).
78 JM, *Federalist* 54 (LoA, pp. 310–13).
79 JM, *Speech in the Federal Convention on the General and State Governments*, 21 June 1787 (LoA, p. 108).
80 JM, *Federalist* 14 (LoA, p. 170).
81 JM, *Federalist* 45 (LoA, p. 264).
82 JM, *Speech at the Virginia Ratifying Convention on Ratification and Amendments*, 24 June 1788 (LoA, p. 404).
83 Bowen, op. cit., p. 79.
84 JM, *Remarks in the Federal Convention on the Power to Negative State Laws*, 8 June 1787 (LoA, p. 100).
85 Joseph Addison, "The Spacious Firmament on High"; JM *Autobiography*, p. 1; Ketcham, op. cit., pp. 40–41.
86 Alexander Pope, "An Essay on Man," Epistle III, 11, 293–94.
87 JM, *Federalist* 51 (LoA, p. 295).
88 "An Essay on Man," Epistle I, 11, 247–54.

CHAPTER 10: James Madison: Practice

1 Ralph Ketcham, *James Madison: A Biography* (Charlottesville: University Press of Virginia, 1990), p. 277.
2 Jack Rakove, *James Madison and the Creation of the American Republic*, 3rd edition (New York: Longman, 2006), p. 93.
3 Andrew Burstein and Nancy Isenberg, *Madison and Jefferson* (New York: Random House, 2010), p. 189.
4 Ketcham, op. cit., pp. 277–78, 280, 283, 286–87; Burstein and Isenberg, op. cit., p. 191.
5 JM, *Speech at the Virginia Ratifying Convention on Ratification and Amendments*, 24 June 1788, in James Madison, *Writings*, Jack N. Rakove, ed. (Library of America, 1999 [LoA]), p. 405.
6 Gordon S. Wood, *Empire of Liberty: A History of the Early Republic, 1789–1815* (New York: Oxford University Press, 2009), pp. 66–67.
7 JM to Richard Peters, 19 August 1789 (LoA, p. 471); Burstein and Isenberg, op. cit., p. 197.
8 JM to Thomas Jefferson, 17 October 1788 (LoA, pp. 420–22).
9 Ketcham, op. cit., p. 276; JM to George Eve, 2 January 1789 (LoA, pp. 427–28).
10 JM, *Speech in Congress Proposing Constitutional Amendments*, 8 June 1789 (LoA, pp. 437–38).
11 Ibid. (LoA, p. 443); Burstein and Isenberg, op. cit., p. 198.
12 JM, *Remarks in Congress on Proposed Constitutional Amendments*, 15 August 1789 (LoA, p. 470).
13 83 U.S. 36.

14 Ketcham, op. cit., p. 118.
15 JM, *Autobiography* (MS, Library of Congress), p. 9; Ketcham, op. cit., p. 308.
16 Ketcham, op. cit., pp. 307–9.
17 Ibid., pp. 311–12.
18 JM, *Autobiography*, p. 9.
19 Burstein and Isenberg, op. cit., p. 223.
20 Ibid., p. 205.
21 Richard Brookhiser, *Gentleman Revolutionary: Gouverneur Morris, The Rake Who Wrote the Constitution* (New York: Free Press, 2003), p. 199; David B. Mattern and Holly C. Shulman, ed., *The Selected Letters of Dolley Payne Madison* (Charlottesville: University of Virginia Press, 2003 [DPM]), p. 197; John C. Hamilton, *Life of Alexander Hamilton* (Boston: Houghton, Osgood, 1879), VII, 686.
22 Wood, op. cit., p. 147.
23 JM to William Bradford, 9 November 1772 (LoA, p. 4).
24 JM, "Republican Distribution of Citizens," *National Gazette*, 5 March 1792 (LoA, pp. 511–13).
25 JM, "Fashion," *National Gazette*, 22 March 1792 (LoA, pp. 513–14).
26 The oil portrait, by Boston-born, London-based Mather Brown, is in the Smithsonian's National Portrait Gallery.
27 JM, "The Union: Who Are Its Real Friends?" *National Gazette*, 2 April 1792 (LoA, pp. 517–18).
28 JM, *Speech in Congress Opposing the National Bank*, 2 February 1791 (LoA, pp. 480–81).
29 Ibid. (LoA, pp. 482–89).
30 JM, "The Union, Who Are Its Real Friends?" (LoA, p. 518).
31 Ketcham, op. cit., pp. 226–27.
32 JM to Henry Lee, 25 June 1824 (LoA, pp. 803–4); JM, *Speech in Congress on the Jay Treaty*, 6 April 1796 (LoA, p. 574).
33 JM, *Veto Message to Congress*, 3 March 1817 (LoA, pp. 718–20); JM, *Speech in Congress Opposing the National Bank*, 2 February 1791 (LoA, p. 482); JM to Thomas Jefferson, 8 February 1825 (LoA, p. 808). Article I, Section 8 of the Constitution gives Congress the power to build only post roads for the mail, not a network of roads and canals for commerce.
34 JM, *Federalist* 44 (LoA, pp. 255–56); Alexander Hamilton, *Opinion on the Constitutionality of a National Bank*, 23 February 1791 (Hamilton LoA, pp. 613–14).
35 Ketcham, op. cit., p. 291.
36 Ibid., pp. 419–22; Burstein and Isenberg, op. cit., p. 392.
37 Wood, op. cit., p. 144.
38 Hamilton, op. cit., pp. 620–21, 637).
39 Wood, op. cit., p. 243.
40 Ibid., pp. 93, 263.
41 Ibid., p. 250.
42 JM, *Report on the Alien and Sedition Acts*, 7 January 1800 (LoA, p. 651); Ketcham, op. cit., pp. 394–95; Burstein and Isenberg, op. cit., p. 336.

43 Burstein and Isenberg, op. cit., pp. 344–45.
44 Ibid., pp. 336–67, 328.
45 Ketcham, op. cit., p. 396.
46 Burstein and Isenberg, op. cit., p. 340.
47 JM to Edward Everett, 28 August 1830 (LoA, pp. 851–52); JM to James Robertson, 27 March 1832 (LoA, p. 853); LoA, p. 950.
48 JM, *Virginia Resolutions Against the Alien and Sedition Acts*, 21 December 1798 (LoA, pp. 590–91).
49 JM, *Report on the Alien and Sedition Acts*, 7 January 1800 (LoA, pp. 647–48).
50 JM, *Virginia Resolutions Against the Alien and Sedition Acts*, 21 December 1798 (LoA, p. 589).
51 Ketcham, op. cit., p. 399.
52 JM to Edward Everett, 28 August 1830 (LoA, pp. 842–44).
53 JM to Nicholas P. Trist, May 1832 (LoA, p. 860).
54 Ketcham, op. cit., p. 646; JM to William Cabell Rives, 12 March 1833 (LoA, p. 865).
55 JM, *Advice to My Country*, 1834 (LoA, p. 866).
56 Irving Brant, *The Fourth President: A Life of James Madison* (Indianapolis: Bobbs-Merrill, 1970), p. 646.
57 Catherine Drinker Bowen, *Miracle at Philadelphia* (Boston: Little, Brown, 1966), p. 13.
58 Ketcham, op. cit., p. 89.
59 Bowen, op. cit., p. 29.
60 Ketcham, op. cit., p. 360.
61 Ibid., p. 258.
62 January 1, 1788, quoted in Burstein and Isenberg, op. cit., p. 166.
63 Ketcham, op. cit., p. 407.
64 Ibid., pp. 88, 108–9.
65 Ibid., pp. 663, 110.
66 Ibid., p. 376.
67 Catherine Allgor, *A Perfect Union: Dolley Madison and the Creation of the American Republic* (New York: Henry Holt, 2006), p. 27; Ketcham, op. cit., p. 378.
68 DPM, p. 16.
69 Allgor, op. cit., p. 232.
70 DPM, pp. 10–14.
71 Ibid., pp. 14–15.
72 Catharine Coles to DPM, 1 June 1794 (DPM, p. 27).
73 JM to DPM, 22 August 1794 (DPM, p. 28).
74 DPM to Eliza Collins Lee, 16 September 1794 (DPM, pp. 31–32).
75 JM to Thomas Jefferson, 2 September 1793 (LoA, p. 547); Ketcham, op. cit., p. 343.
76 Burstein and Isenberg, op. cit., pp. 291, 302.
77 Ketcham, op. cit., p. 355.
78 Ibid., p. 666.

79 Thomas Jefferson to Judge Spencer Roane, 6 September 1819 (Jefferson LoA, p. 1425); Ketcham, op. cit., p. 411.
80 Allgor, op. cit., pp. 46–48; Ketcham, op. cit., p. 408.
81 David McCullough, *John Adams* (New York: Simon & Schuster, 2001), p. 553.
82 Wood, op. cit., p. 558.
83 Ibid., pp. 315–16.
84 Ibid., p. 359.
85 Ketcham, op. cit., pp. 284–85.
86 Thomas Hobbes, *Leviathan*, C. B. Macpherson, ed. (Baltimore: Penguin, 1968), p. 160.
87 Ketcham, op. cit., p. 432.
88 Wood, op. cit., p. 288.
89 Allgor, op. cit., p. 59; Ketcham, op. cit., pp. 446–47.
90 DPM, p. 45.
91 Allgor, op. cit., p. 84.
92 Ibid., pp. 84–86.
93 Ibid., pp. 86–88.
94 Ibid., p. 85.
95 Ibid., p. 90.
96 Ibid., pp. 96–98.
97 Ibid., p. 91.
98 Wood, op. cit., p. 351.
99 Ibid., pp. 351–52.
100 Ibid., pp. 308, 254.
101 JM, "Who Are the Best Keepers of the People's Liberties?" *National Gazette*, 22 December 1792 (LoA, pp. 532–33).
102 Wood, op. cit., p. 10.
103 Ibid., pp. 329, 318–19.
104 Ibid., pp. 327–28.
105 Ibid., pp. 396–97.
106 Allgor, op. cit., p. 178.
107 Ketcham, op. cit., pp. 498–99.
108 Allgor, op. cit., pp. 67–71, 156.
109 DPM, p. 46.
110 Allgor, op. cit., p. 144.
111 Ibid., p. 200.
112 DPM, p. 96.
113 Allgor, op. cit., p. 174.
114 DPM, p. 94.
115 Ibid., pp. 95–97.
116 Allgor, op. cit., p. 243.
117 Ibid., p. 195.
118 DPM, p. 96.
119 Allgor, op. cit., p. 183.

120 Ibid., p. 190.
121 Ibid., pp. 247–48; Wood, op. cit., pp. 662–63.
122 Wood, op. cit., p. 276.
123 Thomas Jefferson, *First Annual Message*, 8 December 1801 (Jefferson LoA, p. 504).
124 Wood, op. cit., pp. 293, 298.
125 Ibid., pp. 292–93.
126 Ibid., pp. 620–23, 625.
127 "Administrative History," *Papers Relating to the British Seizure of American Ships, 1793–1801* (Special Collections, Witchita State University Libraries).
128 Wood, op. cit., p. 640.
129 Ibid., pp. 621, 646; Ketcham, op. cit., pp. 451, 456.
130 Ketcham, op. cit., pp. 452–53; Wood, op. cit., pp. 641–43, 647.
131 Ketcham, op. cit., pp. 456–57, 463.
132 Wood, op. cit., p. 655.
133 Ibid., pp. 656–57.
134 Ketcham, op. cit., pp. 465–66.
135 Ibid., pp. 474–75; JM, *First Inaugural Address*, 4 March 1809 (LoA, p. 681).
136 Wood, op. cit., pp. 664–67, 684.
137 Burstein and Isenberg, op. cit., p. 508.
138 JM, *War Message to Congress*, 1 June 1812 (LoA, pp. 685–92).
139 Ketcham, op. cit., pp. 508–9, 513, 537; Wood, op. cit., pp. 660–61, 695.
140 Wood, op. cit., pp. 299–300; Ketcham, op. cit., p. 532.
141 Ketcham, op. cit., pp. 481–82.
142 Ibid., p. 521.
143 Wood, op. cit., p. 664.
144 Ketcham, op. cit., p. 532.
145 Ibid., p. 566; Donald R. Hickey, *The War of 1812: A Short History* (Urbana: University of Illinois Press, 1995), p. 20.
146 Wood, op. cit., p. 672.
147 Ibid., pp. 673, 684, 692.
148 Ibid., p. 677.
149 Burstein and Isenberg, op. cit., pp. 487–91; Ketcham, op. cit., pp. 500–501.
150 Richard Rush to Benjamin Rush, 20 June 1812, quoted in Henry Adams, *History of the United States During the First Administration of Madison*, Part 2 (New York: Charles Scribner's Sons, 1890), p. 229.
151 Hickey, op. cit., pp. 23–24; Wood, op. cit., p. 679.
152 Hickey, op. cit., pp. 26–27.
153 Ibid., pp. 27–28.
154 Wood, op. cit., pp. 635–39, 681–82, 684–86.
155 Ibid., pp. 683–84, 688–90; Ketcham, op. cit., pp. 573–74; Allgor, op. cit., p. 311.
156 DPM to Edward Coles, 13 May 1813 (DPM, p. 176).
157 DPM to Lucy Payne Washington Todd, 23 August 1814 (DPM, pp. 193–94).
158 Allgor, op. cit., pp. 315–18; Wood, op. cit., p. 691.

159 Wood, op. cit., pp. 695, 689–90.
160 Hickey, op. cit., pp. 65–69; Ketcham, op. cit., pp. 594, 596.
161 Allgor, op. cit., p. 321; Ketcham, op. cit., pp. 596–97; Wood, op. cit., pp. 696–97.
162 Ketcham, op. cit., p. 606.
163 JM to Spencer Roane, 2 September 1819 (LoA, p. 736); Ketcham, op. cit., p. 403.
164 Ketcham, op. cit., p. 337.
165 Ralph Ketcham, *The Madisons at Montpelier: Reflections on the Founding Couple* (Charlottesville: University of Virginia Press, 2009), p. 1.
166 Ibid., p. 32.
167 Ibid., p. 84.
168 Ibid., p. 93.
169 Wood, op. cit., p. 734.
170 Ketcham, *The Madisons at Montpelier*, pp. 33, 36; Thomas Jefferson to JM, 17 February 1826 (Jefferson LoA, pp. 1514–15).
171 JM to Thomas Jefferson, 24 February 1829 (LoA, pp. 810–11).
172 Ketcham, *The Madisons at Montpelier*, p. 14.
173 Ibid., pp. 11–14.
174 Ibid., p. 37; Allgor, op. cit., p. 373.
175 Allgor, op. cit., pp. 380, 395–96, 398.
176 DPM, p. 325.

ACKNOWLEDGMENTS

It is a pleasure to acknowledge with grateful thanks the many debts I have incurred for kindness and support during the writing of *The Founders at Home*. Above all, sincere thanks to the Manhattan Institute—to its president, Lawrence Mone; its staff; and its trustees, especially its succession of remarkable and strong-minded chairmen, Paul Singer, Roger Hertog, and my dear friend, Charles H. Brunie. Heartfelt thanks to my valued colleagues at the institute's magazine, *City Journal*, where the first versions of these chapters appeared. All—writers and editors alike—have been intellectually stimulating friends for years. Brian Anderson, once my deputy and now my successor as editor, generously gave me space in the journal to develop my vision of the Founding, and managing editor Benjamin Plotinsky read through the manuscript of this book with his incomparably sharp eye and exacting standards, a kindness I'll never forget.

Starling Lawrence, W. W. Norton's editor in chief for almost two decades and my valued, witty, and generous-hearted friend for more than five, saw very early that what I began writing as magazine stories would grow up to be a book. His encouragement, confidence, and counsel have been incalculably precious to me from the start, and his finely honed editorial skill and wise judgment have ensured that the final outcome is as in tune and harmonious as it can be. His capable assistant at Norton, Ryan Harrington, has kept an eye on detail with unfailingly cheerful and intelligent meticulousness.

Those entrusted with the preservation and presentation of the houses I discuss were graciously hospitable in every way. Kind thanks for all their help to William Schroh, the operating chief of Kean University's Liberty Hall Museum, who in colonial-era knee breeches also presides as one of the museum's vibrant docents, and to accomplished author and historian Terry Golway, a member of the Kean faculty and curator of the John T. Kean Center for American History. The warm welcome of Stratford Hall's genial executive director, Paul C. Reber, made my visit to that magical place especially enjoyable and informative, and director of research Judith S. Hynson cheerfully provided more and more pictures of the beautiful house for a picky author to chose among.

My friend Lesley Herrmann, executive director of the Gilder Lehrman Institute, an indispensable advocate and provider of resources for the teaching and learning of American history at every level, introduced me to the staff of Mount Vernon, who made sure that I missed not a corner of the amazing house, even to the extent of climbing what seemed an impossibly steep and flimsy ladder into the lantern on the roof to take in the breathtaking Potomac view, which the ever-resourceful Mount Vernon Ladies' Association has preserved as Washington knew it by buying up the river's opposite bank as far as the eye can see. Hearty thanks to Stephen McLeod and Ellen Stanton for guiding my visit, and to Dawn Bonner and Melissa Wood for endlessly kind and patient help with pictures. I deeply appreciate it.

Allan Weinreb showed me around the John Jay Homestead and gave me a look at some of its hidden treasures, including the museum's newly acquired residence permit that New York's royal governor, Thomas Dongan, issued to John Jay's immigrant grandfather in the 1680s—a most evocative link with a long-vanished past. I'm additionally grateful to him, and to Ronna Dixon of the New York State

Office of Parks, Recreation and Historic Preservation, for providing the illustrations of the Homestead and its contents reproduced here.

Being a front-row spectator to the moving of Hamilton Grange to its new site and its restoration to its original form was an exhilarating adventure that unfolded over several years, and I am eternally grateful to the National Park Service officials who invited me to take part. Thanks to Maria Burks, former commissioner of the National Parks of New York Harbor, to Darren Boch (now superintendent of Paterson Great Falls National Historical Park), Mindi Rambo, Kevin Daley, and Steve Laise. I am especially grateful to Stephen Spaulding, who oversaw the Grange's restoration with infectious intensity and in the process gave me a riveting graduate seminar in historic preservation. It was a thrill, as layers of paint got scraped and dental-picked away, to see Hamilton's moldings regain their original crispness and the sunshine yellow of his walls reemerge into the light. Thanks too to architect Nancy Rankin of John G. Waite Associates for providing the floor plan of the Grange reproduced in these pages.

When I told New-York Historical Society chairman Roger Hertog, then a member of the Thomas Jefferson Foundation's board, that I was planning a pilgrimage to Monticello, he told me that I should surely meet with the foundation's then-president, Daniel P. Jordan. How right he was. At the end of a spirited and convivial visit, I asked Dan, a courtly, reflective student of history, what he thought was the best biography of Jefferson. *Jefferson Himself*, he replied, a narrative of the sage of Monticello's life in his own words, selected and introduced by Dan's old professor, Bernard Mayo. The book was a revelation, and it became an inspiration to me to try to tell the story of the Founding as much as possible in the Founders' own voices. Who could better describe and explain their actions and the worldview out of which they sprang? I loved Monticello itself, arguably America's greatest work of architecture, and warm thanks to Leah Stearns for helping me find just the right photographs to convey its uniqueness to readers.

Montpelier turned out to be another graduate course in historic preservation, with restoration chief John K. Jeanes serving as the intense and charismatic professor. Visiting Madison's house in the midst of an heroic restoration, I came upon John, hard-hatted and shirtless in the Virginia sun, as he was working beside his crew. A word of compliment on the progress so far produced first a stream of eloquence on the privilege of working on such a once-in-a-lifetime project and then a long guided tour through the half-dismantled structure, with fascinating demonstrations of the detective work involved in determining what Madison's house looked like during his lifetime, and the methods the restoration sleuths used to figure out where the various fragments they found as they dismantled—a hearthstone, a door case—had originally stood. A later visit proved to be Historic Preservation 202: The Finer Points. What a lucky meeting that turned out to be.

For hospitality at Montpelier, I also want to thank former Montpelier Foundation chief Michael C. Quinn, now head of the American Revolution Center, and Lynn Dakin Hastings. For help with pictures I am deeply grateful to C. Douglas Smith, executive director of the foundation's Center for the Constitution, Tiffany Cole, Jeni Spencer, and Meg Kennedy.

Much appreciated help with other illustrations came from Judith Thomas of the Pennsylvania Academy of the Fine Arts; Andrea Ashby of Independence National Historical Park; Julie Cochrane of the Royal Museums, Greenwich, England; Jerry Bloomer of the R. W. Norton Art Foundation; and Thomas Haggerty and Camila Pawlowski of the Bridgeman Art Library. And hearty thanks for assistance to the Century Association's curator, Jonathan P. Harding, and its librarian, W. Gregory Gallagher.

Organizations such as the Mount Vernon Ladies' Association and the Thomas Jefferson Foundation, which preserve Mount Vernon and Monticello and offer a wealth of further resources for students of the American Founding, are among the nation's premier philanthropies. I can't help singling out for praise and thanks one further nonprofit organization, the Library of America, which publishes beautifully crafted editions of the classics of American literature, including the writings of the nation's major statesmen. I have found its immaculately edited and annotated editions of Washington, Jefferson, Madison, and Hamilton, as well as its volumes of the debates over the Constitution, invaluable.

Though I have tried as much as possible to depend on the words of the Founders and their contemporaries as my sources, anyone who writes on the Founding necessarily stands on the shoulders of such giants in the field as biographers Ron Chernow and Ralph Ketcham and historians Bernard Bailyn, David Hackett Fischer, and Gordon S. Wood. My debts to recent scholars are too numerous to mention here, but accompanying my acknowledgments to them in the endnotes is a bountiful measure of gratitude and respect. I do want to single out for thanks my good friend Richard Brookhiser, however. I had the pleasure of editing his "Alexander Hamilton, New Yorker" when it appeared in *City Journal.* An early version of his *Alexander Hamilton, American*, it first alerted me to the power of compact biographies such as the series he has so gracefully written to illuminate the entire era of the Founding.

At a time when I felt I'd run aground, my wife, Barbara Crehan, floated me off the sandbar with insight, tact, and calm persistence in the face of irascible grumpiness. "How about a trip to Virginia to see Mount Vernon and Monticello?" she said. "Old houses; Founding Fathers—you'd like that." I did; and I'm grateful, not just for the shove but for the intellectual companionship. These places were new and fascinating to both of us. "Everybody says Locke, Locke," Barbara, a onetime renaissance literature professor, would observe as we drove, "but I keep hearing Coke, Coke"—and our discussions of the Jacobean chief justice and his penchant for inventing supposedly immemorial precedents, discussions that started forty years ago, set me off on an interesting train of thought about the intellectual background of the American Revolution, in which Lord Justice Coke indeed plays a key role. So: enduring thanks, for this as for much else. And heartfelt thanks too to my dear children, Julia and Alec, and my son-in-law, Trevor Brown, for their enthusiastic encouragement from the time I first haltingly outlined for them what I wanted to say about Monticello years ago in Maine right through to advice and criticism on matters large and small up to this present moment—and beyond.

INDEX